D0787385

How to Find Out About Financial Aid

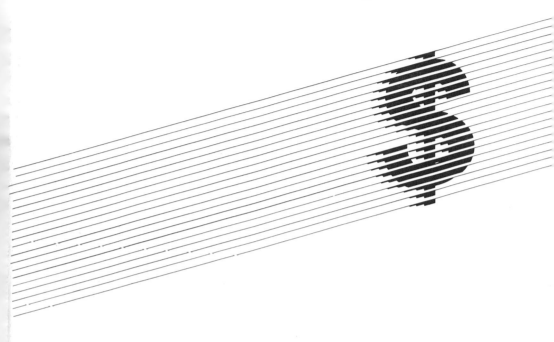

A Guide to Over 700 Directories Listing

- Scholarships •
- Fellowships •
- Loans •
- Grants •
- Awards •
- Internships •

Gail Ann Schlachter

Reference Service Press

Los Angeles

Library of Congress Cataloging in Publication Number:
85-043486

ISBN Number:
0-918276-05-5

10 9 8 7 6 5 4 3 2 1

Reference Service Press is a library-oriented reference book publishing company specializing in the preparation of directories of financial aid for special needs groups (including women, minorities and the disabled).

Reference Service Press
3540 Wilshire Boulevard, Suite 310
Los Angeles, California 90010
(213) 251-3743

Manufactured in the United States of America

To Morris Polan
A valued colleague and a special friend

Contents

Scholarships

Fellowships

Grants

Table of Contents

Awards and Prizes

Loans

Internships

Databases and Search Services

Publishers Directory

Indexes

Introduction

PURPOSE

During the past decade, there have been dramatic changes in the area of financial aid. Federal funds for education have been reduced and reapportioned; the number of publicly-funded scholarships and fellowships has declined, while the number of publicly-funded loans has increased. There has been substantial growth in the funds available to special needs groups (particularly minorities and women) but a reduction in the money available for programs based on merit rather than need. The amount available for grants is down somewhat but still relatively plentiful. Internship opportunities (particularly those that offer monetary support) are on the upswing. In all, there is more than $16 billion available annually in the form of publicly-or privately-funded scholarships, fellowships, grants, awards, loans, and internships.

Yet, until now, no single guide has provided a comprehensive list of the hundreds of directories that describe these financial aid opportunities. Even the standard bibliographic sources have proved to be of limited value. For example, the *American Reference Book Annual*, which has offered professional reviews of financial aid directories for the past 12 years, has covered less than a total of 100 different titles in the annual editions issued between 1980 and 1985. Sheehy's *Guide to Reference Books* provides even less direction; the number of listings of financial aid directories has been limited to less than 30 in each edition. Similarly, the reference publications that focus on either the appropriate format (directories) or subject (financial aid) have offered less than comprehensive listings. Gale's *Directory of Directories*, while more inclusive than the general bibliographic guides, identifies less than 200 financial aid directories (many of which have not released new editions since 1980). Judith Lewis' pamphlet, "Searching for Outside Resources of Financial Aid" (available without charge from the United States International University in San Diego), identifies 155 financial aid directories, but only those aimed at college students (and a number of these are out of date or no longer available). Even more focused is Charlotte Georgi's *Fund Raising, Grants, and Foundations: A Comprehensive Bibliography*, which concentrates on general grants publications and lists fewer than 50 directories. As a result, librarians and financial aid officers have had difficulty determining all the appropriate sources to add to their professional collections or to use to help their clients. Students and researchers in search of financial assistance have also had little bibliographic guidance in identifying relevant directories.

In order to fill this bibliographic gap, *How to Find Out About Financial Aid: A Guide to Over 700 Directories Listing Scholarships, Fellowships, Grants, Awards, Loans, and Internships* has been prepared. It was compiled after an extensive search through a variety of resources: major bibliographic sources and review publications; acquisitions lists from such organizations as the Foundation Center; current publishers' catalogs; on-site visits to a number of major libraries, including the Library of Congress and the Foundation Center Library; and personal contact or correspondence with a number of individuals active in the area of financial aid. The Guide is designed to identify, classify, describe, and evaluate the more than 700 directories published since 1980 that focus on American recipients or would tend to be included in the collections of larger American libraries. The compilation is intended to assist reference and collection development librarians, financial aid officers, career counselors, students, researchers, and anyone else interested in obtaining financial support for education, research, travel, training, career development, or innovative effort.

SCOPE

A number of criteria were established to determine which publications to select for inclusion in the Guide.

Directory-type listings: Only works that list scholarships, fellowships, grants, awards/prizes, loans, and/or internships (in either print or online format) are described in the Guide. Monographs discussing financial aid in general are omitted, as are bibliographies listing materials on financial aid, studies, reports, functional works, journals, and self-help manuals that describe financial aid or fundraising procedures.

Broad listings: In general, the Guide focuses on directories identifying funding opportunities offered by a variety of organizations. Small pamphlets promoting the programs of a single sponsor (e.g., American Chemical Society, Business and Professional Women's Foundation) are usually excluded. Exceptions are made, however, for representative publications issued by such organizations as the AFL-CIO and the National Science Foundation, since the number and diversity of the programs covered is substantial.

Current listings: Because the information related to financial aid rapidly becomes dated, only those directories issued or scheduled to be issued since 1980 are covered in the Guide. Directories with earlier imprints may be referred to in an annotation, but they are not separately listed unless they served as a predecessor to a currently-issued title.

Materials of interest to American users: The Guide is intended primarily for an American audience. Consequently, almost all of the items cited are English-language publications. While a number of international and foreign titles are identified (particularly from Canada, the United Kingdom, and Australia), these are included only because they are perceived to have value for an American user and/or they tend to be included in the collections of larger American libraries.

Cataloged materials: Only those directories that have been commercially available and are likely to be cataloged in larger libraries are identified. Processed materials (such as those issued by academic institutions for the benefit of their students), lists published solely as articles in journals, and directories that are currently out of print (and no plans exist to update later) are generally omitted.

ARRANGEMENT

The Guide consists of four distinct parts. The first six chapters describe and, where appropriate, evaluate printed financial aid directories published since 1980. Chapter seven reviews sources of financial aid information that are available online. The last chapter provides up-to-date addresses and telephone numbers for the publishers responsible for the directories listed in the first seven chapters. There is also a set of four indexes; these provide access to the more than 900 entries by name, title, geographic coverage, and subject focus.

Financial Aid Directories. In order to permit quick and easy access to the information on particular types of financial aid, the first six chapters of the Guide group over 700 directories by type of programs described in the publications. In the following order, the chapters cover:

Scholarships: programs that support studies at the undergraduate level in the United States or abroad; usually no return of service or repayment is required.

Fellowships: programs that support graduate/postgraduate education or research in the United States or abroad; usually no return of service or repayment is required.

Grants: programs that provide funds to support research, innovative efforts, travel, or projects (some of which may be educational in nature) in the United States or abroad; in a number of cases, proposals may be submitted by institutions or organizations only; in others, individuals may submit proposals directly.

Awards and prizes: programs granted in recognition or support of creative work or public service in the United States or abroad.

Loans: programs that provide money that eventually must be repaid— with or without interest.

Internships: programs that provide work experience opportunities and (often) monetary support for students, professionals, and other workers interested in short-term placements.

Each of these six chapters is subdivided, first by discipline or group (General, Social Sciences, Humanities, Sciences, Special Population Groups) and then 1) by geographic coverage for the General sections (e.g., International, United States, California); 2) by topics, for the Social Sciences, Humanities, and Sciences sections (e.g., Librarianship, Music, Technology); and 3) by intended audience, in the Special Population Groups section (e.g., the Disabled, Ethnic Groups, Women). Within each of these subsections, the entries are arranged alphabetically by title.

To facilitate bibliographic access as well as the ordering process, every attempt has been made to provide as complete a bibliographic citation as possible for the directories described in the Guide. Included in each entry (where relevant) are: title, author, edition, place, publisher, date, number of pages or frequency, series, Library of Congress (LC) card number, International Standard Book Number (ISBN), International Standard Serial Number (ISSN), and price. For a number of reasons, however, it was not always possible to supply all of these bibliographic components. First of all, many items lacked LC, ISBN, and ISSN numbers (this was especially true of small press directories). In addition, although a series or serial might have gone through a number of publishers or frequencies of publication, its publication history may never have been recorded. Further, standard reference sources (and even the publications themselves) frequently contained contradictory bibliographic information. Whenever bibliographic records were at variance, OCLC data were given preference, particularly if the Library of Congress had produced the records. Finally, although a wide range of standard reference sources were consulted—including *Books in Print, Forthcoming Books in Print, American Reference Book Annual, Standard Periodicals Directory, Directory of Directories,* and *Ulrich's International Periodical Directory*—it was sometimes difficult to determine current pricing. While every effort was made to provide the latest information available, prices tend to change frequently and, therefore, the figures supplied in the citations should be taken as a guide rather than as definitive. To be sure you have the most up-to-date prices for the directories of interest, it is best to contact the publishers directly (addresses and telephone numbers—along with available toll free numbers—are provided in Chapter 8 of the guide).

All 905 entries in the first seven chapters of the Guide are annotated. The directory profiles are designed to provide information on purpose, scope, arrangement, limitations, and special features. In addition, whenever appropriate, publication history is traced (to identify previous editions and tricky name changes) and publication value is assessed. Expendable publications, standard sources, and "must buys" are indicated.

Because many of the directories included in the Guide focus on more than one type of program or emphasize more than one subject area, titles are listed in all relevant chapters and sections/subsections. For example, *Grants and Fellowships of Interest to Historians* is covered under the "Social Sciences— History" section of both the Grants and the Fellowships chapter. The *Montana and Wyoming Foundations Directory* is listed twice in the Grants chapter, once in the "General—Montana" section and once in the "General—Wyoming" section. In all cases, however, a full description of the title is provided only once, in the section that seemed most appropriate. The reader is always directed to the entry with the fullest annotation.

Online Directories. Not all of the directories included in the Guide are printed publications. Chapter 7 focuses on financial aid "directories" that involve searching an online version. These sources take two forms: as databases that are accessed by computers and as scholarship search services that are accessed upon customer request. Included in this chapter are over 20 of these automated directories, with references made to any available print version.

Publishers' Directory. The final chapter lists all of the publishers responsible for the directories covered in the Guide and supplies the latest available address and telephone number (including toll free numbers) for each. This chapter constitutes the most up-to-date "who's who" in financial aid directory publishing. Since a substantial proportion of the titles included in the Guide are issued by small presses or organizations not ordinarily involved in publishing, many of the addresses provided in this chapter will not be found in the standard reference sources.

Indexes. The Guide provides four indexes to facilitate the search for appropriate financial aid opportunities. Name, Title, Geographic, and Subject Indexes follow a word-by-word arrangement and refer the user to the appropriate entry by number.

 Name Index. This index provides an alphabetical listing of the authors, editors, compilers, translators, and illustrators listed on the title pages of the directories cited in the first six chapters of the Guide. References are made only to the main entry (where the fullest annotation may be found). Since not all directories credit individual authors, a number of the publications (particularly those that are serial in nature or those prepared by organizations) are not represented here.

 Title Index. The current, previous, and variant names of all publications (print and online) cited in the first seven chapters of the Guide (either as separate entries or as references in annotations describing other titles) are indexed here. Over 700 titles are included in this index.

 Geographic Index. This index enables the reader to identify by city, state, region, and country the geographic coverage of the financial aid directories listed in the first seven chapters of the Guide. Since one directory can be cited in several subsections (e.g., a directory describing grant programs offered in New York, New Jersey, and Pennsylvania is listed in three subsections), each of these entries is indexed.

Subject Index. This index allows the reader to identify by subject all of the financial aid directories described in the first seven chapters of the Guide. Over 125 separate subject terms are used. Extensive "see" and "see also" references facilitate the search for appropriate directories. As in the Geographic Index, reference is generally made to all entries where the directory is cited. Thus, a directory describing grants available to both writers and musicians would be listed in two subsections of the Grants chapter, "Humanities—Literature" and "Humanities—Music," and indexed under both subject terms.

HOW TO USE THE GUIDE

To Locate Directories Listing a Particular Type of Financial Assistance. If you are looking for directories listing a particular type of financial aid (e.g., a scholarship for undergraduate courses, a grant for independent study, an award for outstanding achievement), turn to the appropriate chapter: Scholarships (for undergraduate study), Fellowships (for graduate study), Grants (for research, study, travel, or creative efforts), Awards (in recognition of outstanding achievement), Loans (for financial assistance that must be repaid), or Internships (for work experience programs).

To Locate Directories Listing Financial Aid for Particular Subjects. Each of the first six chapters (Scholarships, Fellowships, Grants, Awards, Loans, and Internships) is divided into sections (an initial "General" section, followed by sections arranged by discipline or group) and then into topical subsections (following the same basic arrangement). Be sure to check the "General" section as well as the "General" subsection and the subject-oriented subsections in the discipline in which you are interested. For example, if you want to identify all the directories that list financial assistance for undergraduate study in the communications field in the United States, you would go to the Scholarships chapter, read all the entries in the "General—United States" section, and then all the entries in both the "Humanities—General" and the "Humanities—Communications and Mass Media" sections. Since directories covering multiple subjects are listed in every appropriate location (in the "General" sections/subsections, if there is broad coverage; in the specific subject subsections, if there is more focused coverage), you can browse through any of the sections or subsections in the Guide without first consulting an index. However, if you are looking for directories dealing with a specific subject, it will be more efficient if you turn first to the Subject Index. To facilitate your search, the type of programs covered (scholarships, fellowships, grants, awards, loans, and internships) are clearly indicated for each subject term. Extensive cross-references are also provided.

Introduction

To Locate Directories Listing Financial Aid Programs Open to Members of a Particular Group. In addition to listing directories by subject, this Guide also groups directories by special audience intended: the disabled, ethnic groups, foreign students, military personnel and veterans, reentry students, and women. To locate all directories listing programs for these groups, identify first the type of program in which you are interested, go to the appropriate chapter (Scholarships, Fellowships, Grants, Awards, Loans, Internships), turn to the section focusing on "Special Population Groups" and read through the entries in the subsection covering the group in which you are interested. For example, if you were looking for directories that identify financial aid programs for Hispanic American graduate students, you would use the "Special Population Groups—Ethnic Groups" section in the Fellowships chapter. Remember, the "General" sections and subsections also will identify directories that may list programs for special population groups, so be sure to check there as well. Another way to locate directories focusing on programs open to special population groups is to look up the specific group in which you are interested in the Subject Index.

To Locate Financial Aid Directories Focusing on Particular Geographic Areas. The Geographic Index permits easy access to directories listing financial aid programs open to residents of or tenable in a particular country, state, region, or city. "See" and "see also" references are used liberally, and index entries for a particular geographic area are subdivided by type of program: scholarships, fellowships, grants, awards, loans, and internships. In addition, the "General" sections of each of the first six chapters in the Guide are subdivided geographically (International; United States; names of specific states). You can browse through these sections to quickly identify the general directories that provide basic geographic coverage. For example, if you were interested in determining which sources listed grants available to nonprofit agencies in California, you would turn to the Grants chapter and read through all of the entries in the "General—California" section.

To Locate the Description of a Particular Financial Aid Directory. If you know the name of a particular financial aid directory and the type of assistance covered in the listing (e.g., scholarships, fellowships, grants), then go directly to the appropriate chapter and section/subsection. For example, *Children's Books: Awards & Prizes* is described in the Awards and Prizes chapter, under the "Humanities—Literature" heading. If you are looking for a specific directory and do not find it in the subsection you have checked, be sure to refer to the Title Index to see if it is covered elsewhere in the Guide. To save time, always check the Title Index first if you know the name of a specific directory and are not sure under which subsection it has been annotated.

To Locate Directories Written by a Specific Author. The Name Index makes it easy to identify all the directories covered in the Guide that were prepared by a specific individual. Authors, editors, compilers, translators, and illustrators are listed here. However, since many directories do not credit a specific individual on their title page, a number of the directories included in the Guide are not referenced in this index.

To Order a Directory Listed in the Guide. Although every effort has been made to provide the latest available pricing for each of the directories cited in the Guide, some of the information is by its very nature outdated by the time the Guide reaches the reader. Pricing figures, then, should be viewed as indicative rather than definitive. The most current pricing information for any publication can be obtained only by contacting the publisher. Turn to Chapter 8, Publishers' Directory, to locate the most recently available address and telephone number (including toll free numbers) for each of the over 300 publishers represented in the Guide. The companies are arranged alphabetically, and liberal cross-references are provided for variant names.

PLANS TO UPDATE THE DIRECTORY

This Guide focuses on financial aid directories issued at least once since 1980. The bibliographic information, pricing, descriptions, and evaluations are current as of mid-1986. If the current rate of change in the financial aid field continues in the future, the Guide will be updated on a periodic basis.

ABOUT THE AUTHOR

For the past two decades, Dr. Gail Schlachter has worked as a library administrator, a library educator, and a manager of library-related publishing companies (currently as president of Reference Service Press). Active in the library community, Dr. Schlachter has recently been elected to the Councils of both the American Library Association and the California Library Association. In addition, for the last nine years she has served as the Reference Book Review Editor for RQ (published by the Reference and Adult Services Division of the American Library Association). Well known for her lectures on the need to increase financial aid for special needs groups, Dr. Schlachter has written a series of directories on the topic: *Directory of Financial Aids for Women* (published biennially since 1978); *Directory of Financial Aids for Minorities* (published biennially since 1984); and *Financial Aid for the Disabled and Their Dependents* (first edition published in 1987). She is also the author of two award-winning bibliographic guides: *Minorities and Women: A Guide to Reference Literature in the Social Sciences*, which was chosen as an "Outstanding Reference Book of the Year" by Choice; and *Reference Sources in Library and Information Services*, which was selected to receive the first "Knowledge Industry Publication's Award for Outstanding Contribution to Library Literature" in 1985.

ACKNOWLEDGEMENTS

A debt of gratitude is owed to the publishers that contributed review copies, the libraries that provided unlimited access to their collections of financial aid directories (particularly the Library of Congress, the Foundation Center, and the Grantsmanship Center in Los Angeles), and the numerous librarians who helped untangle difficult bibliographic problems. Special thanks go to Morris Polan, University Librarian; Suzanne Sullivan, Assistant University Librarian for Reference Service; Alan P. Stein, Head of Humanities/Social Sciences Reference; and the rest of the Humanities/Social Sciences reference department staff at California State University, Los Angeles. The generous support and cooperation of these groups has helped to make this publication a current and extensive survey of available publications. In addition, Hal Bayer, Rosemary Boyle, Jane Gadson, Danny Maynard, Irene Wheatly, Chris Wisniewski, and their colleagues at AMTEC (Lakewood, California) deserve special acknowledgement for their significant contributions, not only to the development of the database and manipulation software used to format the content of this book, but to the design and layout of the finished product as well.

OTHER RELATED PUBLICATIONS ISSUED BY REFERENCE SERVICE PRESS

In addition to *How to Find Out About Financial Aid*, Reference Service Press publishes a number of directories identifying financial aid programs aimed at special need groups, including the *Directory of Financial Aids for Women*, which lists over 1,500 scholarships, fellowships, grants, awards, loans, and internships set aside primarily or exclusively for women; the *Directory of Financial Aids for Minorities*, which provides the only current and comprehensive listing of financial aid established for Asian Americans, Black Americans, Hispanic Americans, Native Americans, and ethnic minorities in general; and *Financial Aid for the Disabled and Their Dependents*, which is the first directory to list and describe the hundreds of scholarships, fellowships, loans, awards, and grants-in-aid available solely to the disabled in America. For more information about these or other related publications, write to Reference Service Press' marketing department at 3540 Wilshire Boulevard, Suite 310, Los Angeles, CA 90010

Scholarships

Scholarships provide financial assistance for students pursuing undergraduate education in any type of postsecondary institution: vocational/technical schools, two-year colleges, four-year colleges, and universities. Usually no return of service or repayment is required. Included in this chapter are 175 references to directories that focus solely on scholarships or list substantial numbers of scholarships available on the state, national, or international level—making this the second largest "type of program" chapter in the Guide. Of these entries, 80 are general in nature, 20 focus on the social sciences, 21 concentrate on the humanities, 9 deal with the sciences, and the remainder (45 entries) are aimed at special population groups (especially ethnic groups). If you are looking for a specific scholarship directory and you do not find it in this chapter, be sure to check the Title Index to see if it is covered elsewhere in the Guide.

GENERAL

International

1 **Annual Register of Grant Support: A Guide to Support Programs of Government Agencies, Foundations, and Business and Professional Organizations.** Wilmette, IL: National Register, 1969– . Annual. 69–18307. ISSN 0066–4049. $87 (1985–86 ed.).

Although it focuses on North American programs, the *Annual Register* also describes a number of scholarships sponsored abroad. A more comprehensive list can be found, however, in the *Grants Register* (described in the Grants chapter). For more information on the *Annual Register*, see the annotation in the "Grants—General—United States" section of this bibliography.

2 **College Blue Book.** New York: Macmillan, 1923– . Biennial. 79–66191. ISSN 0069–5572. $185 (20th ed.).

A number of the scholarships described in Volume 5 of the *Blue Book*'s 20th edition may be used for study abroad. For more information about this publication, see the annotation in the "Scholarships—General—United States" section.

3 **Directory of Financial Aid for American Undergraduates Interested in Overseas Study and Travel.** Washington, DC: Adelphi University, 1982. v.p. 83–10055. ISBN 0–88461–007–1. $9. Pap.

Over 100 programs designed to support study and travel by U.S. undergraduates outside of the United States are covered in this directory. Entries provide information on application procedures, application deadline, purpose, subject areas covered, geographic restrictions, eligibility, duration, and stipend. The programs are arranged alphabetically and indexed by country and subject.

4 **Directory of Financial Aids for International Activities.** Minneapolis: Office of International Programs, University of Minnesota, 1978– . Irreg. 78–64527. ISSN 0163–0199. $20 (1985 ed.). Pap.

The fourth (1985) edition of this directory (314p.) provides information on more than 450 individual opportunities for academic staff, graduate and undergraduate students, advanced scholars, and young professionals for study, research, travel, and teaching abroad. The directory also contains sections on grants to individuals for study in a degree program at a foreign institution and grants to individuals. This listing is aimed at citizens and residents of the United States, but many of the awards described are open to individuals of any nationality. The programs are arranged according to the name of the funding agency. Each entry presents the following information:

name and address of funding source, application deadline date, purpose of the award, subject area, geographic area, eligibility requirements, time period for use of funds, stipend, and source and date of information. There are geographic, subject, type, and level of eligibility (undergraduate, graduate, and postdoctoral) indexes.

5   **Directory of Research Grants.** Phoenix: Oryx, 1975– . Annual. 76–47074. ISSN 0146–7336. $74.50 (1986 ed.). Pap.

Although the emphasis is on U.S. programs, some scholarships, fellowships, loans, and research grants sponsored by other countries are also included. For more information about the publication, see the annotation in the "Grants—General—United States" section of this bibliography.

6   **Fellowships, Scholarships, and Related Opportunities in International Education.** Knoxville: Division of International Education, University of Tennessee, 1967– . Annual. 82–5141. ISSN 0735–8830. $8 (1986 ed.). Pap.

In the latest edition of this directory, over 120 scholarships, fellowships, and grants for study, research, and teaching in the United States and abroad are listed and described. For more information about the publication, see the annotation in the "Fellowships—General—International" section of this bibliography.

7   **Financial Aid for First Degree Study at Commonwealth Universities.** London: Association of Commonwealth Universities, 1974– . Biennial. 81–644396. ISSN 0260–0749. Pap.

This biennially-issued pamphlet (generally less than 40 pages) describes approximately 100 different scholarships and awards open to Commonwealth students who wish to pursue a first degree at a Commonwealth university outside of their own country. Most of the listed awards are for students from developing countries. Organizations and program titles are indexed.

8   **Scholarships Abroad: Scholarships Offered to British Students by Overseas Governments and Universities.** London: British Council, 1977– . Annual.

This annual guide identifies scholarships and fellowships available to British students who are interested in studying abroad. Over 300 programs sponsored by non-British institutions and governments are described. These programs are tenable for either a full academic year or a shorter period.

9 Study Abroad: International Scholarships, International Courses. Paris: United Nations Educational, Scientific, and Cultural Organization (dist. by Unipub), 1948– . Biennial. ISSN 0081–895X. $20.50 (1983–85 ed.). Pap.

This directory of worldwide study opportunities at the university level has been issued since 1948. Over 250,000 opportunities to study in more than 107 countries under the auspices of 1,000 national and 100 international organizations are described in two sections of the latest edition. The first section focuses on scholarships offered by international organizations and by national institutions. The entries are arranged by country and by discipline/ profession. Each entry provides information on sponsoring agency, address, number of scholarships and type, subject's eligibility, amount, closing date, and address for application. The second section is arranged by country and lists areas of study by broad disciplinary headings. The following information is provided: sponsoring agency, address, type of course, eligibility, where held, duration, fees, scholarships offered, and application deadline and address. Detailed subject indexes are provided, as well as access by international organizations, national institutions, and countries. The text is in French, Spanish, and English. The work is complicated to use, but the value of the information makes the effort worthwhile.

10 Summer Study Abroad. New York: Institute of International Education, 1947–1980. Annual. (The Learning Traveler, v. 2). 80–647933. ISSN 0271–1702.

Since 1980, this annual publication has been issued under the title *Vacation Study Abroad* (described elsewhere in this section of the bibliography).

11 U.S. College-Sponsored Programs Abroad: Academic Year. Ed. by Gail A. Cohen. New York: Institute of International Education, 1964– . Annual. (The Learning Traveler, v. 1). 83–645013. ISSN 0196–6251. $9.95, U.S.; $14, elsewhere (1984 ed.). Pap.

Described in this annual guide are over 800 study-abroad programs on both the undergraduate and graduate level that are offered during the academic year by American colleges and universities in foreign countries. Excluded from the listing are programs offered only during the summer months, programs offered by nondegree-granting institutions, and intern programs. In addition to information on relevant scholarships and fellowships, the directory also describes courses, costs, credits, housing, and language of the sponsoring institution. The entries are arranged by country and indexed by field of study. A bibliography relating to higher education abroad is also included. Earlier editions of the directory were issued under the title *Undergraduate Study Abroad.*

12 **Vacation Study Abroad.** Ed. by Edrice Howard. New York: Institute of International Education, 1981– . Annual. (The Learning Traveler, v. 2). 85–3528. ISSN 0271–17202. $15.95 (1986 ed.). Pap.

This is an annual guide to more than 900 seminars, short courses, and summer sessions in over 60 countries available to students, teachers, and others planning to study or train abroad during vacation times. Listed are programs sponsored by U.S. colleges and universities as well as by foreign institutions and private organizations. Not only does the directory describe courses, costs, and accommodations, it also provides information on scholarships and fellowships. Indexing is by field of study. A bibliography relating to higher education abroad completes the work. Until 1980, this publication was issued under the title *Summer Study Abroad*.

United States

13 **The A's & B's: Your Guide to Academic Scholarships.** By Victoria A. Fabisch. Alexandria, VA: Octameron Associates, 1985– . Annual. $4 (1986 ed.). Pap.

Published from 1979 through 1984 as *The A's and B's of Academic Scholarships* and *The A's and B's of Merit Scholarships*, this pamphlet lists the major awards offered by 1,200 colleges to students in the top third of their class who have combined SAT scores of 900 or more. Most entries provide information—in tabular form—on number of awards, value range, class standing, study fields, renewability, restrictions, and application date. A short section (generally four pages) identifies some noninstitution-based awards; however, this listing just touches the surface. In addition to being released as a separate publication, this work is also reprinted in its entirety in Peterson's Guide's *Your Own Financial Aid Factory: The Guide to Locating College Money* (described elsewhere in this section of the bibliography).

14 **AFL-CIO Guide to Union Sponsored Scholarships, Awards and Student Financial Aid, 1986.** Washington, DC: AFL-CIO, 1986. v.p. Free to union members; $3 to others. Pap.

This guide contains a selected list of AFL-CIO sponsored scholarships available from international and national unions, local unions, and AFL-CIO state and local central bodies. It is intended to aid union members, their dependents, and certain other students in the search for financial assistance to cover the cost of attending colleges and other postsecondary institutions. In all, over 2,000 scholarships worth more than $2.5 million are described. The information presented was obtained from questionnaires, union newspaper articles, and a limited phone survey of AFL-CIO State Federations and other affiliates. A bibliography of other sources of information about financial aid completes the work.

15   AFS: The 1985/86 College Connection. 3d ed. New York: American Field Service, 1985. 79p. Free. Pap.

A growing number of colleges and universities across the United States are offering scholarships for alumni of American Field Service (AFS) high school exchange programs. These institutions are identified in AFS's *College Connection* catalog. In the third edition, 97 institutions awarding scholarships to students who have spent a summer or school year in one of 70 AFS countries are described. In addition, the catalog lists 63 colleges and universities that recognize the value of the AFS experience and offer scholarship assistance based on need. The entries are arranged alphabetically by academic institution and contain a description of the school, a summary of the programs offered, a list of financial assistance available to AFS returnees at the school, and a contact name, address, and telephone number.

16   American Universities and Colleges. Comp. by the American Council on Education. New York: Walter de Gruyter, 1928– . Irreg. 28–5598. ISSN 0066–0922. $99.50 (1983 ed.).

Based primarily on pre-1981 data, the latest volume in this set (which updates the 1973 edition) provides information on 1,700 institutions granting baccalaureate or higher degrees. The entries are arranged by state and then alphabetically by institution. Among the information categories presented in the entries (e.g., admission requirements, degree requirements, fees and expenses, chief executive and admissions officers), one deals with financial aid in 1979/80. Because both finances and financial aid at these schools have changed substantially since the time period covered, more accurate publications to use are the latest editions of *Peterson's Annual Guide to Undergraduate Study* (described elsewhere in this section) and *Peterson's Annual Guide to Graduate Study* (described in the "Fellowships—General—United States" section).

17   Annual Guide to Undergraduate Study. Princeton, NJ: Peterson's Guides, 1971–1975. Annual. 79–5391. ISSN 0091–0465.

From 1971 to 1984, data on two-year and four-year colleges were included in the same Peterson's Guides publications: in the *Annual Guide to Undergraduate Study* (1971 to 1975) and in *Peterson's Annual Guide to Undergraduate Study* (1976–1984). Since 1984, the data have been split into two separate works: *Guide to Four-Year Colleges* and *Guide to Two-Year Colleges*. For more information, see the descriptions of these two guides elsewhere in this section of the bibliography.

18   **Annual Register of Grant Support: A Guide to Support Programs of Government Agencies, Foundations, and Business and Professional Organizations.** Wilmette, IL: National Register, 1969– . Annual. 69–18307. ISSN 0066–4049. $87 (1985–86 ed.).

Despite its title, this annual covers scholarships, fellowships, and loans as well as grant opportunities. For more information, see the annotation in the "Grants—General—United States" section of this bibliography.

19   **Barron's Guide to the Two-Year Colleges, Volume 1: College Descriptions.** Woodbury, NY: Barron's Educational Series, 1960– . Triennial. 78–8611. $9.95 (1986 ed.). Pap.

Nearly 1,500 descriptions of two-year college programs are presented in this standard reference tool. The entries are grouped into three sections: two-year colleges, two-year colleges that provide residential facilities; and four-year colleges that offer two-year programs. In addition to brief information on the amount and type of financial aid available at each of the listed schools, the following data are provided: enrollment, gender ratio, affiliation, accreditation, calendar, environment, programs, student-teacher ratio, library holdings, admission requirements and procedures, tuition, and other expenses. An alphabetically arranged list of institutions constitutes the index. Volume 2 in the set is an *Occupational Program Selector*, designed to help students choose an occupation.

20   **Barron's Profiles of American Colleges, Volume 1: Descriptions of the Colleges.** Woodbury, NY: Barron's Educational Series, 1964– . Triennial. 75–4924. $28.95, cloth; $12.95, pap. (1986 ed.).

A companion to *Barron's Guide to the Two-Year Colleges* (described above), this directory provides a comprehensive list of accredited four-year U.S. colleges (those granting bachelor's degrees). In addition to brief information on financial aid, the entry profiles cover such topics as enrollment, admission requirements, student-faculty ratio, programs of study, and student life. Similar information on the institutions can be found in (1) the four volumes that make up Barron's regional directories: *The Midwest, The Northeast, The South,* and *The West* and (2) Barron's series of condensed specialized directories: *Barron's Compact Guide to Colleges* (1978– . 78–15174. $4.95, pap. 1986 ed.); *Barron's Guide to the Best, Most Popular, and Most Exciting Colleges* (1981– . 82–16474. $9.95, pap. 1986 ed.); and *Barron's Guide to the Most Prestigious Colleges* (1981– . 84–9314. $9.95, pap. 1986 ed.).

21 **Bear's Guide to Finding Money for College.** By John Bear. Berkeley, CA: Ten Speed Press, 1984. 157p. 84–50044. ISBN 0–89815–126–0. $5.95. Pap.

This informal and sometimes irreverent introduction to financial aid for college students identifies a surprisingly large number of specific financial aid programs in addition to providing the usual chatty instructions and encouragement found in trade-oriented paperbacks. The guide is carefully researched, sensibly organized, and well written. Over 100 athletic, military, and corporate scholarships are listed and very briefly described. In addition, over 200 fellowships, grants-in-aid, and other special awards are similarly covered. There is a lot of information here for $5.95.

22 **Career Opportunities News.** Garrett Park, MD: Garrett Park Press, 1983– . Bimonthly. 83–8288. ISSN 0739–5043. $30/yr.

Designed to assist the job seeker, this bimonthly newsletter provides current information about a variety of careers. In addition, it contains announcements of scholarships, fellowships, foundation grants, and seminars. A separate section deals with women's interests.

23 **Chronicle Four-Year College Databook.** Moravia, NY: Chronicle Guidance Publications, 1980– . Annual. 79–644820. ISSN 0192–3670. $17.75 (1986 ed.). Pap.
24 **Chronicle Two-Year College Databook.** Moravia, NY: Chronicle Guidance Publications, 1980– . Annual. 79–644821. ISSN 0191–3662. $15.95 (1986 ed.). Pap.
25 **Chronicle Vocational School Manual.** Moravia, NY: Chronicle Guidance Publications, 1980– . Annual. 82–643014. ISSN 0276–0371. $15.50 (1986 ed.). Pap.

Taken together, these three volumes provide a current and comprehensive survey of 2,600 two-year schools, 2,000 four-year schools, and 3,700 postsecondary vocational schools. The information presented is taken from questionnaires sent to institutions listed in the *Community, Technical and Junior College Directory* and the *Higher Education Directory*. All three Chronicle Guidance publications follow the same organizational pattern. In each, the final section, which presents the school data in tabular form, provides brief information on financial aid in addition to data on enrollment, admissions, and costs. These publications supersede *Chronicle Guide to Four-Year College Majors* (ISSN 0164–0194) and *Chronicle College Charts* (ISSN 0163–9242). Similar but more detailed information can be found in Peterson's *Guide to Two-Year Colleges* and *Guide to Four-Year Colleges* (described elsewhere in this section of the bibliography).

26 Chronicle Student Aid Annual. Moravia, NY: Chronicle Guidance
Publications, 1978– . Annual. 79–640360. ISSN 0190–339X. $16.50
(1985 ed.). Pap.

Information on financial aid programs offered nationally or regionally by
approximately 700 private and public organizations is provided in this annual
directory. The financial aid sponsors include private organizations, clubs,
foundations, sororities and fraternities, federal and state governments, and
national and international labor unions. The scope of the assistance programs
listed extends from the incoming freshman through the baccalaureate,
graduate, and postdoctoral levels. The types of programs listed include essay
awards, loans, scholarships, grants, and postdoctoral fellowships. The
programs are indexed by subject and sponsor. Prior to 1978, this directory
was issued as the *Student Aid Annual* (ISSN 0585–4555) and the *Student Aid
Manual* (76–18697. ISSN 0145–8043).

27 Clark's Guide: Directory of Non-need Financial Aid. Ed. by Charles A.
Clark. Quincy, IL: Advanced Acceptance Program, 1982. 177p. $10.
Pap.

Prepared as a reference guide for students, parents, and counselors interested
in financial aid not based on financial need, this directory is arranged by type
of program (e.g., academic scholarships, art scholarships, athletic
scholarships) and, for each of the 2,000 sponsoring organizations, provides
the following information: address, name of scholarship, type of award,
number offered, value of each, total amount of funds available, required test
scores, required grades and class rank, and other requirements. The value of
this listing is limited by the fact that few portable programs are covered; most
are sponsored by specific colleges or universities. A more useful (and more
current) list of non-need programs can be found in *Winning Money for
College,* which is described elsewhere in this section of the bibliography.

28 The College Aid Checkbook: A Guide to College Financial Aid. Clifton,
NJ: Army ROTC, 1985. n.p. Free. Pap.

Nearly 70 percent of all college families receive some type of financial aid to
cover educational expenses. This checkbook-sized pamphlet was prepared by
the Army ROTC (in conjunction with the College Board and the American
Association for Counseling and Development) as a starting point to identify
major private and public scholarships, grants, loans, and work programs. It is
written primarily for high school students and their parents. Only minimal
information is provided (for example, no addresses or telephone numbers are
included). The listing is current as of March, 1985.

29 College Blue Book. New York: Macmillan, 1923– . Biennial. 79–66191. ISSN 0069–5572. $185 (20th ed.).

First issued in 1923 as a single volume work, this reference publication has grown to a 1985 (20th) edition of five volumes. Each volume provides information on a different area of higher education (e.g., tabular data on American colleges; degrees offered, by college and by subject). Volume 5 of the set is devoted to scholarships, fellowships, loans, and grants available to undergraduate and graduate students (718p. $44. ISBN 0–02–695790–6). It identifies over $100 million offered by more than 2,000 programs. Arranged by discipline and subdivided by specific subject, the volume is indexed by sponsor, title, interest field, and levels of awards (a cumbersome but feasible way of locating all of the programs scattered throughout the volume for undergraduate, graduate, professional, and/or seminary study). A landmark work—but one marred by numerous typographical errors—the 20th edition is one of the first sources students in search of financial assistance should check.

30 The College Cost Book, 1980– . Prep. by the College Scholarship Service. New York: College Entrance Examination Board, 1980– . Biennial. 80–648095. ISSN 0270–8493. $10.95 (1985–86 ed.). Pap.

The 1985–86 edition (244p. ISBN 0–87447–210–5) indicates costs at more than 3,500 two- and four-year public, private, and proprietary institutions. Figures are given for tuition and fees, books and supplies, room and board, transportation, other expenses, and total student budget. The only financial data given in this school-by-school section is (1) if need analysis documents are required for financial aid; and (2) the deadline for financial aid applications. Of more value to the seeker of financial support is the appendix, which lists colleges by state that offer tuition and/or fee waivers and special tuition payment plans for senior citizens, minority students, the unemployed or children of unemployed, and for family members enrolled simultaneously. From 1970 through 1979, this publication was issued under the title *Student Expenses at Postsecondary Institutions.*

31 College Financial Aid and the Employee Tuition Benefit Programs of the Fortune 500 Companies. By Joseph P. O'Neill. Princeton, NJ: Conference University Press, 1981. 91p. 81–166448. Pap.

In February, 1981, the Conference of Small Private Colleges published its first survey of employee tuition benefits, entitled *College Financial Aid and the Employee Tuition Benefit Programs of the Fortune 500 Companies.* This became the basis of the 1984 publication distributed by Peterson's Guides, *Corporate Tuition Aid Programs* (which is described elsewhere in this section of the bibliography).

32   **The College Financial Aid Emergency Kit.** By Joyce Lain Kennedy and
Herm Davis. Cardiff, CA: Sun Features, 1986. 52p. ISBN
0–937238–05–1. $3.50. Pap.

Written by Kennedy, a nationally syndicated career columnist, and Davis,
the head of College Student Financial Aid Services (a scholarship search
service described in the "Databases and Search Services" chapter of this
bibliography), this small booklet presents hints on a variety of topics, from
filling out a financial application to negotiating more effectively with financial
aid officers. Approximately 50 sources of private and public funding are
identified. Also included are a glossary, resource guide, and calendar of
"what to do when."

33   **The College Handbook.** New York: College Entrance Examination
Board, 1940– . Annual. 41–12971. $15.95 (1985 ed.). Pap.

One of the basic tools for high school students and counselors, the 1985
edition of this annual (over the years the frequency has varied) provides
alphabetically arranged profiles of over 3,000 two-year and four-year colleges.
The information included in the entries was compiled from data supplied by
the institutions themselves. Financial aid (and how to apply for it) is one of
the categories covered. Very brief information is supplied.

34   **The College Money Handbook: The Complete Guide to Expenses,
Scholarships, Loans, Jobs, and Special Aid Programs at Four-Year
Colleges.** Princeton, NJ: Peterson's Guides, 1983– . 83–62921. Annual.
ISSN 0883–5578. $15.95 (1987 ed.). Pap.

The bulk of this book consists of "College Cost and Aid Profiles," which in
tabular form provide address, enrollment, expenses, a summary of
undergraduate financial aid, need-based freshmen aid profiles, non-need
freshmen awards, money saving options available, and financial aid
application procedures for 2,500 four-year colleges in the United States.
Indexes access the information by non-need aids, athletic programs, co-op
programs, ROTC programs, and guaranteed tuition/tuition repayment plans.

35   **Corporate Tuition Aid Programs: A Directory of College Financial Aid
for Employees at America's Largest Corporations.** By Joseph P.
O'Neill. 2d ed. Princeton, NJ: Conference University Press (dist. by
Peterson's Guides), 1986. 250p. 83–63528. ISBN 0–87866–482–3.
$14.95. Pap.

In February, 1981, the Conference of Small Private Colleges published its
first survey of employee tuition benefits, entitled *College Financial Aid and
the Employee Tuition Benefit Programs of the Fortune 500 Companies*. In
1984, the next "edition" of that survey was published by Conference
University Press (and distributed by Peterson's Guides) as *Corporate Tuition*

Aid Programs. In 1986, an update of that survey was released. It describes the tuition aid programs of 650 of America's largest industrial and service corporations (employing more than 17 million Americans, i.e., one quarter of the American work force). Using a large, detailed chart of company-by-company data, the directory answers such questions as: Which employees are eligible for tuition benefits? How long must one be employed to be eligible? How much of the tuition costs will a company pay? When does the company reimburse the employee? What kinds of courses may employees take under the program? The introduction includes sections that supplement the table and help readers to interpret the data. It also provides summary statistics based on the data in the tables. For example, 64 percent of the companies with tuition plans reimburse employees for certain kinds of nonjob-related courses; no company with a plan requires an employee to pay more than 50 percent of tuition for courses covered by the plan; 60 percent of the corporations responding give new employees immediate access to tuition reimbursement plans. Joseph P. O'Neill is the Executive Director of the Conference of Small Private Colleges, the organization that sponsored and published the survey of tuition aid programs on which this book is based.

36 Cutting College Costs. By Bruce H. Donald. New York: E.P. Dutton, 1982. 238p. 82–12792. ISBN 0–525–48009–9. $7.95. Pap.

General information and practical advice is offered to middle-income parents of college-bound students in this 1982 guide. The emphasis is on determining eligibility for financial aid, improving chances of acquiring aid, using financial planning (e.g., trusts, annuities) to cover costs, applying for federal aid programs, locating no-need scholarships, and employing cost-saving tactics (e.g., college credit by examination). Only a limited number of specific programs are identified: selected federal programs, state financial aid programs, and—in the appendix—no-need merit scholarships.

37 Directory of Research Grants. Phoenix: Oryx, 1975– . Annual. 76–47074. ISSN 0146–7336. $74.50 (1986 ed.). Pap.

Some scholarships, fellowships, and loans are described in this annual directory, in addition to research grants. For more information about the publication, see the annotation in the "Grants—General—United States" section of this bibliography.

38 Directory of Scholarships and Loan Funds. Irving, TX: Boy Scouts of America, 1985. 9p. Free. Pap.

While the Boy Scouts of America does not offer scholarships (except for the Eagle and Elks Scholarships), the association has compiled this free booklet to identify about 40 scholarships and loans of interest to Scouts and Explorers. Both institution-specific and unrestricted programs are described.

The brief entries indicate sponsoring organization, address, purpose, eligibility, remuneration, and deadline. In all, approximately 40 sources of financial assistance for current and former members of the Boy Scouts are covered.

39 Don't Miss Out: The Ambitious Student's Guide to Scholarships and Loans. By Robert Leider and Anna Leider. Alexandria, VA: Octameron Associates, 1976– . Annual. 84–643340. ISSN 0277–6987. $4 (1986 ed.). Pap.

Strategies for seeking financial aid for college students are outlined in this pamphlet (currently about 90 pages long). Each annual edition is divided into five parts, one of which identifies sample or representative programs: e.g., no-need, athletic, health careers, programs for particular careers, programs for minorities and women, programs for graduate students. Very brief information is provided for each of these programs, generally address, purpose, eligibility, and stipend. In addition to being issued as a separate publication, this work is also reprinted in its entirety in *Your Own Financial Aid Factory: The Guide to Locating Money for College* (described elsewhere in this section of the bibliography) and has been distributed by the National Association of Secondary School Principals as *Student's Guide to Scholarships & Loans.*

40 Encyclopedia of U.S. Government Benefits: A Complete, Practical, and Convenient Guide to United States Government Benefits Available to the People of America. Ed. by Beryl Frank. 11th ed. New York: Dodd Mead, 1985. 518p. 84–8018. ISBN 0–396–08438–9. $22.95.

Among the benefits described in this publication are scholarships available from the federal government. For more information about the publication, see the annotation in the "Grants—General—United States" section of this bibliography.

41 Fellowships, Scholarships, and Related Opportunities in International Education. Knoxville: Division of International Education, University of Tennessee, 1967– . Annual. 82–5141. ISSN 0735–8830. $8 (1986 ed.). Pap.

In the latest edition of this directory, over 120 scholarships, fellowships, and grants for study, research, and teaching in the United States and abroad are listed and described. For more information about the publication, see the annotation in the "Fellowships—General—International" section of this bibliography.

42 **Financial Aid for College through Scholarships and Loans: A Guide to Meeting College Expenses.** By Elizabeth Hoffman. 4th ed. Wellesley Hills, MA: Richards House, 1985. 169p. 85–185928. ISBN 0–930702–03–4. $7.95. Pap.

This directory focuses on major public programs (federal and state) and privately-sponsored sources (funded by businesses, churches, clubs, the health professions, trade unions, private trusts and foundations, and veterans organizations). Scholarships and loans are covered. Omitted are awards for students at particular high schools (if the guidance officer is the contact person), awards at specific colleges, most contests, graduate fellowships, and local awards in towns under 50,000 people. The entries are arranged by source of funding and indexed by subject, title, and organization. Program profiles contain the following information: address, program title, eligibility, remuneration, deadline, and contact person. Despite the general nature of its title, this work focuses on programs restricted to residents of Massachsuetts. It provides extensive coverage for that area. Earlier editions were issued under the title *FACTS: Financial Aid for College through Scholarships and Loans.*

43 **Financial Aids for Higher Education.** Prep. by Oreon Keeslar. Dubuque, IA: William C. Brown, 1963– . Biennial. 76–645208. ISSN 0364–8877. $32.95 (1986 ed.). Pap.

Each biennial edition of this directory contains detailed information on over 5,000 programs (scholarships, loans, and contests) sponsored by professional associations, national fraternal organizations, religious groups, charities, service organizations, national corporations, small businesses, labor unions, travel clubs, and state and national governments. The main section of each edition consists of an alphabetical listing of programs by official title. Each entry describes applicant eligibility and restrictions, remuneration, application process and deadlines, and sources of additional information. There is an index that provides access to sources of financial aid by sponsor, common name, field of specialization, type of program, and restrictions. A bibliography completes the source. Between 1963 and 1971, the directory was issued under the titles *National Catalog of Scholarships and Other Financial Aids for Students Entering College* and *National Catalog of Financial Aids for Students Entering College.* Since the early 1970s, it has been published as *Financial Aids for Higher Education,* with various subtitles. One of the most reliable listings of scholarships, loans, and awards/prizes, this directory belongs in any core collection of financial aid sources.

44   Financing College Education. By Kenneth A. Kohl. 3d ed. New York: Harper, 1983. 288p. 82–48232. ISBN 0–06–090994–3. $5.95. Pap.

This concise guide provides information on financial planning for a college education. Kohl reviews and evaluates various sources of financial assistance, including work-study programs, scholarship funds, and loans available to middle- and low-income students. Few specific programs are described. The first edition of this work was published in 1979 (229p. 78–20172).

45   Five Federal Financial Aid Programs: A Student Guide. Washington, DC: U.S. Department of Education, 1985/86. 43p. Free. Pap.

There are 12.3 million citizens in the United States who are continuing their education beyond high school. This is twice as many people in postsecondary study than in the Soviet Union, 10 times as many as in France, and 15 times as many as in the United Kingdom. In 1986, of the $24 billion that our nation spent on education, more than $11.8 billion was given to postsecondary students who needed help in paying their higher education costs. These funds were supplied through five federal programs: Pell Grants, Supplemental Educational Opportunity Grants, College Work-Study, National Direct Student Loans, and Guaranteed Study Loans/PLUS Loans. *Five Federal Financial Aid Programs*, distributed without charge by the U.S. Department of Education, describes these programs in detail, indicating purpose, remuneration, application procedures, eligibilities, recipient responsibilities, and notification process. The booklet concludes with a glossary and a list of U.S. Department of Education Regional Offices.

46   Foundation Grants to Individuals. Ed. by Claude Barilleaux. 4th ed. New York: Foundation Center, 1984. 242p. 84–185951. ISBN 0–87954–097–4. $18. Pap.

Many of the grant opportunities for individual applicants identified in the fourth edition of this directory are, in fact, scholarships and loan programs. For more information about the publication, see the annotation in the "Grants—General—United States" section of this bibliography.

47   Get Your Money, Honey: A Student's Guide to Staying Alive. By Shakurra Amatulla. 2d ed. Washington, DC: For Us Publications, 1984. 69p. 84–1647. ISBN 0–915383–01–2. $4.95. Pap.

Shakurra Amatulla is the editor/publisher of *For Us Women Newsletter*, a national monthly periodical identifying competitions for women and nonprofit organizations (described more fully in the "Awards and Prizes—General" section of this bibliography). The first 40 pages of *Get Your Money, Honey* consist of advice presented in a chatty style; subsections cover the psychological aspects of preparing for the financial aid search and the practical techniques of "going for the money." Pages 41 through 64 describe specific programs. The profiles are arranged by educational level. The emphasis is on undergraduate and graduate education; only nine postgraduate and twelve postdoctorate programs are listed. Entries are restricted to name and address of the sponsoring organization. The limited information provided limits the utility of the book. The first edition of this work was published in 1983 (68p. 83–20699. ISBN 0–915383–00–4).

48   Guide to Four-Year Colleges. Princeton, NJ: Peterson's Guides, 1985– . Annual. (Peterson's Annual Guide to Undergraduate Study). ISSN 0737–3163. $14.95 (1987 ed.). Pap.

Peterson's Guides issues a series of directories that have been useful to a generation of high school students. *Guide to Four-Year Colleges* has become one of their most popular titles. The 1987 edition (2,250p. ISBN 0–87866–527–7) covers more than 1,900 accredited institutions that grant baccalaureate degrees in the United States and Canada. It is arranged in five sections (e.g., messages from college admissions directors, special supplement on ROTC programs), one of which provides brief information on the financial aid available at each institution. The entries are indexed by school name. The online version of this directory is *Peterson's College Database* (described in the "Databases and Search Services" chapter), which permits computerized access to over 3,000 colleges and universities with two- and four-year degree programs in the United States and Canada. The information on undergraduate colleges included in the *Guide to Four-Year Colleges* has been issued by Peterson's Guides since 1971, but under a variety of titles. From 1971 through 1975, the material was published as the *Annual Guide to Undergraduate Study*; from 1976 to 1984, the work was published as *Peterson's Annual Guide to Undergraduate Study*. These two publications incorporated data on both four-year and two-year colleges. Since 1984, the data on four-year colleges has been released separately as *Guide to Four-Year Colleges*.

49   Guide to Two-Year Colleges. Princeton, NJ: Peterson's Guides, 1985– . Annual. 84–644469. ISSN 0737–3171. $10.95 (1987 ed.). Pap.

The 1987 edition of this annual guide lists 1,450 institutions that grant associate degrees in the United States and Canada. Concise profiles describe each of these institutions; in addition to typical directory-type data, the profiles provide brief information on the types of financial aid available. The online version of this directory is *Peterson's College Database* (described in the "Databases and Search Services" chapter of this bibliography), which permits computerized access to over 3,000 Canadian and American two-year and four-year degree programs. The information on two-year colleges included in the *Guide to Two-Year Colleges* has been issued by Peterson's Guides since 1971, but under a variety of titles. From 1971 through 1975, the material was published as the *Annual Guide to Undergraduate Study*; from 1976 to 1984 as *Petersons's Guide to Undergraduate Study*. These two publications incorporated data on both two-year and four-year colleges. Since 1984, the data on two-year colleges has been issued separately in the *Guide to Two-Year Colleges*.

50 How to Understand and Apply for Financial Aid. By Kitty Miller. Allentown, PA: Log Cabin, 1984. 16p. ISBN 0–932080–08–1. $1.25. Pap.

Like the Octameron booklets described elsewhere in this section of the bibliography, this pamphlet is aimed at students, counselors, and parents. The general information it provides on scholarships, grants, loans, and college work study is covered in more depth in the free government publication *Five Federal Financial Aid Programs: A Student Guide* (also described in this section). Despite its low price, there is not enough unique content to make this a necessary purchase.

51 Lovejoy's Guide to Financial Aid. By Robert Leider. New York: Monarch Press, 1985. 267p. 84–062593. ISN 0–671–49714–6. $9.95. Pap.

Intended to provide "clear and simple advice for the consumer to help target financial aid and save money," this guide is written by Robert Leider (president of Octameron Associates) in the same informal and chatty style that characterizes all of the Octameron booklets (described elsewhere in this section of the bibliography). Few specific financial aid programs are identified. Those that are included tend to be ones also covered in the more comprehensive standard financial aid directories (e.g., Keeslar's *Financial Aid for Higher Education* and the *Chronicle Student Aid Annual*, both described in this section).

52 Mortgaged Futures: How to Graduate from School without Going Broke. By M. J. Dennis. Washington, DC: Hope Press, 1986. 175p. 85–27245. ISBN 0–9615878–2–2. $9.95. Pap.

Written by the Associate Dean for Student Services at Georgetown University of Dentistry, this 175–page paperback was prepared "(1) to delineate the issues involved in student financial planning and debt management, (2) to provide information on the financial aid application process, (3) to compile a resource and reference guide, (4) to assist students and parents in recognizing the need for establishing student financial planning and debt management programs, and (5) to stimulate creative thought in parents and students seeking ways to finance postsecondary education." While most of the book consists of case studies, financial tables, a bibliography, a glossary, and discussions of the financial aid application procedures, there is one chapter that provides a "Financial Aid Resource List." Included in this chapter are a short list of financial aid directories, the state agencies that supply information on loan and scholarship programs, and a sampling of public and private financial aid programs. A similar publication that provides a more extensive list of specific financial aid programs is *Bear's Guide to Finding Money for College* (described elsewhere in this section of the bibliography).

53 National Catalog of Scholarships and Other Financial Aids for Students Entering College. Prep. by Oreon Keeslar. Dubuque, IA: William C. Brown, 1963–1971. Biennial. 80–11707.

A continuation of the works Keeslar had done for the California State Department of Education (the *Catalog of Scholarships and College Entrance Requirements for High School Graduates* and *Financial Aids for Students Entering College: A Catalog of Scholarships and Entrance Requirements*), this directory has undergone a number of name changes. Currently, it is being published as *Financial Aids for Higher Education* (described elsewhere in this section of the bibliography).

54 National College Databank: The College Book of Lists. Ed. by Karen C. Hegener. Princeton, NJ: Peterson's Guides, 1984. 861p. 84–14798. ISBN 0–87866–268–5. $11.95. Pap.

This guide to accredited colleges and universities that offer associate's or bachelor's degrees is divided into 10 sections, one of which deals with "Financial Aid"; others cover such topics as "Admissions Information," "Expenses," and "Entrance Difficulty Data." Each section is further divided into specific characteristics, e.g., student body size, freshmen attrition. Within these subdivisions, the institutions are either listed by name or grouped by state. Finding information in the guide is complicated by two factors: there is no index and the placement of characteristics is unpredictable (for example, sports scholarships are covereed in the "Campus Life Characteristics" section, not the "Financial Aid" section.

55 Need a Lift? To Educational Opportunities, Careers, Loans, Scholarships, Employment. Prep. by the American Legion Educational and Scholarship Program. Indianapolis: American Legion, 1969– . Annual. $1 (1986 ed.). Pap.

This annually revised guide to sources of financial aid is distributed for a $1 charge from the American Legion (P.O. Box 1055, Indianapolis, IN 46206). It is primarily intended as a source book for children of veterans, although it also contains general information of interest to any student pursuing postsecondary education. The booklet presents descriptions of scholarships, fellowships, loans, and state educational benefits valued at over $4 billion.

Also provided is an annotated bibliography of sources for further information.

56 New York Times Selective Guide to Colleges. New York: Times Books, 1982. 1v. 84–64018.

Only one volume was issued under this title. In 1983, the publication was renamed *Selective Guide to Colleges* (described elsewhere in this section of the bibliography) and two volumes have come out under the new title.

57 Peterson's Annual Guide to Undergraduate Study. Princeton, NJ: Peterson's Guides, 1976–1984. Annual. 77–641842. ISSN 0147–8451.

Prior to 1984, data on two-year and four-year colleges were included in the same Petersons's Guides publications: *Peterson's Annual Guide to Undergraduate Study* (1976 to 1984) and *Annual Guide to Undergraduate Study* (1971 to 1975). Since 1984, the data have been split into two separate works: *Guide to Four-Year Colleges* and *Guide to Two-Year Colleges*. For more information, see the descriptions of these two guides elsewhere in this section of the bibliography.

58 Peterson's State and Federal Aid Programs for College Students. Princeton, NJ: Peterson's Guides, 1986. 56p. ISBN 0–87866–525–0. $3. Pap.

This concise booklet contains a description of the five major federal aid programs available to undergraduate college students: Pell Grants, College Work-Study, National Direct Student Loans, Guaranteed Student Loans, PLUS Loans, and Supplemental Educational Opportunity Grants. It also lists state-sponsored aid programs, indicating contact name and address in each state. The information included here duplicates what has been presented in the Octameron booklets (e.g., *College Loans from Uncle Sam*) and in the free federal pamphlet *Five Federal Financial Aid Programs: A Student Guide* (described elsewhere in this section of the bibliography).

59 Rich or Poor, A College Scholarship Is Possible: A Guide to Scholarships without Financial Need, 1981–82. By Justin B. Galford. Livingston, NJ: Ellen Roberts Press, 1981. 26p. $3. Pap.

Like *Clark's Directory of Non-need Financial Aid*, this small directory is a good idea not well executed. Chatty in presentation, with generalizations rather than specifics, the typescript pamphlet identifes few programs of financial assistance. Those that are mentioned tend to be tenable only at specific academic institutions rather than portable (like the National Merit Scholarships). Furthermore, the lack of systematic organization makes the booklet difficult to use as a reference source. The 1981 edition is a revision of a 1980 pamphlet (30p.).

60 **The Scholarship Book: The Complete Guide to Private-Sector Scholarships, Grants and Loans for Undergraduates.** By Daniel J. Cassidy and Michael J. Alves. Englewood Cliffs, NJ: Prentice-Hall, 1984. 391p. 84–11683. ISBN 0–13–792342–2, cloth; -334–1, pap. $28.50, cloth; $14.95, pap.

The title of this directory does not exactly describe its contents. The listing is not restricted to "scholarships, grants, or loans"; fellowships, internships, and contest prizes are also described. In addition, despite the subtitle, the directory is not limited to the "private-sector"; programs sponsored by the U.S. Public Health Service and other public agencies are included as well. Furthermore, this is not a book for "undergraduates" only; graduate fellowships, grants, and traineeships—such as those sponsored by Japan-United States Frienship Committee—also show up in the listings. Finally, the compilation is far from "complete," even for undergraduate programs. Many of the financial aids identified in Keeslar's *Financial Aids for Higher Education* and the *Chronicle Student Aid Annual* (both described elsewhere in this section of the bibliography) are not covered here. What is this then? The directory is a somewhat random assortment of various types and levels of programs arranged by major field of study and indexed by majors, specific fields, and sponsoring organization/program title. Entries specify program name, sponsoring organization, address, telephone number, amounts, deadlines, distinctive areas, and other information. The data presented were taken from co-author Daniel Cassidy's National Scholarship Search Service (described in the "Databases and Search Services" chapter of this bibliography), but seemingly without much selectivity. There's a lot of information here for the money but not much focus.

61 **Scholarship Booklet for Undergraduates.** By Jerry Adams. lst ed. Orland, IN: Education Unlimited, 1981. 46p. $10. Pap.

It's not clear what Adams intended the scope of this listing to be. While he states in the introduction that excluded from this booklet are "the foundations that restrict their scholarship awards to; (sic) children of...veterans, and...those of specific races, sexes, or ancestry," there are programs described for "daughters of veterans" and "women and girls of Hawaii." The arrangement of the publication also seems confusing. The entries are arranged either by topic (from accounting to teaching) or by state (the bigger section). However, some subject-related programs, like the "Soil Conservation Society Scholarship," are covered in the geographic but not the subject section. If you are interested in general scholarship programs, better organized and more up-to-date sources to use are the *Financial Aids for Higher Education Catalog* and the *Chronicle Student Aid Annual* (both described elsewhere in this section of the bibliography).

62 Scholarships, Fellowships and Loans. Prep. by S. Norman Feingold and Marie Feingold. Bethesda, MD: Bellman Publishing, 1949– . Irreg. 49–49180. $80 (v. 8, 1986).

Issued irregularly since 1949 (the latest edition came out in 1986), this comprehensive guide to student aid provides detailed information on scholarships, fellowships, grants, and loans available to undergraduate and graduate students. The directory is arranged alphabetically by sponsoring agency and is indexed by field of interest. Until the seventh volume was issued, entries were cumulated from one volume to the other. Since volume 7, however, each edition is unique; no information is duplicated. Therefore, be sure to check all recent volumes when using this source. Volume 8, the 1986 edition, provides information on over $1 billion awarded annually by 1,400 financial aid programs. Each entry identifies qualifications, funds, purpose, application process, and background. The Vocational Goals Index pinpoints for whom the award is geared: i.e., level of study, subject of study, geographic area, affiliation requirements, and citizenship. The source is kept up-to-date by *Scholarships, Fellowships and Loans News Service and Counselors Information Services* (described below).

63 Scholarships, Fellowships and Loans News Service and Counselors Information Services. Bethesda, MD: Bellman Publishing, 1980– . Quarterly. 81–642576. ISSN 0277–6502. $32/yr.

This quarterly looseleaf supplement to Feingold's *Scholarships, Fellowships and Loans* (described above) presents up-to-date information on scholarship changes, new student aid awards, and research on financial aid. Also included are annotated bibliographies of relevant books, articles, and professional journals. There is an annual index. Up until 1980, the service was titled *Scholarships, Fellowships and Loans News Service*; with issue 4 of the 1980 volume, the newsletter merged with *Counselors Information Services* to form *Scholarships, Fellowships and Loans News Service and Counselors Information Services.*

64 Selected List of Fellowship Opportunities and Aids to Advanced Education for United States Citizens and Foreign Nationals. Washington, DC: National Science Foundation, 1984. 76p. Free. Pap.

Despite its title, this free pamphlet presents concise descriptions of undergraduate scholarships, loans, and work-study experiences as well as fellowship opportunities. For more information about this publication, see the annotation in the "Fellowships—General—United States" section of this bibliography.

65 **Selective Guide to Colleges.** New York: Times Books, 1983– . Biennial. 85–40267. ISSN 0738–243X. $10.95 (1986–87 ed.). Pap.

Unlike many of the other college directories listed in this bibliography, this publication is written in a narrative rather than outline form. For each edition, data are collected from college presidents, admissions officers, and students. Profiles (averaging nearly two pages) for approximately 300 academic institutions provide brief information on financial aid as well as academics, student body, housing, social life, and extracurricular activities. Each college is rated on a scale of 1 to 5, on the basis of quality of life, social life, and academics. In 1982, the directory was issued as the *New York Times Selective Guide to Colleges*; since 1983, it has been titled *Selective Guide to Colleges*.

66 **Student Aid Annual.** Moravia, NY: Chronicle Guidance Publications, 1955–1974. Annual. ISSN 0585–4555.

From 1955 through 1974, this publication was known as *Student Aid Annual*, from 1955 through 1978 as *Student Aid Manual*, and since 1979 as *Chronicle Student Aid Annual* (described elsewhere in this section of the bibliography).

67 **Student Aid Manual.** Moravia, NY: Chronicle Guidance Publications, 1975–1978. Biennial. 76–18697. ISSN 0145–8043.

Since 1979, this publication has been issued as the *Chronicle Student Aid Annual* (see description elsewhere in this section).

68 **Student Expenses at Postsecondary Institutions.** New York: College Entrance Examination Board, 1970–1979. Annual. 74–167315. ISSN 0361–0039.

Since 1980, this publication has been issued under the title *The College Cost Book* (described elsewhere in this section of the bibliography).

69 **What Every Veteran Should Know.** East Moline, IL: Veterans Information Service, 1937– . Annual, with monthly supplements. ISSN 0083–9108. $6.00; $18, with supplements (1981 ed.). Pap.

Published since 1937, the latest edition of this guide (1981. ISBN 0–346–32464–5) describes the federal benefits that veterans and their dependents are eligible to receive. Instructions are provided on the best ways to obtain assistance. Entries are arranged by subject and thoroughly indexed.

70 **Winning Money for College: The High School Student's Guide to Scholarship Contests.** By Alan Deutschman. Princeton, NJ: Peterson's Guides, 1984. 209p. 83–22151. ISBN 0–87866–261–8. $7.95. Pap.

Written by a Princeton student who won several awards himself, this guide covers 50 national scholarship competitions that award cash prizes for use at any college chosen by the winner. The listing focuses on public speaking, science, citizenship, and related areas. The programs included in the book all provide some form of monetary reward; are based on talent, achievement, and competitive performance (rather than such personal characteristics as race or financial need); may be used at a college or university of the winner's choice; and are open to national competition. Excluded are local programs, athletic awards, and programs open only to nomination. Entries include information about eligibility requirements, the number and value of available scholarships, requirements for contest entrance, background information and rules, deadlines, strategies and inside advice, interviews with previous winners or program officials, and contact names. The dates and statistics refer to 1983 contests only. Samples of winning entries are included in the book. While the listing is somewhat arbitrary in its coverage and far from exhaustive, its inexpensive price makes it a worthwhile acquisition.

71 **Your Own Financial Aid Factory, 1985—1986: The Guide to Locating College Money.** By Robert Leider. 5th ed. Princeton, NJ: Peterson's Guides, 1985. 212p. 80–11185. ISBN 0–87866–295–2. $7.95. Pap.

The fifth edition of this consumer guide to student financial aid incorporates five pamphlets that have been published individually by Octameron Associates: *Don't Miss Out*: a step-by-step exploration of the financial aid process; *The A's and B's of Academic Scholarships*: a brief description of scholarships awarded at 845 colleges; *College Grants from Uncle Sam*: an explanation of the federal government's needs analysis procedures; *College Loans from Uncle Sam*: a description of the $10 billion loan program available from the federal government; and *Earn & Learn: Cooperative Education Opportunities*: a description of the cooperative education programs supported by the federal government. The first edition of this work was issued in 1980. Sometimes, this title is referred to as *Robert Leider's Your Own Financial Aid Factory*.

Florida

72 **Financial Aid Sources for Florida Students.** Tallahassee: Office of Student Financial Assistance, Florida Department of Education. Annual. Free. Pap.

The purpose of this booklet is to provide a starting point for Florida students who plan to continue their education beyond high school and will find financial assistance to do so. A two-page chart lists and describes financial aid programs sponsored by both the federal government and the Florida state government. Entries cover eligibility, remuneration, and application procedures.

Illinois

73 **Financial Aids to Illinois Students.** Springfield: Illinois Office of Education, 1967– . Biennial. 76–641298. ISSN 0085–0543. Free. Pap.

Identified in this biennial directory are scholarships, grants, and loans offered to Illinois students by veteran's associations, private organizations, and colleges and universities. Entries include sponsoring organization address and descriptions of assistance available. Much of this part of the publication is taken from the American Legion's annual *Need a Lift?*. Presented in the rest of the directory are lists offering Veterans Administration-approved programs and academic institutions in Illinois (specifying telephone number, whether or not coed, whether or not public, enrollment, tuition and fees, cost of room and board, and dormitory capacity). First published in 1967 (160p. 68–7442) and issued irregularly for many years, this directory is now released on a biennial basis.

Massachusetts

74 **Financial Aid for College through Scholarships and Loans: A Guide to Meeting College Expenses.** By Elizabeth Hoffman. 4th ed. Wellesley Hills, MA: Richards House, 1985. 169p. 85–185928. ISBN 0–930702–03–4. $7.95. Pap.

Despite the general nature of the title of this publication, the emphasis is on scholarships and loans open to Massachusetts residents. For more information about the publication, see the annotation in the "Scholarships— General—United States" section of this bibliography.

75 **Massachusetts Foundation Directory Supplement: Sources of Private Support for Individuals.** Boston: Associated Grantmakers of Massachusetts, 1984. 109p. 84–71466. ISBN 0–912427–02–7. $12. Pap.

The Associated Grantmakers of Massachusetts was established "to promote effective philanthropy." One of the ways the association has attempted to achieve this purpose is by compiling this guide to sources of private support for Massachusetts residents. Described here are 340 financial aid programs sponsored by private foundations, corporations, service organizations, and labor unions. Of those, 280 provide funds to individuals to meet the cost of higher education, 53 offer assistance in financial emergencies, and seven support artistic activities. Each of the organizations listed is based in Massachusetts and gives annual grants of at least $1,500 to individuals. The entries are arranged by type of support offered (e.g., educational, cultural) and contain the following information: purpose, geographic restrictions, types of support, eligibility, remuneration, application procedures, deadline, trustees, staff, contact person, and publications. A very useful resource, this directory shoud serve as a model for states interested in compiling geographically-based listings.

Minnesota

76 **Dollars for Scholars Student Aid Catalog: Minnesota Edition.** By Marlys C. Johnson and Linda J. Thompson. Princeton, NJ: Peterson's Guides, 1982. v.p. 81–23503. ISBN 0–87866–194–8. $7.95. Pap.

This listing was prepared by staff of the Citizens' Scholarship Foundation of America (CSFA), a national nonprofit, tax-exempt organization dedicated to stimulating student aid opportunities in the private sector. It is based on material from CSFA's files of student aid programs at the national and state levels. The catalog is divided into four "directories." Directory 1 contains an abbreviated listing of 900 aid programs restricted to Minnesota residents, subdivided into 15 interest areas (e.g., agriculture, business, engineering, theology). Each entry in this section specifies abbreviated name of the award, type of aid, gender code for eligibility, year or years in college for which this aid may be used, and entry number in Directory 2, where a more detailed description can be found (including information on sponsoring organization address, number and type of awards given each year, application deadline, remuneration, and purpose of the program). These two directories are duplicated exactly in the other volume in this series: *Dollars for Scholars Student Aid Catalog: New Hampshire Edition.*

New Hampshire

77 **Directory of Charitable Funds in New Hampshire: For General Charitable Purposes and Scholarship Aid.** 3d ed. Concord, NH: Office of the Attorney General, 1976. 107p. 77–624167. $2. Pap.

78 **Cumulative Supplement.** Concord, NH: Office of the Attorney General, 1977– . Annual. $2 (1984 ed.). Pap.

More than half the listings in the 1976 directory and each of the supplements describe scholarships open to New Hampshire residents. For more information about the publication, see the annotation in the "Grants— General—New Hampshire" section of this bibliography.

79 **Dollars for Scholars Student Aid Catalog: New Hampshire Edition.** By Linda J. Thompson and Marlys C. Johnson. Princeton, NJ: Peterson's Guides, 1982. v.p. 81–23502. ISBN 0–87866–193–X. $5.95. Pap.

This listing was prepared by the staff of the Citizen's Scholarship Foundation of America (CSFA), a national nonprofit, tax-exempt organization dedicated to stimulating student aid opportunities in the private sector. It is based on material from CSFA's files of student aid programs at the state and national levels. The catalog is divided into four "directores." Directory 1 contains an abbreviated listing of 400 aid programs restricted to New Hampshire residents, subdivided into 15 interest areas (e.g., agriculture, business, engineering, theology). Each entry in this section specifies abbreviated name of the award, type of aid, gender code for eligibility, year or years in college for which the aid may be used, and entry number in Directory 2, where a more detailed description can be found (including information on sponsoring organization address, number and type of awards given each year, application deadline, remuneration, and purpose of the program). Directories 3 and 4 follow the same pattern but cover 900 national programs. These two sections are duplicated exactly in the other volume issued in the series: *Dollars for Scholars Student Aid Catalog: Minnesota Edition* (described in the "Scholarships—General—Minnesota" section of this bibliography).

Wyoming

80 **Student Financial Aids and Scholarships at Wyoming Colleges.** Laramie, WY: Division of Financial Aid, University of Wyoming. Annual. Free.

This very useful and well-done publication, distributed without charge by the University of Wyoming's Division of Financial Aid, identifies specific financial aid programs available at each of Wyoming's postsecondary institutions. Brief descriptions (purpose, amount awarded, number awarded) are provided. In addition, scholarships available to Wyoming residents that may be used at any institution are also covered selectively.

SOCIAL SCIENCES

Anthropology

81 **Funding for Anthropological Research.** Ed. by Karen Cantrell and Denise Wallen. Phoenix: Oryx, 1986. 308p. 85–43472. ISBN 0–89774–154–4. $74.50. Pap.

Published in 1986, this directory identifies 700 scholarships, fellowships, grants, and loans from 200 government agencies, private and corporate foundations, associations, institutes, museums, libraries, and professional societies that would be of interest to "professional anthropologists and graduate anthropology students." For more information about the publication, see the annotation in the "Grants—Social Sciences—Anthropology" section of this bibliography.

Athletics

82 **Association for Intercollegiate Athletics for Women Directory.**
Washington, DC: Association for Intercollegiate Athletics for Women,
1977– . Biennial. 84–12725. ISSN 0361–5898. $10. Pap.

This biennial directory provides a complete listing of AIAW-member
institutions and indicates scholarship offerings at each of them. From 1972 to
1974, the publication was issued as *Directory, AIAW Member Institutions.*
The volume for 1975–76 combined with the *AIAW Handbook of Policies and
Operating Procedures* and was published as the *AIAW Handbook-Directory.*
Since 1977, it has been issued as the *Association for Intercollegiate Athletics
for Women Directory.*

83 **Callahan's College Guide to Athletics and Academics in America.** By
Timothy R. Callahan. New York: Harper & Row, 1984. 259p.
83–48333. ISBN 0–06–015249–4, cloth; –464081–7, pap. $17.95, cloth;
$9.95, pap.

Issued in 1981 as *The College Guide to Athletics and Academics in the
Northeast* and in 1982 as *Callahan's Compact College Guide to Athletics and
Academics in America* (both published by Callahan's Guides, this new edition
has a slight title change and a new publisher. But the book's format,
arrangement, and content remain basically the same. This directory provides
information on approximately 300 colleges commonly attended by student
athletes. Brief (one page) descriptions on each school cover academic
environment, names of information and athletic directors, athletic division
and conference, conference and national rankings, and won and lost records.
Very limited information on grants-in-aid (average amount and number) is
given for each school.

84 **College: What Every Athlete Needs to Know.** By Bob Florence.
Chicago: Contemporary Books, 1981. 213p. 80–65921. ISBN
0–8092–7109–5. $12.95, cloth.

Compiled by a former collegiate basketball star who subsequently worked as
a professional player, sports columnist, television sports commentator, and
director of an athletes' training program, this directory of scholarships and
athletic programs is divided into three major sections. The first two sections,
"Men's Senior College" and "Men's Junior College," are reprinted from the
National Directory of College Athletics and do not provide financial aid
information. The third section,"Women's Sports Scholarships," reprints a
1980 list of programs/scholarships prepared by the Women's Sports
Foundation. That list has been updated annually since then and is available
for only $2 from the Women's Sports Foundation (see the description of
Women's Sports and Fitness Magazine: Scholarship Guide Issue elsewhere in

this section). A much better purchase than Florence's work for approximately the same money is *The Directory of Athletic Scholarships* (described elsewhere in this section of the bibliography).

85 The College Guide to Athletics and Academics in the Northeast. Comp. by Tim Callahan. Essex Junction, VT: Callahan's Guides, 1981. 154p.

Subsequent editions of this work have been issued under the titles *Callahan's Compact Guide to Athletics and Academics in America* (1982. 247p. 82–73347) and *Callahan's College Guide to Athletics and Academics in America* (described elsewhere in this section of the bibliography).

86 The Complete Guide to Women's College Athletics: Includes over 10,000 Women's Athletic Scholarships and Recruiting Rules and Regulations. By Carolyn Stanek. Chicago: Contemporary Books, 1981. 244p. 80–70635. ISBN 0–8092–5986–4, cloth; -5985–6, pap. $14.95, cloth; $7.95, pap.

In 1980, approximately 700 colleges offered more than $7 million to women athletes. Stanek prepared this guide to assist women high school students interested in obtaining financial assistance for participating in college sports. The bulk of her work provides practical advice, including what to expect in the recruitment process, how to find a good coach, and how to locate a summer sports camp. Of particular value is Appendix 1, which identifies Women's Sports Foundation scholarships. The programs are listed by institution (within geographic groups) and described in terms of sports programs and financial assistance available. In addition, there is a list of women's sports camps, a four-page bibliography listing books and articles on women in sports, and an index to topics and names. Since this compilation is now several years out of date, women interested in college athletics will be better served by first checking *Women's Sports and Fitness Magazine*'s scholarship guide (described elsewhere in this section of the bibliography).

87 The Directory of Athletic Scholarships: Where They Are and How to Get Them. By Barry Green and Alan Green. New York: Putnam, 1981. 363p. 81–4499. ISBN 0–399–12620–1. $14.95.

The title of this directory might be misleading. This is not a guide to scholarships, but a listing of colleges and universities that participate in intercollegiate competitions and offer athletic scholarships. In all, over 40 major and minor sports for both men and women—from archery to wrestling—in more than 1,000 junior and community colleges, four-year colleges, and universities are covered. The main section of the book provides an annotated listing of schools (with their athletic conference affiliation); each entry specifies school name, address and telephone number of the men's and women's athletic departments, male and female athletic conference memberships, male and female sports offered, and the availability of scholarships for these sports. A sports-by-sports index provides the only other access to these entries. A discussion of the recruitment process (including summaries of Title IX and the NCAA) and directory information for 26 collegiate sports professional associations complete the volume. The cloth edition of the directory was published by Putnam; a paper edition was issued by Perigee Books ($6.95).

88   Directory   of   Undergraduate   Physical   Education   Programs. Washington, DC: National Association for Sport and Physical Education, 1979– . Irreg. 79–106845. $11.95 (1982 ed.).

This guide presents information on schools granting undergraduate degrees in physical education and recreation. Included in the general description of each school is an indication of the financial assistance available. A companion volume, *Directory of Graduate Physical Education Programs* (described in the "Fellowships—Social Sciences—Athletics" section), identifies available fellowships for graduate education.

89   Financial Aid for College-bound Athletes. By Marlene Lazar and Stephen H. Lazar. New York: Arco, 1982. 323p. 82–1607. ISBN 0–6680–5499–9, cloth; -5500–6, pap. $14.95, cloth; $8.95, pap.

This guide provides information on 38 collegiate and/or intercollegiate sports (e.g., archery, baseball, bowling, football, frisbee) arranged into two categories: alphabetically by schools in each state; alphabetically by sport. Over 800 entries specify names and addresses for each school, team sports offered, number of athletic scholarships or loans available in each sport, athletic conferences in which each institution participates, availability of out-of-state tuition waivers, deadlines for application, and whether or not the school offers a degree program in physical education. An index of colleges completes the volume.

90   Financial Aid for Student/Athletes, 1982–1983 Edition. By Charles A. Clark III and Patricia Zwick-Clark. Quincy, IL: Advanced Acceptance Program, 1982. 109p. $5. Pap.

This directory was compiled "to assist the high school athlete who intends to pursue a specific activity on the college level and wishes to compete for any available funds associated with that sport." Entries, arranged by state and school, contain minimal information: address and sports for which there are funds. Neither program names nor remuneration are specified. For more comprehensive coverage of athletic scholarships available at the college level, see *Financial Aid for College-bound Athletes* (described elsewhere in this section of the bibliography).

91   **United States Tennis Association College Tennis Guide.** Princeton, NJ: United States Tennis Association, 1979– . Annual. 84–11370. $5. Pap.

Basic information on a number of junior colleges, liberal arts colleges, and universities that offer tennis programs is given in this annual directory. Full and partial tennis scholarships are indicated.

92   **Women's Sports and Fitness Magazine: Scholarship Guide Issue.** San Francisco: Women's Sports Foundation, 1979– . Annual. 85–643170. ISSN 8750–653X. $2. Pap.

This annual list, published in the January issue of *Women's Sports and Fitness Magazine*, currently provides the most comprehensive information on athletic scholarships for women offered at 800 academic institutions in 24 different sports (more than twice as many as covered in the first guide). The guide lists colleges and universities offering scholarships alphabetically by state. Each entry specifies school name, address, and telephone number; name and title of contact person; kinds of scholarships available; their value; and number offered. Most entries also indicate the national athletic association with which the school is affiliated. Reprints of the annual article are available for $2 from the Women's Sports Foundation (195 Mouton Street, San Francisco, CA 94123).

Business and Economics

93   **Financial Aid for Minorities in Business.** Ed. by Howard F. Wehrle, III and Ruth N. Swann. Garrett Park, MD: Garrett Park Press, 1980. 48p. 80–144474. $3. Pap.

One in a series of booklets covering financial assistance programs for minorities, this compilation identifies selected scholarships, fellowships, and grants in the field of business that were available in 1980. The listing is generally unannotated. Despite its title, many of the programs included are not restricted just to minority applicants but are open equally to all segments of the population. A number of the entries are general in nature and there is considerable duplication among booklets in the Garrett Park Press "Financial Aid for Minorities" series. During the past few years, there have been dramatic changes in the financial aid available to minorities, and this listing is now seriously out of date. For more current and comprehensive coverage, see the *Directory of Financial Aids for Minorities* described in the "Scholarships—Special Population Groups—Ethnic Groups" section of this bibliography.

94   **Free Money for Professional Studies.** By Laurie Blum. New York: Barnes and Noble, 1985. 204p. (Blum's Guides to College Money). 85–42725. ISBN 0–06–464104–0. $5.95. Pap.

This guide identifies state-based organizations awarding scholarships, fellowships, and grants to their residents, miscellaneous awards available to special applicants (e.g., deaf children, veteran's dependents), and selected financial aid programs appropriate for "professional studies" (including business administration). For more information about the publication, see the annotation in the "Fellowships—Sciences—Health Sciences" section of this bibliography.

Education

95   **Financial Aid for Minorities in Education.** Ed. by Mary T. Christian and Ruth N. Swann. Garrett Park, MD: Garrett Park Press, 1980. 58p. 80–153221. $3. Pap.

One in a series of booklets covering financial assistance programs for minorities, this compilation identifies selected scholarships, fellowships, and grants in the field of education that were available in 1980. The list is generally unannotated. Despite its title, many of the programs included are not restricted just to minority applicants but are open equally to all segments of the population. A number of the entries are general in nature and there is considerable duplication among booklets in the Garrett Park Press "Financial Aid for Minorities" series. During the last few years, there have been dramatic changes in the financial aid available to minorities, and this listing is now seriously out of date. For more current and comprehensive coverage, see the *Directory of Financial Aids for Minorities* described in the "Scholarships—Special Population Groups—Ethnic Groups" section of this bibliography.

Geography

96   **Guide to Departments of Geography in the United States and Canada.** Washington, DC: Association of American Geographers, 1985– . Annual. 85–641423. ISSN 0072–8497. $9 (1985 ed.). Pap.

This guide identifies most of the geography departments in the United States and Canada that offer majors and/or graduate programs of study. It provides information on financial aid available, as well as on other school-related characteristics. For more information about the publication, see the annotation in the "Fellowships—Social Sciences—Geography" section of this bibliography.

Librarianship

97 **Financial Assistance for Library Education.** Chicago: American
Library Association, 1970– . Annual. 73–649921. ISSN 0569–6275. $1
(1986–87 ed.). Pap.

This annual directory identifies scholarships, fellowships, grants-in-aid, loans,
and other financial aids for library education in the United States and
Canada. For more information about this publication, see the annotation in
the "Fellowships—Social Sciences—Librarianship" section of this
bibliography.

Law

98 **Financial Aid for Minorities in Law.** Ed. by Novelle J. Dickensen and
Ruth N. Swann. Garrett Park, MD: Garrett Park Press, 1981. 63p.
80–153225. $3. Pap.

This booklet, published in 1981, lists scholarships, fellowships, and grants
open to minorities interested in the legal profession. For more information
about the publication, see the annotation in the "Fellowships—Social
Sciences—Law" section of this bibliography.

99 **Free Money for Professional Studies.** By Laurie Blum. New York:
Barnes and Noble, 1985. 204p. (Blum's Guides to College Money).
85–42725. ISBN 0–06–464104–0. $5.95. Pap.

This guide identifies state-based organizations awarding scholarships,
fellowships, and grants to their residents, miscellaneous awards available to
special applicants (e.g., deaf children, veterans' dependents), and selected
financial aid programs appropriate for "professional studies" (including law).
For more information about the publication, see the annotation in the
"Fellowships—Sciences—Health Sciences" section of this bibliography.

Substance Abuse

100 **Guide to International Drug Abuse Demand Reduction Resources:
Scholarships/Fellowships.** Rockville, MD: U.S. National Institute on
Drug Abuse, 1982. 72p. Free. Pap.

This guide was compiled "to provide information about financial resources
which are available from 33 organizations which may be used in the drug
abuse field." The programs described are designed for professionals,
paraprofessionals, and organizations or agencies concerned with manpower
development in the drug abuse field. Approximately 100 scholarships and
fellowships are covered. Entries are arranged in alphabetical order and the
length of description provided varies, depending on the specificity and extent
of information supplied by the funding source. In general, the entries identify

purpose, eligibility requirements, fields of study, remuneration, and contact person.

HUMANITIES

General

101   Free Money for Humanities Students. By Laurie Blum. New York: Barnes & Noble, 1985. 204p. (Blum's Guides to College Money). 85–42554. ISBN 0–06–464107–4. $5.95. Pap.

This is one in a series of three *Blum's Guides to College Money*. The other two cover professional studies and sciences (and are described elsewhere in this directory). Each volume is exactly the same size (204 pages) and the same 160–page section is repeated in all three books: a 138–page state-by-state listing of organizations awarding scholarships and grants to their residents and a 22–page list of miscellaneous awards available to various applicants (e.g., deaf children, veteran's dependents). Each of these entries contains only brief information: sponsoring organization address and telephone number, eligibility, remuneration, deadline, and contact person. The remaining 44 pages identify selected financial aid programs specifically of interest to humanities' students. More complete lists of programs for the various disciplines in the humanities are available in a number of other directories described in this bibliography.

102   The National Directory of Grants and Aid to Individuals in the Arts, International. By Daniel Millsaps. 5th ed. Washington, DC: Washington International Arts Letter, 1983. 246p. (The Arts Patronage series, no. 11). 70–11269. ISBN 0–912072–12–1. ISSN 0270–5966. $15.95. Pap.

According to its editors, this paperback directory lists "most grants, prizes, and awards for professional work in the U.S. and abroad, and information about universities and schools which offer special aid to students." For more information about the publication, see the annotation in the "Grants—Humanities—General" section of the bibliography.

103   Washington International Arts Letter. Washington, DC: Washington International Arts Letter (WIAL), 1962– . 10 issues/yr. 68–6506. ISSN 0043–0609. $54/yr.

This monthly newsletter provides information on fellowships, scholarships, awards, and grants open to institutions and individuals involved in the arts.

For more information about the publication, see the annotation in the "Grants—Humanities—General" section of the bibliography.

Communications and Mass Media

104   Editor & Publisher Journalism Awards Directory. Ed. by Jerome H. Walker. New York, Editor & Publisher Company. Annual. $3. Pap.

This directory describes over 200 scholarships, fellowships, and awards available in the field of journalism, with a total value of over $2 million. The focus is on programs for reporters, columnists, editors, cartoonists, and photographers. The entries are arranged alphabetically within four main sections: national and international awards; regional awards; noncompetitive contests; and special scholarships, fellowships, and grants for journalism. The following information is provided for each program: sponsoring organization, address, requirements, and deadlines. Many entries also list the previous year's winners. Issued annually in January, this pamphlet is reprinted from the December issue (of the previous year) of *Editor & Publisher* magazine.

105   Film/Television: Grants, Scholarships, Special Programs. Comp. by Judy Chaikin and Lucinda Travis. Ed. by Virginia M. Clark. 2d ed. Los Angeles: American Film Institute, 1984. 33p. (Factfile #12). $5. Pap.

This small directory provides information on scholarships and special programs as well as on grants available to students, practitioners, and researchers interested in working in the areas of film and television. For more information about the publication, see the annotation in the Grants— Humanities—Communications and Mass Media" section of this bibliography.

106   Financial Aid for Minorities in Mass Communications. By Leslie L. Lawton and Ruth N. Swann. Garrett Park, MD: Garrett Park Press, 1981. 62p. 81–211245. $3. Pap.

One in a series of booklets covering financial assistance programs for minorities, this compilation identifies selected scholarships, fellowships, and grants in the fields of communication and mass media that were available prior to 1981. The listing is generally unannotated. Despite its title, many of the programs included are not restricted just to minority applicants but are open equally to all segments of the population. A number of the entries are general in nature and there is considerable duplication among booklets in the Garrett Park Press "Financial Aid for Minorities" series. During the past few years, there have been dramatic changes in the financial aid available to minorities, and this listing is now seriously out of date. For more current and comprehensive coverage, use the *Directory of Financial Aids for Minorities* described in the "Scholarships—Special Population Groups—Ethnic Groups" section of this bibliography.

107 Honor Awards Handbook. Ed. by Milton L. Levy. Berkeley, CA: Honor Awards Handbook, 1957–1964. 3v. 84–7113.

Published in 1957, 1960, and 1964 under the title *Honor Awards Handbook*, this directory changed its name in 1968 to *Media Awards Handbook* (described in the "Awards and Prizes—Humanities—Communications and Mass Media" section of this bibliography).

108 Journalism Career and Scholarship Guide. Princeton: Dow Jones Newspaper Fund, 1979– . Annual. 85–644315. Free. Pap.

This booklet is a guide to available financial aid for students majoring in journalism or communciations from news organizations, professional societies, journalism-related groups, colleges, and universities. The guide provides valuable information on what to study in college, where to study journalism and mass communications, where the jobs are, and how to find them. Over $3 million in financial aid for more than 3,000 journalism students is also described. Scholarships under $100 are not included. The listing is arranged into two main sections. Part 1 deals with aid offered through schools and departments of journalism in American and Canadian colleges and universities, as well as by newspapers and professional societies. Part 2 lists miscellaneous sources of scholarships and those grants designed for minority students. The entries are arranged by state and indexed by sponsor. The booklet is available without charge from the Dow Jones Newspaper Fund (P.O. Box 300, Princeton, NJ 08540). Until the 1979 edition, the publication was known as the *Journalism Scholarship Guide and Directory of College Journalism Programs*.

109 Journalism Career Guide for Minorities. Prep. by the American Society of Newspaper Editors. Princeton, NJ: Dow Jones Newspaper Fund, 1984. 48p. Free. Pap.

This free booklet, available from the Dow Jones Newspaper Fund (P.O. Box 300, Princeton, NJ 08540), provides information "about careers and educational requirements for minority students considering careers in print journalism." One section deals with scholarships, fellowships, internships, and special training programs for minorities as well as with general scholarship/fellowship opportunities. Most of the material presented here is taken directly from the *Journalism Career and Scholarship Guide* (described elsewhere in this section of the bibliography).

110   Journalism Directory. Ed. by Nancy Doubledee Barclay. Columbia, SC: Association for Education in Journalism and Mass Communications, 1983– . Annual. 83–646324. ISSN 0735–3103. $16 (1985 ed.). Pap.

While the *Journalism Directory* is primarily a reference guide to more than 300 schools and departments of journalism/mass communications, the annual also contains a small section on "National Funds, Fellowships and Foundations in Journalism." For more complete coverage of financial aid programs available in the areas of communications and journalism, see the *Journalism Career and Scholarship Guide* described elsewhere in this section.

111   Journalism Scholarship Guide and Directory of College Journalism Programs. Princeton: Dow Jones Newspaper Fund, 1962–1979. Annual. Pap.

Since 1979, this publication has been issued as the *Journalism Career and Scholarship Guide* (see description in this section of the bibliography).

112   Media Awards Handbook: Radio, Television, Newspaper, Magazine, Allied Fields & Industries. Ed. by Milton L. Levy. Danville, CA: Media Awards Handbook, 1980. n.p. 68–24272. ISBN 0–910744–03–3. $20. Pap.

Intended as "a workbook for those professionals who want to know as much detail as possible about the various Contests and Awards with the thought of entering them for their work," this directory also lists some scholarships, fellowships, and grants. For more information about this publication, see the annotation in the "Awards and Prizes—Humanities—Communications and Mass Media" section of this bibliography.

Fine Arts

113   American Art Directory. Ed. and comp. by Jaques Cattell Press. New York: Bowker, 1952– . Biennial. 80–609. ISSN 0065–6968. $85 (1984 ed.).

Revised biennially in even numbered years, this directory lists art museums, associations, and schools in the United States and Canada, along with art museums and schools abroad. A separate section in each volume focuses on art-related agencies and activities, including scholarships and fellowships (16 pages of programs are provided in a recent edition). From 1898–1948, this publication was issued by Macmillan under the title *American Art Annual.*

114 **Architecture Schools in North America: Members and Affiliates of the ACSA.** Princeton, NJ: Peterson's Guides, 1976– . Irreg. 83–12070. $11.95 (1982 ed.). Pap.

This guide identifies the architecture schools in the United States and Canada that are affiliated with the Association of Collegiate Schools of Architecture (ACSA). The main body of the text is an alphabetical list of the eligible institutions. In the latest (1982) edition, each entry is approximately two pages in length and, in addition to the typical school-related data, presents information on scholarship aid. Prior to 1976, the guide was published by the Association of Collegiate Schools of Architecture and then by Dover Publications; since 1976, it has been issued by Peterson's Guides.

Literature

115 **How to Enter and Win Fiction Writing Contests.** By Alan Gadney. New York: Facts On File, 1981. 200p. 81–2182. ISBN 0–87196–519–4, cloth; -552–6, pap. $14.95, cloth; $6.95, pap.

More than 400 national and international scholarships, grants, and contests for literature are covered in this guide. For more information about the publication, see the annotation in the "Awards and Prizes—Humanities— Literature" section of this bibliography.

116 **How to Enter and Win Non-Fiction & Journalism Contests.** By Alan Gadney. New York: Facts On File, 1981. 205p. 81–2179. ISBN 0–87196–518–6, cloth; -553–4, pap. $14.95, cloth; $6.95, pap.

Nearly 400 national and international scholarships, contests, festivals, and grants open to nonfiction writers are identified and described in this directory. For more information about the publication, see the annotation in the "Awards and Prizes—Humanities—Literature" section of this bibliography.

117 **Literary Market Place: The Directory of American Book Publishing with Names & Numbers.** New York: Bowker, 1972– . Annual. 81–640008. ISSN 0161–2905. $59.95 (1986 ed.). Pap.

Originally designed as a register of personnel in publishing and allied fields, over the years this annual has been expanded to include 12,000 entries in a dozen major sections. One of these sections focuses on awards, scholarships, fellowships, and grants-in-aid of interest to the American writer. For more information about the publication, see the annotation in the "Awards and Prizes—Humanities—Literature" section of this bibliography.

Music

118 **British Music Yearbook.** London: Adam & Charles Black (dist. by Schimer Books), 1975– . Annual. 75–649724. ISSN 0306–5928. $29.95 (1984 ed.).

In addition to information about awards and prizes, this yearbook also describes music scholarships and grants tenable either in Britain or abroad. For more information about the publication, see the annotation in the "Awards and Prizes—Humanities—Music" section of this bibliography.

119 **Music Industry Directory.** Chicago: Marquis Professional Publications, 1983– . Irreg. 83–645913. ISSN 0740–476X. $67.50 (1983 ed.).

Three chapters in the 1983 edition of this directory describe various financial aid programs and awards available to musicians. One chapter consists of a reproduction of the National Federation of Music Clubs' scholarships and awards chart. For more information about the *Music Industry Directory*, see the annotation in the "Awards and Prizes—Humanities—Music" section of this bibliography.

120 **The Musician's Guide.** New York: Music Information Service, 1954–1980. Irreg. 54–14954. ISSN 0580–3160.

From 1954 through 1980, Music Information Service published six volumes of this directory. In 1983, Marquis began issuing the publication as an annual, under the title *Music Industry Directory*. For more information, see the annotation for *Music Industry Directory* in the "Awards and Prizes—Humanities—Music" section of this bibliography.

Performing Arts

121 **Lively Arts Information Directory.** Ed. by Steven R. Wasserman and Jacqueline Wasserman O'Brien. 2d ed. Detroit: Gale, 1985. 1,040p. 81–20060. ISBN 0–8103–0321–3. $165.

Over 6,700 scholarships, foundations, grants, awards, publications, special libraries, and schools offering study in theater, music, dance, filmmaking, radio, and television are described in the second edition of this directory. For more information about the publication, see the annotation in the "Awards and Prizes—Humanities—Performing Arts" section of this bibliography.

SCIENCES

General

122   Financial Aid for Minorities in Science. Ed. by Ruth N. Swann and
Sharon F. White. Garrett Park, MD: Garrett Park Press, 1980. 49p. $2.
Pap.

One in a series of booklets covering financial assistance programs for
minorities, this compilation identifies selected scholarships, fellowships, and
grants in the sciences that were available prior to 1980. The listing is
generally unannotated. Despite its title, many of the programs included are
not restricted just to minority applicants but are open equally to all segments
of the population. A number of the entries are general in nature and there is
considerable duplication among booklets in the Garrett Park Press
"Financial Aid for Minorities" series. During the past few years, there have
been dramatic changes in the financial aid available to minorities, and this
listing is now seriously out of date. For more current and comprehensive
coverage, use the *Directory of Financial Aids for Minorities* described in the
"Scholarships—Special Population Groups—Ethnic Groups" section of this
bibliography.

123   Free Money for Science Students. By Laurie Blum. New York: Barnes
& Noble, 1985. 204p. (Blum's Guides to College Money). 85–42724.
ISBN 0–06–464108–0. $5.95. Pap.

This is one in a series of three *Blum's Guides to College Money*. The other two
cover humanities and professional studies. Each volume is exactly the same
size (204 pages) and the same 160–page section is repeated in all three books:
a state-by-state listing of organizations awarding scholarships and grants to
their residents and a list of miscellaneous awards available to various
applicants (e.g., deaf children, veteran's dependents). Each of these entries
contains only brief information: sponsoring organization address and
telephone number, eligibility, remuneration, deadline, and contact person.
The remaining 44 pages identify selected financial aid programs specifically
of interest to science students. More complete lists of programs for the
various disciplines in the sciences are available in a number of other
directories described in this bibliography.

Engineering

124   Financial Aid for Minorities in Engineering. Ed. by Clayton G.
Holloway and Ruth N. Swann. Garrett Park, MD: Garrett Park Press,
1981. 52p. 81–161268. $3. Pap.

One in a series of booklets covering financial assistance programs for
minorities, this compilation identifies selected scholarships, fellowships, and

grants in the field of engineering that were available prior to 1981. The listing is generally unannotated. Despite its title, many of the programs included are not restricted just to minority applicants but are open equally to all segments of the population. A number of the entries are general in nature and there is considerable duplication among booklets in the Garrett Park Press "Financial Aid for Minorities" series. During the past few years, there have been dramatic changes in the financial aid available to minorities, and this listing is now seriously out of date. For more current and comprehensive coverage, see the *Directory of Financial Aids for Minorities* described in the "Scholarships—Special Population Groups—Ethnic Groups" section of this bibliography.

125 Students' Guide to Engineering Schools. 3d ed. New York: National Action Council for Minorities in Engineering (NACME), 1986. n.p. Free. Pap.

The National Action Council for Minorities in Engineering (NACME) is a "nonprofit organization founded as a catalyst in the minority engineering education effort." It was established more than a decade ago by company executives, educators, professional society officers, and members of minority organizations to increase the number of underrepresented minorities who graduate from accredited engineering schools. The *Students' Guide to Engineering Schools*, prepared by NACME, describes in tabular form every accredited undergraduate engineering college in the United States. Three basic categories are covered: undergraduate engineering curriculum, support activities, and financial aid offered (indicating whether or not grants, loans, tuition remission programs and/or work programs are available). This free booklet concludes with a description of NACME's Incentive Grants program and a list of Incentive Grants participating schools in 1985/86.

Health Sciences

126 Financial Aid for Minorities in Allied Health. Ed. by Lois S. Cofield and Ruth N. Swann. Garrett Park, MD: Garrett Park Press, 1980. 58p. 81–129225. $2. Pap.

This booklet, published in 1980, lists scholarships, fellowships, and grant programs open to minorities interested in health care. For more information about the publication, see the annotation in the "Fellowships—Sciences—Health Sciences" section of this bibliography.

127 **Financial Aid for Minorities in Medicine.** Ed. by Sterling H. Hudson III and Ruth N. Swann. Garrett Park, MD: Garrett Park Press, 1981. 66p. 81–184828. $3. Pap.

This booklet focuses on scholarships, grants, and fellowships that were open to minorities interested in the medical field prior to 1981. For more information about the publication, see the annotation in the "Fellowships—Sciences—Health Sciences" section of this bibliography.

128 **Free Money for Professional Studies.** By Laurie Blum. New York: Barnes and Noble, 1985. 204p. (Blum's Guides to College Money). 85–42725. ISBN 0–06–464104–0. $5.95. Pap.

This guide identifies state-based organizations awarding scholarships, grants, and fellowships to their residents, miscellaneous awards available to special applicants (e.g., deaf children, veteran's dependents), and selected financial aid programs appropriate for "professional studies" (dentistry, medicine, nursing, optometry, pharmacology, psychiatry, veterinary medicine, business, and law). For more information about the publication, see the annotation in the "Fellowships—Sciences—Health Sciences" section of this bibliography.

129 **Scholarships and Loans for Nursing Education.** New York: National League for Nursing, 1984– . Annual. 80–102098. ISBN 0–88737–128–0. $7.25 (1985 ed.). Pap.

In addition to providing information about the general process of and requirements for applying for financial aid, this booklet describes six federal financial aid programs and 50 sources of private aid available to students interested in nursing (grouped into the following categories: resources for registered nurses only; for RNs and beginning students of nursing; for beginning students only; for minority students only; and scholarships and loans for constituent leagues). The descriptions specify purpose, eligibility, remuneration, number awarded, application process, and deadline. A short, unannotated bibliography of 10 general directories of financial aid completes the pamphlet. From 1974 through 1983, this publication was issued under the title *Scholarships and Loans for Beginning Education in Nursing.*

130 **Student Financial Aid: Speech-Language Pathology and Audiology.** Rockville, MD: American Speech—Language—Hearing Association, 1981. 21p. Free. Pap.

According to the introduction, this booklet "has been prepared to help students planning a career in speech-language pathology and audiology." The listing is divided into four parts: scholarships (federal, state and local, and other programs), loans, aids for graduate education (college work-study and individual college programs), and a two-page bibliography of other financial aid publications. Brief information is provided for most of the entries.

Although the publication is aimed at students interested in speech-language pathology and audiology, less than half of the programs identified deal specifically with those specialties.

SPECIAL POPULATION GROUPS

The Disabled

131 **Financial Aid for the Disabled and Their Dependents.** By Gail Ann Schlachter. Los Angeles: Reference Service Press, 1987– . Biennial. (Directories of Financial Aid for Special Needs Groups). $29.95 (1987/88 ed.).

This is the first comprehensive and up-to-date listing of scholarships, fellowships, awards, loans, and grants-in-aid that have been established for disabled individuals and their dependents. Planned as a biennial, the first volume identifies over 500 programs open to this special needs group in 1987/88. The following information is provided for each of the entries: program title, sponsoring organization, address, telephone number, purpose of program, eligibility, financial data, duration, special features, limitations, number awarded, and deadline date. Also included in the directory are a list of state sources of educational benefits, addresses of state agencies designed to help the disabled (those dealing with vocational rehabilitation, special education, crippled children, employment, etc.), an annotated bibliography of nearly 200 directories listing general financial aid programs, and a set of indexes that provide access by program title, sponsoring organization, geographic coverage, subject, specific disability, and deadline date. Excluded from the compilation are programs aimed at individuals and organizations involved in helping the disabled; these programs are partially covered in the *Handicapped Funding Directory* (described in the "Grants—Special Population Groups—The Disabled" section) and *Directory of Biomedical and Health Care Grants* (described in the "Grants—Sciences—Health Sciences" section).

Ethnic Groups

132 **Career Development Opportunities for Native Americans.** Washington, DC: U.S. Bureau of Indian Affairs, 1980. 56p. Free. Pap.

First issued in 1975, this booklet was revised in 1980 to "incorporate information relative to a vast range of educational opportunities, including information concerning Adult Education and Vocational-Technical programs, as well as college and university aids." The listings are divided into three sections: programs restricted to Native American studies; programs and/or schools specifically for Native American applicants (includes information on Bureau of Indian Affairs, Tribal, institutional, and organizational opportunities); and programs open to students of any background (nearly one-third of the pamphlet). A short bibliography and an index complete the work. The listing is now severely out of date and no longer in print.For a current listing of similar programs, see the *Directory of Financial Aids for Minorities* (described elsewhere in this section of the bibliography).

133   Directory of Financial Aids for Minorities. By Gail Ann Schlachter. Los Angeles: Reference Service Press, 1984– . Biennial. (Directories of Financial Aid for Special Needs Groups). 83–25068. ISBN 0–918276–03–9. ISSN 0738–4122. $37.50 (1986–1987 ed.).

Updating the first biennially-issued volume (which covered 1984/1985), the 1986/1987 edition includes nearly 40 percent more entries and revisions of approximately 50 percent of the original entries. The directory consists of more than 1,500 entries, divided into four sections: a descriptive list of 1,200 scholarships, fellowships, loans, grants, internships, awards, and prizes set aside for Asian Americans, Black Americans, Hispanic Americans, Native Americans, and minorities in general; a list of state sources of educational benefits; an annotated bibliography of over 200 directories published since 1980 that identify general financial aid programs, and a set of indexes that provide access by program title, sponsoring organization, geographic coverage, subject field, and application deadline. This is the most comprehensive and current list of financial aid programs established for minority group members.

134   Directory of Special Programs for Minority Group Members: Career Information Services, Employment Skills Banks, Financial Aid Sources. Prep. by Willis L. Johnson. 3d ed. Garrett Park, MD: Garrett Park Press, 1980. 612p. 73–93533. ISSN 0093–0501. $20. Pap.

Compiled for minority group members and publishers in 1980, this is a listing of 4,100 national, regional, and area programs and employment services; economic assistance, job retraining, and student financial aid programs sponsored by federal agencies; and special financial and academic assistance offered by individual colleges and universities. For those planning for the future, the directory also includes 280 sources of career information, 160 summer employment and internship opportunities, 280 job training programs, and a number of sources of scholarships, fellowships, and loans available in 1980. In addition, there are a glossary, a list of 100 talent banks that identify minority candidates for employment in a number of fields, a selective bibliography of sources, and indexes to the organizations and programs in the publication. The first edition of this directory was published in 1973, with a separate section on employment assistance services for women (384p.). The second edition was released in 1975 (400p.). A fourth edition is planned.

135   Federal Programs of Assistance to American Indians; A Report Prepared for the Senate Select Committee on Indian Affairs of the United States Senate. By Richard S. Jones. Washington, DC: G.P.O., 1985. 295p. (Committee Print 99th Congress, 1st Session). Free. Pap.

Described in this committee report are (1) programs specifically designed to benefit Indian tribes and individuals; (2) programs that specifically include Indians or Indian tribes as eligible beneficiaries; and (3) programs that may not specifically name Indians or Indian tribes as eligible beneficiaries but which are of special interest to Indians. For more information about the publication, see the annotation in the "Grants—Special Population Groups— Ethnic Groups" section of this bibliography.

136   Financial Aid for Minorities in Allied Health. Ed. by Lois G. Cofield and Ruth N. Swann. Garrett Park, MD: Garrett Park Press, 1980. 58p. 81–129225. $2. Pap.

Now considerably out of date, this directory provides a selective listing of scholarships, fellowships, and grants available in 1980 to minorities interested in allied health fields. For more information about the publication, see the annotation in the "Scholarships—Sciences—Health Sciences" section of this bibliography.

137   Financial Aid for Minorities in Business. Ed. by Howard F. Wehrle, III and Ruth N. Swann. Garrett Park, MD: Garrett Park Press, 1980. 48p. 80–144474. $3. Pap.

Selected scholarships, fellowships, and grants in the field of business that were available to minorities in 1980 are listed in this directory. For more information about the publication, see the annotation in the "Scholarships— Social Sciences—Business and Economics" section of this bibliography.

138   Financial Aid for Minorities in Education. Ed. by Mary T. Christian and Ruth N. Swann. Garrett Park, MD: Garrett Park Press, 1980. 58p. 80–153221. $3. Pap.

One in a series of booklets covering financial assistance programs for minorities, this compilation identifies selected scholarships, fellowships, and grants in the field of education that were available in 1980. For more information about the publication, see the annotation in the "Scholarships— Social Sciences—Education" section of this bibliography.

139   Financial Aid for Minorities in Engineering. Ed. by Clayton G. Holloway and Ruth N. Swann. Garrett Park, MD: Garrett Park Press, 1981. 52p. 81–161268. $3. Pap.

Focusing on the field of engineering, this mostly unannotated list selectively identifies scholarships, fellowships, and grants open to minority students prior to 1981. For more information about the publication, see the annotation in the "Scholarships—Sciences—Engineering" section of this bibliography.

140   Financial Aid for Minorities in Law. Ed. by Novelle J. Dickensen and Ruth N. Swann. Garrett Park, MD: Garrett Park Press, 1981. 63p. 80–153225. $3. Pap.

Aimed at minorities interested in legal studies, this (mostly unannotated list) identifies scholarships, fellowships, and grants that were available in 1981. For more information about the publication, see the annotation in the "Fellowships—Social Sciences—Law" section of this bibliography.

141   Financial Aid for Minorities in Mass Communications. By Leslie L. Lawton and Ruth N. Swann. Garrett Park, MD: Garrett Park Press, 1981. 62p. 81–211245. $3. Pap.

Included in this listing are references to scholarships, fellowships, and grants open to minorities interested in the fields of mass media and communications. For more information about the publication, see the annotation in the "Scholarships—Humanities—Communications and Mass Media" section of this bibliography.

142   Financial Aid for Minorities in Medicine. By Sterling H. Hudson III and Ruth N. Swann. Garrett Park, MD: Garrett Park Press, 1981. 66p. 81–184828. $3. Pap.

This listing, published in 1981, identifies selected scholarships, along with fellowships and grants, open to minorities interested in medical studies. For more information about the publication, see the annotation in the "Fellowships—Sciences—Health Sciences" section of this bibliography.

143   Financial Aid for Minorities in Science. Ed. by Ruth N. Swann and Sharon F. White. Garrett Park, MD: Garrett Park Press, 1980. 49p. $2. Pap.

Published in 1980, this mostly unannotated listing selectively identifies scholarships, fellowships, and grants open to minorities interested in the sciences. For more information about the publication, see the annotation in the "Scholarships—Sciences—General" section of this bibliography.

144 Higher Education Opportunities for Minorities and Women...Annotated Selections. Washington, DC: G.P.O., 1982– . Annual. 84–11125. $5.50 (1986 ed.). Pap.

Formerly published as *Selected List of Postsecondary Opportunities for Minorities and Women* (1977–1981. Annual. 82–21846), this directory lists financial aid programs for minorities and women at the postsecondary level. The programs are arranged by field of study: architecture, business administration, engineering, science, health, speech pathology and audiology, theology, and U.S. Department of Education programs. Entries specify program purpose, eligibility, remuneration, application deadline, etc. In addition to describing loan, scholarship, and fellowship opportunities, the publication also provides some basic information on how and where to seek general assistance to pursue educational and career goals.

145 Hispanic Financial Resource Handbook. Comp. by the Hispanic Student Program. Columbus, Office of Student Life, Ohio State University, 1982– . Annual. $5 (1985 ed.). Pap.

This comb-bound handbook was first compiled in 1982 (and revised annually since then) to "assist Hispanic students and professionals in obtaining financial aid information which is especially geared toward Hispanic and other minorities." The 1985 edition is divided into three sections: programs for individual Hispanics (undergraduate, graduate, and professional individuals), arranged by field and level of study; programs for Latin Americans (undergraduate, graduate, and professional individuals), arranged by field and level of study; and summer opportunities for high school, undergraduate, and graduate students, arranged alphabetically. Entries include the following information: sponsoring organization address and telephone number, title of award, area of study, remuneration, eligibility, application process, and deadline. A short, unannotated bibliography of other financial aid directories completes the work. While many more programs for Hispanic and other ethnic minority groups are described more fully in the *Directory of Financial Aids for Minorities* (see annotation elsewhere in this section of the bibliography), *Hispanic Financial Resource Handbook* provides a good starting point at a reasonable price.

146 Journalism Career Guide for Minorities. Prep. by the American Society of Newspaper Editors. Princeton, NJ: Dow Jones Newspaper Fund, 1984. 48p. Free. Pap.

One section of this free booklet deals with scholarships, fellowships, internships, and special training programs for minorities interested in journalism as well as with general scholarship/fellowship opportunities. For more information about the publication, see the annotation in the

"Scholarships—Humanities—Communications and Mass Media" section of this bibliography.

147   **Minority Organizations: A National Directory.** Ed. by Katherine W. Cole. 2d ed. Garrett Park, MD: Garrett Park Press, 1982. 814p. 79–640122. ISBN 0–912048–30–1. ISSN 0162–9034. $30 Pap.

Over 7,100 minority organizations or groups operating minority service programs are described in this edition—almost three times as many entries as included in its predecessor (published in 1978). The organizations listed include professional associations, student groups, civil rights agencies, and research and publication centers. Entries for each summarize organizational activities. A geographical and activity index helps identify such aspects as employment services, publications, and financial aid programs. For a more current and comprehensive list of financial aid for minorities, see the biennial *Directory of Financial Aids for Minorities* (described elsewhere in this section).

148   **Sources of Financial Aid Available to American Indian Students.** Comp. by Kenneth Tsosie and Alan J. Cherino. Las Cruces, NM: Indian Resource Development, 1984. 37p. Free. Pap.

In 1985, this pamphlet was issued under the title *Student Financial Aid for American Indians* (described elsewhere in this section).

149   **Student Financial Aid for American Indians.** Comp. by JoAnn Willie, with the assistance of Marjorie Burr, Alan Cherino, and Emerson Jackson, Jr. Las Cruces, NM: Indian Resource Development, 1985. 44p. Free. Pap.

This booklet is available without charge from the Indian Resource Development (Box 3 IRD, Las Cruces, NM 88003). Despite its title, only a few of the sources of financial aid established exclusively for American Indians are identified here (less than 20). The rest of the pamphlet is concerned with general information (e.g., federal aid programs, tips), descriptions of additional financial aid programs that are open to all minorities, and a 22–page description of colleges and universities in the southwest that have special programs for American Indian students (some information on financial aid at those instituitons is provided). The booklet is funded by the State of New Mexico and is updated annually. The 1984 edition was published under the title *Sources of Financial Aid Available to American Indian Students.*

Foreign Students

150 **A Foreign Students' Selected Guide to Financial Assistance for Study and Research in the United States.** Ed. by Joe Lurie with Jonathan Miller. Garden City, NY: Adelphi University Press, 1983. 327p. ISBN 0–88461–010–1. $22.50. Pap.

Prepared by the International/Intercultural Programs Vice President of the American Field Service, this directory identifies sources of financial assistance for foreign nationals who wish to study and/or conduct research in the United States. There is a total of 232 undergraduate entries and 173 graduate entries from 298 American colleges and universities. These entries are classified by institutions, scholarships for specific countries or regions of the world, and state location. Institution profiles specify eligibility requirements, areas of study, value, type and number of awards, application procedures, deadlines, and award announcements. Only one half of the undergraduate awards and one third of the graduate programs described here are reserved for foreign nationals; the rest are open to American citizens and foreign nationals equally.

151 **Higher Education in the United States: Opportunities for Foreign Students.** By Edith Gann. New York: Institute of Human Relations, American Jewish Committee, 1982. 8p. Pap.

This guide is based on information published by educational associations, large foundations, federal agencies, and other institutions. Its stated purpose is "to acquaint qualified foreign students in many fields with help that is available through public and private sources." However, only 20 programs are covered. For these, brief information is provided on eligibility requirements, availability, and application procedures. For more comprehensive coverage of financial aid programs open to foreign nationals in the United States, see *A Foreign Students' Selected Guide to Financial Assistance for Study and Research in the United States*, described elsewhere in this section of the bibliography.

152 **Private Sector Funding Available to Foreign Scholars and Students in the United States.** Prep. by Ellen Wise Sivon. Rev. ed. Washington, DC: National Association for Foreign Student Affairs, 1985. 54p. 84–242345. ISBN 0–912207–09–4. $2.95. Pap.

A relatively small number of awards are given through U.S. private sector sources to foreign students and scholars in the United States. This directory, first published in 1984 and then revised in 1985, identifies these sources of nongovernmental funding for the postsecondary studies and research of foreign students and scholars in the United States. It is intended "as a sourcebook for foreign students and scholars already in the United States who are seeking additional financial resources to complete their U.S. education." Approximately 50 sources of support from professional societies, scientific and medical organizations, scholarly institutes, foundations, and civic organizations are described. The entries, arranged alphabetically by sponsoring organization, provide the following information: title and address of the sponsoring organization, purpose of the award, eligibility criteria, financial data, and application procedures. There are two indexes; by level and by field of study. A two-page bibliography completes the work.

153   Selected List of Fellowship Opportunities and Aids to Advanced Education for United States Citizens and Foreign Nationals. Washington, DC: National Science Foundation, 1984. 76p. Free. Pap.

This free pamphlet presents concise descriptions of scholarships, fellowships, loans, and work-study experiences available to foreign students in the United States as well as to American citizens. For more information about the publication, see the annotation in the "Fellowships—General—United States" section of this bibliography.

Military Personnel and Veterans

154   Educational Assistance and Opportunities Information for Army Family Members. Alexandria, VA: Adjutant General's Office, U.S. Department of the Army, 1984. v.p. Free. Looseleaf.

Issued previously as *Dependents' Education: Educational Scholarships, Loans, and Financial Aids*, this directory identifies associations and other groups that provide financial assistance to Army personnel and relatives of military personnel. Also covered are state offices responsible for assisting the dependents of military personnel who are missing in action, killed in action, or prisoners of war. Entries are arranged by type of program and specify sponsoring organization name and address, program parameters, and financial assistance available.

155   Federal Benefits for Veterans and Dependents. Prep. by U.S. Veterans Administration. Washington, DC: G.P.O., 1969– . Annual. 85–641702. ISSN 0883–3370. $1.75 (1986 ed.). Pap.

This booklet provides a comprehensive summary of benefits (including scholarships) available to veterans and their dependents. For more information about the publication, see the annotation in the "Grants— Special Population Groups—Military Personnel and Veterans" section of this bibliography.

156 **How the Military Will Help Pay for College: The High School Student's Guide to ROTC, the Academics, and Special Programs.** By Don M. Betterton. Princeton, NJ: Peterson's Guides, 1985. 177p. 85–12409. ISBN 0–87866–362–2. $6.95. Pap.

Written with the cooperation of ROTC officers, Academy admissions officers, and other military personnel, this is one of only a few financial aid books that examine the assistance the military can offer in covering postsecondary educational costs. It brings together information about one of the country's largest "financial aid" programs, the "trade of government dollars for a college education in the military." Part I of this popularly-oriented guide describes the military scholarship options open to graduating high school seniors going directly to college: Army ROTC, Navy ROTC, Air Force ROTC, special academic and leadership programs, West Point, Anapolis, Air Force Academy, Coast Guard Academy, and Merchant Marine Academy. Part II covers the scholarship and tuition-payment programs open to men and women who go into the armed forces after graduation from high school, e.g., DANTES program, and the new GI Bill. The last section, consisting of six appendices, provides an overview of all ROTC host units, Army ROTC units, officers' height/weight requirements, and military pay and benefits. The book is filled with charts and comparison tables. There is no index.

157 **Once a Veteran: Benefits, Rights, Obligations. 1985 Edition.** Washington, DC: American Forces Information Service, U.S. Department of Defense (for sale by G.P.O.), 1985. 43p. $2. Pap.

This inexpensive pamphlet provides up-to-date information on the benefits (including scholarships available), rights, and obligations of American veterans. For more information about the publication, see the annotation in the "Grants—Special Population Groups—Military Personnel and Veterans" section of this bibliography.

158 **Scholarship Pamphlet for USN, USMC, USCG Dependent Children.** Washington, DC: U.S. Naval Military Personnel Command, U.S. Navy Department. Annual. Free. Pap.

Scholarships and other educational assistance programs available to dependents of Navy, Marine Corps, and Coast Guard personnel are listed in this free pamphlet. The Dependents' Scholarship Program, the Navy Relief Society Educational Fund, financial aids for Marine Corps dependents only, NROTC, Social Security benefits and VA programs are among the sources covered. Entries indicate source, eligibility, and application address. Also included are addresses of state agencies providing assistance and a very brief list of reference sources for students, parents, and counselors.

159 State Veterans' Laws: Digests of State Laws Regarding Rights, Benefits, and Privileges of Veterans and Their Dependents. Washington, DC: G.P.O., 1945– . Irreg. 60–62289. Free. Pap. Microfiche to depository libraries.

This congressional report covers the scholarships, fellowships, loans, and grants available to veterans on the state level. For more information about the publication, see the annotation in the "Grants—General—United States" section of this bibliography.

160 United States Code, Title 38: Veteran's Benefits. Washington, DC: G.P.O. Irreg. $25, U.S.; $31.25, elsewhere. Looseleaf.

This looseleaf subscription service contains the exact text of laws relating to veterans' benefits (including the financial aid programs established by the federal government). For more information about the publication, see the annotation in the "Grants—Special Population Groups—Military Personnel and Veterans" section of this bibliography.

161 The Viet Vet Survival Guide: How to Get through the Bureaucracy and Get What You Need and Are Entitled To. Ed. by Craig Kubey, et al. New York: Facts On File, 1986. 256p. ISBN 0–8160–1379–9. $19.95.

Included in this first self-help book for Vietnam veterans is information on scholarships, fellowships, loans, and grants-in-aid that are available for this group from the federal government. For more information about the publication, see the annotation in the "Grants—Special Population Groups— Military Personnel and Veterans" section of this bibliography.

Reentry Students

162 Back to School: The College Guide for Adults. By William C. Haponski and Charles E. McCabe. Princeton, NJ: Peterson's Guides, 1982. 229p. 82–315. ISBN 0–87866–197–2. $7.95. Pap.

Aimed at the fastest-growing segment of the college population, this guide describes innovative academic, counseling, and financial aid programs of value to the adult student. Also provided are tips on such matters as dealing with college bureaucracy and balancing the demands of work, family, and school. Much of the information in this volume is now considerably dated.

163 Better Late Than Never: Financial Aid for Older Women Seeking Education and Training. Washington, DC: Women's Equity Action League (WEAL), 1982. 43p. $3. Pap.

Aimed at reentry students (particularly women), this pamphlet identifies selected scholarship and fellowship programs open to returning and nontraditional students. For more information about the publication, see the annotation in the "Scholarships—Special Population Groups—Women" section of this bilbliography.

164 Finding Financial Resources for Adult Learners: Profiles for Practice. New York: College Entrance Examination Board, 1985. 56p. 85–172422. ISBN 0–87447–206–7. $8.95. Pap.

Traditionally, most financial aid sources have not been available to part-time students. And, for those programs that were, they generally were not of sufficient duration to support the part-time student through graduation. Recently, new college and community sources have been established to assist this special (and growing) segment of the college student population. In this selective guide, 70 of these community- and campus-based sources of financial aid are identified and described (including credit for prior learning, loans, tuition plans, scholarships, and work programs). Entries indicate purpose, amount of financial assistance available, numbers awarded, and contact person. The programs reported were selected for their innovativeness and/or representativeness. No attempt is made in the listing to be comprehensive. Thus, the publication serves more as a model for interested institutions than as a guide that can be of specific assistance to part-time students.

165 Happier by Degrees: The Complete Guide for Women Returning to College or Just Starting Out. By Pam Mendelsohn. 2d ed. Berkeley, CA: Ten Speed, 1986. 266p. 79–19380. $8.95. Pap.

A small portion of this book specifically addresses financial aid: the chapter on "Financing Your Education" briefly discusses aid from the federal government, aid from state governments, aid from academic institutions, Aid for Families with Dependent Children, employers' subsidies, and other scholarships and opportunities; the appendix providing "A Selected Listing of Financial Resources for Women" describes about 20 basic financial aid programs established for women and a dozen directories identifying programs for women; and one section of the bibliography lists "Sources of Information about Financial Aid for Students." For more information about this publication, see the annotation in the "Scholarships—Special Population Groups—Women" section of this bibliography.

166 Paying for Your Education: A Guide for Adult Learners. 2d ed. New York: College Entrance Examination Board (dist. by Scribner's), 1983. 160p. 82–73562. ISBN 0–87447–152–4. $7.95. Pap.

Updating the first edition (1980. 65p. 80–117810), this guide is written for adult learners, particularly unemployed students and women returning to college who are in need of financial assistance. Presented in the volume is information on how to locate possible sources of aid, organize a campaign to obtain finances, compare aid awards offered by various colleges, and reduce the time and cost required to complete a degree. One section of the source addresses the seven most frequently posed questions about financial assistance. Specific programs are not described.

Women

167 Association for Intercollegiate Athletics for Women Directory. Washington, DC: Association for Intercollegiate Athletics for Women (AIAW), 1977– . Biennial. 84–12725. ISSN 0361–5898. $10. Pap.

This biennial directory provides a complete listing of AIAW-member institutions and indicates scholarship offerings at each of them. For more information about the publication, see the annotation in the "Scholarships—Social Sciences—Athletics" section of this bibliography.

168 Better Late Than Never: Financial Aid for Older Women Seeking Education and Training. Washington, DC: Women's Equity Action League (WEAL), 1982. 43p. $3. Pap.

Developed under the auspices of WEAL's intern program, this directory identifies a sampling (about 60) of the scholarships and fellowships open to returning and nontraditional students. The listing is arranged into three main sections. The first describes programs that offer a counseling component along with financial aid; the second deals with federal financial aid resources and includes information on veterans benefits; the third covers nongovernment resources. Entries provide information on address, telephone, contact person, aid offered, services, program requirements, and application deadline. These sections are followed by a briefly annotated bibliography of related publications and two indexes: by sponsoring organization and by program. Despite its title, this directory does not focus solely on women's programs; many of the financial aid resources listed are open equally to men and women.

169 The Complete Guide to Women's College Athletics: Includes over 10,000 Women's Athletic Scholarships and Recruiting Rules and Regulations. By Carolyn Stanek. Chicago: Contemporary Books, 1981. 244p. 80–70635. ISBN 0–8092–5986–4, cloth; -5985–5, pap. $14.95, cloth; $7.95, pap.

Stanek prepared this guide to assist women high school students interested in obtaining financial assistance for participating in college sports. For more information about the publication, see the annotation in the "Scholarships—Social Sciences—Athletics" section of this bibliography.

170 Directory of Financial Aids for Women. By Gail Ann Schlachter. Los Angeles: Reference Service Press, 1978– . Biennial. (Directories of Financial Aid for Special Needs Groups). 84–24582. ISSN 0732–5215. $37.50.

First published in 1978, this is the only extensive and regularly updated list of scholarships, fellowships, loans, grants, internships, and awards/prizes designed primarily or exclusively for women. The directory is divided into four separate sections: a descriptive list of more than 1,100 national and international financial aid programs set aside for women, a list of state sources of educational benefits, an annotated bibliography of over 150 directories listing general financial aid programs, and a set of indexes that provide access by program title, sponsoring organization, geographic coverage, deadline date, and subject. The 1978 edition of the directory was published solely by Reference Service Press; the 1982 and the 1985/86 editions were co-published by Reference Service Press and ABC-CLIO. Beginning with the 1987/88 edition, the directory will be again published exclusively by Reference Service Press.

171 Educational Financial Aids: A Guide to Selecting Fellowships, Scholarships, and Internships in Higher Education. Washington, DC: American Association of University Women, 1984. 35p. $5. Pap.

This updated pamphlet (earlier versions were issued in 1976 and 1981) "divides financial aid offerings according to educational level: undergraduate, graduate, postdoctoral, and internships/traineeships." For more information about the publication, see the annotation in the "Fellowships—Special Population Groups—Women" section of this bibliography.

172 Financial Aid: A Partial List of Resources for Women. Prep. by the Project on the Status and Education of Women. Washington, DC: Association of American Colleges, 1984. 15p. $2.50. Pap.

This informative pamphlet was prepared by the Project on the Status and Education of Women to identify selected financial aid programs for women. It was first issued in 1982 and then updated in 1984. One half of the booklet consists of general tips for cutting school expenses, e.g., different ways to attend school, getting credit for prior experiences, brushing up on skills. The next section of the pamphlet lists approximately 80 scholarships and grants available to women students, including older women, minority women, women considering nontraditional careers, and others at all levels of postsecondary education. In addition, the booklet includes a resource section; brief descriptions are provided for 55 books and pamphlets that might be helpful in locating money for college. Slightly more than 100 publications and programs are covered, many of which are aimed at men as well as at women.

173 Happier by Degrees: The Complete Guide for Women Returning to College or Just Starting Out. By Pam Mendelsohn. 2d ed. Berkeley, CA: Ten Speed, 1986. 266p. 79–19380. $8.95. Pap.

Nearly half of today's college students are over the age of 25 and many of this group are women. Mendelsohn's revision of a guide first published in 1980 by E. P. Dutton is aimed at them. It is based on extensive interviews with over 100 women, their dependents and companions, and faculty and staff familiar with the needs of reentry students. It discusses, in an informal and anecdotal way, juggling home with school, selecting a college and getting admitted, handling the reactions of family members and friends, providing for children's after-school activities, and coping with illnesss and other "unexpecteds." A small portion of the book specifically addresses financial aid: the chapter on "Financing Your Education" briefly discusses aid from the federal government, aid from state governments, aid from academic institutions, Aid for Families with Dependent Children, employers' subsidies, and other scholarship opportunities; the appendix providing "A Selected Listing of Financial Resources for Women" describes about 20 basic financial aid programs established for women and a dozen directories identifying programs for women; and one section of the bibliography lists "Sources of Information about Financial Aid for Students." For a more extensive listing of scholarships, fellowships, grants, loans, awards, and internships open to reentry women, see the *Directory of Financial Aids for Women* (described elsewhere in this section of the bibliography).

174 Higher   Education   Opportunities   for   Minorities   and Women...Annotated Selections. Washington, DC: G.P.O., 1982– . Annual. 84–11125. $5.50 (1986 ed.). Pap.

Issued annually, this pamphlet describes scholarships, fellowships, and loans open to women and minorities at the postsecondary level. For more information about the publication, see the annotation in the "Scholarships—Special Population Groups—Ethnic Groups" section of this bibliography.

175 Women's Sports and Fitness Magazine: Scholarship Guide Issue. San Francisco: Women's Sports Foundation, 1979– . Annual. 85–643170. ISSN 8750–653X. $2. Pap.

This annual list, published in the January issue of *Women's Sports and Fitness Magazine,* currently provides the most comprehensive information on athletic scholarships for women offered at 800 academic institutions in 24 different sports. For more information about the publication, see the annotation in the "Scholarships—Social Sciences—Athletics" section of this bibliography.

Fellowships

Fellowships provide financial assistance for students pursuing graduate/postgraduate education or research in the United States or abroad. Usually no return of service or repayment is required. Included in this chapter are 148 references to directories that focus solely on fellowships or include substantial numbers of fellowships on the national or international level in their listings. Of these, 43 are general in nature, 30 focus on the social sciences, 27 concentrate on the humanities, 18 deal with the sciences, and 30 are aimed at special population groups. If you are looking for a specific fellowship directory and you do not find it in this chapter, be sure to check the Title Index to see if it is covered elsewhere in the Guide.

GENERAL

International

176 **Annual Register of Grant Support: A Guide to Support Programs of Government Agencies, Foundations, and Business and Professional Organizations.** Wilmette, IL: National Register, 1969– . Annual. 69–18307. ISSN 0066–4049. $87 (1985–86 ed.).

Although it focuses on North American programs, the *Annual Register* also describes a number of fellowships sponsored abroad. A more comprehensive list can be found, however, in the *Grants Register* (described elsewhere in this section). For more information on the *Annual Register*, see the annotation in the "Grants—General—United States" section of this bibliography.

177 **Awards for Commonwealth University Academic Staff.** London: Association of Commonwealth Universities (avail. from International Publication Service), 1972– . Biennial. 80–647312. $17.50 (5th ed.). Pap.

Described in this biennial are nearly 700 fellowships, visiting professorships, and grants open to Commonwealth university staff interested in studying, teaching, or conducting research in another Commonwealth country. In addition, some of the programs listed are aimed at staff members of non-Commonwealth countries. This publication supersedes *United Kingdom Postgraduate Awards*, which from 1955/56 to 1966/67 was issued as an annual and from 1967/69 to 1970/72 was issued as a biennial.

178 **Awards for Postgraduate Study in Australia.** 6th ed. Victoria, Aust.: Graduate Careers Council of Australia, 1984. Free. Pap.

Information on fellowships and grants for graduate and postdoctoral study/ research at Australian universities is provided in this pamphlet. Entries are arranged by field of study. The publication is available without cost from the Graduate Careers Councils of Australia (P.O. Box 28, Parkville, Victoria 3052, Australia), although $5 is charged for airmail postage and handling.

179 **Canadian Directory of Awards for Graduate Study.** Ottawa: Association of Universities and Colleges of Canada, 1981– . Biennial. 82–39014. ISSN 0711–8635. $10, Canadian. Pap.

Over 800 awards available to college graduates from sources in Canada, the United Kingdom, the United States, and numerous other countries are identified and described in this biennially-issued directory. The focus is on awards tenable in Canada that are open to students from Canada or abroad. These awards are grouped into the following categories: humanities, social studies, natural and applied sciences, medical sciences, and multiple areas of study. Each category is subdivided by countries where the award may be used. The entries are indexed by award name and subject. A bibliography of source materials is is appended. The text is in both English and French. Between 1951 and 1954, the directory was issued under the title *Post-Graduate Scholarships Open to Canadian Students*. Next, it was released under variations of the title *Awards for Graduate Study and Research*. Since 1981, it has been published as *Canadian Directory of Awards for Graduate Study*. In French, the title of the directory is *Repertoire Canadien des Bourses d'Etudes Superieures*.

180 College Blue Book. New York: Macmillan, 1923– . Biennial. 79–66191. ISSN 0069–5572. $185 (20th ed.).

A number of the fellowships described in Volume 5 of the *Blue Book*'s 20th edition may be used for study abroad. For more information about this publication, see the annotation in the "Scholarships—General—United States" section.

181 Directory of Financial Aids for International Activities. 4th ed. Minneapolis: Office of International Programs, University of Minnesota, 1978– . Irreg. 78–645627. ISSN 0163–0199. $20 (1985 ed.). Pap.

The fourth (1985) edition provides information on more than 450 fellowships, scholarships, and grants for academic staff, graduate and undergraduate students, advanced scholars, and young professionals for study, research, travel, and teaching abroad. For more information about this publication, see the annotation in the "Scholarships—General—International" section.

182 Directory of Research Grants. Phoenix: Oryx, 1975– . Annual. 76–47074. ISSN 0146–7336. $74.50 (1986 ed.). Pap.

Although the emphasis is on U.S. programs, some fellowships, scholarships, loans, and research grants sponsored by other countries are also included. For more information about the publication, see the annotation in the "Grants—General—United States" section of this bibliography.

183 Fellowship Guide to Western Europe. Ed. by Siri Belgum. 5th ed. New York: Council for European Studies, 1981. 99p. $5. Pap.

This guide is intended to "assist students of European society in finding funds for travel and study in Europe." In the fifth edition, published in 1981, the scope of the listing is expanded from the social sciences to include the fine arts, humanities, and sciences. The programs described are sponsored by foundations, organizations, and academic institutions. Fellowships offered by individual American universities open only to their registered students are omitted, as are fellowships awarded by invitation only or those offered at irregular intervals. Entries are grouped by field of study (ranging from anthropology to social work) and by specific countries in western Europe, including the United Kingdom. The following information is provided: address, program title, purpose, eligibility requirements, remuneration, duration, and application procedures. A sponsoring organization index completes the work.

184 Fellowships, Scholarships, and Related Opportunities in International Education. Knoxville: Division of International Education, University of Tennessee, 1967– . Annual. 82–5141. ISSN 0735–8830. $8 (1986 ed.). Pap.

In the latest edition of this directory, over 120 fellowships, scholarships, and grants for study, research, and teaching in the United States and abroad are listed and described. The programs covered are open to U.S. students and faculty. Most awards are for experiences outside the United States. Entries are arranged alphabetically and include the following information: area of study, country of study, eligibility, stipend, application deadline, and address. A "Field of Study Index" provides additional access.

185 Fulbright Grants and Other Grants for Graduate Study Abroad. New York: Institute of International Education. 1986. 78p. 84–12172. Free. Pap.

This annual pamphlet is available without charge from the Institute of Interntional Education. The 1986–1987 edition lists Institute-administered fellowships and grants available to U.S. graduate students for study abroad. For more information, see the description of *Fulbright Grants and Other Grants for Graduate Study Abroad* in the "Grants—General—International" section of this bibliography.

186 Fulbright Senior Scholars Awards Abroad. Washington, DC: Council for International Exchange of Scholars, 1984– . Annual. 84–10416. Free. Pap.

This free pamphlet from the Council for International Exchange of Scholars (11 Dupont Circle, Suite 300, Washington, DC 20036) identifies fellowships and grants open to U.S. citizens who are interested in lecturing and/or conducting advanced research abroad.

187 Grants for Graduate Study Abroad. New York: Institute of International Education, 1965– . Annual. ISSN 0270–9880. Free. Pap.

This free annual booklet lists fellowships and grants available to American students for predoctoral study, research, and professional training abroad. For more information about the publication, see the annotation in the "Grants—General—International" section of this bibliography.

188   **The Grants Register: Postgraduate Awards in the English Speaking World.** Ed. by Norman Frankel. New York: St. Martin's Press, 1969– . Biennial. 77–12055. $39.50 (1985–87 ed.).

This biennial directory describes fellowships, grants, and prizes open to nationals of the United States, Canada, the United Kingdom, Ireland, Australia, New Zealand, South Africa, and the developing countries. For more information about the publication, see the annotation in the "Grants—General—International" section of this bibliography.

189   **How to Get Money for Research.** By Mary Rubin and the Business and Professional Women's Foundation. Foreword by M. Chamberlain. Old Westbury, NY: Feminist Press, 1983. 78p. 83–1444. ISBN 0–935312–18–8. $6.95. Pap.

Both international and national fellowships "for and about women at the pre- and post-doctoral levels" are described in this directory. For more information, see the annotation in the "Grants—General—United States" section of this bibliography.

190   **IREX Program Announcement, 1986–87.** New York: International Research and Exchanges Board (IREX), 1986. 15p. Free. Pap.

This free pamphlet provides descriptions of the exchange programs (fellowships and grants) with Eastern European countries and the Soviet Union that are administered by IREX each academic year. For more information about the publication, see the annotation in the "Grants—General—International" section of this bibliography.

191   **Scholarships Abroad: Scholarships Offered to British Students by Overseas Governments and Universities.** London: British Council, 1977– . Annual.

This annual guide identifies scholarships and fellowships available to British students who are interested in studying abroad. Over 300 programs sponsored by non-British institutions and governments are described. These programs are tenable for either a full acadmeic year or a shorter period.

192   **Scholarships Guide for Commonwealth Postgraduate Students.** London: Association of Commonwealth Universities (dist. by International Publications Service), 1972– . Biennial. 77–643818. $25 (1985–87 ed.). Pap.

Similar in organization to *Awards for Commonwealth University Academic Staff* (described elsewhere in this section of the bibliography), this biennial publication identifies fellowships, grants, and assistantships available to graduates of Commonwealth universities who wish to undertake postgraduate study or research at a Commonwealth university outside their own country. Program entries are arranged geographically and contain information on eligibility requirements, remuneration, duration, etc. In addition, there are appendices that list awards tenable at nonuniversity institutions and awards tenable in the United Kingdom by graduates of that country. Also included is an index to award titles and organizations. In the latest edition (1985–1987. 356p. ISBN 0–85143–090–2), nearly 1,300 programs are covered. Graduates of postsecondary schools in non-Commonwealth countries are eligible to compete for many of the awards listed here. From 1955 through 1971, this publication was issued under the title *United Kingdom Post-graduate Awards.*

193 **U.S. College-Sponsored Programs Abroad: Academic Year.** Ed. by Gail A. Cohen. New York: Institute of International Education, 1964– . Annual. (The Learning Traveler, v. 1). 83–645013. ISSN 0196–6251. $9.95, U.S.; $14, elsewhere (1984 ed.). Pap.

Described in this annual guide are scholarships and fellowships at 800 study-abroad programs offered by American colleges and universities in foreign countries. For more information about the publication, see the annotation in the "Scholarships—General—International" section of this bibliography.

194 **United Kingdom Post-graduate Awards.** London: Association of Commonwealth Universities, 1955–1971. Biennial. 72–623777.

Issued first as an annual (1955–1966; published by the Association of Universities of the British Commonwealth), this listing was released as a biennial from 1967 through 1971. Since 1972, the directory has been published under the title *Scholarships Guide for Commonwealth Postgraduate Students* (described elsewhere in this section of the bibliography).

195 **Vacation Study Abroad.** Ed. by Edrice Howard. New York: Institute of International Education, 1981– . Annual. (The Learning Traveler, v. 2). 85–3528. ISSN 0271–1202. $15.95 (1986 ed.). Pap.

Not only does this annual directory describe costs and accommodations for more than 900 seminars, short courses, and summer sessions abroad, but it also provides information on available fellowships and scholarships. For more information about the publication, see the annotation in the "Scholarships—General—International" section of this bibliography.

United States

196 **Aids to Individual Scholars: Competitions to Be Held in 1985–1986.** New York: American Council of Learned Societies, 1985. 18p. Free. Pap.

The Council's programs of fellowships and grants are designed to advance research. Competitions are not limited to members of the Council's constituent societies. Younger scholars and independent scholars who do not hold academic appointments are strongly encouraged to apply. This booklet, distributed without charge by the Council (228 East 45th Street, New York, NY 10017), lists the fellowships and grants sponsored by the Council as well as those co-sponsored by the Council and the Social Sciences Research Council. It is updated biennially. For a similar listing, see *Social Science Research Council Fellowships and Grants to Be Offered for Training and Research* (described elsewhere in this section of the bibliography).

197 **Annual Register of Grant Support: A Guide to Support Programs of Government Agencies, Foundations, and Business and Professional Organizations.** Wilmette, IL: National Register, 1969– . Annual. 69–18307. ISSN 0066–4049. $87 (1985–86 ed.).

Despite its title, this annual covers fellowships, scholarships, and loans as well as grant opportunities. For more information, see the annotation in the "Grants—General—United States" section of this bibliography.

198 **Bear's Guide to Finding Money for College.** By John Bear. Berkeley, CA: Ten Speed Press, 1984. 157p. 84–50044. ISBN 0–89815–126–0. $5.95. Pap.

In addition to the providing the usual chatty instructions and encouragement found in trade-oriented paperbacks, this guide briefly describes over 200 fellowships, grants-in-aid, and other special awards. For more information about the publication, see the annotation in the "Scholarships—General—United States" section of this bibliography.

199 **Career Opportunities News.** Garrett Park, MD: Garrett Park Press, 1983– . Bimonthly. 83–8288. ISSN 0739–5043. $30/yr.

Designed to assist the job seeker, this bimonthly newsletter provides current information about a variety of careers. In addition, it contains announcements of fellowships, scholarships, foundation grants, and seminars. A separate section deals with women's interests.

200 **Chronicle Student Aid Annual.** Moravia, NY: Chronicle Guidance Publications, 1978– . Annual. 79–640360. ISSN 0190–339X. $16.50 (1985 ed.). Pap.

In addition to scholarship programs, a number of fellowships, awards, loans, and grants are described in this annual directory. For more information about the publication, see the annotation in the "Scholarships—General—United States" section of this bibliography.

201 **College Blue Book.** New York: Macmillan, 1923– . Biennial. 79–66191. ISSN 0069–5572. $185 (20th ed.).

Volume 5 of the 20th edition (718p. $44. ISBN 0–02–695790–6) identifies over $100 million in fellowships, scholarships, grants, and loans available to graduate and undergraduate students. For more information about this publication, see the annotation in the "Scholarships—General—United States" section.

202 **Directory of Research Grants.** Phoenix: Oryx, 1975– . Annual. 76–47074. ISSN 0146–7336. $74.50 (1986 ed.). Pap.

Fellowships, loans, and some scholarships are described in this annual directory, in addition to research grants. For more information about the publication, see the annotation in the "Grants—General—United States" section of this bibliography.

203 **Fellowships, Scholarships, and Related Opportunities in International Education.** Knoxville: Division of International Education, University of Tennessee, 1967– . Annual. 82–5141. ISSN 0735–8830. $8 (1986 ed.). Pap.

In the latest edition of this directory, over 120 fellowships, scholarships, and grants for study, research, and teaching in the United States and abroad are listed and described. For more information about this publication, see the annotation in the "Fellowships—General—International" section.

204 **Financial Aid for Graduate & Professional Education.** By Patricia McWade. 2d ed. Princeton, NJ: Peterson's Guides, 1986. 12p. ISBN 0–87866–400–9. $1.25. Pap.

This small pamphlet provides an introduction to the types of financial aid available to graduate students. It is very similar to the first edition, which was published in 1985. Except for five major federal financial aid programs (which are covered more completely in the federal government's free pamphlet *Five Federal Financial Aid Programs*, described in the "Scholarships—General—United States" section), individual financial aid programs are not covered. A few directories of financial aid are identified.

65

The guide is written by Patricia McWade, the Assistant Dean for Admissions and Financial Aid at Harvard's Graduate School of Arts and Sciences.

205 Get Your Money, Honey: A Student's Guide to Staying Alive. By Shakurra Amatulla. 2d ed. Washington, DC: For Us Publications, 1984. 69p. 84–1647. ISBN 0–915383–01–2. $4.95. Pap.

Pages 41 through 64 describe specific programs. The emphasis is on scholarships and fellowships; only nine postgraduate and twelve postdoctorate programs are listed. For more information, see the description of *Get Your Money, Honey* in the "Scholarships—General—United States" section of this bibliography.

206 Grants for Graduate Students, 1986—88. Ed. by Andrea Leskes. Princeton, NJ: Peterson's Guides, 1986. 400p. 86–1847. ISBN 0–87866–483–1. ISSN 0889–1613. $29.95. Pap.

This directory describes over 600 fellowships and grants open to American graduate students. For more information about the publication, see the annotation in the "Grants—General—United States" section of this bibliography.

207 The Grants Register: Postgraduate Awards in the English Speaking World. Ed. by Norman Frankel. New York: St. Martin's Press, 1969– . Biennial. 77–12055. $39.50 (1985–87 ed.).

This biennial directory describes fellowships, grants, and prizes open to nationals of the United States, Canada, the United Kingdom, Ireland, Australia, New Zealand, South Africa, and the developing countries. For more information about the publication, see the annotation in the "Grants—General—International" section of this bibliography.

208 Guide to American Graduate Schools. New York: Penguin, 1967– . Irreg. 67–20675. $14.95 (1986 ed.). Pap.

Nearly 700 graduate institutions (not all accredited by appropriate professional/regional associations) are described in the fifth edition of this directory (1986). They are listed in alphabetical order in the main body of the text and each entry provides the usual school descriptions (location, tuition, enrollment, admissions requirements, etc.) as well as information on financial aid. More complete information is available in *Peterson's Annual Guide to Graduate Study* (described elsewhere in this section of the bibliography).

209 How to Get Money for Research. By Mary Rubin and the Business and Professional Women's Foundation. Foreword by M. Chamberlain. Old Westbury, NY: Feminist Press, 1983. 78p. 83–1444. ISBN 0–935312–18–8. $6.95. Pap.

There are 81 fellowships and grants "for and about women at the pre- and post-doctoral levels" described in this directory. For more information, see the description of *How to Get Money for Research* in the "Grants—General— United States" section.

210 An Independent Sector Resource Directory of Education and Training Opportunities and Other Services. By Sandra Trice Gray. Washington, DC: Independent Sector, 1986– . Annual. $18 (1986 ed.). Pap.

One of the four sections in this annual identifies fellowships, internships, and grants for individuals interested in nonprofit work. For more information about the publication, see the annotation in the "Internships—General— United States" section of this bibliography.

211 Need a Lift? To Educational Opportunities, Careers, Loans, Scholarships, Employment. Prep. by the American Legion Educational and Scholarship Program. Indianapolis: American Legion, 1969– . Annual. $1 (1986 ed.). Pap.

This annually revised booklet presents descriptions of fellowships, scholarships, loans, and state educational benefits valued at over $4 billion. For more information about the publication, see the annotation in the "Scholarships—General—United States" section of this bibliography.

212 Peterson's Annual Guide to Graduate Study. Princeton, NJ: Peterson's Guides 1976– . Annual. 77–64195. ISSN 0163–6111. $100 (1985 ed., 5 v.). Pap.

In its latest edition (1985), this annually updated guide consists of five volumes: *Graduate and Professional Programs: An Overview* (850p. ISBN 0–87866–234–0. $15.95. Pap); *Graduate Programs in the Humanities and Social Sciences* (1,576p. ISBN 0–87866–236–9. $22.95. Pap.); *Graduate Programs in the Biological, Agricultural, and Health Sciences* (1,975p. ISBN 0–87866–235–7. $25.95. Pap.); *Graduate Programs in Physical Sciences and Mathematics* (640p. ISBN 0–87866–237–5. $19.95. Pap.); and *Graduate Programs in Engineering and Applied Sciences* (885p. ISBN 0–87866–238–3. $21.95. Pap.). The five volumes can be purchased individually (see above) or collectively ($100 for the set). In all, over 1,350 schools and 23,500 programs in the United States and Canada are covered. The data presented were gathered through questionnaires. Information on financial aid at each school is presented, along with the usual directory-type data.

213   The Scholarship Book: The Complete Guide to Private-Sector Scholarships, Grants and Loans for Undergraduates. By Daniel J. Cassidy and Michael J. Alves. Englewood Cliffs, NJ: Prentice-Hall, 1984, 391p. 84–11683. ISBN 0–13–792342–2, cloth; -334–1, pap. $28.50, cloth; $14.95, pap.

Despite its title, this directory covers a number of fellowships and other programs for graduate students as well as scholarships, grants, internships, loans, and competitions for undergraduate students. For more information about the publication, see the annotation in the "Scholarships—General—United States" section of this bibliography.

214   Scholarships, Fellowships and Loans. Prep. by S. Norman Feingold and Marie Feingold. Bethesda, MD: Bellman Publishing, 1949– . Irreg. 49–49180. $80 (v. 8, 1986).

This comprehessive guide to student aid provides detailed information on fellowships, scholarships, grants, and loans available to undergraduate and graduate students in the United States. For more information about the publication, see the annotation in the "Scholarships—General—United States" section of this bibliography.

215   Scholarships, Fellowships and Loans News Service and Counselors Information Services. Bethesda, MD: Bellman Publishing, 1980– Quarterly. 81–642576. ISSN 0277–6502. $32/yr.

Use this newsletter to update Feingold's *Scholarships, Fellowships and Loans* (described above). For more information on the newsletter, see the annotation in the "Scholarships—General—United States" section of this bibliography.

216   Selected List of Fellowship Opportunities and Aids to Advanced Education for United States Citizens and Foreign Nationals. Washington, DC: National Science Foundation, 1984. 76p. Free. Pap.

This pamphlet is distributed without charge by the National Science Foundation (Room 235, 1800 G Street, N.W., Washington, DC 20550). It presents concise descriptions of about 100 major graduate, and postdoctoral fellowships, loans, work-study assignments, and scholarship programs funded by various organizations, foundations, and government agencies. For each program, the following information is provided: number, remuneration, eligibility, restrictions, application procedures, and sources of additional information. A short bibliography of other publications listing fellowships, scholarships, and student loans completes the work. The current publication was formed by a merger of *A Selected List of Major Fellowship Opportunities and Aids to Advanced Education for Foreign Nationals* and *A Selected List of Major Fellowship Opportunities and Aids to Advanced Education for United States Citizens.* A previous edition was published in 1980 (61p.).

217 Student Aid Annual. Moravia, NY: Chronicle Guidance Publications, 1955–1974. Annual. ISSN 0580–4555.

From 1955 through 1974, this publication was known as *Student Aid Annual,* from 1975 through 1978 as *Student Aid Manual,* and since 1979 as *Chronicle Student Aid Annual* (described in the "Scholarships—General—United States" section of this bibliography).

218 The Student Guide to Fellowships and Internships. By students of Amherst College. New York: Dutton, 1980. 402p. 80–67575. ISBN 0–5254–3155–4, cloth; -3147–3, pap. $15.95, cloth; $7.95, pap.

Despite its title, only one chapter in this book addresses fellowships, and only national fellowships are described there. For more information about the publication, see the annotation in the "Internships—General—United States" section of this bibliography.

SOCIAL SCIENCES
General

219 ARIS Funding Messenger: Social and Natural Sciences Report. San Francisco: Academic Research Information System, 1976– . 8 times/ yr., plus supplements. 84–8697. ISSN 0747–9921. $79, individuals; $165, institutions.

This current awareness service presents up-to-date information on hundreds of grant and fellowship opportunities in the social and natural sciences. For more information about the publication, see the annotation in the "Grants— Social Sciences—General" section of this bibliography.

220 Social Science Research Council Fellowships and Grants to Be Offered for Training and Research. New York: Social Science Research Council. Annual. Free. Pap.

This annual pamphlet, distributed without charge by the Social Science Research Council, provides a listing and short description of Council research grants and of Foreign Affairs Fellowship Grants co-sponsored by the Council and the American Council of Learned Societies. These programs (dissertation fellowships and advanced research grants) apply to both the social sciences and humanities. They are open to American and foreign citizens on the advanced graduate or postgraduate levels. Also included in each annual pamphlet is a short list of grants from other agencies. Unless otherwide specified, funds are provided by the National Endowment for the

Humanities, the Ford Foundation, and the William & Flora Hewlett Foundation.

Anthropology

221 Funding for Anthropological Research. Ed. by Karen Cantrell and Denise Wallen. Phoenix: Oryx, 1986. 308p. 85–43472. ISBN 0–89774–154–4. $74.50. Pap.

Published in 1986, this directory identifies 700 fellowships, loans, scholarships, and grants from 200 government agencies, private and corporate foundations, associations, institutes, museums, libraries, and professional societies that would be of interest to "professional anthropologists and graduate anthropology students." For more information about the publication, see the annotation in the "Grants—Social Sciences—Anthropology" section of this bibliography.

Athletics

222 Directory of Graduate Physical Education Programs. Washington, DC: National Association for Sport and Physical Education, 1979– . Irreg. 79–106841. $11.95.

This guide presents information on schools granting graduate degrees in physical education and recreation. Included in the general description of each school is an indication of the financial assistance available. A companion volume, *Directory of Undergraduate Physical Education Programs* (described in the "Scholarships—Social Sciences—Athletics" section), identifies available scholarships for undergraduate education.

Business and Economics

223 Barron's Guide to Graduate Business Schools. Ed. by Eugene Miller. 5th ed. Woodbury, NY: Barron's, 1986. 732p. 86–14080. $19.50. Pap.

Nearly 700 business schools (including selected Canadian schools and schools outside North America) are profiled in the fifth edition of this directory. Very brief information on financial opportunities is given for each of the schools. The first edition of the directory was issued in 1978.

224 Financial Aid for Minorities in Business. Ed. by Howard F. Wehrle, III and Ruth N. Swann. Garrett Park, MD: Garrett Park Press, 1980. 48p. 80–144474. $3. Pap.

This booklet, published in 1980, lists fellowships, scholarships, and grant programs open to minorities interested in business administration. For more information about the publication, see the annotation in the "Scholarships—Social Sciences—Business and Economics" section of this bibliography.

225 **Free Money for Professional Studies.** By Laurie Blum. New York: Barnes and Noble, 1985. 204p. (Blum's Guides to College Money). 85–42725. ISBN 0–06–464104–0. $5.95. Pap.

This guide identifies state-based organizations awarding fellowships, scholarships, and grants to their residents, miscellaneous awards available to special applicants (e.g., deaf children, veterans' dependents), and selected financial aid programs appropriate for "professional studies" (including business administration). For more information about the publication, see the annotation in the "Fellowships—Sciences—Health Sciences" section of this bibliography.

226 **Guide to Graduate Study in Economics, Agricultural Economics, and Related Degrees in Business and Administration in the United States of America and Canada.** Ed. by Wyn F. Owen and Larry R. Cross. Boulder, CO: Economics Institute, 1984. 500p. ISBN 0–88036–003–8. $33.

Individual graduate programs in economics, agricultural economics, and administration are described in this directory. In addition to providing typical directory-type information for each of the departments, the entries indicate whether or not financial assistance is available, for either native or foreign students. The first six editions of this directory (last one published in 1982) were issued by Richard D. Irwin as *Guide to Graduate Study in Economics and Agricultural Economics in the United States of America and Canada.*

Education

227 **Chronicle of Higher Education.** Washington, DC: Chronicle of Higher Education, 1966– . Weekly. ISSN 0009–5982. $48/yr., surface mail; $222/yr., air mail.

Information on both fellowships and grants are included in this weekly news service. For more information about the publication, see the annotation in the "Grants—General—United States" section of this bibliography.

228 **Financial Aid for Minorities in Education.** Ed. by Mary T. Christian and Ruth N. Swann. Garrett Park, MD: Garrett Park Press, 1980. 58p. 80–153221. $3. Pap.

This booklet, published in 1980, lists fellowships, scholarships, and grant programs open to minorities interested in the field of education. For more information about the publication, see the annotation in the "Scholarships—Social Sciences—Education" section of this bibliography.

229   Graduate Programs and Faculty in Reading. Ed. by Paula Blomenberg. 4th ed. Newark, DE: International Reading Association, 1981. 383p. 73–159461. ISBN 0–87207–928–7. $15.50. Pap.

More than 300 graduate level programs in reading in the United States and Canada are described in the fourth edition of this directory. The data presented were collected by questionnaire. Programs are listed by state or province and then by institution. Available financial aid is indicated in each program entry.

230   The Grant Advisor. Arlington, VA: Toft Consulting, 1983– . Monthly, except July. 83–2781. ISSN 0740–5383. $85/yr.

This monthly newsletter, aimed at colleges and universities, identifies faculty fellowships and grant opportunities as well as institutional grant programs from federal agencies, private foundations, corporations, and professional organizations. For more information about the publication, see the annotation in the "Grants—Social Sciences—Education" section of this bibliography.

231   Grants for Study Visits by University Administrators and Librarians. London: Association of Commonwealth Universities, 1979– . Biennial. Pap.

This biennially-issued pamphlet describes approximately 40 fellowships, research grants, and travel grants available to university administrators and university librarians from Commonwealth countries who wish to undertake study visits in other countries. For more information about the publication, see the annotation in the "Grants—Social Sciences—Librarianship" section of this bibliography.

Geography

232   Guide to Departments of Geography in the United States and Canada. Washington, DC: Association of American Geographers, 1985– . Annual. 85–641423. ISSN 0072–8497. $9 (1985 ed.). Pap.

This guide identifies most of the geography departments in the United States and Canada that offer majors and/or graduate programs of studies. Entries note the usual school-related items (e.g., degrees offered, number of students, names and degrees of faculty members, admissions requirements), some not-so-usual categories (e.g., thesis and dissertation titles), and information about available financial aid. From 1969 through 1984, this work was issued under the title *Guide to Graduate Departments of Geography in the United States and Canada.*

History

233 **Fellowships and Grants of Interest to Historians.** Washington, DC: American Historical Association, 1976–1977. Annual. Pap.

Since 1978, this annual publication has been issued as *Grants and Fellowships of Interest to Historians* (described in the "Grants—Social Sciences— History" section).

234 **Grants and Fellowships of Interest to Historians.** Washington, DC: American Historical Association, 1978– . Annual. 83–644237. ISSN 0275–830X. $4, members; $5, nonmembers (1985/86 ed.). Pap.

This annual listing identifies and describes nearly 200 fellowships, internships, awards, prizes, and travel grants of interest to graduate students, postdoctoral researchers, and scholars in history. For a more complete annotation, see the description of *Grants and Fellowships of Interest to Historians* in the "Grants—Social Sciences—History" section of this bibliography.

Librarianship

235 **Financial Assistance for Library Education.** Chicago: American Library Association, 1970– . Annual. 73–649921. ISSN 0569–6275. $1 (1986–87 ed.). Pap.

This comprehensive summary of fellowships, scholarships, grants-in-aid, loans, and other financial aids for library education is available from the American Library Association (50 East Huron Street, Chicago, IL 60611) for $1 to cover postage. The booklet is an annually revised list of awards from state library agencies, national and state library associations, local libraries, and academic institutions offering undergraduate or graduate programs in library education in the United States or Canada. Scholarships of less than $200 are not listed. For each entry, the following information is given: granting body, level of program, type of assistance, number available, academic or other requirements, application deadline, and application address. Supplementing the text are a list of graduate library education programs accredited by the American Library Association and indexes to sources of support for nonmaster's degree programs and for special groups of students (e.g., minority group applicants). In earlier editions, the directory was published under the title *Fellowships, Scholarships, Grants-in-Aid, Loan Funds, and Other Financial Assistance for Library Education.*

236   Grants for Study Visits by University Administrators and Librarians.
London: Association of Commonwealth Universities, 1979– . Biennial.
Pap.

This biennially-issued pamphlet describes approximately 40 fellowships,
research grants, and travel grants available to university librarians and
university administrators from Commonwealth countries who wish to
undertake study visits to other countries. For more information about the
publication, see the annotation in the "Grants—Social Sciences—
Librarianship" section of this bibliography.

**237   A Librarian's Directory of Exchange Programs/Study Tours/Funding
Sources and Job Opportunities Outside of the United States.** Ed. by
Diane Stine. Chicago: American Library Association, 1982. 15p. $1.50.
Pap.

This directory covers approximately 75 institutions and organizations that
either provide information on or offer opportunities for exchange programs,
study tours, and job opportunities abroad. Some funding sources are also
identified. The programs listed are designed specifically for librarians. The
entries are arranged by type of program and identify sponsoring organization,
address, and program parameters. Indexing is by organization, geographic
location, and type of eligible librarian (public, academic, etc.).

238   Opportunities and Honors for You and Your Colleagues. Chicago:
American Library Association, 1986. 4p. Free. Pap.

The American Library Association sponsors more than 80 fellowships,
grants, and awards "to honor distinguished service and foster professional
growth." These are described in this small booklet. For more information
about the publication, see the annotation in the "Awards and Prizes—Social
Sciences—Librarianship" section of this bibliography.

Law

239   Barron's Guide to Law Schools. Woodbury, NY: Barron's Educational
Series, 1967– . Irreg. 84–9316. $8.95 (1984 ed.). Pap.

In addition to the usual school-related information (e.g., student-faculty
ratio, number of volumes in library,. average GPA and LSAT scores,
application process), the latest edition (1984. 461p. ISBN 0–8120–2772–8) of
this directory provides information on financial aid available. There is also a
separate chapter devoted to financial aid programs (fellowships and loans)
available from private and public sources to low-income students interested in
legal studies.

240   Financial Aid for Minorities in Law. Ed. by Novelle J. Dickensen and
Ruth N. Swann. Garrett Park, MD: Garrett Park Press, 1981. 63p.
80–153225. $3. Pap.

One in a series of booklets covering financial assistance programs for
minorities, this compilation identifies selected fellowships, scholarships, and
grants in the field of law that were available prior to 1980. The listing is
generally unannotated. Despite its title, many of the programs included are
not restricted just to minority applicants but are open equally to all segments
of the population. A number of the entries are general in nature and there is
considerable duplication among booklets in the Garrett Park Press
"Financial Aid for Minorities" series. During the past few years, there have
been dramatic changes in the financial aid available to minorities, and this
listing is now seriously out of date. For more current and comprehensive
coverage, see the *Directory of Financial Aids for Minorities* described in the
"Scholarships—Special Population Groups—Ethnic Groups" section of this
bibliography.

241   Free Money for Professional Studies. By Laurie Blum. New York:
Barnes and Noble, 1985. 204p. (Blum's Guides to College Money).
85–42725. ISBN 0–06–464104–9. $5.95. Pap.

This guide identifies state-based organizations awarding fellowships,
scholarships, and grants to their residents, miscellaneous awards available to
special applicants (e.g., deaf children, veterans' dependents), and selected
financial aid programs appropriate for "professional studies" (including law).
For more information about the publication, see the annotation in the
"Fellowships—Sciences—Health Sciences" section of this bibliography.

Political Sciences

242   Guide to Graduate Study in Political Sciences. Washington, DC:
American Political Science Association, 1972–1981. Annual. $10,
members; $12, nonmembers (1981 ed.). Pap.

This annual, which was suspended in 1981, identified master's and doctoral
programs in political science offered at American academic institutions
between 1972 and 1981. The entries are arranged alphabetically by institution
and, in addition to information on admissions, retention, and graduation,
provide brief information on financial aid programs offered. Completing each
annual are faculty and institution indexes and statistical analyses of the
number, sex, and education of students admitted to the programs.

243 Research Support for Political Scientists: A Guide to Sources of Funds
     for Research Fellowships, Grants, and Contracts. Comp. by Stephen F.
     Szabo. 2d ed. Washington, DC: American Political Science
     Association, 1981. 126p. 78–102488. ISBN 0–915654–43–1. $6. Pap.

Updating the first edition, which was issued in 1978 (154p. ISBN
0–915654–22–9), this directory was prepared to guide political scientists to
sources and strategies for locating financial support for research. Not
intended to be exhaustive, the source provides a sampling of the agencies that
have funded research by political scientists in the past. The listing is divided
into four main sections: research fellowships (the largest), doctoral
dissertation grants and fellowships, private foundation research grants, and
U.S. government grants and contracts. For each of the programs listed, the
following information is provided: priorities and focus, application and
selection, funding policy, contacts, and examples of funded projects. A
bibliography of basic sources of information on research support, a list of
federal agencies supporting social research (as of 1981), and instructions for
preparing proposals complete the work. There are no indexes. Published in
1981, many of the listings are now substantively out of date.

Psychology

244 American Psychological Association's Guide to Research Support. Ed.
     by Ralph E. Dusek, et al. Washington, DC: American Psychological
     Association, 1984. 463p. 84–71433. ISBN 0–912704–91–8. $25. Pap.
245 Addendum. Washington, DC: American Psychological Association,
     1986. 117p. $17.50. Pap.

The 1984 revised edition and 1986 addendum of this directory cover more
than 180 federal and 55 nonfederal sources of research support for the
behavioral sciences. Some of these are fellowship programs. For more
information about these publication, see the annotation in the "Grants—
Social Sciences—Psychology" section of this bibliography.

246 Graduate Study in Psychology and Associated Fields. Washington,
     DC: American Psychological Association, 1983– . Annual. 84–641215.
     ISSN 0742–7220. $15.50 (1984, with 1985 addendum). Pap.

The latest edition of this guide (1984, with 1985 addendum. 546p.) describes
graduate programs in psychology and allied fields offered by more than 300
Canadian and American institutions of higher learning. Entries include
information not only on admission requirements, but on financial assistance
as well. From 1969 through 1982, this directory was issued as *Graduate
Study in Psychology* (Annual. 72–626834. ISSN 0072–5277).

Sociology

247 Guide to Graduate Departments of Sociology. Washington, DC: American Sociological Association, 1969– . Annual. ISSN 0091–7052. $4, members; $10, nonmembers (1986 ed.). Pap.

This annual directory provides up-to-date information on graduate departments of sociology. Entries are arranged alphabetically by college or university name and contain basic information about the departments (including address and telephone number, chair of the department, graduate degrees offered, graduate student enrollment, special programs, and faculty). The financial aid available at each school is briefly identified.

Substance Abuse

248 Guide to International Drug Abuse Demand Reduction Resources: Scholarships/Fellowships. Rockville, MD: U.S. National Institute on Drug Abuse, 1982. 72p. Free. Pap.

Approximately 100 fellowships and scholarships open to professionals, paraprofessionals, and organizations or agencies concerned with manpower development in the drug abuse field are described in this directory. For more a more complete annotation, see the description of *Guide to International Drug Abuse Demand Reduction Resources* in the "Scholarships—Social Sciences—Substance Abuse" section of this bibliography.

HUMANITIES

General

249 Aid to Artists/Aide aux Artists. Ottawa: Canada Council. Annual. 77–70101. ISSN 0703–6043. Free. Pap.

The Canada Council is an organization created by Parliament in 1957 to promote the arts in Canada. Its funds, which come from an annual Parliamentary appropriation, are used to provide financial assistance and services to both individuals and arts organizations in the performing arts, writing and publishing, the visual and media arts, and architecture. The purpose of this bilingual (English and French) brochure is to describe the various forms and amounts of assistance (fellowships, research grants, travel grants) offered to individual artists by the Council. Entries specify information about eligibility, projected program of work, remuneration, length of tenure, renewability, limitations, and application procedures. They are arranged by form of assistance or discipline. The publication is updated annually and is available without charge from the Canada Council (255 Albert Street, Ottawa, Ontario K1P 5V8 Canada).

250   ARIS Funding Messenger: Creative Arts and Humanities Report. San Francisco: Academic Research Information System, 1976– . 8 times/ yr., plus supplements. 84–8702. ISSN 0747–993X. $46, individuals; $95, institutions.

This current awareness service provides up-to-date information about regional, national, and international fellowships, grants, and awards in the humanities, performing arts, and visual arts. For more information about the publication, see the annotation in the "Grants—Humanities—General" section of this bibliography.

251   Directory of Grants in the Humanities. Phoenix: Oryx, 1986– . Annual. 86–2385. ISSN 0887–0551. $74.50 (1986 ed.). Pap.

This new annual directory identifies fellowships and grants in literature, languages, history, anthropology, philosophy, ethics, religion, the fine arts, and performing arts (including painting, dance, photography, sculpture, music, drama, crafts, folklore, and mime). For more information about the publication, see the annotation in the "Grants—Humanities—General" section of this bibliography.

252   Free Money for Humanities Students. By Laurie Blum. New York: Barnes & Noble, 1985. 204p. (Blum's Guides to College Money). 85–42554. ISBN 0–06–464107–4. $5.95. Pap.

This guide identifies state-based organizations awarding grants and scholarships to their residents, miscellaneous awards available to special applicants (e.g., deaf children, veteran's dependents), and selected financial aid programs specifically of interest to humanities' students. For more information about the publication, see the annotation in the "Scholarships—Humanities—General" section of this bibliography.

253   Gadney's Guide to 1800 International Contests, Festivals & Grants in Film & Video, Photography, TV-Radio Broadcasting, Writing, Poetry, Playwriting, Journalism. By Alan Gadney. 2d ed. Glendale, CA: Festival Publications, 1980. 610p. 80–66803. ISBN 0–930828–03–8, cloth; 02–X, pap. $22.95, cloth; $15.95, pap.

This guide describes over 1,800 national and international fellowships, festivals, competitions, prizes, awards, grants, and loans open to those interested in film, video, photography, TV-radio broadcasting, writing, poetry, playwriting, and journalism. For more information about the publication, see the annotation in the "Awards and Prizes—Humanities—General" section of this bibliography.

254 **Grants in the Humanities: A Scholar's Guide to Funding Sources.** By William E. Coleman. 2d ed. New York: Neal-Schuman, 1984. 175p. (Neal-Schuman Grants series). 83–27069. ISBN 0–918212–80–4. $24.95.

Fellowships as well as grants are described in the second edition of this directory. For a more complete annotation, see the description of *Grants in the Humanities* in the "Grants—Humanities—General" section.

255 **Guide to the National Endowment for the Arts.** Washington, DC: U.S. National Endowment for the Arts. Annual. Free. Pap.

This is one of a number of publications issued without charge by the National Endowment for the Arts (1100 Pennsylvania Avenue, N.W., Washington, DC 20506) that describe fellowships and grants sponsored by the agency. These programs are open to both U.S. citizens and permanent residents. An example of the other useful pamphlets published by the Endowment is *Crafts: Visual Arts Programs Guidelines.*

256 **The National Directory of Grants and Aid to Individuals in the Arts, International.** By Daniel Millsaps. 5th ed. Washington, DC: Washington International Arts Letter, 1983. 246p. (The Arts Patronage series, no. 11). 70–11269. ISBN 0–912072–12–1. ISSN 0270–5966. $15.95. Pap.

According to its editors, this paperback directory lists "most grants, prizes, and awards for professional work in the U.S. and abroad, and information about universities and schools which offer special aid to students." For more information about the publication, see the annotation in the "Grants—Humanities—General" section of this bibliography.

257 **Ocular: The Directory of Information and Opportunities for the Visual Arts.** Denver: Ocular, 1976– . Quarterly. $14/yr.

Provided in each issue of this quarterly journal is a section identifying financial aid for visual artists, including fellowships, grants, and awards. For more information about this publication, see the annotation in the "Grants—Humanities—General" section of this bibliography.

258 **Social Science Research Council Fellowships and Grants to Be Offered for Training and Research.** New York: Social Science Research Council. Annual. Free. Pap.

This annual pamphlet describes dissertation fellowships and advanced research grants in both the humanities and social sciences that are open to American and foreign citizens on the advanced graduate or postgraduate levels. For more information about the publication, see the annotation in the "Fellowships—Social Sciences—General" section of this bibliography.

259 **Washington International Arts Letter.** Washington, DC: Washington International Arts Letter (WIAL), 1962– . 10 issues/yr. 68–6506. ISSN 0043–0609. $54/yr.

This monthly newsletter provides information on fellowships, scholarships, awards, and grants open to institutions and individuals involved in the arts. For more information about the publication, see the annotation in the "Grants—Humanities—General" section of this bibliography.

Communications and Mass Media

260 **Editor & Publisher Journalism Awards Directory.** Ed. by Jerome H. Walker. New York: Editor & Publisher Company. Annual. $3. Pap.

Each year, this directory describes over 200 fellowships, scholarships, and awards available in the United States and abroad for reporters, columnists, editors, cartoonists, and photographers. For more information about the publication, see the annotation in the "Scholarships—Humanities—Communications and Mass Media" section of this bibliography.

261 **Financial Aid for Minorities in Mass Communications.** By Leslie L. Lawton and Ruth N. Swann. Garrett Park, MD: Garrett Park Press, 1981. 62p. 81–211245. $3. Pap.

This booklet, published in 1981, lists fellowships, grants, and scholarships open to minorities interested in communications and mass media. For more information about the publication, see the annotation in the "Scholarships—Humanities—Communications and Mass Media" section of this bibliography.

262 **Honor Awards Handbook.** Ed. by Milton L. Levy. Berkeley, CA: Honor Awards Handbook, 1957–1964. 3v. 84–7113.

Published in 1957, 1960, and 1964 under the title *Honor Awards Handbook*, this directory changed its name in 1968 to *Media Awards Handbook* (described in the "Awards and Prizes—Humanities—Communications and Mass Media" section of this bibliography).

263 **How to Enter and Win Video/Audio Contests.** By Alan Gadney. Ed. by Carolyn Porter. New York: Facts On File, 1981. 193p. 81–2221. ISBN 0–87196–520–8, cloth; -551–8, pap. $14.95, cloth, $6.95, pap.

This volume describes over 400 national and international fellowships, grants, contests, and festivals open to television and video tape producers. For more information about the publication, see the annotation in the "Awards and Prizes—Humanities—Communications and Mass Media" section of this bibliography.

264 Journalism Career Guide for Minorities. Prep. by the American Society of Newspaper Editors. Princeton, NJ: Dow Jones Newspaper Fund, 1984. 48p. Free. Pap.

One section of this free booklet deals with fellowships, scholarships, internships, and special training programs for minorities interested in journalism as well as with general scholarship/fellowship opportunities. For more information about the publication, see the annotation in the "Scholarships—Humanities—Communications and Mass Media" section of this bibliography.

265 Journalism Directory. Ed. by Nancy Doubledee Barclay. Columbia, SC: Association for Education in Journalism and Mass Communciations, 1983– . Annual. 83–646324. ISSN 0735–3103. $16 (1985 ed.). Pap.

One section of this annual covers "National Funds, Fellowships and Foundations." For more information about the publication, see the annotation in the "Scholarships—Humanities—Communications and Mass Media" section.

266 Media Awards Handbook: Radio, Television, Newspaper, Magazine, Allied Fields & Industries. Ed. by Milton L. Levy. Danville, CA: Media Awards Handbook, 1980. n.p. 68–24272. ISBN 0–910744–03–3. $20. Pap.

Intended as a "workbook for those professionals who want to know as much detail as possible about the various Contests and Awards with the thought of entering them for their work," this directory also lists some fellowships, scholarships, and grants. For more information about this publication, see the annotation in the "Awards and Prizes—Humanities—Communications and Mass Media" section of this bibliography.

Fine Arts

267 American Art Directory. Ed. and comp. by Jaques Cattell Press. New York: Bowker, 1952– . Biennial. 80–609. ISSN 0065–6968. $85 (1984 ed.).

A separate section in each biennial volume focuses on art-related agencies and activities, including fellowships and scholarships (16 pages of programs are provided in a recent edition). For more information about this publication, see the annotation in the "Scholarships—Humanities—Fine Arts" section of this bibliography.

Language and Linguistics

268 **Guide to Grants & Fellowships in Languages & Linguistics.**
Washington, DC: Linguistic Society of America, 1984– . Biennial.
84–12438, ISSN 0024–3906. $3 (1985 ed.). Pap.

Published biennially, this directory lists and describes fellowships and grants
in the fields of language and linguistics sponsored by institutions,
associations, foundations, and government agencies located in the United
States. For more information about the publication, see the description in the
"Grants—Humanities—Language and Linguistics" section of this
bibliography.

Literature

269 **Dramatists Sourcebook: Complete Opportunities for Playwrights,
Translators, Composers, Lyricists, and Librettists.** Ed. by M. Elizabeth
Osborne. New York: Theatre Communications Group, 1982– .
Annual. 82–644562. ISSN 0733–1606. $10.95 (1985–86 ed.). Pap.

There are a number of separate sections in this sourcebook that describe
various financial aid programs for dramatists, including fellowships, grants,
awards and prizes, colonies and residencies, and emergency funds. For more
information about the publication, see the annotation in the "Awards and
Prizes—Humanities—Literature" section of this bibliography.

270 **How to Enter and Win Fiction Writing Contests.** By Alan Gadney,.
New York: Facts On File, 1981. 200p. 81–2182. ISBN 0–87196–519–4,
cloth; -552–6, pap. $14.95, cloth; $6.95, pap.

More than 400 national and international fellowships, scholarships, grants,
and contests for literature are covered in this guide. For more information
about the publication, see the annotation in the "Awards and Prizes—
Humanities—Literature" section of this bibliography.

271 **How to Enter and Win Non-Fiction & Journalism Contests.** By Alan
Gadney. New York: Facts On File, 1981. 205p. 81–2179. ISBN
0–87196–518–6, cloth; -553–4, pap. $14.95, cloth; $6.95, pap.

Nearly 500 national and international fellowships, scholarships, contests,
festivals, and grants open to nonfiction writers are identified and described in
this directory. For more information about the publication, see the
annotation in the "Awards and Prizes—Humanities—Literature" section of
this bibliography.

272 **International Directory of Writers Groups & Associations, 1984–1985.**
Comp. by John Hall. Alexandria, MN: Inkling, 1984. 186p. ISBN
0–932620–54–X. $19.50. Pap.

In addition to providing typical directory-type information for many of the
organizations listed in this international compilation, some of the entries also
indicate sponsored fellowships and awards. For more information about the
publication, see the annotation in the "Grants—Humanities—Literature"
section of this bibliography.

273 **Literary Market Place: The Directory of American Book Publishing
with Names & Numbers.** New York: Bowker, 1972– . Annual.
81–640008. ISSN 0161–2905. $59.95 (1986 ed.). Pap.

Originally designed as a register of personnel in publishing and allied fields,
over the years this annual has been expanded to include 12,000 entries in a
dozen major sections. One of these sections focuses on awards, scholarships,
fellowships, and grants-in-aid of interest to the American writer. For more
information about the publication, see the annotation in the "Awards and
Prizes—Humanities—Literature" section of this bibliography.

Performing Arts

274 **Lively Arts Information Directory.** Ed. by Steven R. Wasserman and
Jacqueline Wasserman O'Brien. 2d ed. Detroit: Gale, 1985. 1,040p.
81–20060. ISBN 0–8103–0321–3. $165.

Over 6,700 fellowships, grants, foundations, scholarships, awards,
publications, special libraries, and schools offering study in theater, music,
drama, filmmaking, radio, and television are described in the second edition
of this directory. For more information about the publication, see the
annotation in the "Awards and Prizes—Humanities—Performing Arts"
section of this bibliography.

Philosophy

275 **Grants and Fellowships of Interest to Philosophers.** Newark, DE:
American Philosophical Association, 1972– . Annual. $2.50. Pap.

This annually-issued directory identifies fellowships and grant opportunities
for graduate and postdoctoral study and research in the United States and
abroad. For more information, see the description of *Grants and Fellowships
of Interest to Philosophers* in the "Grants—Humanities—Philosophy" section.

SCIENCES

General

276   ARIS Funding Messenger: Social and Natural Sciences Report. San Francisco: Academic Research Information System, 1976– . 8 times/yr., plus supplements. 84–8697. ISSN 0747–9921. $79, individuals; $165, institutions.

This current awareness service provides up-to-date information on hundreds of fellowship and grant opportunities in the sciences and social sciences. For more information about the publication, see the annotation in the "Grants—Social Sciences—General" section of this bibliography.

277   Financial Aid for Minorities in Science. Ed. by Ruth N. Swann and Sharon F. White. Garrett Park, MD: Garrett Park Press, 1980. 49p. $2. Pap.

This booklet, published in 1980, lists fellowships, scholarships, and grants open to minorities interested in the sciences. For more information about the publication, see the annotation in the "Scholarships—Sciences—General" section of this bibliography.

278   Free Money for Science Students. By Laurie Blum. New York: Barnes & Noble, 1985. 204p. (Blum's Guides to College Money). 85–42724. ISBN 0–06–464108–0. $5.95. Pap.

This guide identifies state-based organizations awarding fellowships, grants and scholarships to their residents, miscellaneous awards available to special applicants (e.g., deaf children, veteran's dependents), and selected financial aid programs specifically of interest to science students. For more information about the publication, see the annotation in the "Scholarships—Sciences—General" section of this bibliography.

279   National Science Foundation Guide to Programs. Washington, DC: National Science Foundation. Annual. Free. Pap.

Described in this free annual pamphlet are fellowships and grants sponsored by the National Science Foundation and administered by the foundation in cooperation with foreign countries. For more information about the publication, see the annotation in the "Grants—Sciences—General" section of this bibliography.

Engineering

280 **Financial Aid for Minorities in Engineering.** Ed. by Clayton G. Holloway and Ruth N. Swann. Garrett Park, MD: Garrett Park Press, 1981. 52p. 81–161268. $3. Pap.

This booklet, published in 1981, lists fellowships, scholarships, and grant programs open to minorities interested in engineering. For more information about the publication, see the annotation in the "Scholarships—Sciences—Engineering" section of this bibliography.

Health Sciences

281 **Admission Requirements of American Medical Colleges.** Washington, DC: Association of American Medical Colleges, 1951–1964. Annual.

This annual directory was issued from 1951 through 1954 as *Admission Requirements of American Medical Colleges* and from 1955 through 1964 as *Admissions Requirements of American Colleges, Including Canada.* Since 1965, the annual has been entitled *Medical School Admission Requirements* (described elsewhere in this section of the bibliography).

282 **ARIS Funding Messenger: Medical Sciences Report.** San Francisco: Academic Research Information System, 1976– . 8 times/yr., plus supplements. 84–8696. ISSN 0747–9913. $79, individuals; $165, institutions.

This current awareness service provides up-to-date information on hundreds of fellowships and grants in the biological and medical sciences. For more information about the publication, see the annotation in the "Grants—Sciences—Health Sciences" section of this bibliography.

283 **Directory of Biomedical and Health Care Grants.** Phoenix: Oryx, 1985– . Annual. 85–15562. $74.50 (1986 ed.). Pap.

The second edition of this directory, issued in 1986, identifies 2,000 health-related fellowships and grants, ranging from nutrition to health care delivery needs for the aged. For more information about the publication, see the annotation in the "Grants—Sciences—Health Sciences" section of this bibliography.

284 **Directory of Psychiatry Residency Training Programs.** Ed. by Carolyn B. Robinowitz and Zebulor Taintor. Washington, DC: American Psychiatric Association, 1982– . Biennial. 84–1012. ISSN 0740–8250. $15. (1986 ed.). Pap.

Aimed at medical students interested in applying for a general or child psychiatry residency program, this directory also identifies applicable postgraduate fellowships. For more information about the publication, see the annotation in the "Internships—Sciences—Health Sciences" section of this bibliography.

285   Financial Aid for Minorities in Allied Health. Ed. by Lois S. Cofield and Ruth N. Swann. Garrett Park, MD: Garrett Park Press, 1980. 58p. 81–129225. $2. Pap.

One in a series of booklets covering financial assistance programs for minorities, this compilation identifies selected scholarships, fellowships, and grants in the allied health area that were available in 1980. The listing is generally unannotated. Despite its title, many of the programs included are not restricted just to minority applicants but are open equally to all segments of the population. A number of the entries are general in nature and there is considerable duplication among booklets in the Garrett Park Press "Financial Aid for Minorities" series. During the last few years, there have been dramatic changes in the financial aid available to minorities, and this listing is now seriously out of date. For more current and comprehensive coverage, see the *Directory of Financial Aids for Minorities* described in the "Scholarships—Special Population Groups—Ethnic Groups" section of this bibliography.

286   Financial Aid for Minorities in Medicine. By Sterling H. Hudson III and Ruth N. Swann. Garrett Park, MD: Garrett Park Press, 1981. 66p. 81–184828. $3. Pap.

Another in Garrett Park Press' "Financial Aid for Minorities" series, this booklet identifies fellowships, grants, and some scholarships in the medical field that were available prior to 1981. Like the other pamphlets in the series, this listing is infrequently annotated, includes programs open to all segments of the population as well as programs restricted to minorities, and duplicates many of the listings found in other Garrett Park Press booklets. Because of the publication date, this listing should be used with caution. For more current and comprehensive coverage, see the *Directory of Financial Aids for Minorities* described in the "Scholarships—Special Population Groups— Ethnic Groups" section of this bibliography.

287   Free Money for Professional Studies. By Laurie Blum. New York: Barnes and Noble, 1985. 204p. (Blum's Guides to College Money). 85–42725. ISBN 0–06–464109–0. $5.95. Pap.

This is one in a series of three *Blum's Guides to College Money*. For the purposes of this volume, "professional studies" are defined to include dentistry, medicine, nursing, optometry, pharmacology, psychiatry, veterinary medicine, business, and law. The other two volumes in the set cover sciences and the humanities (and are described elsewhere in this bibliography). Each volume is exactly the same size (204 pages) and the same 160–page section is repeated in all three books: a 130–page state-by-state listing of organizations awarding scholarships and grants to their residents and a 22–page listing of miscellaneous awards available to various applicants (e.g., deaf children, veterans' dependents). Each of these entries contains only brief information: sponsoring organization address and telephone number, eligibility, remuneration, deadline, and contact person. The remaining 44 pages identify selected financial aid programs specifically of interest to students involved in "professional studies." More complete lists of programs for the various disciplines in the professions are available in a number of other directories described in this bibliography.

288 Medical Research Funding Bulletin. Bronxville, NY: Science Support Center, 1972– . 3 times/month. 85–14532. $48/yr.

Each issue identifies up to 40 fellowships and research grants in medical sciences offered by federal and private organizations. For more information about the publication, see the annotation in the "Grants—Sciences—Health Sciences" section of this bibliography.

289 Medical School Admission Requirements, United Sates and Canada. Washington, DC: Association of American Medical Colleges, 1965– . Annual. 82–8187. ISSN 0738–6060. $9.75. Pap.

Issued annually, this directory provides "current and official information on pre-medical preparation and admissions" at over 120 medical schools in the United States, Puerto Rico, and Canada. It also includes information related to financial aid. Covered in various sections of each edition are undergraduate financial planning, sources of financial aid at the medical school and post-M.D. levels, and financial resources for disadvantaged and minority students. From 1951 through 1964, this directory was published as *Admission Requirements of American Medical Colleges* (1951–1954) and *Admission Requirements of American Medical Colleges, Including Canada* (1955–1964).

290 Minority Student Opportunities in United States Medical Schools. Washington, DC: Association of American Medical Colleges, 1970– . Biennial. 79–640963. ISSN 0085–3488. $7.50 (1985 ed.). Pap.

Similar in structure to *Medical School Admission Requirements* (described elsewhere in this section of the bibliography), this directory presents data on minority student opportunities in U.S. medical schools. The information is collected biennially by the AAMC's Office of Minority Affairs. Program profiles for medical schools are arranged geographically. The entries specify recruitment procedures, admission process, academic aid programs, summer enrichment programs, student financial assistance, and other pertinent data.

291   **Student Financial Aid: Speech-Language Pathology and Audiology.**
Rockville, MD: American Speech—Language—Hearing Association,
1981. 21p. Free. Pap.

Aimed at students planning careers in speech-language pathology and
audiology, this listing identifies loans, scholarships, and aids for graduate
education. For more information about the publication, see the annotation in
the "Scholarships—Sciences—Health Sciences" section of this bibliography.

Mathematics

292   **Assistantships and Fellowships in Mathematical Sciences.** Providence,
RI: American Mathematical Society, 1953– . (December issue of
Notices of the American Mathematical Society). Annual. 77–404. ISSN
0002–9920. $7. Pap.

Every year, the December issue of *Notices* presents a comprehensive list of
assistantships and fellowships in mathematics available at about 280 U.S. and
Canadian universities. Entries for the nearly 400 departments of math,
applied math, statistics, and computer science covered contain the following
information: address, type of assistantship, number to be awarded, amount of
stipend, tuition and fees, services required, and degrees awarded. The issue
also includes information on financial support for study and travel abroad by
U.S. students and a section on financial support for study in the United States
by foreign students. Over 100 programs are described.

Technology

293   **Graduate Assistantship Directory in the Computer Sciences.** New
York: Association for Computing Machinery, 1966– . Annual.
79–1510. ISSN 0072–5234. $10. Pap.

Over 140 graduate programs in computer science and allied fields are
described in the latest edition of this directory, which is published by the
Association for Computing Machinery for its student members and
participating graduate institutions.The directory is also available for sale to
the general public. Entries indicate financial aid available to qualified
students as well as such institution-related information as degrees offered,
institution size, faculty size, enrollment, computer equipment available, and
contact persons.

SPECIAL POPULATION GROUPS

The Disabled

294 **Financial Aid for the Disabled and Their Dependents.** By Gail Ann Schlachter. Los Angeles: Reference Service Press, 1987– . Biennial. (Directories of Financial Aid for Special Needs Groups). $29.95 (1987/ 88 cd.).

This is the first comprehensive and up-to-date listing of scholarships, fellowships, loans, awards, and grants-in-aid that have been established for disabled individuals and their dependents. For more information about the publication, see the annotation in the "Scholarships—Special Population Groups—The Disabled" section of this bibliography.

Ethnic Groups

295 **Directory of Financial Aids for Minorities.** By Gail Ann Schlachter. Los Angeles: Reference Service Press, 1984– . Biennial. (Directories of Financial Aid for Special Needs Groups). 83–25068. ISBN 0–918276–03–9. ISSN 0738–4122. $37.50 (1986–1987 cd.).

The latest edition of this biennial directory includes a descriptive list of more than 1,200 fellowships, scholarships, loans, grants, internships, awards, and prizes set aside for Asian Americans, Black Americans, Hispanic Americans, Native Americans, and minorities in general. For more information about the publication, see the annotation in the "Scholarships—Special Population Groups—Ethnic Groups" section of this bibliography.

296 **Directory of Special Programs for Minority Group Members: Career Information Services, Employment Skills Banks, Financial Aid Sources.** Prep. by Willis L. Johnson. 3d ed. Garrett Park, MD: Garrett Park Press, 1980. 612p. 73–93533. ISSN 0093–9501. $20. Pap.

In addition to listing career information services and employment skills banks, this directory identifies a number of sources of fellowships, scholarships, and loans for minority groups members that were available in 1980. For more information about the publication, see the annotation in the "Scholarships—Special Population Groups—Ethnic Groups" section of this bibliography.

297 **Financial Aid for Minorities in Allied Health.** Ed. by Lois G. Cofield and Ruth N. Swann. Garrett Park, MD: Garrett Park Press, 1980. 58p. 81–129225. $2. Pap.

Now considerably out of date, this directory provides a selective listing of fellowships, scholarships, and grants available in 1980 to minorities interested in allied health fields. For more information about the publication, see the annotation in the "Scholarships—Sciences—Health Sciences" section of this bibliography.

298 Financial Aid for Minorities in Business. Ed. by Howard F. Wehrle, III and Ruth N. Swann. Garrett Park, MD: Garrett Park Press, 1980. 48p. 80–14474. $3. Pap.

Selected fellowships, scholarships, and grants in the field of business that were available to minorities in 1980 are listed in this directory. For more information about the publication, see the annotation in the "Scholarships— Social Sciences—Business and Economics" section of this bibliography.

299 Financial Aid for Minorities in Education. Ed. by Mary T. Christian and Ruth N. Swann. Garrett Park, MD: Garrett Park Press, 1980. 58p. 80–153221. $3. Pap.

One in a series of booklets covering financial assistance programs for minorities, this compilation identifies selected fellowships, scholarships, and grants in the field of education that were available in 1980. For more information about the publication, see the annotation in the "Scholarships— Social Sciences—Education" section of this bibliography.

300 Financial Aid for Minorities in Engineering. Ed. by Clayton G. Holloway and Ruth N. Swann. Garrett Park, MD: Garrett Park Press, 1981. 52p. 81–161268. $3. Pap.

Focusing on the field of engineering, this mostly unannotated list selectively identifies fellowships, scholarships, and grants open to minority students prior to 1981. For more information about the publication, see the annotation in the "Scholarships—Sciences—Engineering" section of this bibliography.

301 Financial Aid for Minorities in Law. Ed. by Novelle J. Dickensen and Ruth N. Swann. Garrett Park, MD: Garrett Park Press, 1981. 63p. 80–153225. $3. Pap.

Aimed at minorities interested in legal studies, this (mostly unannotated) list identifies fellowships, scholarships, and grants that were available in 1981. For more information about the publication, see the annotation in the "Fellowships—Social Sciences—Law" section of this bibliography.

302 Financial Aid for Minorities in Mass Communications. By Leslie L. Lawton and Ruth N. Swann. Garrett Park, MD: Garrett Park Press, 1981. 62p. 81–211245. $3. Pap.

Included in this listing are references to scholarships, fellowships, and grants open to minorities interested in the fields of mass media and communications. For more information about the publication, see the annotation in the

"Scholarships—Humanities—Communications and Mass Media" section of this bibliography.

303   Financial Aid for Minorities in Medicine. By Sterling H. Hudson III and Ruth N. Swann. Garrett Park, MD: Garrett Park Press, 1981. 66p. 81–184828. $3. Pap.

This listing, published in 1981, identifies selected fellowships, grants, and scholarships open to minorities interested in medical studies. For more information about the publication, see the annotation in the "Fellowships—Sciences—Health Sciences" section of this bibliography.

304   Financial Aid for Minorities in Science. Ed. by Ruth N. Swann and Sharon F. White. Garrett Park, MD: Garrett Park Press, 1980. 49p. $2. Pap.

Published in 1980, this mostly unannotated listing selectively identifies fellowships, scholarships, and grants open to minorities interested in the sciences. For more information about the publication, see the annotation in the "Scholarships—Sciences—General" section of this bibliography.

305   Higher   Education   Opportunities   for   Minorities   and Women...Annotated Selections. Washington, DC: G.P.O., 1982– . Annual. 84–11125. Free. Pap.

Issued annually, this pamphlet describes fellowships, scholarships, and loans open to minorities and women at the postsecondary level. For more information about the publication, see the annotation in the "Scholarships—Special Population Groups—Ethnic Groups" section of this bibliography.

306   Hispanic Financial Resource Handbook. Comp. by the Hispanic Student Program. Columbus: Office of Student Life, Ohio State University, 1982– . Annual. $5 (1985 ed.). Pap.

This comb-bound handbook was first compiled in 1982 (and revised annually since then) to "assist Hispanic students and professionals in obtaining financial aid information which is especially geared toward Hispanic and other minorities." Brief descriptions are provided for applicable fellowships, scholarships, loans, and grants. For more information about the publication, see the annotation in the "Scholarships—Special Population Groups—Ethnic Groups" section of this bibliography.

307   Journalism Career Guide for Minorities. Prep. by the American Society of Newspaper Editors. Princeton, NJ: Dow Jones Newspaper Fund, 1984. 48p. Free. Pap.

One section of this free booklet deals with scholarships, fellowships, internships, and special training programs for minorities interested in journalism as well as with general scholarship/fellowship opportunities. For more information about the publication, see the annotation in the "Scholarships—Humanities—Communications and Mass Media" section of this bibliography.

308 Minority Student Opportunities in United States Medical Schools. Washington, DC: Association of American Medical Colleges, 1970– . Biennial. 79–640963. ISBN 0085–3488. $7.50 (1985 ed.). Pap.

This directory presents data on minority student opportunities in U.S. medical schools (including information on student financial assistance). For more information about the publication, see the annotation in the "Fellowships—Sciences—Health Sciences" section of this bibliography.

Foreign Students

309 A Foreign Students' Selected Guide to Financial Assistance for Study and Research in the United States. Ed. by Joe Lurie with Jonathan Miller. Garden City, NY: Adelphi University Press, 1983. 327p. ISBN 0–88461–010–1. $22.50. Pap.

This source identifies fellowships and scholarships available to foreign nationals who wish to study and/or conduct research in the United States. For more information about the publication, see the annotation in the "Scholarships—Special Population Groups—Foreign Students" section of this bibliography.

310 Private Sector Funding Available to Foreign Scholars and Students in the United States. Prep. by Ellen Wise Sivon. Rev. ed. Washington, DC: National Association for Foreign Student Affairs, 1985. 54p. 84–242345. ISBN 0–912207–09–4. $2.95. Pap.

Approximately 50 private sector-sponsored fellowships, grants, and scholarships for foreign students and scholars already in the United States are described in this directory. For more information about the publication, see the annotation in the "Scholarships—Special Population Groups—Foreign Students" section of this bibliography.

311 Selected List of Fellowship Opportunities and Aids to Advanced Education for United States Citizens and Foreign Nationals. Washington, DC: National Science Foundation, 1984. 76p. Free. Pap.

This free pamphlet presents concise descriptions of fellowships, scholarships, loans, and work-study experiences available to foreign students in the United States as well as to American citizens. For more information about the publication, see the annotation in the "Fellowships—General—United States" section of this bibliograpy.

Military Personnel and Veterans

312 Educational Assistance and Opportunities Information for Army Family Members. Alexandria, VA: Adjutant General's Office, U.S. Department of the Army, 1984. v.p. Free. Looseleaf.

This directory identifies associations and other groups that provide fellowships, scholarships, loans, and grants-in-aid to army personnel and relatives of military personnel. For more information about the publication, see the annotation in the "Scholarships—Special Population Groups— Military Personnel and Veterans" section of this bibliography.

313 Once a Veteran: Benefits, Rights, Obligations. 1985 Edition. Washington, DC: American Forces Information Service, U.S. Department of Defense (for sale by G.P.O.), 1985. 43p. $2. Pap.

This inexpensive pamphlet provides up-to-date information on the benefits (including fellowships available), rights, and obligations of American veterans. For more information about the publication, see the annotation in the "Grants—Special Population Groups—Military Personnel and Veterans" section of this bibliography.

314 State Veterans' Laws: Digests of State Laws Regarding Rights, Benefits, and Privileges of Veterans and Their Dependents. Washington, DC: G.P.O., 1945– . Irreg. 60–62289. Free. Pap. Microfiche to depository libraries.

This congressional report covers the fellowships, loans, scholarships, and grants available to veterans on the state level. For more information about the publication, see the annotation in the "Grants—General—United States" section of this bibliography.

315 United States Code, Title 38: Veteran's Benefits. Washington, DC: G.P.O. Irreg. $25, U.S.; $31.25, elsewhere. Looseleaf.

This looseleaf subscription service contains the exact text of laws relating to veterans' benefits (including the financial aid programs established by the federal government). For more information about the publication, see the annotation in the "Grants—Special Population Groups—Military Personnel and Veterans" section of this bibliography.

316 The Viet Vet Survival Guide: How to Get through the Bureaucracy and Get What You Need and Are Entitled To. Ed. by Craig Kubey, et al. New York: Facts On File, 1986. 256p. ISBN 0–8160–1379–9. $19.95.

Included in this first self-help book for Vietnam veterans is information on fellowships, scholarships, loans, and grants-in-aid that are available for this group from the federal government. For more information about the publication, see the annotation in the "Grants—Special Population Groups—Military Personnel and Veterans" section of this bibliography.

Reentry Students

317 **Better Late Than Never: Financial Aid for Older Women Seeking Education and Training.** Washington, DC: Women's Equity Action League (WEAL), 1982. 43p. $3 Pap.

Aimed at reentry students (particularly women), this pamphlet identifies selected scholarship and fellowship programs open to returning and nontraditional students. For more information about the publication, see the annotation in the "Scholarships—Special Population Groups—Women" section of this bibliography.

Women

318 **Better Late Than Never: Financial Aid for Older Women Seeking Education and Training.** Washington, DC: Women's Equity Action League (WEAL), 1982. 43p. $3. Pap.

This listing identifies a sampling (about 60) of the fellowships and scholarships open to returning and nontraditional students. For more information about the publication, see the annotation in the "Scholarships—Special Population Groups—Women" section of this bibliography.

319 **Directory of Financial Aids for Women.** By Gail Ann Schlachter. Los Angeles: Reference Service Press, 1978– . Biennial. (Directories of Financial Aid for Special Needs Groups). 84–24582. ISSN 0732–5215. $37.50. (1985–86 ed.).

This is the only extensive and regularly updated listing of fellowships, loans, grants, scholarships, awards/prizes, and internships designed primarily or exclusively for women. For more information about the publication, see the annotation in the "Scholarships—Special Population Groups—Women" section of this bibliography.

320 **Educational Financial Aids: A Guide to Selecting Fellowships, Scholarships, and Internships in Higher Education.** Washington, DC: American Association of University Women, 1984. 35p. $5. Pap.

This updated pamphlet (earlier versions were issued in 1976 and 1981) "divides financial aid offerings according to educational level: undergraduate, graduate, postdoctoral, and internships/traineeships." It has been expanded to include information also about loans and additional financial aid directories. The entries are designed to supply information on program title, purpose, requirements for selection, stipends, application procedure, and sponsoring organization's address (no telephone numbers are provided). Although the listing is aimed at women, many of the programs covered are open equally to men (e.g., Purina Research Fellowships in Animal Science, Rotary's Teacher of the Handicapped Scholarship). While more expensive, the *Directory of Financial Aids for Women* (described elsewhere in this section of the bibliography) identifies many more programs established primarily or exclusively for women and provides more current information.

321   Financial Aid: A Partial List of Resources for Women. Prep. by the Project on the Status and Education of Women. Washington, DC: Association of American Colleges, 1984. 15p. $2.50. Pap.

Selected fellowships, scholarships, and grants available to women students are briefly described in this pamphlet. For more information about the publication, see the annotation in the "Scholarships—Special Population Groups—Women" section of this bibliography.

322   Higher   Education   Opportunities   for   Minorities   and Women...Annotated Selections. Washington, DC: G.P.O., 1982– Annual. 84–11125. $5.50 (1986 ed.). Pap.

Issued annually, this pamphlet describes fellowships, scholarships, and loans open to women and minorities at the postsecondary level. For more information about the publication, see the annotation in the "Scholarships— Special Population Groups—Ethnic Groups" section of this bibliography.

323   Women & Fellowships, 1981. By Judith Nies. Washington, DC: Women's Equity Action League (WEAL), 1981. 28p. $3.50. Pap.

This report of the Women's Equity Action League is an update of a 1976 report, which itself was based on a 1974 report. The 1981 revision was prepared with the assistance of the WEAL Intern Program and supported by a grant from the Ford Foundation. It presents data on the selection of women applicants by four major fellowship programs (e.g, Rhodes Scholarships); discusses the importance of fellowships in postgraduate education; and describes about two dozen major fellowships by program focus, indicating the percentage of successful women applicants in previous years (only one of these is a program designed primarily or exclusively for women). Four pages of bibliography (sources on specific fellowships and general sources on fellowships and foundations) complete the work. A new revision of the pamphlet is in process.

Grants

Grants provide funds to support research, innovative efforts, travel, or projects (some of which may be educational in nature). Many are restricted by geographic location, purpose of the proposed program, or type of applicant (in many cases, proposals may be submitted by institutions or organizations only). Included in this chapter—the largest in the Guide—are over 350 references to directories listing grants available on the international, national, and/or state levels. Of these directories, nearly half (175) are general in their subject coverage: 23 have international scope, 70 have national scope, and 82 provide state coverage (only 6 states do not have at least one state-based listing of grants available in that area). Of the remaining entries, 63 focus on grants in the social sciences, 58 cover the humanities, 22 deal with the sciences, and 35 are aimed at special population groups. If you are looking for a specific grants directory and you do not find it in this chapter, be sure to check the Title Index to see if it is covered elsewhere in the Guide.

GENERAL

International

324 **Annual Register of Grant Support: A Guide to Support Programs of Government Agencies, Foundations, and Business and Professional Organizations.** Wilmette, IL: National Register, 1969– . Annual. 69–18307. ISSN 00664049. $87 (1985–86 ed.).

Although it focuses on North American programs, the *Annual Register* also describes a number of grants sponsored abroad. A more comprehensive listing, however, can be found in the *Grants Register* (described elsewhere in this section). For more information on the *Annual Register*, see the annotation in the "Grants—General—United States" section of this bibliography.

325 **Awards for Commonwealth University Academic Staff.** London: Association of Commonwealth Universities (avail. from International Publication Service), 1972– . Biennial. 80–647312. $17.50 (5th ed.). Pap.

Described in this biennial are grants, fellowships, and visiting professorships open to Commonwealth university staff interested in studying, teaching or conducting research in another Commonwealth country. For more information about the publication, see the annotation in the "Fellowships—General—International" section of this bibliography.

326 **Awards for Postgraduate Study in Australia.** 6th ed. Victoria, Aust.: Graduate Careers Council of Australia, 1984. Free. Pap.

Information on grants and fellowships for graduate and postdoctoral study/research at Australian universities is provided in this pamphlet. For more information about the publication, see the annotation in the "Fellowships—General—International" section of this bibliography.

327 **Canadian Directory of Awards for Graduate Study.** Ottawa: Association of Universities and Colleges of Canada, 1981– . 82–39014. ISSN 0711–8635. $10, Canadian. Pap.

Over 800 grants and fellowships available to college graduates from sources in Canada, the United Kingdom, the United States, and numerous other countries are identified in this biennially-issued directory. For more information about the publication, see the annotation in the "Fellowships—General—International" section of this bibliography.

328   Canadian Directory to Foundations. Concord, Ont.: Canadian Centre for Philanthropy, 1966– . Quadrennial. 83–30525. ISSN 0820–7682. $69 (6th ed.).

Canada's major reference source for foundation research, information, and grant solicitation, this directory gives detailed data on over 700 Canadian foundations controlling $1.5 billion in capital assets. American foundations granting in Canada are also covered. These foundations made over 10,000 grants (totaling over $200 million) to Canadian charitable organizations in 1983. The following information is provided for each of the foundations: address, founding date, source of funds, purpose, interests, eligibility, requirements, limitations, geographic scope, receipted gifts, total assets, total grants, number of grants, grant range, publications, offices, application procedures, application deadlines, and contact person. The entries are indexed by subject, geographic coverage, key people, and foundation name. Use this source to answer such questions as: Which Canadian foundations (or American foundations giving in Canda) have supported my type of project in the past? What are their special interests? Within what dollar range are their grants given? Where is the foundation located? When should I send them my proposal? What do I send and to whom? The first edition of the directory was published in 1966, and subsequent editions were released in 1969, 1973, 1978, and 1982. Over the years, both the title and publisher of the directory have varied. For example, the first edition was published by the Association of Universities and Colleges of Canada as *Canadian Universities' Guide to Foundations and Similar Granting Agencies*. In 1973, the directory changed its name to a variation of the current version: *A Canadian Directory to Foundations and Other Granting Agencies*. A companion volume to the directory is *Foundation 500*, also published by the Canadian Centre for Philanthropy. It provides ordered lists of all the foundations in the directory, listing them by total dollar value of grants, by total assets, and by geographic location.

329   Canadian Universities' Guide to Foundations and Similar Granting Agencies. Ottawa: Information Division, Association of Universities and Colleges of Canada, 1966–1969. 2v. 83–31140. ISSN 0820–7674.

In 1973, this directory changed its name to *Canadian Directory to Foundations and Other Granting Agencies* (161p. 74–156208) and is currently being published every four years under the title *Canadian Directory to Foundations* (described elsewhere in this section).

330   Charities Digest: A Classified Digest of Charities. London: Family Welfare Association, 1882– . Annual.

First published in 1882 under the title *Annual Charities Register and Digest*, this directory has been issued annually since then. Recent editions have listed over 2,000 English charities, trusts, and associations. The entries, which contain typical directory-type information, are grouped in various categories, e.g., blind, deaf, hospitals, animal welfare, religious organizations. There is a detailed index to the information on the charitable organizations as well as an index to the advertisers.

331 College Blue Book. New York: Macmillan, 1923– . Biennial. 79–66292. ISSN 0069–5572. $185 (20th ed.).
A number of the grants described in Volume 5 of the *Blue Book*'s 20th edition may be used for research or study abroad. For more information about this publication, see the annotation in the "Scholarships—General—United States" section.

332 Directory of Financial Aid for American Undergraduates Interested in Overseas Study and Travel. Washington, DC: Adelphi University, 1982. v.p. 83–10055. ISBN 0–88461–007–1. $9. Pap.
Over 100 grants and scholarships designed to support study and travel by U.S. undergraduates outside of the United States are covered in this directory. For more information about this publication, see the annotation in the "Scholarships—General—International" section.

333 Directory of Financial Aids for International Activities. 4th ed. Minneapolis: Office of International Programs, University of Minnesota, 1978– . Irreg. 78–645627. ISSN 0163–0199. $20 (1985 ed.). Pap.
The fourth (1985) edition provides information on more than 450 grants, scholarships, and fellowships for academic staff, graduate and undergraduate students, advanced scholars, and young professionals for study, research, travel, and teaching abroad. For more information about this publication, see the annotation in the "Scholarships—General—International" section.

334 Directory of Grant-Making Trusts. Tonbridge, Eng.: Charities Aid Foundation, 1968– . Biennial. 81–645033.
This directory describes over 2,200 grant-making charitable trusts in the United Kingdom. Program profiles specify trust name, address, founding date, Charity Commission registry number, trustees, purpose, limitations, giving policies, areas of grant interest, financial activity, types of grants, types of recipients, application procedures, and publications. The entries are arranged alphabetically by name of the trust and indexed by grant interest, trust name, subject, and geographic restrictions. The directory (issued by Charities Aid Fund from 1968 to 1973 and Charities Aid Foundation since 1975) is updated biennially, in odd-numbered years.

335 Directory of Research Grants. Phoenix: Oryx, 1975– . Annual. 76–47074. ISSN 0146–7336. $74.50 (1986 ed.). Pap.

Although the emphasis is on U.S. research grants (and other types of financial aid), some programs sponsored by other countries are also included. For more information about the publication, see the annotation in the "Grants—General—United States" section of this bibliography.

336 Fellowships, Scholarships, and Related Opportunities in International Education. Knoxville: Division of International Education, University of Tennessee, 1967– . Annual. 82–5141. ISSN 0735–8830. $5. Pap.

In the latest edition of this directory, over 120 grants, scholarships, and fellowships for study, research, and teaching in the United States and abroad are listed and described. For more information about this publication, see the annotation in the "Fellowships—General—International" section.

337 Fulbright Grants and Other Grants for Graduate Study Abroad. New York: Institute of International Education, 1986. 78p. 84–12172. Free. Pap.

This annual pamphlet is available without charge from the Institute of International Education. The 1986–87 edition lists Institute-administered fellowships and grants available to U.S. graduate students for study abroad. The arrangement is by country in which the recipient will study or conduct research. Entries specify recommended fields of study or investigation, language requirements, duration, selection procedures, financial data, application process, special features, and limitations. A similar publication for more advanced scholars is *Fulbright Senior Scholars Awards Abroad (described below).*

338 Fulbright Senior Scholars Awards Abroad. Washington, DC: Council for International Exchange of Scholars, 1984– . Annual. 84–10416. Free. Pap.

Issued as a complement to *Fulbright Grants and Other Grants for Graduate Study Abroad* (described elsewhere in this section), this free pamphlet from the Council for International Exchange of Scholars (11 Dupont Circle, Suite 300, Washington, DC 20036) identifies grants and fellowships for university lecturing and advanced research abroad. The programs covered are open to U.S. citizens who are recent Ph.Ds, advanced Ph.D. candidates, and teachers of English. Prior to 1984, this pamphlet was published under the titles *Fulbright Lecturing and Research Awards* and *Fulbright Awards Abroad.*

339 Grants for Graduate Study Abroad. New York: Institute of International Education, 1965– . Annual. 79–3853. ISSN 0270–9880. Free. Pap.

United States Government Grants for Graduate Study (ISSN 0443–3629) merged with *Fellowships Offered by Foreign Governments, Universities, and Private Donors* (ISSN 0534–185X) to form *Grants for Graduate Study Abroad.* Provided free upon request from the Institute of International Education (809 United Nations Plaza, New York, NY 10011), this annual booklet lists fellowships and grants available to American students for predoctoral study, research, and professional training abroad. The entries are arranged by country (Afghanistan through Zaire) and include the following information: recommended fields of study, nonrecommended fields of study, duration, dependents' support, language requirements, eligibility, housing arrangements, and stipend.

340 The Grants Register: Postgraduate Awards in the English Speaking World. Ed. by Normal Frankel. New York: St. Martin's Press, 1969– . Biennial. 77–12055. $39.95 (1985–87 ed.).

Despite its title, this directory is not restricted to grants listings; it also includes fellowships, exchanges, vocational study, travel grants, grants-in-aid, competitions, prizes, and other awards (including awards for refugees, war veterans, minority groups, and students in unexpected financial difficulties). Published every two years (in even-numbered years, but dated for odd-numbered years, e.g., 1985–1987 came out in 1984), the *Grants Register* provides up-to-date information on over one million awards from more than 2,000 awarding bodies other than universities; listed are awards offered by governmental agencies, international agencies, national organizations, and private agencies. Emphasis is on awards for nationals of the United States, Canada, the United Kingdom, Ireland, Australia, New Zealand, South Africa, and the developing countries. The programs included are selected for graduate students, young professionals, academics, scholars, vocational trainees, veterans, minorities, the handicapped, etc. The following information is provided for each program: remuneration, eligibility, deadline, application procedures, subject areas covered, purpose, number offered, where tenable, awarding organization, and address for application and/or further information. A bibliography of additional financial aid resources is included, as are a subject index and an index of awards and awarding bodies. The latest biennial edition issued covers 1985–1987 (854p. ISBN 0–312–34409–0). It complements the information included in the other standard general financial aid directories, including the *Annual Register of Grant Support*, the *Directory of Research Grants*, and *Foundation Grants to Individuals* (each described in the "Grants—General—United States" section of this bibliography).

341   How to Get Money for Research. By Mary Rubin and the Business and Professional Women's Foundation. Foreword by M. Chamberlain. Old Westbury, NY: Feminist Press, 1983. 78p. 83–1444. ISBN 0–9835312–18–8. $6.95. Pap.

Both international and national grants are described in this directory. For more information, see the annotation in the "Grants—General—United States" section of this bibliography.

342   International Foundation Directory. Ed. by H. V. Hodson. 3d ed., rev. and enl. London: Europa (dist. by Gale), 1983. 401p. 84–181779. ISBN 0–8103–2032–0. $78.

The title of this directory can be misleading. This is not a listing of foundations around the world. Rather, this is a directory of foundations and trusts that operate on an international basis (although some national foundations are also included). Not all geographic locations are equally represented. The emphasis is on international foundations in North America and Europe. Some coverage is also provided for South America, Japan, and other areas of Asia. Profiles are presented for more than 700 foundations, arranged alphabetically by country and then by foundation name within the country. The entries provide brief information in the following categories: history of the organization, activities and interests, publications issued (if any), financial status, officers and trustees, and addresses and telephone numbers. Additional access to the entries is provided through the name and broad subject categories indexes. The first edition of the directory was published in 1974 (396p. 73–90303); the second edition was released in 1979 (378p. 79–23803). While by no means complete, the third edition (1983) is the most curent of the major lists of international foundations.

343   International Philanthropy: A Compilation of Grants by U.S. Foundations, 1980. Comp. by Martha R. Keens and Josephine E. Case. New York: Foundation Center, 1981. 240p. 82–13992. ISBN 0–87954–050–8. o.p. Pap.

This volume, a revision of the 1978 edition prepared by Jean Ann Martinson, is based on the 1980 Foundation Center's Grants Index database. From the 21,500 grants made by 408 foundations totaling nearly $1.2 billion that were listed in the database at that time, 1,400 were identified as international in scope and included in this directory. For the purpose of this listing, international grants were defined as those "with a foreign recipient, an international classification code, or descriptive text or indexing indicating international programs or focus." The volume is divided into three sections. The first section provides two ordered lists of the 1,400 grants: by foreign recipients and by domestic recipients. Each of these entries specifies foundation name and state, recipient name and location, dollar amount, date of authorization, and purposes of the grant. The current address of each foundation is given in the appendix. The next section consists of computer-generated statistics on the number of grants and aggregate dollar amounts by foundation, geographic location, and general program area. The final section contains a set of five indexes. The first four indexes provide access to the grants listed in Section I by foundation name, program name, key phrase, and geographic focus. The fifth index identifies foundation grants to colleges and universities. This directory, which was the precursor to *COMSEARCH Broad Topics* (described in the "Grants—General—United States" section of this bibliography), is now out of print.

344 IREX Program Announcement, 1986–87. New York: International Research and Exchanges Board (IREX), 1986. 15p. Free. Pap.

This annual pamphlet (published annually since 1968) is available without charge each May from International Research and Exchanges Board (655 Third Avenue, New York, NY 10017). It provides descriptions of the exchange programs (grants and fellowships) with Eastern European countries and the Soviet Union that are administered by the Board for each academic year. The programs covered are open to U.S. college or university faculty, eligible scholars, and advanced doctoral candidates who have completed all Ph.D. requirements except the dissertation. Entries specify program name, description, eligibility requirements, name and address of corresponding organization, host country provisions, and period of stay abroad.

345 Scholarships Guide for Commonwealth Postgraduate Students. London: Association of Commonwealth Universities (dist. by International Publications Service), 1972– . Biennial. 77–643818. $25 (1985–87 ed.). Pap.

In the most recent edition of this biennial (1985–1987), over 1,300 grants, fellowships, and assistantships available to graduates of Commonwealth universities are described. For more information about the publication, see the annotation in the "Fellowships—General—International" section of this bibliography.

346 United Kingdom Post-graduate Awards. London: Association of Commonwealth Universities, 1955–1971. Biennial. 72–623777.

Issued first as an annual (1955–1971; published by the Association of Universities of the British Commonwealth), this listing was released as a biennial from 1967 through 1971. Since 1972, the directory has been published under the title *Scholarships Guide for Commonwealth Postgraduate Students* (described in the "Fellowships—General—International" section of this bibliography).

United States

347 Aids to Individual Scholars: Competitions to Be Held in 1985–1986.
New York: American Council of Learned Societies, 1985. 18p. Free.
Pap.

Both grants and fellowships to advance general research are described in this
free booklet issued biennially by the American Council of Learned Societies.
For more information about the publication, see the annotation in the
"Fellowships—General—United States" section of this bibliography.

348 **American Association of Fund-Raising Counsel's Directory of**
Members. New York: American Association of Fund-Raising Counsel,
1935– . Annual. Free. Pap.

There are organizations in the United States whose primarily business is
providing consultation and fund-raising activities for interested groups. One
way of locating these organizations is by referring to this directory, which
lists members of the American Association of Fund-Raising Counsel. The
booklet, which is updated annually, is distributed without charge upon
request from the Counsel (25 West 43rd Street, New York, NY 10036).

349 **Annual Register of Grant Support: A Guide to Support Programs of**
Government Agencies, Foundations, and Business and Professional
Organizations. Wilmette, IL: National Register, 1969– . Annual.
69–18307. ISSN 0066–4049. $87 (1985–86 ed.).

Nearly 3,000 programs sponsored by government agencies, private
foundations, corporations, unions, church groups, and educational and
professional associations are described in the latest edition of this directory
(1985–86 ed. 923p.). The programs provide grant support in the humanities,
international affairs, race and minority concerns, education, environmental
and urban affairs, social sciences, physical sciences, life sciences, technology,
and other areas. Each entry contains the following information: organization
name; address and telephone number; major field(s) of organizational
interest; name(s) of grant program(s); purpose; nature of support available;
amount of support per award; number of applicants and recipients for most
recent years; legal basis for program; eligibility requirements; application
instructions; and deadline. The work is indexed by subject, sponsor,
geographic requirements, and personnel. Over the years, both the subtitle and
publisher have varied. Beginning with 1985, the annual has been published by
the National Register Publishing Company (taking over from Marquis
Academic Media) under the title *Annual Register of Grant Support: A
Directory of Funding Sources.*

350 **Annual Survey of Corporate Contributions.** New York: Conference Board, 1974– . Annual. 76–24946. ISSN 0146–0986. $25, associates; $125, non-associates (1985 ed.). Pap.

Charitable giving plays a major role in the social activities of U.S. corporations. This annual report, issued by the Conference Board, summarizes corporate funding activities during the previous year. It has been published annually since 1974 (in 1972 and 1973, the publication was issued as the *Biennial Survey of Company Contributions*). The 1985 edition (by Linda Cardillo Platzer. 37p.) analyzes the corporate contributions budget (especially in comparison to profit, employee size, and geographic areas of giving) and the subject areas supported by the surveyed corporations. Half of the book contains statistical tables covering such topics as: corporate contributions as a percent of pretax income, level of support for minorities, and industry classes benefiting from company support. Because the data are aggregate (individual companies participating are not identified or described separately), this publication will not directly benefit the grantseeker hoping to identify specific funding opportunities.

351 **Bear's Guide to Finding Money for College.** By John Bear. Berkeley, CA: Ten Speed Press, 1984. 157p. 84–50044. ISBN 0–89815–126–0. $5.95. Pap.

In addition to providing the usual chatty instructions and encouragement found in trade-oriented paperbacks, this guide briefly describes over 200 fellowships, grants-in-aid, and other special awards. For more information about the publication, see the annotation in the "Scholarships—General—United States" section of this bibliography.

352 **Biennial Survey of Company Contributions.** New York: Conference Board, 1972–1973. Biennial. 82–642219.

Beginning in 1974, this publication became an annual and changed its title to *Annual Survey of Corporate Contributions* (described elsewhere in this section of the bibliography).

353 **Career Opportunities News.** Garrett Park, MD: Garrett Park Press, 1983– . Bimonthly. 83–8288. ISSN 0739–5043. $30/yr.

Designed to assist the job seeker, this bimonthly newsletter provides current information about a variety of careers. In addition, it contains announcements of foundation grants, fellowships, scholarships, and seminars. A separate section deals with women's interests.

354 Catalog of Federal Domestic Assistance. Prep. by the U.S. General Services Administration. Washington, DC: G.P.O., 1965– . Annual. 73–60018. ISSN 0097–7799. $36. Looseleaf.

This is the "what's what" of government grant programs. It is *the* single source of information on programs administered at the federal level. Over 1,000 domestic assistance programs and activities, administered by 60 different federal agencies and departments, are described in this annual publication: grants, loans, loan guarantees and shared revenue; provision of federal facilities, direct construction of goods and services; donation or provision of surplus property, technical assistance, and counseling; statistical and other information services; and service activities or regulatory agencies. These assistance programs are available to state and local governments, public and private organizations and institutions, and individuals. Excluded are automatic payment programs not requiring application; personal recruitment programs of individual federal departments other than the Civil Service Program; and inactive or unfunded programs. Each program entry contains information on purpose, availability, authorizing legislation, administering agency, and sources of additional information. The catalog is organized into three indexes: a functional index, a subject index, and an agency program index. It is issued once a year in looseleaf notebook form (usually published in June and distributed in August) and is updated six months after publication. At $36/year, this is a best buy. The catalog is also available in online form as the *Federal Assistance Program Retrieval System* (see the annotation in the "Databases and Search Services" section of this bibliography).

355 Chronicle Student Aid Annual. Moravia, NY: Chronicle Guidance Publications, 1978– . Annual. 79–640360. ISSN 0190–339X. $16.50 (1985 ed.). Pap.

In addition to scholarship programs, a number of grants, awards, loans, and fellowships are described in this annual directory. For more information about the publication, see the annotation in the "Scholarships—General—United States" section of this bibliography.

356 The College Aid Checkbook: A Guide to College Financial Aid. Clifton, NJ: Army ROTC, 1985. n.p. Free. Pap.

This checkbook-sized pamphlet was written as a starting point to identify major private and public grants, scholarships, loans, and work program. For more information about the free publications, see the annotation in the "Scholarships—General—United States" section of this bibliography.

357 College Blue Book. New York: Macmillan, 1923– . Biennial. 79–66191. ISSN 0069–5572. $185 (20th ed.).

Volume 5 of the 20th edition (718p. $44. ISBN 0–02–695790–6) identifies over $100 millon in grants, scholarships, fellowships, and loans available to graduate and undergraduate students. For more information about this publication, see the annotation in the "Scholarships—General—United States" section.

358 Commerce Business Daily. Chicago: U.S. Department of Commerce, 1979– . Daily. 79–643799. ISSN 0095–3423. $86/yr., sent second class; $165/yr., sent first class.

Listed in this daily publication are government procurement invitations, contract awards, subcontracting leads, sales of surplus property, foreign business opportunities, and research and development sources sought. Each entry briefly describes the service or item involved and gives the address and the contact for the particular action as well as the deadline established. Also appearing on occasion in the publication are Requests for Proposal (RFP) notices. The information on contracts included here is less complete than can be found in the *Federal Register* (described elsewhere in this section). However, at $86 per year sent second class ($165 per year sent first class), the *Daily* is considerably less expensive than the *Register* (at $300 per year). Since October 1982, the information included in this publication is also available to be searched online (see the descriptions of *Commerce Business Daily* and *CBD Plus* in the "Databases and Search Services" chapter).

359 COMSEARCH Printouts: Broad Topics. New York: Foundation Center, 1983– . Annual. $28 each. Pap.

This is the newest component in the Foundation Center's COMSEARCH series (which identifies foundations making grants in a particular subject field or geographic location). *Broad Topics* covers giving in 11 subject areas: arts and cultural programs; business and employment; children and youth; higher education; hospitals and medical care programs; museums; science programs; social science programs; women and girls; international and foreign programs; and minorities. Each of these printouts identifies all grants reported to the Foundation Center in that category during the previous year. The printouts also provide an index of foundations with addresses and notes about specific limitations in their giving, a key word index for that field, and an index of all recipient organizations listed.

360 COMSEARCH Printouts: Geographic. New York: Foundation Center. Annual. $25 each. Pap.

This is a series of computer-produced guides to foundation giving in key geographic areas. The printouts list and describe actual grants made to organizations in two cities (Washington, D.C. and New York City), 11 states, and four regions (Northeast, Southeast, Northwest, and Rocky Mountains). Each of those 17 printouts provides the same grant data as is offered in the *Foundation Grants Index Annual* (described elsewhere in this section), but the entries here are arranged according to geographic specifications.

361 COMSEARCH Printouts: Special Topics. New York: Foundation Center. Annual. $15 each. Pap.

This is a series of computer-produced guides to foundations making grants in special categories. These categories are the ones most frequently requested from the Foundation Center's specialized databases. Some of the topics available include: the 1,000 largest U.S. foundations by asset size; the 1,000 largest U.S. foundations by annual grant totals; 1,300 operating foundations adminstering their own projects or programs.

362 COMSEARCH Printouts: Subjects. New York: Foundation Center. Annual. $15 each, pap; $5 each, microfiche. $175 for all printouts or microfiche.

This is a series of computer-produced subject guides to foundation grant giving. The printouts provide the same grant data as can be found in the *Foundation Grants Index Annual* (described elsewhere in this section), but the listing is arranged according to specific subjects. There are currently 114 printouts available in eight major areas (communications, education, health, cultural activities, population groups, science and technology, social sciences, welfare, and other). Some of the specific subjects covered include: library and information services, mentally retarded and disabled, blacks, child abuse, and refugee and relief services.

363 Corporate Foundation Profiles: Complete Analysis of the Largest Company-Sponsored Foundations. 4th ed. New York: Foundation Center, 1985. 593p. 80–69622. ISBN 0–87954–135–0. $55. Pap.

Over 230 of the largest company-sponsored foundations are covered in detail in this publication. Each of the listed foundations either has assets totaling more than $1 million or gives more than $100,000 annually. Entries (averaging three to six pages) are drawn from *Source Book Profiles* (described elsewhere in this section) and include address and telephone number; a complete list of officers, directors, and chief program staff; information about the parent company; current financial data (total assets, expenditures, grants); background data on each foundation and its key officers; representative grants arranged by subject; application guidelines and procedures; and a statistical and analytical review of the foundation's grantmaking program. Indexing is by subject, type of support, and geographic restrictions. In addition, summary financial data are provided for 400 more corporate foundations.

364 **Corporate Fund Raising Directory, 1980/81– .** Hartsdale, NY: Public Service Materials Center, 1980– . Biennial. 80–115325. ISSN 0736–8615. $79.50 (1985–86 ed.). Pap.

Up-to-date information on the $3.5 billion given away each year by over 500 of America's top corporations is provided in the 1985–86 edition (1985. 400p. ISBN 0–914977–02–4) of this directory. Companies that fund through foundations as well as those that give directly are covered. Listed alphabetically by foundation name, entries specify who to approach, primary areas of giving, typical grants, total amount of grants, any geographic limitations, and deadlines. The information was compiled primarily from telephone interviews. The state locations of corporate headquarters are listed in the index. In this edition, for the first time, the directory identifies corporations expecting to increase their contributions in future years, notes corporations that contribute executives and materials as well as dollars, and indicates which corporations will send guidelines on their giving policies and procedures.

365 **Corporate Giving Yellow Pages: Philanthropic Contact Persons for 1,300 of America's Leading Public and Privately Owned Corporations.** Ed. by David E. Sharpe, et al. Washington, DC: Taft Corporation, 1983– . Biennial. 85–61522. $57.50 (1985 ed.). Pap.

It is often more effective to address an initial inquiry to a specific contact person at a potential granting source than to submit an undirected letter. The 1985 edition of this directory (101p. ISBN 0–914756–71–0) identifies the funding contact persons at 1,300 major corporate giving programs and corporate foundations in the United States (200 more than in the previous edition). More than half of the listed companies have direct giving programs (these are identified by "dg" after the name; foundation giving is indicated by "fdn"). Entries are arranged by organization name and specify only contact name, company address, and telephone numbers. An asterisk identifies the corporations that are described in the *Taft Corporate Giving Directory* (see annotation elsewhere in this section). Entries are indexed by state location and field of interest. Two editions have been issued to date, in 1983 and in 1985.

366 Corporate 500: The Directory of Corporate Philanthropy. San
Francisco: Public Management Institute (dist. by Gale), 1980– . Irreg.
82–643221. ISBN 0–916664–41–4. ISSN 0197–937X. $265 (1985 ed.).
Pap.

This directory, first issued in 1980, summarizes and analyzes in detail
information about the contributions programs of the most influential
corporations in America. The fourth edition (942p.), published in 1985,
provides not only a picture of each corporation's grant pattern, but an
overview as well of the entire field of corporate giving (which in 1985
exceeded $2 billion). The 500 corporations described in the 1985 edition are
those known to be the most active in supporting nonprofit organizations and
public agencies. Included are those corporations that make direct
contributions as well as those that make donations through a foundation
funded by the corporation. Arranged by corporation, each entry provides
name, address, and phone number of the company; details of eligibility;
geographic preferences; financial profile; application procedures; areas of
funding interest; policy statement; restrictions and special requirements;
number of grants given; amount and range of grants; sample grant recipients;
contribution committee members; and special analyses by the research staff of
the Public Management Institute. Additional access to the information is
offered through a series of 11 indexes, including: areas of interest, activities
eligible, geography (two parts), corporate headquarters, board and committee
members, contact people, and grant recipients.

367 Directory of Research Grants. Phoenix: Oryx, 1975– . Annual.
76–47074. ISSN 0146–7336. $74.50 (1986 ed.). Pap.

After a decade of publication, the *Directory of Research Grants* was
thoroughly revised and expanded (by one-third) in 1985. In the latest edition
(1986), over 4,000 grants, contracts, fellowships, and loan programs for
research, training, and innovative effort sponsored by more than 600
organizations are described. The emphasis is on U.S. programs, although
some sponsored by other countries are included. Currently, entries are
arranged by program title (prior to the 1986 edition, they were organized by
subject or academic discipline). Annotations include requirements,
restrictions, value, names and addresses, and application procedures. The
programs are indexed by subject, with over 1,600 subject terms. A
bibliography is appended. The information available in this publication may
also be searched online through SDC Information Services and Dialog
Information Services (both described in the "Databases and Search Services"
chapter). This directory belongs in financial aid collections.

368 **Encyclopedia of U.S. Government Benefits: A Complete, Practical, and Convenient Guide to United States Government Benefits Available to the People of America.** Ed. by Beryl Frank. 11th ed. New York: Dodd Mead, 1985. 518p. 84–8018. ISBN 0–396–08438–9. $22.95.

As the title states and the subtitle repeats, this work is intended as a guide to the services and benefits provided by the federal government. It describes such assistance programs as Social Security, Medicare, small business loans, federal crop insurance, veterans' benefits, and government federal scholarships. Not all programs described provide financial assistance. Many of them cover such nonmonetary programs as braille books for the blind, immigration and naturalization, wildlife service, and mine safety. The entries, which range from a paragraph to several pages, are arranged alphabetically and the text is indexed by subject. In most cases, the address of the appropriate government agency is provided at the end of each entry. However, telephone numbers are not included. Numerous illustrations and photographs supplement the text. The eleventh edition of this work was published in 1985. Previous editions were issued in 1965, 1967, 1968, 1969, 1970, 1971, 1973, 1977, and 1981. Because of the "encyclopedic" nature of the work, the information presented would be useful only to those users who have just begun their search for financial assistance. And, caveat emptor. Much of the information presented is quite a bit out of date.

369 **Federal Funding Guide.** Arlington, VA: Government Information Services, 1980– . Annual. 82–643112. ISSN 0273–4435. $122.95 (1985 ed.). Pap.

The focus of this guide is on federal programs that provide grants and loans to local, county, and state governments, nonprofit organizations, and community and volunteer groups. The over 300 programs covered each year are indexed by program title and listed by subject category, e.g., arts and cultural activities, senior citizens, housing, transportation. The guide does not cover education programs because they are dealt with in the *Guide to Federal Funding for Education* (described in the "Grants—Social Sciences—Education" section), which is published by GIS's affiliate, Education Funding Research Council. The entries indicate eligibility, type of aid, purpose, contact person, restrictions, funding potential, application procedures, deadline date, and legislative authority. In total, nearly $60 billion of funding is identified. Nonprofits can apply for well over half of these funds. Supplementing the main, looseleaf volume are quarterly-issued guides, which cover the latest developments, provide new financial figures, and present recently-released requirements and rule changes. While the supplements make the main guide more current, still much of the information presented duplicates the *Catalog of Federal Domestic Assistance* and is less up to date than presented in the *Federal Register*.

370 Federal Grants & Contracts Weekly. Arlington, VA: Capitol
Publications, 1974– . Weekly (51 issues). 79–5100. ISSN 0194–2247.
$191/yr.

Each week, close to $100 million in federal funding opportunities are
announced. The *Federal Grants & Contracts Weekly* acts as an "early
warning" system, to alert readers to all federal grant announcements as well
as to research, training, and technical services contracts. Each eight-page
issue is published on Monday and contains information on Requests for
Proposals (RFPs), closing dates for grant programs, procurement-related
regulatory news, contract awards, updates on federal budget action, and
profiles on grant programs and federal agencies. This information used to be
available online through NewsNet as *Grants & Contracts Weekly*; however,
the online versioin was recently suspended.

371 Federal Register. Prep. by the U.S. Office of Federal Register.
Washington, DC: G.P.O., 1936– . Daily (Monday through Friday,
except legal holidays). 36–26246. $300/yr., pap.; $175/yr, microfiche.

The *Federal Register* is issued every week day except holidays. It is the
official source for the publication of public regulations and legal notices
issued by federal executive agencies and independent agencies. By law, all
agency documents of public interest, documents required to be published by
acts of Congress, federal agency documents of general applicability and legal
effect, presidential proclamations, and Executive Orders are presented here.
Thus, this is an excellent place to check for the latest information (including
deadline date) on federally funded programs. But the information does not
come cheap. A subscription costs $300 a year. There is a separately published
Federal Register Index that is issued monthly; each issue is cumulative, with
the December issue serving as the annual cumulative index. Libraries receive
copies of the *Federal Register* several days after publication. More current
information can be obtained by calling the Federal Register Information
Desk in Washington, D.C. at (202) 523–5227.

372 Federal Research Report. Silver Spring, MD: Business Publishers,
1975– . Weekly. 78–667. $117/yr.

This newsletter identifies federal and foundation funds for R & D in such
diverse areas as education, environment and energy, health and safety,
transportation, science and mathematics, art and humanities, and social
sciences. Each weekly issue provides concise descriptions of grant
opportunities, which include information on addresses and telephone
numbers, contact persons, deadlines, and other related data. The information
presented here is also available online, through NewsNet's *Federal Research
Report* database (described in the "Databases and Search Services" chapter).

373 Fellowships, Scholarships, and Related Opportunities in International Education. Knoxville: Division of International Education, University of Tennessee, 1967– . Annual. 82–5141. ISSN 0735–8830. $8 (1986 ed.). Pap.

In the latest edition of this directory, over 120 grants, scholarships, and fellowships for study, research, and teaching in the United States and abroad are listed and described. For more information about the publication, see the annotation in the "Fellowships—General—International" section of this bibliography.

374 For Us Women Newsletter. Washington, DC: For Us Publications, 1983– . Monthly. 83–7501. ISSN 0737–5395. $16.50/yr.

This eight-page monthly newsletter provides information on grants as well as on contests of interest to individuals and nonprofit organizations. For more information about the publication, see the annotation in the "Awards and Prizes—General—United States" section of this bibliography.

375 Foundation Center National Data Book. New York: Foundation Center, 1974–1979. Biennial. 77–86479. ISSN 0730–1677.

This directory continued *The Foundation Center 1972 Data Bank* for three editions (1974 through 1979). In 1981, its title changed to *National Data Book* (described elsewhere in this section of the bibliography).

376 The Foundation Center 1972 Data Bank. New York: Foundation Center, 1972. 2v.

This is the first edition of a directory now issued under the title *National Data Book* (described elsewhere in this section of the bibliography).

377 The Foundation Directory. New York: Foundation Center, 1960– . Biennial. ISSN 0071–8092. $65 (10th ed.).

The Foundation Center is the only nonprofit organization in the country that focuses on the activities of private foundations. This directory is the standard work on nongovernmental grantmaking foundations. It lists nonprofit, nongovernmental organizations with assets in excess of $1 million or which made grants in excess of $100,000 in one year. More than 4,500 foundations are identified. These represent only 10 percent of all grantmaking foundations but over 90 percent of all grant money distributed ($4 billion annually). Data on the foundations, arranged by state and then by name of agency, include: purpose, finances, person to contact, number of grants awarded, and average amount of the award. Entries are indexed by type of support awarded; field of interest; foundation name; geographic location; and donors, trustees, and administrators. The supplements issued between biennial editions (see below) list foundations by state for which recent fiscal data are available on microfiche. The *Directory* is also available to be searched online; see the description of *Foundation Directory (Database)* in the "Databases and Search Services" chapter of this bibliography.

378   The Foundation Directory Supplement. New York: Foundation Center, 1982– . Biennial. $30 (1984 ed.). Pap

This supplement provides updated information on grantmaking foundations between biennial editions of the *Foundation Directory* (described above). In each supplement, approximately 2,000 entries are presented, each supplying new fiscal data; changes in staff, trustees, officers, addresses, telephone numbers, deadlines, application procedures, and funding priorities; and information on major foundations that terminated during the previous year. Subject, foundation, and personnel indexes complete the work. To "update" this updating service, use the *Foundation Directory (Database)*, described in the "Databases and Search Services" chapter of this bibliography.

379   The Foundation Grants Index Annual: A Cumulative Listing of Foundation Grants. New York: Foundation Center, 1971– . Annual. 72–76081. ISSN 0090–1601. $44 (1985 ed.). Pap.

The *Foundation Grants Index Annual* provides detailed subject access to the 34,000 grants made in excess of $5,000 during the year of record by approximately 500 major foundations with a total value of more than $1.8 million. This represents about 47 percent of all foundation giving. The grants are listed alphabetically by foundation under state division. Entries include the amount and date of the grant, name and location of the recipients, a description of the grant, and any known limitations in the foundation's giving pattern. The entries are indexed by key word, subject category, and recipient. While not comprehensive, the *Index* is useful in representing current grants made by large national foundations, thus providing insight into their current interest. You can use the index to find foundations active in your field, check for foundations that made grants in your geographic area, review the recent grants of 500 large foundations, and identify which nonprofits have been successful in obtaining grants. The information in the *Foundation Grants Index* is also available in *COMSEARCH* printouts (described elsewhere in this section), where all of the grants in each category are selected and arranged by computer. To update the information presented in the *Index*, use the *Foundation Grants Index Bimonthly* (described below) and/or the *Foundation Grants Index* database, described in the "Databases and Search Services" chapter of this bibliography.

380   **Foundation Grants Index Bimonthly.** New York: Foundation Center,
       1983– . Bimonthly. 83–1428. ISSN 0735–2522. $20.
This bimonthly subscription service updates the *Foundation Grants Index
Annual* (see description above). It continues the "Grants Index" bimonthly
section of the *Foundation News.* In each bimonthly issue, the main section
identifies the most recent grants of $5,000 or more awarded by private,
corporate, and community foundations that are reported to the Foundation
Center. Each grant record specifies the recipient organization's name and
location, the date the grant was authorized, the amount awarded, the purpose
of the grant, and the source of the information. The grants listed in each
bimonthly issue are indexed by grant recipient and project fields. Use this
section to identify foundations that have recently supported organizations
similar to yours. The next section in the bimonthly index notes recent
changes in the addresses, telephone numbers, personnel, program interests,
application guidelines, and other important data taken from annual reports,
news releases, newsletters, IRS returns, other private documents, and
correspondence between foundations and the Foundation Center. The last
section in each issue lists directories, grant indexes, and other reference
guides to grantmaking organizations (including annual reports, information
brochures, and newsletters).

381   **Foundation Grants to Individuals.** Ed. by Claude Barilleaux. 4th ed.
       New York: Foundation Center, 1984. 242p. 84–185951. ISBN
       0–87954–097–4. $18. Pap.
This is the only publication devoted entirely to foundation grant
opportunities (including some scholarships and loans) for individual
applicants. Updating the 1977, 1979, and 1982 editions, the fourth edition
provides full descriptions of nearly 1,000 foundations annually making grants
of at least $2,000 to individuals. These foundations represent more than $8.5
billion in assets and together give over $96 million to individuals annually.
Approximately 125 foundations appear in this edition for the first time, as do
foundation telephone numbers, names of trustees and staff, and sample
grants. All information from the earlier editions has been fully revised:
addresses, program descriptions, interview and deadline requirements, and
financial data. The work is organized by type of grant awarded (e.g.,
scholarships, general welfare, medical assistance), subdivided by eligibility
requirements and means of access (including "Grants to Foreign Individuals"
and "Grants to Employees of Specific Companies"). Multiple avenues of
access are provided through the following indexes: subject, state restrictions,
travel provisions, company-related grants, student grants, and foundations.
In addition to foundation listings, there are several useful articles on
approaching foundations and a bibliography of information sources for
individuals.

382   Foundation 500: An Index to Foundation Giving Patterns. Ed. by
David M. Lawson. New York: Douglas M. Lawson Associates, 1975– .
Irreg. 77–640049. ISSN 0145–6067. $29.95 (1984 ed.). Looseleaf.

The latest (1984) edition of the *Foundation 500*, issued in looseleaf form, is
intended to be "a desk-top research guide to the giving programs and
geographical distribution of 500 of the nation's top foundations." The data
reported were collected from annual reports, IRS reports, and the
foundations themselves. Rather than provide narrative entries for the
purpose, scope, requirements, and support offered by each company, as most
directories have done, Lawson concentrates on the subject giving areas and
reports in tabular form on the number of grants over $1,000 each company
gave in each of nearly 70 areas (e.g., music, medical research, aged,
handicapped, drug abuse, youth). Addresses, officers, telephone numbers,
number and total amount of grants awarded, and average size of grants are
indicated in the "Alphabetical Index." The scope of this publication is
limited, but its price is reasonable ($29.95 for the 1984 looseleaf edition). The
next edition is expected in 1987.

383   Foundations. By Harold M. Keele and Joseph C. Kiger. Westport, CT:
Greenwood, 1984. 516p. (Greenwood Encyclopedia of American
Institutions, no. 8). 83–10750. ISBN 0–313–22556–7. ISSN 0271–9509.
$49.95.

More like an encyclopedia than a directory, this volume focuses on the
history and philosophy of 234 of the largest American foundations, ranging
from the Ford Foundation ($2.5 billion in assets) to the Samuel H. Kreese
Foundation ($30 million in assets). Information is provided on the beginnings
of the foundation, motivation of the donors, needs they wanted addressed,
development of priorities in grant giving, administration of the grants, and
sources of further information about the foundation. Some of the entries were
prepared from information sent by the foundations; others were
supplemented by or created from information taken from the foundations'
annual reports, brochures, and/or other directories. As a result, the articles
vary in length, style, detail, and readability. Completing the volume are five
appendices: assets, family-connected foundations, locations, chronology, and
genealogy. Overall, grantseekers will find this source less useful than the
publications put out by the Foundation Center, Taft, etc.

384   Fund Raising for Museums: The Essential Book for Staff and Trustees.
By Hedy A. Hartman. Bellevue, WA: Hartman Planning and
Development Group, 1985. 530p. 85–151339. $85. Looseleaf.

Museums are defined in their broadest sense in this source book; aquariums,
aboretums, botanical gardens, zoos, and historical museums are all included.
The main section of the work consists of a listing of corporations,

foundations, and government agencies that have funded museum projects in the past. The entries are arranged by sponsoring organization and contain information on address and telephone number, financial activities, application guidelines, and typical grants. Several indexes are provided, including types of museums funded and geographic coverage.

385 Getting Yours: The Complete Guide to Government Money. By Matthew Lesko. Rev. Ed. New York: Penguin, 1984. 292p. 84–60953. ISBN 0–14046–652–5. $7.95. pap.

There are over 1,000 government programs annually providing $190 million in loans and guarantees and $207 billion in grants and payments to individuals, nonprofit organizations, and state and local governments. Covered here are financial assistance programs for mortgages, agricultural subsidies, business activities, research and education, social security, health care, unemployment compensation, and job training. Lesko lists 800 ways for "getting yours." Similar coverage is provided in the first edition, published in 1982 by Viking in cloth (346p. 81–52256. ISBN 0–67033–764–1) and Penguin in paper (346p. 81–11979. ISBN 0–14046–510–3). Most of the information included in this work can be found in much greater detail in the *Catalog of Federal Domestic Assistance* (see description elsewhere in this section of the bibliography).

386 Government Assistance Almanac: The Guide to All Federal Programs Available to the American Public. By J. Robert Dumouchel. Washington, DC: Foggy Bottom Publications, 1985– . Annual. 85–7164. ISSN 0883–8690. $19.95 (1985 ed.). Pap.

This is another publication based on the *Catalog of Federal Domestic Assistance* (described elsewhere in this section). Unlike the Ready Reference series (also described in this section), Dumouchel's work summarizes rather than reproduces all the information in the 1985–1986 *Catalog*'s 1,200 pages. Furthermore, it adds its own index, provides a system of finding federal office contacts, and costs less than the *Catalog*. If you are interested in the essentials rather than the details of current federal programs, this volume could prove less cumbersome to use than the *Catalog*'s looseleaf system.

387 Government Programs and Projects Directory: A Guide to National Programs and Projects Administered by the Executive Department and Independent Agencies of the United States Government. Ed. by Anthony T. Kruzas and Kay Gill. Detroit: Gale, 1983–84. 3v. 83–645478. ISBN 0–8103–0422–8. ISSN 0737–5255. $135. Pap.

This directory focuses on programs and projects administered by the executive department and independent agencies of the U.S. government. Among the 1,574 programs covered are the Food Stamps Program, the

Cooperative Forestry Assistance Program, and the Solar Energy Program. Arranged by sponsoring organization, the entries contain information on the name of the program or project, sponsoring organization address, legislative authorization, project scope and purpose, funding, and source of information used to prepare the entry (these include government reports, fact sheets, program guides, the *Catalog of Federal Domestic Assistance*, and questionnaire responses from the sponsoring agencies). Indexing is by name and keyword.

388   Grant Information System. Comp. by Betty L. Wilson and William K. Wilson. Phoenix: Oryx, 1976–1984. Annual, with quarterly updates.

The Oryx Press *Grant Information System* provided information on more than 2,000 American federal and state agencies and private foundations, associations, and corporations. It was composed of several *Faculty Alert Bulletins* as well as the monthly *Elhi Funding Sources Newsletter* (78–0721. ISSN 0149–3450). The service was suspended in 1984 and replaced by the *GRANTS* database (described in the "Databases and Search Services" chapter) and the series of annual directories being generated from the database (e.g., *Directory of Grants in the Humanities*).

389   Grant Making Corporations That Publish Guidelines. Hartsdale, NY: Public Service Materials Center, 1984. 47p. ISBN 0–91497–705–9. $8.95. Pap.

Even the best and most comprehensive of the grant directories cannot supply the fullness of information that can be found in corporate guidelines for giving. This publication identifies 241 corporations that issue guidelines and provides the addresses, telephone numbers, and contact persons for them. The entries are arranged by name of parent company. There is no index. The Public Service Materials Center also issues another pamphlet that concentrates on publications issued by funding agencies; it is a revision of a 1976 release: *Foundations That Send Their Annual Reports* (2d ed. 1984. 45p. $8.95, pap.).

390   Grants for Graduate Students, 1986—88. Ed. by Andrea Leskes. Princeton, NJ: Peterson's Guides, 1986. 400p. 86–1847. ISBN 0–87866–483–1. ISSN 0889–1613. $29.95. Pap.

Compiled by the Office of Research Affairs at the University of Massachusetts' Graduate School and originally intended for use by the students there, this listing has now been edited by Andrea Leskes and published by Peterson's Guides. It identifies over 600 grants and fellowships open to students at the graduate level. The entries are indexed by subject and title and contain the following information: purpose, number awarded, amount awarded, ratio of awards to applicants, eligibility requirements, application deadlines, and contact names and addresses. No other directory focuses only on graduate students.

391 The Grants Register: Postgraduate Awards in the English Speaking World. Ed. by Norman Frankel. New York: St. Martin's Press, 1969– . Biennial. 77–12055. $39.50 (1985–87 ed.).

This biennial directory describes grants, fellowships, and prizes open to nationals of the United States, Canada, the United Kingdom, Ireland, Australia, New Zealand, South Africa, and the developing countries. For more information about the publication, see the annotation in the "Grants— General—International" section of this bibliography.

392 The Grantseeker for State and Local Government. Washington, DC: Revenue Sharing Advisory Service, 1981– . Biweekly. $108/yr.

This biweekly newsletter attempts to cover all current federal funding opportunities and to provide advance notice of funding priorities, new programs under consideration in Congress, and some examples of state and local projects that were successfully funded.

393 The Grantsmanship Center News. Los Angeles: Grantsmanship Center, 1973– . Bimonthly. ISSN 0364–3115. $28/yr.

The Grantsmanship Center is the oldest and largest fund-raising training organization in the country, offering 250 workshops annually in over 75 cities. The *Grantsmanship Center News* has been published bimonthly since 1973 and it offers (1) lively and informative how-to articles covering such topics as obtaining grants, writing proposals, planning programs, managing nonprofit organizations, and developing resources; (2) case histories that document successful and unsuccessful proposals; (3) interviews with government and foundation officials; (4) news and comment from Washington, D.C.; (5) deadlines; (6) federal regulations and summaries; and (7) funding notes. In addition, it periodically features an up-to-date "Basic Grantsmanship Library" article (the seventh edition was recently published), which identifies core resources (especially government publications) for a funding library.

394 Guide to Federal Grants & Financial Aid for Individuals and Nonprofit Organizations. Ed. by Calvin W. Fenton and Charles J. Edwards. Arlington, VA: Fenton Associates (dist. by Kendall/Hall), 1984– . Annual. 85–23486. $125 (1985 ed.). Pap.

Described in this guide are 494 grants issued by the federal government in such areas as agriculture, arts and humanities, business and commerce, crime and deliquency, defense, education, and energy. The entries are arranged by federal agency and indexed by subject. Each program description contains the following information: purpose, eligibility, funds available, application process, notification procedures, type of assistance available, and requirements. Special note should be taken of the price. All of the information included in the guide, and more, is available in the *Catalog of Federal Domestic Assistance* (described elsewhere in this section) for one fourth the cost. However, many users will find Fenton and Edward's guide easier to use than the *Catalog*. Furthermore, it is updated in bimonthly supplements.

395   How to Get Money for Research. By Mary Rubin and the Business and Professional Women's Foundation. Foreword by M. Chamberlain. Old Westbury, NY: Feminist Press, 1983. 78p. 83–1444. ISBN 0–935312–18–8. $6.95. Pap.

This book was prepared "to help women researchers, and those doing research about women, locate sources of funds for their work and take actions that maximize their chances of obtaining funding." It is an expanded and updated version of the *Research Funding Sourcebook: A Guide for Women Researchers and Researchers on Women*, a typed list of grants available to women and a selected bibliography of other directories prepared by Mary Rubin and issued by the Business and Professional Women's Foundation in 1980. Although the introduction to *How to Get Money for Research* indicates that the listing included in the book focuses on "funding opportunities for and about women at the pre- and post-doctorate level," a large proportion of the programs described are open equally to men and women (e.g., Tinker Foundation Grants, National Science Foundation Dissertation Program). In all, only 81 programs are covered, along with descriptions of 21 grant and foundation directories, a list of Foundation Center regional collections, and a guide to proposal writing. The 81 program entries are indexed by subject, program title, and sponsoring organization. For a more comprehensive and up-to-date listing of grants (and other types of programs) for and about women, see the latest biennial edition of the *Directory of Financial Aids for Women* (described elsewhere in this section).

396   An Independent Sector Resource Directory of Education and Training Opportunities and Other Services. By Sandra Trice Gray. Washington, DC: Independent Sector, 1986– . Annual. $18 (1986 ed.). Pap.

One of the four sections in this annual identifies fellowships, internships, and grants for individuals interested in nonprofit work. For more information about the publication, see the annotation in the "Internships—General— United States" section of this bibliography.

397 Internal Revenue Service Foundation Reports. Philadelphia, PA: U.S. Internal Revenue Service. Annual. Price varies (see below). Paper and aperture cards.

The Internal Revenue Service requires all private foundations to file two types of annual forms: 990–AR, which provides information on the foundation's managers, financial activities, etc.; and 990–PF, which provides information on income, expenses, officers' salaries, investments, etc. For the smaller foundations, especially, these returns may provide the most current and complete information about their activities. The submitted reports can be purchased on aperture cards (microforms mounted in windows in file cards) or as photocopies. Aperture cards cost $1 for the first card and $.13 for each additional card; photocopies cost $1 for the first page and $.10 for each additional page. Many of the state directories listed in this bibliography are based on information taken from 990–AR and 990–PF forms.

398 National Data Book. 9th ed. New York: Foundation Center, 1985. 2v. 81–71421. ISBN 0–87954–126–1. ISSN 0732–8788. $55. Pap.

This is the only publication that lists *all* foundations giving more than $1 per year. It is the best single source for information on small foundations. The nineth edition contains brief descriptions of 22,000 currently active grantmaking foundations in the United States (five times more than any other published source). A two-volume set, the first volume arranges foundations by state and provides information for each on name, address, principal officers, market value of assets, grants paid, gifts received, fiscal period, and annual reports; the second volume, which features foundations listed by state (and, within each state, from highest to lowest grant amounts), serves as an index to the entries in Volume One. The introduction to the set provides various statistical analyses, including numerical distribution, dollar totals, and percentages of foundation assets. Detailed charts illustrate the geographic concentration of foundation wealth as well as the patterns of economic distribution. Also included is information about community foundations (i.e., 170 grantmakers that focus on the needs of their particular cities). You can use this resource to find the address of any active U.S. foundation, locate all foundations in a particular city or zip code area, profile foundation assets or giving levels by states or region, identify all foundations issuing annual reports, and determine the number and size of small foundations by community. The first edition of this directory was published in 1972 under the title *Foundation Center 1972 Data Bank*. The 1976 and 1979 editions were issued as the *Foundation Center National Data Book*. Since 1981, the directory has been released on a annual basis as *National Data Book*. It is also available as an online database, under the title *National Foundations*, through Lockheed's Dialog system. A search costs approximately $60 an hour and can be done at any library that has online access to Dialog.

399 **National Directory of Arts and Education Support by Business Corporations.** By Daniel Millsaps. 2d ed. Washington, DC: Washington International Arts Letter, 1982. 234p. (The Arts Patronage Series, no 10). 77–79730. ISBN 0–912072–11–3. $75. Pap.

This directory, a revised edition of the *National Directory of Arts Support by Business Corporations*, is more expensive but also more comprehensive than the *Guide to Corporate Giving 3* (see description in the "Grants— Humanities—General" section of the bibliography). Like the other Arts Patronage Series' titles covered in this bibliography, this volume identifies corporations that have been active in giving, in this case, giving to the arts and education. Over 3,000 corporations (including subsidiaries) are covered here. Entries specify headquarters address, officers, kinds of support offered, and examples of typical grants awarded. The listing is arranged by corporation and indexed by geographic location and areas of interest, including dance, fellowships and scholarships, literature, mass media, and theater (in the first edition there was only an index to officers). Use the *Washington International Arts Letter*, issued by the same publisher, to update the information (which was current as of 1982).

400 **National Directory of Corporate Charity.** Comp. by Sam Sternberg. San Francisco: Regional Young Adult Project, 1984. 613p. 84–15950. ISBN 0–9606198–2–8. $80. Pap.

This directory is the result of a 1981 research project sponsored by the San Francisco Regional Young Adult Project. The purpose of the project was to identify the charitable activities of major U.S. corporations. Information is presented here on 1,600 companies with annual revenues of over $200 million. Both donor (1,600 companies) and presumed nondonor companies (1,000 companies) are represented. The information included in the directory was taken from annual reports, questionnaires, reference directories, grants lists, corporate donors, lists of nonprofit organizations, and news releases. The entries are listed by company name and, for donors, specify address, telephone number, any foundations or subsidiaries, program areas, any nonmonetary support offered, amount of money given, range of gift amounts, giving policy, and application procedures. The nondonor entries are much briefer: address, telephone number, and contact person. Indexing is by operating locations of corporations, support categories, and companies and their subsidiaries. Separate sections describe corporate giving patterns, nonprofit status, corporate solicitation campaigns, and relevant readings. The directory is available in both the print version ($80) and a 10–disk set for the IBM-PC ($100) that can be used with most word processing programs.

401 **National Directory of Corporate Public Affairs, '86.** Ed. by Arthur C. Close, with Regina Germain and John P. Gregg. 4th ed. Washington, DC: Columbia Books, 1986. 575p. ISBN 0–910416–56–7. $55. Pap.

Using data from questionnaires, augmented by information taken from printed sources, this directory focuses on companies and individuals involved in public affairs programs. The information is current as of October, 1985. The listing is divided into two sections. The first is an alphabetical catalog of 1,500 companies of varied sizes with public affairs programs. The following information is provided; address of corporate headquarters, address of Washington, D.C. office (if exists), political action committee activity, foundation or corporate giving program, corporate publications, and names of the company's public affairs and related activities personnel. The second section, "The People," consists of an alphabetical list of 10,000 corporate officers engaged in the informational, political, or philanthropic aspects of public affairs in the United States. The entries in both sections are indexed by industry and by geographical location. Because of its currency, this directory is a good source to use to identify appropriate contact people, to determine who has public affairs responsibility in a given company, or to discover where to get more information on a public affairs program.

402 **People in Philanthropy: A Guide to Philanthropic Leaders, Major Donors, and Funding Connections.** Washington, DC: Taft, 1984. 361p. 84–50482. ISBN 0–914756–60–5. $187.

Identified in this "blue book" of the funding world are some of America's wealthiest and most powerful business and community leaders, some of the donors who have created the largest charitable foundations, thousands of foundation trustees, and thousands more corporate personalities who direct the giving of America's largest businesses. The volume is divided into four sections: wealthy people, foundation donors, foundation officers, and corporate officers. Each section contains biographical profiles and is indexed by philanthropic affiliation, state of birth, and alma mater. A companion volume to *People in Philanthropy* is *America's Wealthiest People: Their Philanthropic and Nonprofit Affiliations,* which focuses in greater detail on the charitable activities of America's rich. Included there are 500 in-depth profiles indicating philanthropic, nonprofit, and corporate affiliations. Use these sources to obtain information on the people you may need to contact in your grants activities. It should be noted, however, that personal interaction has a price. *People in Philanthropy* costs $187.

403   **Research Activities and Funding Programs.** Ed. by Anthony T. Kruzas
and Kay Gill. Detroit: Gale, 1983– . Irreg. ISBN 0–8130–0149–0. $200
(1983–84 ed.). Pap.

Issued as part of Gale's *Encyclopedia of Associations*, this is the first attempt
by any publisher to compile information on the research programs and
funding activities of over 1,000 nonprofit, unofficial, and nongovernmental
associations located throughout the United States. International
organizations are included only if they maintain headquarters in the United
States or have a large American membership. Entries provide specific
information on types of programs, fields of interest,and publications of the
associations actively involved in conducting and/or supporting research.
Completing the 1983–84 edition is a comprehensive, cumulative name and
keyword index (which is a single alphabetical index to the organizations
listed).

404   **The Scholarship Book: The Complete Guide to Private-Sector
Scholarships, Grants and Loans for Undergraduates.** By Daniel J.
Cassidy and Michael J. Alves. Englewood Cliffs, NJ: Prentice-Hall,
1984. 391p. 84–11683. ISBN 0–13–792342–2, cloth; -334–1, pap.
$28.50, cloth; $14.95, pap.

Included in this extensive but rather unfocused directory are grants, loans,
scholarships, fellowships, competitons, and internships for undergraduate
and (despite its subtitle) graduate students. For more information about the
publication, see the annotation in the "Scholarships—General—United
States" section of this bibliography.

405   **Scholarships, Fellowships and Loans.** Prep. by S. Norman Feingold
and Marie Feingold. Bethesda, MD: Bellman Publishing, 1949– . Irreg.
49–49180. $80 (v. 8, 1986).

Despite its title, this comprehensive guide covers grants as well as
scholarships, fellowships, and loans. For more information about the
publication, see the annotation in the "Scholarships—General—United
States" section of this bibliography.

406   **Scholarships, Fellowships and Loans News Service and Counselors
Information Services.** Bethesda, MD: Bellman Publishing, 1980– .
Quarterly. 81–642576. ISSN 0277–6502. $32/yr.

Use this newsletter to update Feingold's *Scholarships, Fellowships and Loans*
(described above). For more information on the newsletter, see the annotation
in the "Scholarships—General—United States" section of this bibliography.

407   Source Book Profiles. New York: Foundation Center, 1977– . Quarterly, with annual cumulations. 77–79015. ISBN 0–87954–128–8. $265. Looseleaf.

Of all the Foundation Center's directories, *Source Book Profiles* provides the most detailed treatment but covers the smallest number of foundations. In all, only 1,000 grantmaking organizations are treated, with entries averaging three to six pages each. These foundations account for 79 percent of the total annual giving of all U.S. foundations, more than $2.9 billion in grants annually. Each profile provides information on the foundation's areas of giving, types of grants, and types of recipients. All varieties of foundations are surveyed, including over 200 company-sponsored foundations and more than 25 community foundations. The *Source Book* service operates on a two-year publishing cycle. Subscribers to the current series receive about 125 completely new four- to six-page profiles every quarter, totaling over 500 during the subscription year. Each quarterly installment also includes a completely revised set of indexes to all 1,000 foundations by name, subject interest, type of grants awarded, and city and state of location or concentration of giving. *Foundation Profile Updates*, a bimonthly Foundation Center news service monitoring changes in address, telephone, personnel, or program direction at the 1,000 foundations covered in the *Source Book*, is included in each subscription arrangement, as is *Source Book Profile Series*, a set of 500 foundation profiles extracted from the previous year's *Source Book* entries. This work was first published as a two-volume set, covering 1975–1976, under the title *The Foundation Center Source Book* (1975. 75–334871. ISSN 0362–1170). Beginning in 1977, the publication was issued as an annual, first with bimonthly updates (1977–1981) and then with quarterly updates (beginning in 1982).

408   Student Aid Annual. Moravia, NY: Chronicle Guidance Publications, 1955–1975. Annual. ISSN 0580–4555.

From 1955 through 1974, this publication was known as *Student Aid Annual*, from 1975 through 1978 as *Student Aid Manual*, and since 1979 as *Chronicle Student Aid Annual* (described in the "Scholarships—General—United States" section of this bibliography).

409   Survey of Grant-Making Foundations. Hartsdale, NY: Public Service Materials Center, 1970– . Irreg. 79–2822. ISSN 0190–5163. $19.50 (1985 ed.).

This irregularly issued directory covers over 1,000 foundations with assets in excess of $1 million or awarding grants in excess of $200,000. Entries are arranged alphabetically by foundation name and supply the following information: address, telephone number, contact person, meeting schedule, geographic restrictions, and types of grants awarded.

410 Taft Corporate Giving Directory: Comprehensive Profiles and Analyses of America's Private Foundations. Washington, DC: Taft, 1977– . Annual. 85–19020. ISSN 0882–7176. $287 (1986 ed.).

Taft is one of the oldest, largest, and best known of the information subscription services. This directory, first issued in 1977 and updated annually since then, contains over 500 corporate foundation profiles. The entries are arranged by program name and present information on sponsoring company, grant distribution, type of grants, areas of interest, contact persons, total assets, sample grants, corporate operating location, and Fortune 500 ranking (profiles average one page in length). Multiple indexes are provided: state, field of interest, corporate operating location, contact persons, sponsoring company, and types of grants. Use Taft's monthly *Corporate Updates* and *Corporate Giving Watch* to supplement entries in the annual directory. From 1977 through 1981, this publication was issued as *Taft Corporate Foundation Directory* and from 1982 to 1984 as *Taft Corporate Directory.* Beginning in 1984, with the 1985 edition, the name changed slightly, again, to its present *Taft Corporate Giving Directory.* To complement the listings included here, use the *Corporate 500, Foundation Center Source Book Profiles,* the *Foundation Directory,* and its companion the *Foundation Grants Index Annual* (each described elsewhere in this section of the bibliography).

411 Taft Foundation Reporter: Comprehensive Profiles and Analyses of America's Private Foundations. Washington, DC: Taft, 1977– . Annual. 82–7865. ISSN 0741–6709. $287 (1986 ed.).

This is one of the best, most comprehensive, and most expensive of the grants directories. Included annually in this definitive directory are 600 indepth profiles and analyses of America's private foundations. Lengthy entries provide information on history of the foundation, officers, directors, types of foundations, areas of interest, fiscal activities, types of grants awarded, grants distribution, sample grants, application requirements, and contact persons. Four indexes are suppplied: state, type of grant, field of interest, and officers/ directors by name, place of birth, and alma mater. Two monthly periodicals update the listings included here: *Foundation Giving Watch* provides concise coverage of the new trends and ideas shaping the private funding scene and *Foundation Updates* presents the most current information available on foundations' direct giving programs. Prior to 1980, this directory was issued under the title *Taft Foundation Reporter. National Edition, and Nine Separate Regional Editions.*

412 Taft Trustees of Wealth. Washington, DC: Taft, 1980—1984. Annual. 82–3020. ISSN 0731–2318.

From 1975 through 1979, this annual biographical directory of private corporate foundation officers was issued under the title *Trustees of Wealth: The Taft Guide to Philanthropic Decisionmakers.* Since 1984, the annual has been published as *People in Philanthropy* (described elsewhere in this section of the bibliography).

413 The Top 50 Grant Awarding Foundations in 1982. By Donald Levitan. Newton Center, MA: Grants Advisory Service, 1983. 17p. $9. Pap.

This small booklet identifies the top 50 private funding agencies in the United States (Ford Foundation, number one; Henry Dreyfus Foundation, number 50) and outlines the giving patterns for each. Also provided are contact names, chief executive officers' names, geographic restrictions, addresses, and telephone numbers for each of the listed foundations. For a more comprehensive list of American foundations (and one providing much more information for each agency), see the *Foundation Directory* (described elsewhere in this section of the bibliography).

414 Trustees of Wealth: The Taft Guide to Philanthropic Decisionmakers. Washington, DC: Taft, 1975—1979. Annual. 75–32239.

Since 1979, this annual has been issued under the titles *Taft Trustees of Wealth* and *People in Philanthropy,* both described elsewhere in this section of the bibliography).

415 Where America's Large Foundations Make Their Grants. Ed. by Joseph Dermer. Hartsdale, NY: Public Service Materials Center, 1971– . Irreg. 80–1404. $44.50 (1983–84 ed.).

The latest edition (1983–84. 250p. ISBN 0–686–37909–8) covers 650 foundations with assets of more than $10 million. These foundations control 85 percent of foundation assets and make 80 percent of all foundation grants. Each entry identifies grant recipients, how much they received, and the purpose of their projects. A new segment, "Additional Insights," provides private research information supplied by Dermer's financial development firm.

416 Your 1987/88 Guide to Social Security Benefits. By Leona G. Rubin. New York: Facts On File. To be published in 1987. 192p. ISBSN 0–8160–1567–8, cloth; -1568–6, pap. $15.95, cloth; $7.95, pap.

More than 35 million Americans (with the average age of 30 years) are eligible to receive social security). This guide describes the current social security benefits available to them, covers eligibility requirements, indicates application procedures, and details the appeal process in a question-and-answer format. The 1987/88 edition is the first to be published by Facts on File. Earlier editions were issued under a slightly different title and by a different publisher. For example, the 1986 edition (by Dale Detlefs) was published by Mercer—Meringer as the *Guide to Social Security, 1986.*

Washington, DC

417 **Directory of Foundations of the Greater Washington Area.** Ed. by Elizabeth Frazier. Washington, DC: Community Foundation of Greater Washington, 1984. 125p. 85–648739. ISBN 0–318–03830–7. ISSN 0884–9056. $10. Pap.

Information on 500 foundations located in the greater Washington, D.C. area are described in this directory. Entries are arranged by type of foundation (large, small, publicly supported) and indexed by officers/trustees, foundation name, and asset size. The profiles specify officers/trustees, amounts of grants awarded, and areas of interest. The data reported are based primarily on 990–PF returns filed with the Internal Revenue Service. A glossary of terms completes the volume.

Alabama

418 **Alabama Foundation Directory.** Rev. ed. Birmingham, AL: Reference Department, Birmingham Public Library, 1983. 56p. 84–116103. $5. Pap.

Based on 990–PF and 990–AR returns filed with the IRS, the 1983 edition of this directory describes the funding activities of 184 private Alabama foundations. Entries are arranged alphabetically by foundation and indexed by geographic and interest areas. The following information is provided for each entry: address and telephone number, names of officers and trustees, financial data, grant totals for the last calendar year for which information was available, number and range of grants, and major areas of interest. The first edition of the directory was edited by Anne F. Knight and published by the Friends of the Birmingham Public Library in 1980 (29p. 80–150755).

419 **Foundation Profiles of the Southeast: Alabama, Arkansas, Louisiana, Mississippi.** Comp. by James H. Taylor and John L. Wilson. Williamsburg, KY: James H. Taylor Associates, 1983. 119p. $39.95.

Information on 212 foundations in Alabama, Arkansas, Louisiana, and Mississippi is provided in this directory. The entries, which are arranged by state and then alphabetically by foundation name, indicate principal officer, assets, total grants offered, and sample grants awarded. There is no other access provided to the information.

Arkansas

420 **Foundation Profiles of the Southeast: Alabama, Arkansas, Louisiana, Mississippi.** Comp. by James H. Taylor and John L. Wilson. Williamsburg, KY: James H. Taylor Associates, 1983. 119p. $39.95.

Information on 212 foundations in Arkansas, Alabama, Louisiana, and Mississippi is provided in this directory. For more information about the publication, see the annotation in the "Grants—General—Alabama" section of this bibliography.

421 **Guide to Arkansas Funding Sources: Foundations & Religious Organizations.** Comp. by Jerry Cronin and Cheryl Waller. Hampton, AR: Independent Community Consultants, 1983. 103p. (Arkansas Private Philanthropy Research Series, v. 4). $20.

Approximately 100 grantmakers in or related to Arkansas are covered in this directory. The following information is provided for each foundation: foundation name, address and telephone number, officers' names, employer ID, amount granted, total number of grants, range of grant size, areas of giving, policies (e.g., restrictions on grantmaking activities), and procedures. The entries are arranged alphabetically in three categories: Arkansas foundations; foundations in neighboring states that regularly fund Arkansas programs; and religious organizations that are willing to support secular groups. This directory is number four in the *Private Philanthropy in Arkansas Research* series. Volume one in the series, *Charitable Contributions by Arkansas Businesses* (By David Miller. 1982. 32p. $10.50) supplements the listings found here.

California

422 **Catalog of California State Grants Assistance.** Sacramento: State Agency Grantspeople Exchange and California State Library, 1985. 75p. $8.95. Pap.

The State Agency Grantspeople Exchange (SAGE), a working association of state employees concerned with exchanging information about grants, recognized the lack of a single resource directory to describe the myriad of financial aid programs offered through state agencies in California and issued this directory in 1985. Described in the catalog are 75 programs administered by California governmental agencies that are either funded by state monies or federal "pass through" funds. Because grant programs administered directly by federal agencies are listed in the *Catalog of Federal Domestic Assistance* (described in the "Grants—General—United States" section of this bibliography), they are not covered here. The entries range from "Community Service Employment for Older Americans" to "Floating Restrooms" to "Domestic Violence Crime Prevention Programs." The following information is provided for each program: purpose, limitations, authorization, type of assistance, amount of funds available, eligibility, typical grants, deadline, and contact person (with address and telephone number). California is one of only a few states that has a directory of grants offered in the public sector on the state level (some of the other states are New York, Michigan, and Maryland). In the future, the directory may be issued as an annual.

423 The Directory of Major California Foundations. 1st ed. Attleboro, MA: Logos, 1986. 94p. $19.95. Pap.

Like the other foundation directories published by Logos, e.g., *Directory of Major New Jersey Foundations* (described in the "Grants—General—New Jersey" section), the first edition of this publication covers only the largest and most important of the foundations located in California. The program profiles are arranged alphabetically and provide the following information: activities, geographic restrictions, amounts granted, officers/trustees, contact persons, and examples of typical grants. This is one of the most current but the least comprehensive of the directories describing general California foundations.

424 Guide to California Foundations. San Francisco: Northern California Grantmakers, 1976– . Biennial. 78–58948. $17 (1985 ed.). Pap.

Published biennially since 1976, this state directory gives basic descriptive information on private charitable foundations based in California that either give grants of at least $25,000 a year or have assets of over $500,000. Some corporations and a few smaller foundations are also included. In the 1985 edition, over 700 foundations are covered. These foundations combined control $6.9 million in assets and award more than $500,000 in grants annually. Over 100 of the listed foundations appear for the first time in this edition. For each entry, information is given on purpose and fields of granting interest; total amount, number, and range of grants; geographic limits and other restrictions; contact person, officers, and directors; application deadlines and procedures; and five sample grants reflecting giving patterns. The information is based primarily on 990–PF and 990–AR returns filed with the IRS or records in the California Attorney General's Office and, to a much lesser extent, on data supplied by foundations completing questionnaires. Arranged by foundation name, the directory is indexed by primary interest, geographic area, and name of foundation. Also included are sections on applying for grants, scholarship foundations, and related terms.

425 **National Directory of Corporate Charity: California Edition.** Comp. by Sam Sternberg. San Francisco: Regional Young Adult Project, 1981. 450p. ISBN 0–9606198–0–1. $30. Pap.

Aimed primarily at nonprofit service organizations in California, this directory describes 624 national corporations that have a history of contributing to California groups. California-based companies listed here must have incomes in excess of $100 million; companies based outside of California must have over $500 million. The information presented in the directory was taken from annual reports, questionnaires, reference directories, grants lists, corporate donors lists of nonprofit organizations, and news releases. Arranged alphabetically by name of corporation, entries indicate giving policies, categories of giving, amount of money donated in most recent years, charity program activity, nonmonetary contributions, giftmaking policies, geographic preferences, and contact persons. Indexing is by operating locations of corporations, support categories, and companies and their subsidiaries. Separate sections describe corporate giving patterns, nonprofit strategies, corporate solicitation campaigns, and relevant readings.

426 **Other Than Grants: A Sampling of Southern California's Corporate Gift Matching, Volunteer, and In-Kind Giving Programs.** 2d ed. Los Angeles, California Community Foundation, 1984. 48p. $3. Pap.

The recent substantial budget cuts have turned the attention of the private sector to alternative funding sources. This publication is one of only a few that identify the employee gift matching, in-kind giving, and employee volunteer programs. The listing is not intended to be definitive; rather, it is a sampling of programs and represents only 39 corporations out of the hundreds in Southern California. The entries are arranged by type of program (matching gift, volunteer, and in-kind/non-cash giving); each supplies name and address of the corporation, contact person, and a description of the program.

Colorado

427 **Colorado Foundation Directory.** Denver: Junior League of Denver, 1978– . Irreg. 81–10970. $10 (1984–1985 ed.). Pap.

Over 240 Colorado foundations are described in the fourth (1984–1985) edition of this directory. The information included in the listings is taken from 990–PF and 990–AR returns filed with the IRS and from data supplied by the foundations themselves. The entries are arranged by foundation name; there are no indexes. The following information is presented for each foundation: statement of purpose, sample grants, and officers. Separate sections are provided on proposal writing and budget form. A bibliography and an analysis of foundations by assets, grants, and fields of interest are also included. The first edition of this title was issued in 1978.

Connecticut

428   Connecticut Foundation Directory. Ed. by Michael E. Burns. New Haven: OUA/DATA, 1980. 152p. 80–142336. Pap.

Since 1982, this directory has been issued as the *Guide to Corporate Giving in Connecticut*. For more information about that publication, see the annotation elsewhere in this section of the bibliography.

429   Directory of the Major Connecticut Foundations. Attleboro, MA: Logos, 1982. 49p. $19.95. Pap.

Over 60 Connecticut foundations are described here. The data presented are based on foundation publications, information from the Office of the Attorney General in Hartford, and the 1979 and 1980 990–PF and 990–AR IRS returns. Foundation profiles are arranged alphabetically and specify grant range, geographic limitations, officers, and directors. The entries are indexed by subject.

430   Guide to Corporate Giving in Connecticut. Ed. by Michael E. Burns. Comp. by Anne Washburn. New Haven: OUA/DATA, 1982– . Biennial. 83–139213. $31.50. Pap.

First issued in 1980 as the *Connecticut Foundation Directory*, the 1982 edition of this directory provides information on 769 Connecticut corporate foundations that have offices in the state and annual sales in excess of $10 million. Unlike its predecessor, which relied on information from the 990–PF and 990–AR IRS returns, this source is based on data supplied by the foundations themselves. The entries are arranged alphabetically by foundation name and contain the following information: areas of interest, giving policies, geographic preferences, and contact persons. Indexing is by geographic location. There is a 20–page statistical analysis of the information presented in the directory. This is the first volume issued in OUA/DATA's proposed series on funding in New England states. Once OUA/DATA has published guides to all the New England states, this directory will be issued as a biennial.

Delaware

431   Delaware Foundations. Wilmington: United Way of Delaware, 1983. 120p. $14.50. Pap.

This directory presents information on 111 private foundations in Delaware, lists 27 operating foundations in Delaware, and provides a sampling of 16

out-of-state foundations that have made grants in Delaware. The entries—
which specify purpose, officers, grants awarded, and types of recipients—are
arranged alphabetically by foundation name within the three categories of
foundations covered. They are indexed by foundation name and officers/
trustees. The data reported were taken from 990–PF and 990–AR forms,
annual reports, and questionnaires completed by the foundations. A new
edition is expected in 1986.

Florida

432   The Complete Guide to Florida Foundations. Miami: John L. Adams,
    1985. 239p. $55. Pap.

This is the most current and the most comprehensive but not the most
detailed of the directories listing Florida foundations. While nearly 1,000
organizations are identified here, the directory-type information provided for
each is very brief.

433   Foundation Profiles of the Southeast: Florida. Comp. by James H.
    Taylor and John L. Wilson. Williamsburg, KY: James H. Taylor
    Associates, 1983. 130p. $39.95.

Unlike some of the other volumes in this series of *Foundation Profiles of the
Southeast*, this volume concentrates on only one state. Nearly 800
foundations in Florida are described. The entries are arranged alphabetically
by foundation and provide information on officers, assets, total grants
offered, and typical grants awarded. The data reported are taken from
990–PF and 990–AR returns filed with the Internal Revenue Service. There
are no indexes.

434   Guide to Foundations in Florida. Comp. by the Florida Department of
    Community Affairs. Tallahassee: Bureau of Local Government
    Assistance, 1983. 72p. 84–620738. Free. Pap.

Less comprehensive but more detailed than *Foundation Profiles of the
Southeast: Florida* (described elsewhere in this section of the bibliography),
this free directory lists 437 foundations making grants in Florida. The entries
are arranged alphabetically by foundation name and present information on
purpose, officers, net worth, grant range, total dollar amount of grants
awarded, and total number of grants awarded. No examples of sample grants
are provided. The entries are indexed by geographic location. This is the
second edition of the directory; the first was issued in 1979 (146p.).

Georgia

435 **Foundation Profiles of the Southeast: Georgia.** Comp. by James H. Taylor and John L. Wilson. Williamsburg, KY: James H. Taylor Associates, 1983. 85p. $39.95.

Like the Taylor Associates' volume on Florida, this directory is arranged by foundation name. Nearly 500 foundations are described. The entries provide information on officers, assets, total grants offered, and typical grants awarded. The data reported are taken from 990–PF and 990–AR returns filed with the Internal Revenue Service. There are no indexes.

436 **Georgia Foundation Directory.** Atlanta: Atlanta Public Library, 1983. 250p. Free. Pap.

Nearly 600 foundations in Georgia are listed in this directory. The entries are arranged alphabetically and indexed by geographic interest. The following information is provided for each foundation: address and telephone number, contact person, purpose, range of grants awarded, and sources of information. The listings are based on 1981 data. Previously, this publication was issued under the title *Guide to Foundations in Georgia* (see below).

437 **Guide to Foundations in Georgia.** Atlanta: Atlanta Public Library, 1970–1981. Irreg. 79–623231.

In 1983, this title changed its name to *Georgia Foundation Directory* (described above).

Hawaii

438 **Guide to Charitable Trusts and Foundations in the State of Hawaii.** Honolulu: Alu Like, 1980– . Annual. $35.

Issued annually since 1980, this 300–page directory describes over 100 foundations and church funding sources in Hawaii. The information reported is taken from annual reports and 990–PF and 990–AR IRS returns filed in the State Attorney General's Office. The profiles are arranged by foundation name and specify officers, purpose, foundation date, type of foundation, assets, total giving, number of grants awarded, and activities. A short bibliography (generally three pages) is included in each annual edition, as are sections on forming a tax-exempt organization, proposal writing, local service organizations, national church funding organizations, and mainland foundations.

Idaho

439 **Directory of Idaho Foundations.** 3d ed. Caldwell, ID: Caldwell Public Library, 1984. 23p. $3. Pap.

Less than 90 foundations in Idaho are coverd in this brief listing. The entries are arranged alphabetically by foundation name and indexed by subject. The information in each entry (e.g., assets, grants, major areas of interest) was taken primarily from 990–AR returns filed with the IRS. Appendices list inactive foundations, foundations with designated recipients, and national foundations that have demonstrated interest in funding projects based in Idaho. The first edition (8p.) was issued in 1978 under the same title; the second (12p.) was released in 1980.

Illinois

440 **Illinois Foundation Profile.** Ed. by Leslie Upledger and Susan M. Levy. Chicago: Donors Forum, 1982. 48p. $7.50. Pap.

More a survey than a directory, this 1982 publication draws on data from the 1980 tax returns of 268 foundations located in Illinois to develop a picture of grantmaking activity in the state. The report indicates that funding in Illinois is dominated by large donors (e.g., John D. and Catherine T. MacArthur Foundation accounted for 21 percent of all grants awarded during the study period) and by large recipients. More directly of reference value is the eight-page appendix, which provides a giving profile for each of the foundations studied. Now considerably out of date, only limited copies are available for distribution from the Donors Forum.

Indiana

441 **Indiana Foundations: A Directory.** Ed. by Paula Reading Spear. 2d ed. Indianapolis: Central Research Systems, 1981. 147p. $19.95.

Nearly 300 grantmaking foundations in Indiana that have at least $10,000 in assets or make at least $1,000 a year in grants are described in this directory. The entries are arranged by foundation and indexed by financial criteria, subjects, and counties. The following information is provided: contact persons, officers, areas of interest, and typical grants awarded. Several other listings are also included: restricted foundations, corporate foundations, foundations for student assistance, and dissolved foundations. Although scheduled to be issued as a biennial, no edition later than 1981 has been published to date.

Iowa

442 **Iowa Directory of Foundations.** By Daniel H. Holm. 1st ed. Dubuque, IA: Trumpet Associates, 1984. 108p. 84–50380. $21.75. Pap.

Written by Daniel Holm, then vice president of Trumpet Associates (a consulting firm for nonprofit institutions), this directory concentrates on foundations located in Iowa. The information presented is based on 990–PF reports and data submitted by foundation officers. In all, 247 foundations are described. Program profiles are arranged alphabetically by foundation name and contain the following information: address and telephone number, employer identification number, fair market value of assets, total gifts and grants made in 1982, purpose, activities, officers/trustees, contact persons, and application procedures. The entries are indexed by city.

Kentucky

443 **Foundation Profiles of the Southeast: Kentucky, Tennessee, Virginia.** Ed. by James H. Taylor and John L. Wilson. Williamsburg, KY: James H. Taylor Associates, 1981. 153p. $39.95.

The following information, taken from 1978 and 1979 990–PF and 990–AR IRS return, is provided for 117 foundations in Kentucky, Tennessee, and Virginia: assets, total number and amount of grants, and officers. The entries are arranged alphabetically by foundation name and there are no indexes.

444 **Guide to Kentucky Grantmakers.** Ed. by Nancy C. Dougherty. Louisville, KY: Louisville Foundation, 1982. 19p. $7.50. Pap.

The 101 grantmakers in Kentucky that award $2,000 or more in annual grants are covered in this small directory. The information presented was gathered by the then 77–year old Louisville Foundation. Questionnaires were sent to all the listed foundations; only 16 responded (their entries are the most complete). Data for the other foundations were taken from 1981 990–PF and 990–AR IRS returns. Entries are arranged alphabetically by foundation name and specify assets, total grants paid, number of grants, size of grants, areas of interest, and contact person. No other access to the data is provided.

Louisiana

445 **Foundation Profiles of the Southeast: Alabama, Arkansas, Louisiana, Mississippi.** Comp. by James H. Taylor and John L. Wilson. Williamsburg, KY: James H. Taylor Associates, 1983. 119p. $39.95.

Information on 212 foundations in Louisiana, Mississippi, Arkansas, and Alabama is provided in this directory. For more information about the publication, see the annotation in the "Grants—General—Alabama" section of this bibliography.

Maine

446 A Directory of Foundations in the State of Maine. Portland: Center for Research and Advanced Study, University of Southern Maine, 1973– . Irreg. $5.50 (1983 ed.). Pap.

Based on 990–PF and 990–AR returns filed with the IRS, the fifth edition, issued in 1983 (39p.), covers 74 foundations in the state of Maine. In addition to the descriptive entries arranged alphabetically by city location, the directory contains a section on preparing grant requests, a description of IRS information returns, a bibliography, a list of recent grants, and a subject index. Earlier editions were published in 1973, 1975, 1978, and 1980. The first two editions were issued by Eastern Connecticut State College Foundation. Over the years, the title of the directory has varied slightly. It was originally released as *A Directory of Foundations and Charitable Trusts in the State of Maine.*

447 Guide to Corporate Giving in Maine. Ed. by Michael E. Burns. New Haven, CT: OUA/DATA, 1984– . Biennial. 85–646106. ISSN 0883–2830. $15. Pap.

The charitable activities of 218 Maine corporations are recorded in the first (1984) edition of this directory. Each of the corporations included had annual sales of at least $10 million or employed at least 200 staff members. All corporations have their headquarters or an operating unit located in Maine. The information reported was obtained from questionnaires and includes name of the corporation, address, contact person and telephone number, product, plants, frequency/deadlines, contributions, geographic preference, maximum size of single contribution, average size of contributions, total contributions, and giving interests. Corporate profiles are arranged alphabetically by name and indexed by city of location. This is one in a series of OUA/DATA guides to funding in New England. Once directories have been issued for all the states in New England, this title will be issued as a biennial.

448 Maine Corporate Funding Directory, 1984. By Janet F. Brysh. 2d ed. Portland: Center for Research and Advanced Study, University of Southern Maine, 1984. 77p. $10. Pap.

Unlike the *Directory of Foundations in the State of Maine* (see description in this section of the bibliography), which draws its information from IRS returns, this directory is based on data supplied by 75 corporations. The programs described offer support to the state's nonprofits. The entries, arranged alphabetically by corporate name, indicate areas of interest, geographic limitations, sample grants, and contact persons. Profiles vary in

length. Index access is provided by corporate name and areas of interest. The
first editon of the directory was published under the same title in 1981 (56p.).

Maryland

449 Annual Index Foundation Reports. Baltimore: Maryland Office of the
    Attorney General, 1979– . Irreg. $35 (1982 ed.).

Compiled by the Maryland Office of the Attorney General, the latest edition
(1982. 203p.) provides brief information on 380 foundations in the state:
name, address, employer identification number, foundation manager, and
total assets in book and market value. The source is arranged alphabetically
by foundation name (there are no indexes) and the entries consist of data
taken from 990–AR returns received by the state Attorney General's Office.
The first edition of this directory was published in 1979 under the same title.

450 Catalog of State Assistance Programs. Baltimore: Maryland
    Department of State Planning, 1985. 2d ed. 600p. 75–642476. ISSN
    0097-9309. $5. Pap.

Over $2.25 billion in grants, loans, information, and services available from
the state and federal government to public sector agencies and the general
public in Maryland are described in this directory. Entries specify sponsoring
organization, program title, address, telephone number, contact person, type
of assistance available, eligibility requirements, authorizing legislation,
printed information available, and application procedures. A previous edition
was published in 1983.

Massachusetts

451 Guide to Corporate Giving in Massachusetts. Ed. by Michael E. Burns.
    New Haven: OUA/DATA, 1984– . Biennial. 85–648128. ISSN
    0882-0449. $31.50. Pap.

This is the second volume in OUA/DATA's series on corporate giving in
New England (the first volume is *Guide to Corporate Giving in Connecticut*,
described in the "Grants—General—Connecticut" section of this
bibliography). Over 700 Massachusetts corporations with annual sales
exceeding $10 million or with at least 200 employees and an office in the state
are listed in the directory. Entries are arranged by city location and indexed
by corporation/city. Detailed information is not provided for all the listed
corporations, only those that responded to survey questionnaires or telephone
interviews. The first edition of this directory was published in 1984. Once
OUA/DATA has issued guides covering all the New England states, this
directory will be published as a biennial.

452 Massachusetts Foundation Directory. Boston: Associated Grantmakers of Massachsuetts, 1983. 136p. 83–641108. ISSN 0739–1315. ISBN 0–912427–00–0. $15. Pap.

Nearly 600 grantmaking foundations in Massachusetts that give at least $15,000 annually are covered in this directory. The entries describing the foundations' activities are arranged alphabetically by foundation and indexed by program areas, city, and foundations granting support to individuals. For each of the foundations included in the main section, the following information is provided: trustees, contact person, emphasis, areas of interest, total grants, range, and assets. The data presented were taken from 990–PF and 990–AR returns filed with the IRS and from questionnaries answered by the foundations. Listed in the appendices are smaller Massachusetts foundations, company-sponsored foundations, and recently terminated foundations. A *Supplement* (described in the "Scholarships—General—Massachusetts" section) was issued in 1984 to provide comprehensive information on private support for Massachusetts residents.

Michigan

453 The Michigan Foundation Directory. Prep. by the Council of Michigan Foundations and Michigan League for Human Services. 4th ed. Lansing: Michigan League for Human Services, 1983. 154p. 76–642379. ISSN 0362–1561. $15. Pap.

First published in 1976, this directory is more comprehensive than many of the other state listings. It can serve as a model guide. Cited here are 859 Michigan foundations with assets of more than $200,000 or grants of at least $5,000 per year. The entries are arranged alphabetically, with additional sections for Michigan foundations having assets of $200,000 or making grants of at least $25,000; foundations making grants of $1,000 or more annually; terminated foundations; and special purpose foundations. A geographic listing of foundations by city is also provided. New to this edition is a special section that profiles 48 corporate giving programs. In addition to typical directory information, entries for the larger foundations also specify time of the year requests are preferred, type of initial contact preferred, types of requests the foundation will consider, and whether an application or special format is required. Completing the volume are a survey of Michigan foundation philanthropy, information for grantseeking, and a set of indexes by subject area of interest, donor/trustee/officer, and foundation name.

454 Michigan Local Assistance Manual. Lansing: Michigan State Department of Commerce, 1981. 750p. $ll. Looseleaf.

Like the *Catalog of State Assistance Programs* in Maryland (described in the "Grants—General—Maryland" section), this directory identifies agencies, federal offices, and state universities in Michigan that offer grants, loans, information, and services to local government units. Arrangement is by department. Entries specify sponsoring organization, address and telephone number, contact persons, program title, purpose, type of assistance offered, authorizing legislation, eligibility requirements, and application procedures.

Minnesota

455   **Guide to Minnesota Foundations and Corporate Giving Programs.** By the Minnesota Council on Foundations. 3d ed. Minneapolis: University of Minnesota Press, 1983. 149p. 82–21928. ISBN 0–81661–219–6. $14.95. Pap.

This book, like the 1977 and 1980 editions, is designed to help individuals and organizations seeking grants in Minnesota as well as to aid grantmakers and the general public. Covered in the directory are 420 private, corporate, and community foundations in Minnesota. Information about them is taken primarily from 1980 and 1981 990–PF and 990–AR IRS returns. The 52 corporate sources listed account for 40 percent of the grants awarded annually. Specified in each entry are: statement of purpose, interests, funding limits, financial data, application procedures, geographic orientation, sample grants, and officers. Also included are a section on proposal writing; a description of foundations' review processes; lists of inactive foundations; foundations with designated recipients; foundations making grants only outside of Minnesota; and indexes of foundations, types of organizations, types of organizations funded, and grantmakers by size. The third edition was prepared by the Minnesota Council on Foundations (which published the first two editions) but was published by the University of Minnesota Press.

Mississippi

456   **Foundation Profiles of the Southeast: Alabama, Arkansas, Louisiana, Mississippi.** Comp. by James H. Taylor and John L. Wilson. Williamsburg, KY: James H. Taylor Associates, 1983. 119p. $39.95.

Information on 212 foundations in Mississippi, Alabama, Arkansas, and Louisiana is provided in this directory. For more information about the publication, see the annotation in the "Grants—General—Alabama" section of this bibliography.

Missouri

457   **Directory of Missouri Foundations.** By Wilda H. Swift. St. Louis: Swift Associates, 1985. 126p. 85–194617. ISSN 0884–7223. $15. Pap.

Information from income tax forms and from questionnaires is presented here for 788 grantmakers located in Missouri. Entries specify names of executive officers, mailing address, telephone number, total assets, limitations, geographic restrictions, largest and smallest grants made recently, major interests, and application procedures/deadlines.

Montana

458   The Montana and Wyoming Foundations Directory. 3d ed. Billings: Eastern Montana College Foundation, 1984. 28p. $7. Pap.

Covered in this small directory are 50 Montana and 20 Wyoming foundations. The profiles presented are based on information supplied by the foundations themselves, taken from the *National Data Book* (see description in the "Grants—General—United States" section), and extracted from 990–PF and 990–AR IRS returns. The information provided includes foundation name, address, telephone number, contact person, and areas of funding interest. The entries are arranged by foundation and indexed by name and areas of interest.

Nebraska

459   Nebraska Foundation Directory. Omaha, NE: Junior League of Omaha, 1981. 14p. $3. Pap.

Approximately 150 Nebraska foundations are listed alphabetically by foundation name in this directory. The entries contain information taken from the 1979 and 1980 990–PF and 990–AR returns filed with the IRS. Statement of purpose and officers are identified for each foundation. There are no indexes. The first edition was published in 1979 (77 leaves) under the same title.

Nevada

460   Nevada Foundation Directory. Prep. by Vlasta Honsa and Annetta Yousef. Las Vegas: Clark County Library District, 1985. 64p. 85–157150. $7. Pap.

Information is presented here on 41 foundations located in Nevada. Entries are arranged alphabetically by foundation name and are indexed by fields of interest and geographic location. The following information is provided for each foundation: funding interests, amounts awarded, contact person, and typical grants. The data presented were taken from 990–PF forms filed with the Internal Revenue Service and from interviews with foundation officials. In addition to the descriptions of active foundations in Nevada, the directory also includes lists of inactive or defunct foundations and national foundations that in the past have funded projects in Nevada.

New Hampshire

461 **Directory of Charitable Funds in New Hampshire: For General Charitable Purposes and Scholarship Aid.** 3d ed. Concord, NH: Office of the Attorney General, 1976. 107p. 77–624167. $2. Pap.

462 **Cumulative Supplement.** Concord, NH: Office of the Attorney General, 1977– . Annual. $2 (1984 ed.). Pap.

First issued in 1962, under the title *Directory of Charitable Trusts for Scholarships and General Charitable Uses,* the second and third editions were released in 1967 and 1976 respectively as the *Directory of Charitable Funds in New Hampshire: For General Charitable Purposes and Scholarship Aid.* For the purposes of this directory, "charitable purposes" are defined as "the aid of the needy, the relief of sickness and adversity, the advancement of education and religion, specialized programs which are of benefit to the general public and the community and individual scholarship aid." Omitted are trusts that fund specific charitable organizations and operating charities using their funds to provide services directly to the public. The entries are arranged alphabetically by sponsoring organization and indexed by geographic restrictions and subject interests. Each entry specifies sponsoring organization, founding date, purposes, assets, contact person, and address. A separate section charts the amount of money granted in 1975 by subject area (e.g., library, aged, scholarship, needy, family services) for each sponsoring organization. Each year, a cumulative supplement is issued that identifies changes in original entries, defunct programs, and additions to the 1976 listing. This arrangement is somewhat cumbersome to use, particularly for the "changes" noted. A complete rewrite of the 1976 *Directory* is planned for the near future.

463 **Guide to Corporate Giving in New Hampshire.** Ed. by Michael E. Burns. New Haven, CT: OUA/DATA, 1984– . Biennial. 85–646199. $15. Pap.

Like the other directories in the OUA/DATA series (see, for example, *Guide to Corporate Giving in Connecticut,* described in the "Grants—General—Connecticut" section), this guide provides information on New Hampshire corporate foundations with $10 million in annual sales that have offices in the state. The 239 entries, arranged alphabetically by foundation name, contain the following information: areas of interest, giving policies, geographic preferences, and contact person. The first edition of the directory was issued in 1984. Once OUA/DATA has issued guides to all the New England states, this directory will be scheduled as a biennial.

New Jersey

464 Catalogue of State Programs of Assistance to New Jersey Local Governments. Trenton: New Jersey Department of Community Affairs, 1972–1976. 3v. 73–620522.

Issued in 1972, 1976, and 1979 as the *Catalogue of State Programs of Assistance to New Jersey Local Governments*, this publication changed its name in 1985 to the *New Jersey State Catalog for Local Governments* (described elsewhere in this section of the bibliography).

465 Directory of Major New Jersey Foundations. Attleboro, MA: Logos, 1983. 56p. $19.95. Pap.

Selective in scope, this directory provides descriptions of less than 70 foundations located in New Jersey. Entries are arranged alphabetically by foundation name; there are no indexes. The information provided for each foundation includes activities, geographic restrictions, amounts granted, officers/trustees, contact person, and typical grants. The information is current as of 1982. For more extensive coverage of the same geographic area, see the *New Jersey Mitchell Guide* (described below), which covers 400 foundations and 600 corporations.

466 A Directory of New Jersey Foundations. Comp. by Janet A. Mitchell. Princeton, NJ: Mitchell Guides, 1980. 218p. 80–113117. ISSN 0743–9598.

The first edition of this directory was issued in 1977 (81p. 77–83083). A revision was issued in 1980, under the same title, and the next revision was released in 1983, under the title *New Jersey Mitchell Guide: Foundations, Corporations, and Their Managers* (described elsewhere in this section of the bibliography).

467 New Jersey Mitchell Guide: Foundations, Corporations, and Their Managers. Ed. by Janet A. Mitchell. 4th ed. Princeton, NJ: Mitchell Guides, 1985. 150p. 83–179198. ISSN 0743–9601. $65. Pap.

More up to date but less inclusive than *Foundations in New Jersey: A Directory* (2d ed. Trenton: New Jersey State Library, 1978. v.p.), this guide covers 400 New Jersey foundations with at least $100,000 in assets and which awarded at least $5,000 in 1980 or 1981 grants. Arranged alphabetically by foundation name, the entries present information taken from 990–PF and 990–AR returns filed with the IRS along with data supplied by the foundations themselves. Also included in the volume is a section that describes funding activities of 600 New Jersey-based corporations. Both the foundation and corporation entries are indexed by county and by managers. Appendices provide foundation statistics, list foundations with assets over $1 million, and identify foundations with grant totals over $100,000. There have been two editions issued under this title, one in 1983 and the next one in 1985. These volumes revise and update the 1980 *Directory of New Jersey Foundations* and list deletions from that publication. The first edition of the directory was issued in 1977, also under the title *Directory of New Jersey Foundations*.

468 New Jersey State Aid Catalog for Local Governments. Comp. and ed. by Diane Coyle. 4th ed. Trenton: New Jersey Department of Community Affairs, 1985. 300p. in v.p. $7. Pap.

This catalog was compiled "to help local government officials and concerned citizens avail themselves of over three hundred State assistance programs— grants and services—that are provided by the State of New Jersey for their benefit." The catalog is divided into three sections: information on how to contact state agencies (including addresses, telephone numbers, and maps); techniques to use in obtaining and administering state and federal grants; and a listing of all programs of state aid and assistance. The program entries in the third section ar arranged by sponsoring agency and provide a brief description of the program, the kinds of assistance available, eligibility requirements, and contact person. The entries are indexed by program title and by purpose. The first three editions of this directory (1972, 1976, and 1979) were issued as the *Catalogue of State Programs of Assistance to New Jersey Local Governments*. Along with the *Catalog of California State Grants Assistance* (described in the "Grants—General—California" section), this is one of only a few directories that identify grant programs sponsored by state agencies.

New Mexico

469 New Mexico Private Foundations Directory. Ed. by William G. Murrell and William M. Miller. Tijeras, NM: New Moon Consultants, 1982. 77p. 82–149332. $5.50. Pap.

Covered in this directory are 35 New Mexico foundations, nine corporate funding sources, and six local libraries. The amount of information presented for each varies. For those foundations that responded to the authors' questionnaires, the entries specify contact person, program purpose, areas of interest, financial data, application procedures, meeting times, and publications. For the others, the profiles are brief. The directory is arranged by foundation. Addressed in separate sections are proposal writing, corporate grantsmanship, and sources of additional information. There are no indexes.

New York

470 The Mitchell Guide to Foundations, Corporations and Their Managers: Central New York State. Ed. by Rowland L. Mitchell. Princeton, NJ: Mitchell Guides, 1985. 74p. 85–23786. $25. Pap.

471 The Mitchell Guide to Foundations, Corporations and Their Managers: Long Island. Ed. by Rowland L. Mitchell. Princeton, NJ: Mitchell Guides, 1985. 99p. $30. Pap.

472 The Mitchell Guide to Foundations, Corporations and Their Managers: Upper Hudson Valley. Ed. by Rowland L. Mitchell. Princeton, NJ: Mitchell Guides, 1985. 46p. 85–23785. $25. Pap.

473 The Mitchell Guide to Foundations, Corporations and Their Managers: Westchester. Ed. by Rowland L. Mitchell. Princeton, NJ: Mitchell Guides, 1985. 94p. 85–23788. $30. Pap.

474 The Mitchell Guide to Foundations, Corporations and Their Managers: Western New York State. Ed. by Rowland L. Mitchell. Princeton, NJ: Mitchell Guides, 1985. 95p. 85–23784. $30. Pap.

475 The New York City Mitchell Guide to Foundations, Corporations, and Their Managers. Ed. by Rowland L. Mitchell. Princeton, NJ: Mitchell Guides, 1983. 413p. 84–33954. $75. Pap.

Each of the six volumes in this set covering New York follows the same arrangement. The main sections are organized alphabetically by foundation and by corporation. The entries, which are based on data taken from 990–PF returns filed with the Internal Revenue Service, identify officers, financial data, and typical grants awarded. Indexes of foundations/corporations and managers are provided in each volume. The number of organizations and the extent of geographic coverage varies from title to title. In *Central New York State*, descriptions are presented for 62 foundations and 125 corporations in Binghamton, Corning, Elmira, Geneva, Ithaca, Oswego, Syracuse, and Utica. In *Long Island*, 149 foundations and 125 corporations in Nassau and Suffolk counties are covered. In *Upper Hudson Valley*, information is provided for 61 foundations and 125 corporations in Albany and Glenns Falls, Newburgh, Plattsburgh, Poughkeepsie, and Schenectady. In *Westchester*, 148 foundations and 58 corporations in Putnam, Rockland, and parts of Orange County are described. In *Western New York State*, the coverage extends to 125 foundations and 132 corporations in Buffalo, Jamestown, Niagara Falls, and Rochester. *New York City* includes descriptions of 1,832 foundations and 750 corporations located in that municipal area.

476 State Aid to Local Government. Albany: New York State Department of Audit and Control, 1952– . Annual. Free. Pap.

Like the *Michigan Local Assistance Manual* (described in the Grants— General—Michigan" section of this bibliography), this annual directory lists state agencies in New York that are administering programs of assistance for local governmental units. The state aid programs are divided into 10 categories, nine of which are directly associated with the major functions of local government (e.g., community service, education, environmental control). The tenth section, "General Purpose Aid," identifies funds made available to lessen local tax burdens. Each category begins with the names and addresses of the agencies responsible for administering the programs. This is followed by a summary of actual program expenditures in the previous fiscal year, and a listing of annual total payments in the category since 1961. Finally, there is an individual description of each current program, specifying eligible municipalities, purpose for which aid is used, apportionment formula, governing provisions of state law, and trend of payments since 1961. These descriptions are deleted whenever a program is discontinued.

North Carolina

477 **Foundation Profiles of the Southeast: North Carolina, South Carolina.** Comp. by James H. Taylor and John L. Wilson. Williamsburg, KY: James H. Taylor Associates, 1983. 100p. $39.95.

Descriptions of nearly 500 foundations in North Carolina and South Carolina are arranged alphabetically by foundation. The entries specify officers, assets, total grants, and typical grants awarded. There are no indexes. Data are taken from 990–PF and 990–AR returns filed with the Internal Revenue Service.

Ohio

478 **Charitable Foundations Directory of Ohio.** Columbus, OH: Office of the Attorney General, 1973– . Biennial. 81–622662. $6 (6th ed.). Pap.

Prepared by the Ohio State Attorney General's Office, this biennial directory is intended to benefit individuals and organizations seeking grants and other types of assistance from charitable foundations in Ohio. The sixth edition, issued in 1984 (105p.), includes all organizations reporting to the Attorney General's Office under Ohio Revised Code 109.31 and the Federal Tax Reform Act of 1969, regardless of the extent of assets or distribution. Because of this loose definition of "foundation," there are a surprising number of entries (1,200), some of which are trusts wholly devoted to named recipients and a number with zero assets and grants. The source is arranged alphabetically by foundation and indexed by counties and purpose. Each entry specifies, in addition to the usual data, the name of the individual handling grants, restrictions, trust number, and purpose code. Previous editions were issued in 1973, 1975, 1978, 1980, and 1982.

Oklahoma

479 **Directory of Oklahoma Foundations.** Ed. by Thomas E. Broce. 2d ed. Norman: University of Oklahoma Press, 1982. 284p. 82–6984. ISBN 0–8061–1827–X. $22.50.

The first edition of this directory was issued in 1974 (304p. 73–7430. ISBN 0–80611–123–2). Since then, the state's foundations decreased numerically by 17 percent but increased in terms of awards and assets by 112 percent and 272 percent respectively. The second edition, revised and enlarged, was published in 1982. In it, profiles for 150 Oklahoma foundations are arranged by foundation name and indexed by grant activities. Entries provide information on address, telephone number, name and title of director, goals, grant interests, and financial activities. The data presented in each entry are taken directly from cooperating foundations or off their 1974 through 1981 990–PF and 990–AR returns. The entries are arranged alphabetically and indexed by area of interest.

Oregon

480 **Guide to Oregon Foundations.** By Craig McPherson. 3d ed. Portland, OR: United Way of the Columbia-Willamette, 1984. 215p. 85–106385. $15. Pap.

Over 300 Oregon foundations are described in the third edition of this directory. The data are taken primarily from the 1982 and 1983 990–PF, 990–AR, and CT-12 forms filed with the Oregon Register of Charitable Trusts. Entries are grouped into six categories, including general purpose foundations, special purpose foundations, and national foundations with an active interest in Oregon. Included as appendices are lists of Oregon foundations with assets of $500,000 or more, Oregon foundations making annual grants of $50,000 or more, terminated foundations, inactive foundations, new foundations, national foundation grants to Oregon, and Oregon community foundations. The volume concludes with a regional breakdown of foundations, a glossary of fundraising terms, and an index of foundation names. Previous editions of the directory were published by the Tri-County Community Council in 1977 (262p. 78–106643) and in 1981 (208p. 81–203269).

Pennsylvania

481 **Directory of Pennsylvania Foundations.** Comp. by S. Damon Kletzien, with assistance from Margaret H. Chalfant and Frances C. Ritchey. 2d ed. Philadelphia: Free Library of Philadelphia, 1981. 180p. $18.50.

The main section of this directory consists of over 2,000 Pennsylvania foundations arranged alphabetically within five geographic regions. Each profile of foundations with assets of more than $75,000 or awarding grants in excess of $4,000 gives: representative grants or an analysis of the grantmaking process, funding areas, application guidelines, telephone numbers, and names of trustees, directors, and principal officers. The information presented is taken either from the 1979 and 1980 990–PF and 990–AR returns filed with the IRS or from questionnaires returned by the foundations. Additional sections in the directory cover program planning, proposal writing, approaching foundations, and broadening the foundation search. There are three indexes: officers, directors, and trustees; funding interests; and foundation name. A new edition is being planned.

Rhode Island

482 **Directory of Grant-Making Foundations in Rhode Island.** Providence: Council for Community Services, 1983. 47p. $8. Pap.

Approximately 100 grantmaking foundations in Rhode Island are described in this small directory. The entries are arranged alphabetically by foundation. They contain information on officers/trustees, purpose, geographic restrictions, assets, amounts granted, number awarded, and application process. There are three indexes: foundations by amount granted; foundations by location; and foundations by area of interest. The data presented are taken from 990–PF and 990–AR returns filed with the Internal Revenue Service, information supplied by foundation officers, and information available in the Rhode Island Attorney General's Office. Not covered in the directory are operating foundations, foundations that concentrate on a single beneficiary or limited benificiaries, foundations that make only small grants to needy individuals, and those that serve groups outside of Rhode Island.

483 **Guide to Corporate Giving in Rhode Island.** Ed. by Michael E. Burns. New Haven, CT: OUA/DATA, 1984– . Biennial. 85–646107. $15. Pap.

Compiled as a "first step toward identifying potential resource support," this directory provides information on the charitable activities of 188 Rhode Island corporations. To be included, corporations had to have recorded sales of $10 million annually or have employed at least 200 staff members. All listed corporations have their headquarters or an operating unit located in Rhode Island. The entries are arranged alphabetically and indexed by city location. The information provided includes: name of corporation, address, contact person and telephone number, products, plants, frequency/deadlines, contributions, geographic preferences, minimum size of single contribution, average size of contribution, total contributions, and giving interests. The first edition of this directory was issued in 1984. Once OUA/DATA has prepared guides to all New England states, this directory will be issued as a biennial.

South Carolina

484 **Foundation Profiles of the Southeast: North Carolina, South Carolina.**
Comp. by James H. Taylor and John L. Wilson. Williamsburg, KY:
James H. Taylor Associates, 1983. 100p. $39.95.

Descriptions of nearly 500 foundations in North Carolina and South
Caroliona are arranged alphabetically by foundation in this directory. For
more information about the publication, see the annotation in the "Grants—
General—North Carolina" section of this bibliography.

485 **South Carolina Foundation Directory.** Ed. by Anne K. Middleton. 2d
ed. Columbia: South Carolina State Library, 1983. 51p. 84–62093. $5.
Pap.

There are nearly 200 grantmaking foundations in South Carolina described in
this directory. About 90 percent of these have less than $1 million in assets.
The entries are arranged alphabetically by foundation and indexed by city
and areas of interest. The following information is provided for each of the
foundations: officers, areas of interest, geographical restrictions, assets, total
grants awarded, number awarded, and range of grants. The first edition of the
directory was published in 1978 (53p.) under the same title.

Tennessee

486 **Foundation Profiles of the Southeast: Kentucky, Tennessee, Virginia.**
Ed. by James H. Taylor and John L. Wilson. Williamsburg, KY: James
H. Taylor Associates, 1981. 153p. $39.95.

The funding activities of 117 foundations in Tennessee, Kentucky, and
Virginia are described in this directory. For more information about the
publication, see the annotation in the "Grants—General—Kentucky" section
of this bibliography.

487 **Tennessee Directory of Foundations and Corporate Philanthropy.** Rev.
ed. Memphis: Bureau of Intergovermental Management, 1985. 117p.
$20. Pap.

This directory is divided into two main sections. The first focuses on
grantmaking foundations (83) in Tennessee; the other on grantmanking
corporations (23) in Tennessee. In both sections, the program descriptions are
arranged alphabetically by organization and specify contact person, officers,
areas of interest, geographic restrictions, financial data, sample grants, and
application process. The entries are indexed by name, areas of interest, and
geographic coverage. In a separate section, foundations in Tennessee giving
less than $10,000 per year and major corporations in Tennessee that employ

more than 300 staff members are listed. An earlier editon was published in 1982 (134p.).

Texas

488 Directory of Texas Foundations. Comp. and ed. by William J. Hooper, Jr. Austin: Texas Foundation Research Center, 1978–1982. Annual. 75–311891.

From 1978 through 1982, this annual was issued as the *Directory of Texas Foundations.* Since 1983, the directory has been published as *Hooper Directory of Texas Foundations* (described elsewhere in this section of the bibliography).

489 The Guide to Texas Foundations. Ed. by Jed Riffe. 2d ed. Dallas: Dallas Public Library, 1980. 103p. $10. Pap.

Described in this directory are approximately 200 Texas foundations awarding grants in excess of $30,000 per year. Entries specify statements of purpose, typical grants awarded, officers, and grant amounts. The data were taken from the 1977 and 1978 records in the Texas Attorney General's Office and the Dallas Public Library. Foundation profiles are arranged by city location and indexed by name and areas of interest. The first edition of the directory was published in 1975 (104p.) by the Southern Resource Center.

490 Hooper Directory of Texas Foundations. Comp. and ed. by William J. Hooper, Jr. and Amie Rodnick. Austin: Texas Foundation Research Center, 1983– . Annual. 75–311891. $25 (8th ed.). Pap.

More up to date but also more expensive than the *Guide to Texas Foundations* (described elsewhere in this section of the bibliography), this directory describes over 1,300 grantmaking foundations in Texas. The entries are arranged alphabetically by foundation and indexed by areas of interest, cities, and trustees. Information is provided on areas of interest and contact person. Dissolved foundations and the top 100 foundations in Texas are each listed in separate sections. From 1978 through 1982, the directory was issued under the title *Directory of Texas Foundations.*

Utah

491 A Directory of Foundations in Utah. By Lynn Madera Jacobsen. Salt Lake City: University of Utah Press, 1985. 270p. 85–11228. ISBN 0–87480–245–8. $50. Pap.

This directory contains financial and organizational information on almost 175 public and private foundations in Utah. It also lists officers, advisers, contact persons, recipients, and value of grants awarded. The information is based in part on Internal Revenue Service tax returns from 1980–1981. There is a cross-referenced index of officers, directors, and advisors to Utah foundations. Biennial revisions are planned.

Vermont

492 **Guide to Corporate and Foundation Giving in Vermont.** Ed. by Michael E. Burns. New Haven, CT: OUA/DATA, 1984– . Biennial. $15. Pap.

DATA (Development and Technical Assistance Research Resource Center) is a project of the Office of Urban Affairs (OUA). OUA is the official social action agency of the Archdioceses of Hartford. Like the other volumes in the OUA/DATA series of New England directories, this publication focuses on corporate and foundation giving (in this case, in Vermont). Corporate foundations must have $10 million annual sales and an office or operating unit in the state to be listed. The 188 entries, arranged alphabetically by corporation/foundation name, contain information on areas of interest, giving policies, geographic preferences, and contact persons. Indexing is by geographic location. The first edition of this directory was issued in 1984. Once OUA/DATA has prepared guides to all New England states, this directory will be issued as a biennial.

Virginia

493 **Foundation Profiles of the Southeast: Kentucky, Tennessee, Virginia.** Ed. by James H. Taylor and John L. Wilson. Williamsburg, KY: James H. Taylor Associates, 1981. 153p. $39.95.

The funding activities of 117 foundations in Tennessee, Kentucky, and Virginia are described in this directory. For more information about the publication, see the annotation in the "Grants—General—Kentucky" section of this bibliography.

494 **Virginia Foundations, 1984.** Hampton, VA: Grants Resource Library, 1984. 200p. $10. Pap.

Approximately 500 grantmaking foundations in Virginia are arranged alphabetically in this directory and are described in terms of officers/ directors, assets, total grants offered, and typical grants awarded. The data presented here were taken from the 1980 through 1983 990–PF and 990–AR returns filed with the Internal Revenue Service.

Washington

495 **Charitable Trust Directory.** Olympia, WA: Office of the Attorney General, 1983. 242p. $4. Pap.

Nearly 1,000 Washington foundations are covered in this directory. The information presented is based on registration and reporting forms gathered by the Attorney General's Office under the Washington Charitable Trust Act. The main section of the work is arranged alphabetically by organization. Standard directory-type information is presented for each institution, but the "purpose" category is often listed as "general" or not stated and "officers" are frequently the name of a single officer or bank. There are no indexes.

Wisconsin

496 **Foundations in Wisconsin: A Directory.** Comp. by Susan H. Hopwood. Milwaukee: Foundation Collection, Marquette University Memorial Library, 1975– . Biennial. 75–647625. ISSN 0360–8042. $15 (1984 ed.). Pap.

First issued in 1975 (compiled by Barbara Szyszko. 250p.), the latest edition of this biennial describes nearly 700 Wisconsin foundations (1984. 282p.). Since there are no size qualifications for inclusion, assets vary from more than $10 million to none. Asset data are given at market value. Arranged alphabetically by foundation name, the entries contain information based on 1980 and 1981 990–PF and 990–AR returns filed with the IRS. Additional access to the entries is provided through the country, foundation managers, and funding interest indexes. A listing of terminated, inactive, and operating foundations completes the work.

Wyoming

497 **The Montana and Wyoming Foundations Directory.** 3d. ed. Billings: Eastern Montana College Foundation, 1984. 28p. $7. Pap.

Covered in this small directory are 20 Wyoming and 50 Montana foundations. The profiles presented are based on information supplied by the foundations themselves, taken from the *National Data Book* (see description in the "Grants—General—United States" section), and extracted from 990–PF and 990–AR IRS returns. The information provided includes foundation name, address, telephone number, contact person, and areas of funding interest. The entries are arranged by foundation and indexed by name and areas of interest.

498 Wyoming Foundations Directory. Prep. by Joy Riske. 2d ed. Cheyenne, WY: Laramie County Community College Library, 1982. 54p. $2. Pap.

Information on 45 Wyoming foundations, taken from the 1980 through 1982 990–PF and 990–AR returns filed with the IRS, is presented in this small directory (available from the Laramie County Community College Library, 1400 East College Drive, Cheyenne, WY 82007). Also included are a list of foundations based out of the state that award grants in Wyoming, a list of foundations awarding scholarships and educational loans, and a foundation index. The first edition of the directory was issued in 1981 (49p.). The 1982 edition is now out of print, but a third edition is in process.

SOCIAL SCIENCES

General

499 ARIS Funding Messenger: Social and Natural Sciences Report. San Francisco: Academic Research Information System, 1976– . 8 times/ yr., plus supplements. 84–8697. ISSN 0747–9921. $79, individuals; $165, institutions.

This current awareness service, begun in 1976, presents up-to-date information on public and private funding in the fields of (1) social sciences research, including business, education, law, and the behavioral sciences; (2) natural sciences research, including agriculture, computer sciences, engineering, environmental sciences, mathematics, and space sciences. Each entry provides address, telephone number, concise guidelines, and deadline dates. The reports are issued every six weeks, and supplements are issued as needed, to include deadlines and RFPs announced after a report's publication date. While the price for this service may seem a little steep, its comprehensiveness and currency are well worth the price.

500 Church Funds for Social Justice: A Directory. 2d ed. Minneapolis: Greater Minneapolis Council of Churches, 1984. 94p. $8. Pap.

This directory identifies local, regional, and national church funding sources that are interested in supporting social change organizations. Many faiths are represented, including Jewish, Roman Catholic, Presbyterian, Lutheran, Methodist, Baptist, and Unitarian. The focus is on the Minneapolis area. Each source listed granted a minimum of $500 annually to at least one social change organization working primarily on the local level. The entries are arranged by sponsoring organization and contain the following information: church name, address, telephone number, contact person, type of assistance provided, remuneration, areas of interest, restrictions, application procedures, and sample grants. This directory was first issued in 1983 (106p.) and was updated in 1985, just at the time when state and federal funding in this area was drastically curtailed. By identifying church funding, this publication serves as a "godsend" for social justice groups.

501 Federal Funding Programs for Social Scientists. Comp. by Kathleen Bond. Washington, DC: American Sociological Association, 1980. 84p. (Professional Information series). ISBN 0–317–36341–7. $5. Pap.

This directory is both out of date and limited in its coverage. Only 50 federal programs supporting social science research are described. While the entries are detailed and give examples of funded programs, the information on each is taken from 1977 or earlier editions of the *Catalog of Federal Domestic Assistance*. There is no index, so the user must page through the entire text. At the end of the volume, three brief appendices identify additional sources of information on federal funding opportunities and on some of the federal funding mechanisms.

502 GrantSeekers Guide: Funding Sourcebook. Mt. Kisco, NY: Moyer Bell, 1985. 550p. ISBN 0–918825–05–9, cloth; -10–5, pap. $21.95, cloth; $16.95, pap.

Included in this one-of-a-kind directory are program and financial data on over 170 local and national foundations that have supported economic and social justice programs. The emphasis is on community-based programs. Listed foundations have assets in excess of $1 million or grantmaking budgets in excess of $100,000. Each entry includes the following information: address, contact person, purpose, areas of interest, size of grants, application procedures, grant limitations, and publications. The entries are arranged alphabetically by foundation name within in national and regional sections; they are indexed by foundation name, geographic giving, subject matter, and contact persons. Also included in the volume are sections on technical assistance (including how to approach a grantmaker and how to research a foundation), and a brief, annotated bibliography listing other technical assistance resources. Earlier editions of this directory were issued under the titles *The Grantseekers Guide: A Directory for Social and Economic Justice Projects* and *Directory of Change Oriented Foundations*; both of these editions were published by the National Network of Grantmakers.

503 Public Media Center's Index of Progressive Funders, 1985–86 Edition. Ed. by Bill Hartman. San Francisco: Public Media Center, 1985. 466p. 84–62417. ISBN 0–915287–16–1. $40, nonprofit groups advocating social change; $50, others.

The Public Media Center is a nonprofit advertising agency and communications firm specializing in public interest media campaigns. The

Center has prepared two editions of the *Index of Progressive Funders*; the 1985/86 edition provides the latest information on more than 130 foundations, trusts, church groups, funds, and individual givers who make grants to social change organizations in such areas as disarmament, women's issues, civil rights, economic justice, and citizen advocacy. Entries are arranged alphabetically by sponsoring organization and indexed by subject. There is a separate section for church-related programs. Each entry begins with a brief description of funding interests and priorities, followed by a listing of recent and typical grants. In all, over 5,600 grants—totaling more than $1 million—are identified. This directory provides the most comprehensive and current overview of progressive funding available. The first edition was published in 1983.

504 Social Science Research Council Fellowships and Grants to Be Offered for Training and Research. New York: Social Science Research Council. Annual. Free. Pap.

This annual pamphlet describes advanced research grants and dissertation fellowships in both the social sciences and humanities that are open to American and foreign citizens on the advanced graduate or postgraduate levels. For more information about the publication, see the annotation in the "Fellowships—Social Sciences—General" section of this bibliography.

Anthropology

505 Funding for Anthropological Research. Ed. by Karen Cantrell and Denise Wallen. Phoenix: Oryx, 1986. 308p. 85–43172. ISBN 0–89774–154–4. $74.50. Pap.

Published in 1986, this directory identifies 700 funding programs (fellowships, grants, loans, and scholarships) available from 200 government agencies, private and corporate foundations, associations, institutes, museums, libraries, and professional societies that would be of interest to "professional anthropologists and graduate anthropology students." The entries are arranged by sponsoring organization and indexed by subject and sponsor type. There is a separate list of sponsoring organizations at the end of the volume which duplicates the addresses but omits the telephone numbers found in the profiles. Detailed information is provided for each of the programs covered, including data on purpose and activities, eligibility and limitations, deadlines, funding, subject indexing, and the *Catalog of Federal Domestic Asssitance* program number for federal programs. The book is attractively produced and easy to use for reference purposes. However, no definition for "anthropology" is given (except to indicate that it is being "broadly defined") and a number of the included programs seem to be somewhat outside the scope of the subject (e.g., American Lung Association's

Research Grants, Epilepsy Foundation of America's Research Grants). For the same price, Oryx Press' *Directory of Research Grants*, described in the "Grants—General—United States" section, will cover many of the same programs, and more.

Business and Economics

506   Banker's Handbook of Federal Aid to Financing. Boston, H.S. Spolan, 1971—1976. Irreg. 75–309857.

The first two editions of this directory were published in 1971 and 1974. A supplement was released in 1976. Since 1979, this guide has been issued as *Handbook of Federal Assistance: Financing, Grants* (described elsewhere in this section of the bibliography).

507   Direct Investment and Development in the U.S.: A Guide to Incentive Programs, Laws and Restrictions. Washington, DC: Transnational Investments, 1980. 443p. 80–51673. $75. Pap.

An earlier version of *Directory of Incentives for Business Investment and Development in the United States* (described elsewhere in this section of the bibliography), this guide identifies federal and state incentive programs offered to foreign and domestic investors that were designed to encourage industry and investment in 1980. Entries specify program title, sponsoring organization address and contact person, program description, eligibility, legal provisions, application process, authorizing legislation, and related laws and regulations. A separate section lists state development agencies. In 1979, the directory was published as *U.S. Incentives and Restrictions on Foreign Investment* (413p. 79–64318).

508   Directory of Federal and State Business Assistance, 1986–1987: A Guide for New and Growing Companies. Springfield, VA: National Technical Information Service, 1986. 176p. ISBN 0–934213–05–8. $19. Pap.

Most states now have active programs designed to help new and growing businesses. Available services include venture financing, planning help, product marketing, employee training, export assistance, site location, technology development, and technical/management information. This new guide from the Department of Commerce's National and Technical Information Service (NTIS) provides comprehensive access to both federal sources (180 programs) and state sources (400 programs) of business assistance. Each entry gives a summary of the services offered, a telephone number and address, and eligibility requirements (if any). Use this listing to learn how to get funding for R&D projects, where to get mailing lists of potential overseas buyers, which states provide venture money, how to take advantage of free export assistance, what federal and state contacts offer management consulting, and where to find free evaluations of energy-related inventions. A companion volume to this guide is the *Directory of Federal Laboratory & Technology Resources: A Guide to Services, Facilities, and Expertise,* also published by NTIS, which links U.S. businesses to the capabilities and know-how of hundreds of federal laboratories and research centers willing to share their services.

509 Directory of Incentives for Business Investment and Development in the United States: A State-by-State Guide. Prep. by the National Association of State Development Agencies, National Council for Urban Economic Development. Washington, DC: Urban Institute Press, 1983. 652p. 83–10400. ISBN 0–87766–324–6. $65. Pap.

This directory provides a little different slant to "financial assistance." The focus is on state industrial incentives for business financing and development. The source is divided into two parts. The first part describes each type of incentive or element found in the state programs; the second covers incentive programs by state. In all, 600 state business location and expansion financial incentive programs are described. Each entry specifies program title, name, address, telephone number, terms and conditions of the program, eligibility criteria, application procedure, and volume or level of program activity. Preceding each state section is an overview of the state's economic development, foreign investments, export promotion tax incentives, and nonfinancial assistance. Indexing is by incentive/state. There are separate English and Japanese editions. An update is planned.

510 Directory of State and Federal Funds for Business Development. Babylon, NY: Pilot Books, 1985. 48p. 84–22745. ISBN 0–87576–116–X. $5. Pap.

Many states and local communities are currently trying to expand their industrial base. To attract businesses to their area, these states and communities are offering an array of financial inducements. This pamphlet describes the industrial development programs offered by each of the 50 states, Puerto Rico, and the federal government in 1985. The following information is given for each entry: sponsoring organization, address, telephone number, contact person, and funding available. There is no index.

511 Federal Handbook for Small Business. Washington, DC: G.P.O., 1962–1966. 2v.

The first two editions of the handbook were published under this title. Currently, it is being issued as the *Handbook for Small Business* (described elsewhere in this section of the bibliography).

512 Financial Aid for Minorities in Business. Ed. by Howard F. Wehrle, III and Ruth N. Swann. Garrett Park, MD: Garrett Park Press, 1980. 48p. 80–144474. $3. Pap.

This booklet, published in 1980, lists grants, fellowships, and scholarships open to minorities interested in business administration. For more information about the publication, see the annotation in the "Scholarships— Social Sciences—Business and Economics" section of this bibliography.

513 Free Money for Professional Studies. By Laurie Blum. New York: Barnes and Noble, 1985. 204p. (Blum's Guides to College Money). 85–42725. ISBN 0–06–464104–0. $5.95. Pap.

This guide identifies state-based organizations awarding grants, fellowships, and scholarships to their residents, miscellaneous awards available to special applicants (e.g., deaf children, veterans' dependents), and selected financial aid programs appropriate for "professional studies" (including business administration). For more information about the publication, see the annotation in the "Fellowships—Sciences—Health Sciences" section of this bibliography.

514 Guide to Federal Minority Enterprise and Related Assistance Programs. Rev. ed. Washington, DC: Minority Business Development Agency, U.S. Department of Commerce, 1982. 44p. 83–644813. ISSN 0739–6066. Free. Pap.

This directory was prepared by the Minority Business Development Agency (MBDA) in collaboration with the federal departments included in its Interagency Council for Minority Business Enterprise. The pamphlet is divided into eight sections, only one of which deals specifically with financial assistance. The publication is intended to be issued biennially. The previous edition (1980) was released under the title *Guide to Federal Assistance Programs for Minority Business Development* (81–642274. ISSN 0277–5972).

515 Guide to Government Resources for Economic Development: A Handbook for Nonprofit Agencies and Municipalities. Washington, DC: Northeast-Midwest Institute, 1979– . Irreg. 83–9394. ISSN 0735–6226. $19.95 (1983 ed.). Pap.

Originally published to help members of Congress and their staffs reply to inquiries about federal grants and loans, this guide (in the 1983 edition) continues to focus on "those programs most important to developing overall economic development strategies." Each edition is arranged by major department or agency in the federal government. Lengthy program descriptions are provided. The entries are indexed by type of need, departments, agencies, program titles, and subject. Although announced as an annual, publication has been irregular to date. The 1983 edition was issued under the title *Guide to Government Resources for Economic Development.* Earlier editions had different titles. In 1979 and 1981, the directory was released as *Guide to Federal Resources for Economic Development;* the 1982 edition was entitled *The User's Guide to Government Resources for Economic Development.*

516 Handbook for Small Business: A Survey of Small Business Programs of the Federal Government. Washington, DC: G.P.O., 1962– . Irreg. 85–601200. $7. Pap.

This guide contains highlights and descriptions of selected federal programs that are designed to assist small businesses. It was first published in 1962 under the title *Federal Handbook for Small Business.* The most recent edition was released in 1984 under the title *Handbook for Small Business* (228p.); it was distributed in microfiche to some depository libraries.

517 Handbook of Federal Assistance: Financing, Grants. Boston: Warren, Gorham & Lamont, 1979– . Irreg. 79–57200. $56 (1982 ed.).

The first two editions of this directory were published (1971, 1974) by H.S. Spolan as *Banker's Handbook of Federal Aid to Financing.* A supplement was issued in 1976 under the same title. Since 1979, the directory has been distributed as *Handbook of Federal Assistance.* The latest edition was released in 1982 (ed. by Eric Stevenson. 673p. 82–70715). It identifies more than 700 sources of financial assistance offered by the federal government that can be used in banking. The entries are classified by topic and indexed by type of assistance and type of applicant. The following information is given for each program: type of assistance offered, purpose of program, eligibility, program operation and use, application process, amount of financial assistance, regulations, guidelines, and contact person.

518 Small Business Guide to Federal R&D Funding Opportunities. Washington, DC: National Science Foundation, 1978– . Irreg. 81–602110. $6 (1983 ed.). Pap.

This irregularly-issued directory identifies federal agencies that offer significant research and development programs. Entries specify sponsoring organization, contact persons, scope of the support programs, and areas of major interest. First published in 1978, the latest edition was released in 1983 (136p. 83–602408).

519 The User's Guide to Government Resources for Economic Development. Washington, DC: Northeast-Midwest Institute, 1982. 168p. 82–644121. ISSN 0730–6288. Pap.

The first two editions (1979, 1981) of this directory were issued under the title *Guide to Federal Resources for Economic Development.* It was released in

1982 as *The User's Guide to Government Resources for Economic Development.* Since 1983, the listing has been published as the *Guide to Government Resources for Economic Development: A Handbook for Nonprofit Agencies and Municipalities* (described elsewhere in this section of the bibliography).

Education

520 C.A.S.E. Matching Gift Details. Washington, DC: Council for Advancement and Support of Education, 1982– . Annual. 84–642360. ISBN 0–89964–237–3, cloth; -218–7, pap. $60 (1986 ed.), cloth; $39.95 (1986 ed.), pap.

Published annually since 1982, this directory provides information on nearly 1,000 corporation that match employee gifts to educational institutions and/ or noneducational, nonprofit organizations. The entries indicate organizations that qualify for matching gifts, which employees are eligible, whether or not spouses' or retirees' gifts will be matched, the minimum and maximum dollar amount the company will match, how to obtain the company portion of the match, and how often the money is distributed. In the appendices, a state-by-state breakdown of company contacts is presented, along with a list of all divisions, subsidiaries, and affiliated companies included in the parent company's programs. To update the listings provided here, use C.A.S.E.'s quarterly newsletter, *Matching Gift Notes* (described below).

521 Catalog of Federal Education Assistance Programs: An Indexed Guide to the Federal Government's Programs Offering Educational Benefits to the American People. Washington, DC: G.P.O., 1972– . Biennial. 72–603497. ISSN 0097–7802. $9.50 (1980 ed.). Pap.

This catalog is a compilation of all federal agencies' programs affording educational opportunities, assistance, and benefits, including aid for study abroad. Excluded from the catalog are benefits or assistance available only to current employees of the federal government (either civilian or military) and federal procurement or contracting. Entries provide information on purpose, financial assistance available, and eligibility requirements for the program. The federal officers to contact for additional information on each program are identified. The information presented here is also available online through the *Federal Assistance Programs Retrieval System* (described in the "Databases and Search Services" chapter). Six different indexes are included to help the user identify relevant programs (e.g., authorization index, beneficiary index, and program name index. The programs listed here also appear in the *Catalog of Federal Domestic Assistance* (described in the "Grants—General—United States" section of this bibliography). The latest edition of the *Catalog of Federal Education Assistance Programs* was released in 1980 (718p.) and is now out of print.

522 CFAE Casebook: A Cross Section of Corporate Aid-to-Education Programs. New York: Council for Financial Aid to Education, 1956– . Biennial. $21 (1984 ed.). Pap.

The Council for Financial Aid to Education (CFAE) is a nonprofit service organization that promotes increased voluntary support of higher education by all sources, but especially by the corporate community. It was founded in 1952 by five prominent business leaders: the chairs of U.S. Steel, General Motors, Exxon, Container Corporation, and Armstrong Cork. When the first edition of this directory was published in 1956, corporate support of education was estimated to be $13 million annually. By 1984, when the most recent edition of the casebook was being compiled, the level of support had grown to more than $1 billion, an average annual increase of more than nine percent. The 1984 casebook brings together "details of existing aid-to-education programs so that those interested in starting a program may take advantage of the experience of firms with a going program...and provides companies that have established programs a means of comparing their programs with those of other companies of similar size and characteristics." Unlike *C.A.S.E. Matching Gift Details* (described elsewhere in this section), this work contains only a small sampling of corporate programs offering educational support. The 200 entries are arranged alphabetically and contain information on company name, address, telephone number, contact person, recent educational grants (total amount, purpose, significant policies), support they give to colleges and universities, students, and educational organizations, and materials available. There are indexes by field of business, size of educational support programs, and categories of giving. A related publication of interest issued by the Council for Financial Aid to Education is *What American Corporations Are Doing to Improve the Quality of Precollege Education: A CFAE Sampler* (1985. 21p. Free. Pap). This brief sampler was prepared to describe the extent and variety of corporate aid to pre-college education. It provides a cross-section of corporate efforts in this area.

523 Chronicle of Higher Education. Washington, DC: Chronicle of Higher Education, 1966– . Weekly. ISSN 0009–5982. $44/yr., surface mail; $222/yr., air mail.

Included in each weekly issue of the *Chronicle of Higher Education* are foundation and grant news items and deadline dates. The programs covered here represent all fields of study and are of interest principally to academic teaching faculty, researchers, and administrator.

524   The CISP International Studies Funding Book. Ed. by Walter T. Brown, Robert H. Leder, and Ward Morehouse. 3d ed. New York: Learning Resources in International Studies, 1983. v.p. ISBN 0–939288–01–X. $30, CISP members; $50, others. Spiralbound.

CISP is a cooperative, nonprofit association of 200 colleges and universities (representing over 25,000 faculty members and nearly 1 million students). The *CISP International Studies Funding Book*, published in a binder, is "the cumulation of a long commitment by the Council to provide college and university educators and administrators with updated information on funding and implementing international/intercultural education." The funding book is published in eight sections, including "Foreign Sources of Funding: Key Contacts" and "Sources of Financial Aid: Specific Grants Available." These sections are updated periodically, and new ones are added by enclosures in the monthly issues of *Intercultural Studies Information Services*, which is sent free to CISP members. The third edition of the directory was published in 1983; earlier editions were issued in 1978 and 1980.

525   The Complete Grants Sourcebook for Higher Education. Ed. by David G. Bauer. 2d ed. New York: Macmillan, 1985. 608p. 84–25030. ISBN 0–02–901950–8. $85.

The *Sourcebook* is both a directory to funding sources and a manual on grantseeking. First, it lists and describes more than 500 foundations, corporations, and federal programs that award grants to colleges, universities, and other postsecondary institutions. The arrangement is by funding source (i.e., private foundation, corporation, federal agency), with indexing by type, area of interest, and geographic coverage. Each program entry contains information on areas of interest, eligibility requirements and policies, finances, application procedures, and sample grants. In addition, the publication serves as a guide to successful grantsmanship, describing practical techniques, approaches, methods, and procedures involved in seeking and winning grant support. The first edition of the *Sourcebook* was prepared by the Public Management Institute and published by the American Council on Education in 1980 (605p. 80–18886. ISBN 0–82681–245–7). Both editions were written by David G. Bauer, who has taught more than 7,000 fundraising officials in his workshops and seminars.

526   Directory of Federal Aid for Education: A Guide to Federal Assistance Programs for Education. Santa Monica, CA: Ready Reference, 1982. 383p. 81–23558. ISBN 0–916270–31–9. $47.50. Pap

The stated purpose of this guide is "to provide readers with information on federal domestic assistance programs, projects, services, and activities available for education." Like the other Ready Reference federal aid directories described elsewhere in this bibliography, the material provided in this directory on education generally duplicates the information presented in the *Catalog of Federal Domestic Assistance* (see the annotation in the "Grants—General—United States" section).

527 **Education Funding News.** Washington, DC: Education Funding Research Council, 1971– . Weekly (with quarterly *Congressional Boxscore*). 83–2573. ISSN 0273–4443. $128/yr.

This publication provides current information on new federal programs for education. It updates the Council's annual publication *Guide to Federal Funding for Education* (described elsewhere in this section of the bibliography). The annual subscription to the *News* also includes quarterly issues of the publisher's *Congressional Boxscore*.

528 **Federal Funding Guide for Elementary and Secondary Education.** Washington, DC: Education Funding Research Council, 1975–1980. Annual.

Since 1981, this annual has been issued under the title *Guide to Federal Funding for Education* (described elsewhere in this section of the bibliography).

529 **Financial Aid for Minorities in Education.** Ed. by Mary T. Christian and Ruth N. Swann. Garrett Park, MD: Garrett Park Press, 1980. 58p. 80–153221. $3. Pap.

This booklet, published in 1980, lists grants, fellowships, and scholarships open to minorities interested in the field of education. For more information about the publication, see the annotation in the "Scholarships—Social Sciences—Education" section of this bibliography.

530 **The Grant Advisor.** Arlington, VA: Toft Consulting, 1983– . Monthly, except July. 83–2781. ISSN 0740–5383. $85/yr.

This is a monthly newsletter (except July), aimed at colleges and universities, that identifies faculty fellowship and grant opportunities as well as institutional grant programs from federal agencies, private foundations, corporations, and professional organizations. Each issue is divided into two sections. The first identifies 20 or more programs and provides address, telephone number, program description, eligibility requirements, funding amounts, and deadlines. The second section lists approximately 150 new programs, grouped by major academic divisions; entries specify sponsoring agency, program title, telephone number, deadlines, and cross-references to past review dates. Advice doesn't come cheap. This six-page newsletter costs $85 a year.

531   Grants for Study Visits by University Administrators and Librarians.
London: Association of Commonwealth Universities, 1979– . Biennial.
Pap.

This biennially-issued pamphlet describes approximately 40 research grants,
travel grants, and fellowships available to university administrators and
university librarians from Commonwealth countries who wish to undertake
study visits in other countries. For more information about the publication,
see the annotation in the "Grants—Social Sciences—Librarianship" section
of this bibliography.

532   Guide to Federal Assistance. La Jolla, CA: Wellborn Associates,
1978– . Looseleaf. Updated monthly. ISSN 0278–5064. $315, first yr.;
$281.50/yr., thereafter.

Another in the plethora of directories identifying federal assistance programs,
this one is somewhat unique in that it focuses on education and issues
replacement pages for its looseleaf service on a monthly basis. Program
descriptions are arranged by the federal department or agency administering
them and indexed by department/agency; deadlines, eligibility, and funds;
public laws authorizing the programs; and field, discipline, or category. The
500 entries indicate purpose, eligibility, deadlines, contacts, and related
federal programs. In addition, the guide provides cross-references to the
Catalog of Federal Domestic Assistance and provides lists of contact persons,
inactive but authorized programs, and regional/state offices. Even with the
monthly updating service, the guide still lags behind in reporting the
inevitable day-to-day changes. To identify new assistance grant programs and
changes in existing programs, use the *Federal Register* (described elsewhere in
this section of the bibliography).

533   A Guide to Federal Funding for Education. Ed. by Jeffrey A. Simering.
Mary M. Stump, assoc. ed. Arlington, VA: Education Funding
Research Council, 1981– . Annual. 81–643087. ISSN 0275–8393.
$78.95 (1986 ed.). Looseleaf.

Designed to serve as a single–volume reference source on programs that
provide financial aid to educational agencies and institutions, this publication
covers the fields of elementary, secondary, and higher education.
Introductory narratives for each of the 16 topic program areas (e.g.,
handicapped, desegregation, bilingual education, adult and vocational
education) provide information on the evolution of grant programs, new
developments, and potential funding opportunities for the year covered.
Within each of the topic sections, entries are arranged by program title and
supply information on purpose, eligibility requirements, type of assistance
offered, application procedures, legislative authority, and information
contacts. Indexing is by program title. Although focusing on education, this

guide does not comprehensively cover the field. Less than 200 federal programs are described each year, while well over half of the 1,000 programs listed in the *Catalog of Federal Domestic Assistance* can be labeled educational. From 1975 through 1980, this publication was issued as *Federal Funding Guide for Elementary and Secondary Education* (described elsewhere in this section of the bibliography).

534 **International Funding Guide: Resources and Funds for International Activities at Colleges and Universities.** Washington, DC: American Association of State Colleges and Universities, 1985. 40p. ISBN 0–88044–109–7. $6, members; $7.50, nonmembers.

This is a compilation of resources designed to assist colleges and universities in finding support for their international activities. The guide covers programs sponsored by the federal government, private and service agencies, foundations, and foreign governments and multilateral agencies.

535 **Matching Gift Details: Double Your Dollar, 1983–1984.** Washington, DC: Council for Advancement and Support of Education, 1983. 174p.

This directory covers corporations that match employee gifts to education. The information included here has been subsumed by that presented in the latest edition of *C.A.S.E. Matching Gift Details* (described elsewhere in this section of the bibliography).

536 **Matching Gift Notes: Notes of Interest from CASE.** Washington, DC: Council for the Advancement and Support of Education, 1984– . Quarterly. 84–147. $20, CASE members; $30, nonmembers.

This quarterly newsletter is prepared by the Council for the Advancement and Support of Education's (CASE) National Clearinghouse for Corporate Matching Gift Information. National in scope, it presents information about new matching gift programs, changes in existing ones, and program cancellations or suspensions. Use this publication to update the data provided in CASE's annual directory, *C.A.S.E. Matching Gift Details* (described above).

537 **The Rural Funding Guide: Sources of Funds for Rural Programs at Colleges and Universities.** Washington, DC: American Association of State Colleges and Universities, 1985. 35p. 85–9836. ISBN 0–88044–111–9. $7.50. Pap.

This directory complements the *Urban Funding Guide* (described elsewhere in this section of the bibliography) and provides an overview of major sources of funds available for rural programs in higher education. The following information is provided in each entry: sponsoring association and address, program priorities, funding levels, application deadlines, and contacts.

538   **Serving the Rural Adult: Private Funding Resources for Rural Adult Postsecondary Education.** Prep. by Jacqueline D. Spears. Manhattan, KS: Action Agenda Project, University for Man, 1985. 67p. $7. Pap.

This is a useful directory for rural educators seeking private sources of funding. Over 90 foundations that have supported rural postsecondary projects are identified. Entries specify address and telephone numbers, contact person, purpose, limitations, and application procedures. Also included in the volume are suggestions on how to approach foundations and a list of questions grantmakers might ask.

539   **The Urban Funding Guide: Sources of Funds for Urban Programs at Colleges and Universities.** Washington, DC: American Association of State Colleges and Universities, 1983. 86p. 83–21553. ISBN 0–88044–100–3. $7.50. Pap.

In 1969, the American Association of State Colleges and Universities prepared its first guide to funds for urban programs at postsecondary institutions. In the 15 years since then, colleges and universities have experienced an explosion of knowledge and student enrollment and, at the same time, a dwindling of resources available for urban programs. The most recent information about private and public sector funding for urban programs at academic institutions is available in this publication, compiled by the American Association of State Colleges and Universities in 1983. The purpose of this guide is to provide "summary information on federal grant programs and major non-governmental organizations that can help colleges and universities to plan, develop, or operate programs that respond to the needs created by their urban environment." The guide is divided into three major sections, describing federal/state block grants (pp. 7–13); federal categorical grants (pp. 15–65); and foundation and other nongovernmental sources (pp. 67–76). For each of the 65 programs covered, the following information is given: program name, sponsoring agency, description and priorities, funding information, contact person, address, and telephone number. The entries are arranged by agency in each of the three sections and indexed by subject. A short bibliography identifying resources for program development and proposal writing completes the work.

History

540   **Directory of Resources in Neighborhood Conservation.** Washington, DC: Preservation Reports, 1980. 150p. $12. Pap.

Now considerably out of date, this directory identifies approximately 100 organizations that funded neighborhood conservation programs in 1980. The work begins with a chapter on HUD programs (written prior to the Reagan administration cuts), followed by 12 topical chapters. The entries are arranged alphabetically and provide basic directory-type information.

541   Fellowships and Grants of Interest to Historians. Washington, DC: American Historical Association, 1976–1977. Annual. Pap.

Since 1978, this annual publication has been issued as *Grants and Fellowships of Interest to Historians* (described elsewhere in this section).

542   Funding Sources and Financial Techniques for Historic Preservation. Prep. by Karen Luehrs. Atlanta: Goergia Department of Natural Resources, 1983. 39p. Free. Pap.

Similar to *Sources of Funding for Preservation Projects* (described below), which focuses on New York, this pamphlet identifies "the kinds of grants programs available for preservation purposes in Georgia." It is intended to help individuals and community groups research funding sources, tax incentives, and other alternatives to financing historic preservation. Some federal programs are described as well as those based in Georgia.

543   Grants and Fellowships of Interest to Historians. Washington, DC: American Historical Association, 1978– . Annual. 83–644237. ISSN 0275–830X. $4, members; $5, nonmembers (1985/86 ed.). Pap.

Begun as a 46–page pamphlet, this 100–page annual listing identifies and describes nearly 200 sources of funding for graduate students, postdoctoral researchers, and scholars in the history profession tenable in the United States or abroad. Covered here are fellowships, internships, awards, prizes, and travel grants. The entries are arranged in three sections: support for dissertation and postdoctoral research, support for dissertation study and research, and support for organizations working in the fields of historical research or education. Published in 1976 and 1977 under the title *Fellowships and Grants of Interest to Historians*, the annual changed its name in 1978 to *Grants and Fellowships of Interest to Historians*.

544   Sources of Funding for Preservation Projects. Ed. by Ruth A. Lawlor. Albany: Preservation League of New York State, 1983. 10p. $1.50. Pap.

This small booklet describes approximately 50 sources of funding offered by foundations and government agencies (particularly on the federal level) for historic preservation projects in New York. The entries are listed by sponsoring organization and indexed by type of assistance, form of assistance, eligible recipients, and eligible projects. The following information is provided: address and telephone number of sponsoring organization, program title, eligibility requirements, type of assistance, and form of assistance.

Librarianship

545 **The Bowker Annual of Library and Book Trade Information.** New York: Bowker, 1955– . Annual. 55–12434. ISSN 0068–0540. $79.95 (1986 ed.).

Generally, each edition contains a list of library scholarship sources and up-to-date information on library legislation, funding, and grantmaking agencies. For more information about the publication, see the annotation in the "Awards and Prizes—Social Sciences—Librarianship" section of this bibliography.

546 **Federal Grants for Library and Information Services.** By Nancy Godfrey. Washington, DC: American Library Association's Washington Office, 1986. 48p. $5. Pap.

This recently published pamphlet lists and describes 59 federal grants available in the fields of library and information services. An earlier version, edited by Anne Heanue, was published in 1981 under the same title.

547 **Grant Money and How to Get It: A Handbook for Librarians.** By Richard Boss. New York: Bowker, 1980. 138p. 80–17880. ISBN 0–8352–1274–2. $24.95.

Included in the appendix of this guide is a list of private foundations that provide support to libraries. Because of the publication date, use the information presented here with care.

548 **Grants for Libraries: A Guide to Public and Private Funding Programs and Proposal Writing Techniques.** By Emmett Corry. Littleton, CO: Libraries Unlimited, 1982. 240p. 81–20886. ISBN 0–87287–262–9. $22.50.

Described in this guide are federal library grants programs and foundation grants for various types of libraries and library programs. In addition, information is provided on successful proposal writing, reference sources and services available from foundation centers, a listing of 113 federal support programs for libraries as of FY 1981, a listing of state coordinators of ESEA programs, samples of four projects, abstracts of grants awarded, and a complete proposal for faculty development in information science. Published in 1982, much of the information presented is now out of date. A new edition is scheduled for Fall 1986 release (approximately 300 pages. ISBN 0–87287–534–2. $28.50).

549 Grants for Study Visits by University Administrators and Librarians.
London: Association of Commonwealth Universities, 1979– . Biennial.
Pap.

This biennially-issued pamphlet (generally less than 30 pages) describes
approximately 40 fellowships, research grants, and travel grants available to
university librarians and university administrators from Commonwealth
countries who wish to undertake study visits to other countries. One section
lists grants tenable in one Commonwealth country by staff from another. The
other section identifies grants that support movement between non-
Commonwealth and Commonwealth countries. Courses and conferences for
administrators are listed in an appendix. Organizations and award titles are
indexed.

550 Opportunities and Honors for You and Your Colleagues. Chicago:
American Library Association, 1986. 4p. Free. Pap.

The American Library Association sponsors more than 80 grants,
fellowships, and awards "to honor distinguished service and foster
professional growth." These are described in this small booklet. For more
information about the publication, see the annotation in the "Awards and
Prizes—Social Sciences—Librarianship" section of this bibliography.

Law

551 Directory of Federal Programs: Resources for Corrections. By Tamara
Hatfield, et al. Washington, DC: U.S. Department of Justice, 1981.
544p. in v.p. 81–602140. $10. Pap.

The second edition of this directory was issued in 1982 under the title
Resources for Corrections: A Directory of Federal Programs (described below).

552 Financial Aid for Minorities in Law. Ed. by Novelle J. Dickensen and
Ruth N. Swann. Garrett Park, MD: Garrett Park Press, 1981. 63p.
80–153225. $3. Pap.

This booklet, published in 1981, lists grants, fellowships, and scholarships
open to minorities interested in the legal profession. For more information
about the publication, see the annotation in the "Fellowships—Social
Sciences—Law" section of this bibliography.

553 Free Money for Professional Studies. By Laurie Blum. New York:
Barnes and Noble, 1985. 204p. (Blum's Guides to College Money).
85–42725. ISBN 0–06–464104–0. $5.95. Pap.

This guide identifies state-based organizations awarding grants, scholarships,
and fellowships to their residents, miscellaneous awards available to special
applicants (e.g., deaf children, veterans' dependents), and selected financial

aid programs appropriate for "professional studies" (including law). For more information about the publication, see the annotation in the "Fellowships—Sciences—Health Sciences" section of this bibliography.

554   **Resources for Corrections: A Directory of Federal Programs.** By Susan Ainslie Dunn, 2d ed. Washington, DC: U.S. Department of Justice, 1982. 416p. Free. Pap.

This directory contains 199 entries rerpesenting 27 federal government departments and independent agencies that can offer assistance to state and local corrections agencies, including prisons, jails, and probation, parole, or community programs. For the purposes of this directory, "assistance" is broadly defined: financial, technical, informational, and provision of goods and services. Each entry contains a description of the program, eligibility requirements, past correctional assistance, types of assistance available, and several other categories for information. The first edition of the directory was published in 1981 under the title *Directory of Federal Programs: Resources for Corrections.* The second edition was published in 1982 and there are no plans to update it. Limited copies or loan copies are available from the National Institute of Corrections Information Center, 1790 30th Street, Suite 130, Boulder, CO 80301.

Political Sciences

555   **Research Support for Political Scientists: A Guide to Sources of Funds for Research Fellowships, Grants, and Contracts.** Comp. by Stephen F. Szabo. 2d ed. Washington, DC: American Political Science Association, 1981. 126p. 78–102488. ISBN 0–915654–43–1. $6. Pap.

This listing is divided into four main sections: doctoral dissertation grants and fellowships, private foundation research grants, U.S. government grants and contracts, and research fellowships (the largest section). For more information about this publication, see the annotation in the "Fellowships—Social Sciences—Political Sciences" section of this bibliography.

556   **Search for Security: A Guide to Grantmaking in International Security and the Prevention of Nuclear War.** Washington, DC: Forum Institute, 1985. 281p. $45. Pap.

Similar in structure to the subject-oriented COMSEARCHES prepared by the Foundation Center (described in the "Grants—General—United States" section of this bibliography), this guide identifies private foundations that have funded studies on international security and the prevention of nuclear war. It provides "the first comprehensive analysis of this philanthropic response and its possible future course." The directory is based on material gathered in two questionnaire surveys conducted between November 1984 and March 1985. The data collected are reported in four sections. Part I presents an analysis of the nature and composition of foundations active in international security (with a number of explanatory tables and graphs). Part II provides an analysis of nearly 2,000 foundation grants made in 1984, organized into four activity and seven issue categories (with lists of foundations most active in each of the 11 categories). Part III (the main section) consists of the profiles of 77 foundations that actively contribute to the field of international security and the prevention of nuclear war. The following data are provided for each of these foundations: purpose, history, guidelines, assets, grant range, grant plans, grant summary, deadlines, and programs funded (with summaries attached). The final section reports the results of a survey of 154 national and local organizations working in the field of international security, including detailed data on their sources of support and views about future funding prospects. An index of tables and graphs and an index of profiles complete the work. The analysis of sources of organization income and of foundation grantmaking contained in the guide was partially presented in an earlier (April, 1981) preliminary report issued by the Forum Institute, entitled *Search for Security: A Study of Philanthropy in International Security and the Prevention of Nuclear War.*

557 **Township Funding Opportunities: A Guide to Federal Resources for Small Communities.** Washington, DC: National Association of Towns and Townships, 1981. 55p. $15. Pap.

This pamphlet first provides a brief overview of federal funding in general and then matches specific township needs (e.g., bridges and roads, water systems, sewers and sewage treatment facilities) to specific federal programs. Update this listing by using current issues of the *Catalog of Federal Domestic Assistance* (described in the "Grants—General—United States" section of this bibliography).

Psychology

558 **American Psychological Association's Guide to Research Support.** Ed. by E. Ralph Dusek, et al. 2d ed. Washington, DC: American Psychological Association, 1984. 463p. 84–71433. ISBN 0–912704–91–8. $25. Pap.

559 **Addendum.** American Psychological Association, 1986. 116p. $17.50. Pap.

As part of its mission to support scientific psychology, the American Psychological Association has made a commitment to gather and disseminate information on behavioral science research funding opportunities. The result is this directory, first compiled in 1981 as a "mechanism to inform the scientific community about the factors and focus that affect research funding." The directory was updated in 1984 and expanded to include not only federal funding sources but foundations and other private sector sources as well. The update is divided into six sections. Part I provides an introduction to the guide and to federal research support. The next section covers 180 federal sources of research funding. Parts III and IV list 55 nonfederal sources of research support. Part V identifies additional reading and Part VI indexes the information by personnel (for federal agencies), by federal and nonfederal programs, and by subject. Program profiles include the following information: organization address, program title, priorities and focus, application and selection procedures, funding policy, contact, and examples of funded projects (if applicable and/or available). A 116–page addendum brings the information up to date. This is the only publication on funding that focuses exclusively on the behavioral sciences.

Public Administration

560   **Funding Sources for Fire Departments.** By James C. Smalley. Quincy, MA: National Fire Protection Association, 1983. 104p. (NFPA Publications, FSP-60). 82–62452. ISBN 0–87765–246–5. $15. Pap.

Like other government services, fire departments have discovered that there is tremendous competition for funding. This guide was compiled to help fire department administrators by identifying appropriate public and private funding sources. It is not intended to be definitive; rather, it is meant to provide, "as its title implies, a guide to various sources and types of assistance available from the federal government and non-federal or private sources." The pamphlet is divided into three sections: federal sources, private sources, and sources of additional help (Federal Information Centers, research tools, the Foundation Center libraries). The guide relies heavily on the author's personal experience. The resulting informal structure and conversational style make reference use of the publication somewhat difficult.

Sociology

561   **Directory of Federal Aid for the Aging: A Guide to Federal Assistance Programs Serving the Aged.** Santa Monica, CA: Ready Reference, 1982. 280p. 81–23546. ISBN 0–916270–39–4. $47.50. Pap.

The purpose of this directory is to provide information on federal funding, services, and activities relating to the needs of the aged. As with the other Ready Reference directories of federal aid (described in various sections of this bibliography), the listings in this volume on aging are taken directly from the *Catalog of Federal Domestic Assistance* (see the annotation in the "Grants—General—United States" section). The information presented here, in fact, even follows the format of the catalog (which costs less, covers more areas, and is more current).

HUMANITIES

General

562 ACA Updates. New York: American Council for the Arts, 1979– .
Monthly. 82–20752. ISSN 0300–7065. $20/yr.

This monthly publication of the American Council for the Arts analyzes the
federal and state funding picture. It supersedes *Update* and *ACA Word from
Washington*, which were published from 1967 to 1979. Its focus is on
Washington and the National Endowment for the Arts. Special features
include corporate giving deadlines and lists of coming events in the arts.

563 Aid to Artists/Aide aux Artists. Ottawa: Canada Council. Annual.
77–70101. ISSN 0703–6043. Free. Pap.

The purpose of this bilingual (English and French) brochure is to describe the
various forms and amounts of assistance (research grants, travel grants, and
fellowships) offered to Canadian artists by the Council. For more information
about the publication, see the annotation in the "Fellowships—Humanities—
General" section of this bibliography.

564 ARIS Funding Messenger: Creative Arts and Humanities Report. San
Francisco: Academic Research Information System, 1976– . 8 times/
yr., plus supplements. 84–8702. ISSN 0747–993X. $46, individuals;
$95, institutions.

This current awareness service, operating since 1976, presents up-to-date
information on funding opportunities, agency activities, new programs, and
funding policies in the creative arts and humanities. Arts coverage includes
funding for practicing artists and arts groups in both the performing and
visual arts. Regional, national, and international competitions are
highlighted. Humanities coverage includes information on funding for the
academic study of the traditional humanistic disciplines as well as for
projects emphasizing the broader social and community applications. Both
public and private programs are described. Each entry provides address,
telephone numbers, concise guidelines, and deadline dates. Reports are issued
every six weeks and supplements are issued as needed, to list program
deadlines and RFPs announced after a report's publication date. While the
price for the service may seem a little steep, its comprehensiveness and
currency are well worth it.

565 Cultural Directory II: Federal Funds and Services for the Arts and Humanities. Ed. by Linda Coe. Washington, DC: Smithsonian Institution Press, 1980. 256p. 79–20413. ISBN 0–87474–323–0. $8.95. Pap.

Updating a 1975 edition, this directory describes 270 national, federal, and quasi-federal programs providing funds and services for the arts and humanities. Program profiles contain the following information: scope, purpose, eligibility, specific examples of assisted activities, size and number of awards, and contact persons. Deadlines and telephone numbers are not specified. Included in the 10 appendices are addresses and phone numbers of regional and other relevant offices of the Departments of HEW, HUD, Interior, and Commerce; of Federal Information Centers; of federal bookstores; of the endowments; of state arts agencies; and of the National Trust for Historical Preservation. Much of the information provided here is now quite dated.

566 Directory of Grants in the Humanities. Phoenix: Oryx, 1986– . Annual. 86–2385. ISSN 0887–0551. $74.50 (1986 ed.). Pap.

A spinoff from Oryx Press' *GRANTS* database (described in the "Databases and Search Services" chapter of this bibliography), this new annual directory identifies funding sources in literature, languages, history, anthropology, philosophy, ethics, religion, fine arts, and performing arts (including painting, dance, photography, sculpture, music, drama, crafts, folklore, and mime). The first edition (1986. 256p. ISBN 0–89774–333–4) contains nearly 1,500 entries, each of which includes information on restrictions and requirements, amount of money available, application deadline, renewability, sponsoring organization name and address, and *Catalog of Federal Domestic Assistance* number. More than half of the listing focuses on federal programs; the remainder is devoted to state government programs, university-sponsored programs, and corporate or foundation funding sources. Most of the programs described here are also covered in Oryx Press' more comprehensive *Directory of Research Grants.*

567 Directory of Matching Gift Programs for the Arts. New York: Business Committee for the Arts, 1984. 152p. 84–72475. $5. Pap.

Matching gift programs encourage employers to give to their favorite arts groups, enable businesses to provide special support to those activities of importance to their employees, and provide new sources of support for nonprofit organizations. This directory identifies 255 companies that have established matching gift programs for the arts. The entries are organized by company and provide the following information: address, telephone number, contact person, eligible participants, eligible recipients, and type of match and eligible gifts. The directory was issued in 1984; an addendum will be issued periodically to update the listing.

568   Free Money for Humanities Students. By Laurie Blum. New York: Barnes & Noble, 1985. 204p. (Blum's Guides to College Money). 85–42554. ISBN 0–06–464107–4. $5.95. Pap.

This guide identifies state-based organizations awarding grants and scholarships to their residents, miscellaneous awards available to special applicants (e.g., deaf children, veteran's dependents), and selected financial aid programs specifically of interest to humanities' students. For more information about the publication, see the annotation in the "Scholarships—Humanities—General" section of this bibliography.

569   Funding Sources for Cultural Facilities: Private and Federal Support for Capital Projects. Ed. by Linda Coe. Rev. ed. Salem, OR: National Endowment for the Arts and the Oregon Arts Commission, 1980. ISBN 0–89062–184–5. 72p. $3. Pap.

This dirrectory is divided into two sections: (1) private sources of support for cultural facilities, and (2) federal sources of support. In this directory, "cultural facilities" are defined to include performing arts and cultural centers, museums, libraries, studios and galleries, theaters, and historical buildings used for 'cultural' purposes. The first section of the guide identifies 135 foundations that are possible sources of support for culturally-related capital projects. Those include private (nongovernmental) nonprofit organizations, community foundations, and company-sponsored foundations. The entries are organized alphabetically by state, with a notation for those making grants on a regional or national level. The following information is provided: name, address, telephone number, contact person, restrictions, priorities, and 1977 award examples. There is an alphabetical list of foundations by name and a selected bibliography of additional sources of information at the end of this section. In section two, 21 major federal programs (administered by 10 federal and quasi-federal agencies) providing funds for culturally-related capital projects are described. The entries are arranged alphabetically by agency and supply information on what/for whom, typical grants, purpose of program, and contact person. For a more extensive listing of federal programs in this area, see *Cultural Directory II* (described elsewhere in this section of the bibliography), which covers five times the number of programs listed in Coe's directory.

570 **Gadney's Guide to 1800 International Contests, Festivals & Grants in Film & Video, Photography, TV-Radio Broadcasting, Writing, Poetry, Playwriting, Journalism.** By Alan Gadney. 2d ed. Glendale, CA: Festival Publications, 1980. 610p. 80–66803. ISBN 0–930828–03–8, cloth; -02–X, pap. $22.95, cloth; $15.95, pap.

This guide describes over 1,800 national and international grants, festivals, competitions, prizes, awards, fellowships, and loans open to those interested in film, video, photography, TV-radio broadcasting, writing, poetry, playwriting, and journalism. For more information about the publication, see the annotation in the "Awards and Prizes—Humanities—General" section of this bibliography.

571 **Grants in the Humanities: A Scholar's Guide to Funding Sources.** By William E. Coleman. 2d ed. New York: Neal-Schuman, 1984. 175p. (Neal-Schuman Grants series). 83–27069. ISBN 0–918212–80–4. $24.95.

The second edition of this directory updates its coverage of more than 150 funding sources in the humanities (in a 100–page appendix), identifying type, purpose, areas of support, conditions, deadlines, and addresses for inquiries. Programs are listed that award support (fellowships, grants, tuition remission) or provide facilities (office space, affiliation with a university, secretarial assistance). The research and study opportunities covered are open to those who have completed their professional training. The book also contains a detailed discussion of program writing and budget development, a review of the tax laws affecting grant recipients, an annotated bibliography, a list of Federal Information Centers and Foundation Center Libraries, a calendar of grant deadlines to 1985, and a subject index. First published in 1980 (152p. 79–25697. ISBN 0–918212–21–9), the second edition was released in 1984.

572 **Guide to Corporate Giving 3.** Ed. by Robert A. Porter. New York: American Council for the Arts, 1983. 567p. 82–20732. ISBN 0–91540–039–1. ISSN 0748–1713. $39.95.

The first two editions of this directory were published in 1978 (403p.) and 1981 (378p.) as the *Guide to Corporate Giving in the Arts* (Comp. by Susan E. Wagner. 84–643198. ISSN 0748–1705). The third edition, issued in 1983 as the *Guide to Corporate Giving 3*, describes 700 corporate funding programs and policies in the arts (twice the number of programs treated in the first edition and 40 percent more than in the second edition). These corporations made contributions totaling $1 billion, representing more than one third of the $2.9 billion given by all corporations reported by the Conference Board in its 1981 survey. Company profiles supply names and addresses of contribution officers, total dollars given to the arts, application procedures and requirements, evaluation criteria, and number of grants requested and awarded. The entries are listed in alphabetical order and indexed by state, type of activities supported, and type of support given. In addition to the arts, entries describe grants given in the areas of health and welfare, civic issues, and education. This is one of the best and most reasonably priced funding directories.

573 **Guide to the National Endowment for the Arts.** Washington, DC: U.S. National Endowment for the Arts. Annual. Free. Pap.

This is one of a number of publications issued without charge by the National Endowment for the Arts (1100 Pennsylvania Avenue, N.W., Washington, DC 20506) that describe grants and fellowships sponsored by the agency. These programs are open to both U.S. citizens and permanents residents. An example of the other useful pamphlets published by the Endowment is *Crafts: Visual Arts Programs Guidelines.*

574 **International Cultural Exchange.** New York: Center for Arts Information, 1985. 35p. $3.50. Pap.

Prepared at the request of the National Assembly of State Art Agencies, this booklet identifies and describes more than 60 organizations that facilitate or fund international cultural exchange programs. The first edition (13p.) was published in 1983.

575 **Money Business: Grants and Awards for Creative Artists.** Boston: Artists Foundation, 1978– Irreg. 80–640447. ISSN 0161–5866. $9.50. (1982 ed.). Pap.

The latest edition (1982) reflects changes recommended by the artists who have used the publication in the past and includes a new presentation format and a comprehensive indexing system. The main body of the book identifies 300 foundations, businesses, federal programs, and art councils offering financial aid for poets, fiction writers, playwrights, filmmakers, video artists, composers, choreographers, painters, sculptors, photographers, and other artists. The work is divided into six categories, including state art agencies and the National Endowment for the Arts. Many of the programs listed here are limited to residents of a particular state. Program profiles contain the following information: eligibility requirements, remuneration, application procedures, and deadlines. The information is indexed by organization and artistic discipline.

576   **National Directory of Arts Support by Private Foundations.** By Daniel
      Millsaps. 5th ed. Washington, DC: Washington International Arts
      Letter, 1983. 330p. (The Arts Patronage series, no. 12). 77–79730.
      ISBN 0–912072–13–X. $79.95.

Issued by the same publishers as the *Washington International Arts Letter*
(described elsewhere in this section of the bibliography), this directory
complements *The National Directory of Grants and Aid to Individuals in the
Arts, International* (described below). It focuses on over 1,600
nongovernmental organizations (those not directly supported by tax funds)
that aid group endeavors and art-related organizations. The entries are
arranged by foundation name and specify address, contact person, disciplines
supported, previously issued grants, and assets of the foundation. Additional
access is provided through the geographic index. The first edition of this
publication was issued in 1970 under the title *Private Foundations Active in
the Arts* and the second edition in 1974 under the title *Private Foundations
and Business Corporations Active in Arts/Humanities/Education.* The third
and fourth editions were issued in 1977 and 1980, respectively, under the
current title.

577   **The National Directory of Grants and Aid to Individuals in the Arts,
      International.** By Daniel Millsaps. 5th ed. Washington, DC:
      Washington International Arts Letter, 1983. 246p. (The Arts
      Patronage series, no. 11). 70–11269. ISBN 0–912072–12–1. ISSN
      0270–5966. $15.95. Pap.

According to its editors, this paperback directory lists "most grants, prizes,
and awards for professional work in the United States and abroad, and
information about universities and schools which offer special aid to
students." It identifies approximately 3,000 monetary an other aids for
professional students. The emphasis is on awards obtainable by individuals.
The disciplines covered include architecture, arts management, crafts, dance,
film and video, music, museum administration, theater, visual and plastic
arts, and writing. The source is arranged alphabetically by sponsor and is
indexed by discipline. Each entry contains information on the address, basic
requirements, amount of grant or award, and restrictions, if any. Each entry
is preceded by a symbol indicating the discipline covered by the award and
whether it is for working professionals or for educational purposes. There are
13 subject indexes keyed to these codes. Separate sections cover federal
government sources of assistance and artists' retreats/colonies. This is the
fifth edition of the directory. The first two editions were issued under the title
Grants and Aid to Individuals in the Arts (1970, 1972. 70–112695. ISSN
0533–9626). The third and fourth editions were issued in 1976 and 1980
respectively. A new edition is expected shortly.

578 **Ocular: The Directory of Information and Opportunities for the Visual Arts.** Denver: Ocular, 1976– . Quarterly. $14/yr.

Included in each issue of this quarterly journal is a section identifying financial aid for visual artists, including grants, fellowships, employment assistance, regional and national competitions, and workshops. Awards in the United States and abroad are covered, as are funding programs for both individuals and organizations. The entries are arranged geographically by state and then by sponsoring organization. Information is provided on purpose, address, eligibility, remuneration, application procedures, and deadline dates.

579 **Overview of Endowment Programs.** Washington, DC: National Endowment for the Humanities. Annual. Free.

This free pamphlet provides information on grants available to organizations and individuals in the humanities that are sponsored by the National Endowment for the Humanities (1100 Pennyslvania Avenue, N.W., Washington, DC 20506). There are a number of other Endowment program listings issued without charge by the agency, including *Fellowships for College Teachers and for Independent Study and Research, NEH Extramural Programs*, and *Summer Stipends*.

580 **Private Foundations Active in the Arts.** By Daniel Millsaps. 1st ed. Washington, DC: Washington International Arts Letter, 1970. 138p. (The Arts Patronage series). 77–140925.

Currently, this publication is being issued under the title *National Directory of Arts Support by Private Foundations* (described elsewhere in this section of the bibliography).

581 **Private Foundations and Business Corporations Active in Arts/ Humanities/Education.** By Daniel Millsaps. 2d ed. Washington, DC: Washington International Arts Letter, 1974. 2v. (The Arts Patronage series). 77–140925.

Currently, this publication is being issued under the title *National Directory of Arts Support by Private Foundations* (described elsewhere in this section of the bibliography).

582 **Public/Private Cooperation: Funding for Small and Emerging Arts Programs.** New York: Foundation Center, 1983. 60p. ISBN 0–87954–094–X. o.p. Pap.

A major problem for America's arts organizations has been a lack of sufficient capital. This problem has been particularly difficult for small and emerging organizations, which lack visibility and administrative/ developmental capabilties. In order to provide information on funding for grantseekers in these organizations, the Foundation Center received a grant from the Expansion Arts Program of the National Endowment for the Arts (NEA) to compile a directory of resources. The result is *Public/Private Cooperation*, the first effort of the Foundation Center to identify both private *and* public support for small and emerging arts agencies. The directory provides access to both grants from the NEA's Expansion Arts Program and grants from private/community foundations (as listed in the 12th edition of the *Foundation Grants Index Annual*) for the expansion arts. For the purposes of this compilation, "expansion arts organizations" are defined as those that are "deeply routed in and reflective of a minority, inner city, rural or tribal community." The compilation is divided into six sections. The first lists 453 grants made by NEA by names of the recipient organizations; each entry indicates name and location of the recipient, the amount awarded, the grant duration, and a brief description of the grant. The second section arranges 216 private foundations alphabetically by the state in which they are located and lists 1,257 grants of $5,000 or more by the names of recipient organizations; the following information for each grant is provided: name and location of the recipient organization, amount awarded, date grant paid or authorized, grant duration, brief description of the grant, and source of grant data. Sections 3 through 5 provide index access by grant recipient, subject, and state location. The final section, "Foundations," is an alphabetical list of the foundations included in the volume, with their addresses and grant-giving limitations specified.

583 **Social Science Research Council Fellowships and Grants to Be Offered for Training and Research.** New York: Social Science Research Council. Annual. Free. Pap.

This annual pamphlet describes advanced research grants and dissertation fellowships in both the humanities and social sciences that are open to American and foreign citizens on the advanced graduate or postgraduate levels. For more information about the publication, see the annotation in the "Fellowships—Social Sciences—General" section of this bibliography.

584 **Washington International Arts Letter.** Washington, DC: Washington International Arts Letter (WIAL), 1962– . 10 issues/yr. 68–6506. ISSN 0043–0609. $54/yr.

This is a monthly newsletter providing information on federal and corporate financial assistance programs open to institutions and individuals involved in the arts. Use it to update the information included in the three WIAL directories described in this bibliography: the *National Directory of Arts and Education Support by Business Corporations*; the *National Directory of Arts Support by Private Foundations*; and the *National Directory of Grants and Aid to Individuals in the Arts, International*.

Applied Arts

585 **How to Enter and Win Black & White Photography Contests.** By Alan Gadney. New York: Facts On File, 1982. 204p. 81–12594. ISBN 0–87196–571–2, cloth; -577–1, pap. $14.95, cloth; $6.95, pap

586 **How to Enter and Win Color Photography Contests.** By Alan Gadney. New York: Facts On File, 1982. 204p. 81–12591. ISBN 0–87196–572–0, cloth; -578–X, pap. $14.95, cloth; $6.95, pap.

These twin directories each cover over 500 national and international photography grants, apprenticeships, contests, photofairs, festivals, and awards. For more information about the publications, see the annotation in the "Awards and Prizes—Humanities—Applied Arts" section of this bibliography.

587 **Photographer's Market: Where to Sell Your Photographs.** Ed. by Robin Weinstein. Cincinnati, OH: Writer's Digest, 1978– . Annual. 78–643526. ISSN 0147–247X. $16.95 (1986 ed.).

Included in each annual guide to the photography market are chapters that (1) identify a total of 2,500 organizations making awards or grants to photographers (state arts council funding programs receive special emphasis) and (2) list foundations and grants of interest to the photographer. In both these sections, the entries are arranged alphabetically by sponsoring organization and annotated to include information on purpose, requirements, and remuneration. A monthly supplement, *Photographer's Market Newsletter* (1981– . 81–1971. ISSN 0278–2790), updates the listing. The annual volume and its supplements supersede, in part, *Artist's Market* (described elsewhere in this section).

Communications and Mass Media

588 **The A-V Connection: The Guide to Federal Funds for Audio-Visual Users.** 4th ed. Fairfax, VA: National Audio-Visual Association (now International Communications Industries Association), 1981. 161p. 81–128041. $33.

Less than 50 programs that provide funds for the purchase of audiovisual equipment and materials are described here. Of these, nearly 40 were sponsored by the Department of Education in the early 1980s. Lengthy descriptions of each program are provided, including an explanation of why the agency is interested in audiovisual projects. A glossary and indexes complete the volume. The first three editions of this publication were issued in 1976, 1977, and 1979 under the title *A-V Connection: The Guide to Federal Funds for A-V Programs.* Because of its 1981 publication date, many of the program descriptions are no longer relevant. To update the 1981 listing, use the association's bimonthly newsletter, *Actionfacts*, which provides current information on federal grants available for the purchase of audiovisual materials and equipment.

589 Children's Media Market Place. Ed. by Carol A. Emmens. 2d ed. New York: Neal-Schuman, 1982. 353p. 82–82058. ISBN 0–918212–33–2. ISSN 0734–8169. $29.95. Pap.

In focusing on print and nonprint children's materials, this directory identifies state and federal agency officials concerned with library and media services, grants for children's programming, and national awards for children's materials. For more information about the publication, see the annotation in the "Awards and Prizes—Humanities—Literature" section of this bibliography.

590 Film/Television: Grants, Scholarships, Special Programs. Comp. by Judy Chaikin and Lucinda Travis. Ed. by Virginia M. Clark. 2d ed. Los Angeles, CA: American Film Institute, 1984. 33p. (Factfile #12). $5. Pap.

A revision of the 1977 edition, this small directory provides information on grants, scholarships, and special programs available to students, practitioners, and researchers interested in working in the areas of film and television. The entries are grouped by intended audience and arranged by sponsoring organization. The following information is provided: organization name, address, telephone number, contact person, amounts awarded, and application procedures. Also included are brief sections on organizations, periodicals, and related publications in the field.

591 Financial Aid for Minorities in Mass Communications. By Leslie L. Lawton and Ruth N. Swann. Garrett Park, MD: Garrett Park Press, 1981. 62p. 81–211245. $3. Pap.

This booklet, published in 1981, lists grants, scholarships, and fellowships open to minorities interested in the fields of communication and mass media. For more information about the publication, see the annotation in the "Scholarships—Humanities—Communications and Mass Media" section of this bibliography.

592 Foundation Grants for Schools, Museums, and Libraries: Grants with a Slice for Communications Technology Products. 2d ed. Fairfax, VA: International Communications Industries Association, 1984. 62p. $16.95. Pap.

Historically, private foundations have earmarked substantial portions of their giving budgets to support education through grants to elementary and secondary schools, academic institutions, and museums. Recently, large numbers of foundations have broadened their giving programs to include funding for the acquisition of media, microcomputers, video, and other advanced technologies in schools, libraries, and museums. In 1983, the International Communications Industries Association (formerly the National Audio-Visual Association) polled foundations across the country and found 82 organizations providing funds for the purchase of communications technology products (the results of this survey were presented in 1983, in the first edition of the directory). In the second edition, 161 foundations that made grants to schools or library/museum projects are identified. Program profiles are divided into two sections (schools and museums/libraries), arranged by sponsoring organization, and specify address, telephone number, contact person, geographic restrictions, and educational funding levels or library classification. Foundations that have made grants for the purchase of microcomputers, video, or audiovisual equipment are marked with a star. There is no index. This listing serves as a complement to *The A-V Connection* (described elsewhere in this section of the bibliography), which focuses on federal sources of funding in this area.

593 Foundation Radio Funding Guide I. San Francisco: Audio Independents, 1982. 64p. $15. Pap.

Audio Independents, which was established in 1979 "to foster and support the work of independent radio producers and audio artists," maintains an inhouse database on funding data. This directory was compiled from that file. It lists and describes 60 foundations that have given grants to radio-related projects in 18 states. Many of these are general grant-giving foundations, like Dayton Hudson Foundation, General Mills Foundation, Honeywell Fund, and Exxon Education Foundation. The data reported are taken from 1979 through 1981 annual reports and foundation funding records. Entries supply information on address, contact person, purpose/activities, limitations, funding, and application procedures. Sample grants are listed. The entries are indexed by organization name and by geographic location (the indexes are located in the front of the book).

594 Honor Awards Handbook. Ed. by Milton L. Levy. Berkeley, CA: Honor Awards Handbook, 1957–1964. 3v. 84–7113.

Published in 1957, 1960, and 1964 under the title *Honor Awards Handbook*, this directory changed its name in 1968 to *Media Awards Handbook* (described in the "Awards and Prizes—Humanities—Communications and Mass Media" section of this bibliography).

595   **How to Enter and Win Film Contests.** By Alan Gadney. New York:
      Facts On File, 1981. 195p. 81–2183. ISBN 0–87196–517–8, cloth;
      -524–0, pap. $14.95, cloth; $6.95, pap.

This reference source covers over 350 international film grants, contests,
festivals, and screenings. For more information about the publication, see the
annotation in the "Awards and Prizes—Humanities—Communications and
Mass Media" section of this bibliography.

596   **How to Enter and Win Video/Audio Contests.** By Alan Gadney. Ed.
      by Carolyn Porter. New York: Facts On File, 1981. 193p. 81–2221.
      ISBN 0–87196–520–8, cloth; -551–8, pap. $14.95, cloth; $6.95, pap.

This volume describes over 400 national and international grants, fellowships,
contests, and festivals open to television and video tape producers. For more
information about the publication, see the annotation in the "Awards and
Prizes—Humanities—Communications and Mass Media" section of this
bibliography.

597   **Media Awards Handbook: Radio, Television, Newspaper, Magazine,
      Allied Fields & Industries.** Ed. by Milton L. Levy. Danville, CA:
      Media Awards Handbook, 1980. n.p. 68–24272. ISBN 0–910744–03–3.
      $20. Pap.

Intended as a "workbook for those professionals who want to know as much
detail as possible about the various Contests and Awards with the thought of
entering them for their work," this directory also lists some grants,
scholarships, and fellowships. For more information about this publication,
see the annotation in the "Awards and Prizes—Humanities—
Communications and Mass Media" section of this bibliography.

Fine Arts

598   **How to Enter and Win Fine Arts & Sculpture Contests.** By Alan
      Gadney. New York: Facts On File, 1982. 205p. 81–12580. ISBN
      0–87196–573–9, cloth; -579–8, pap. $14.95, cloth; $6.95, pap.

This volume identifies 343 grants and contests in fine arts and sculpture. For
more information about the publication, see the annotation in the "Awards
and Prizes—Humanities—Fine Arts" section of this bibliography.

Language and Linguistics

599 Guide to Grants & Fellowships in Languages & Linguistics.
Washington, DC: Linguistic Society of America, 1984– . Biennial.
84–12438. ISSN 0024–3906. $3 (1985 ed.). Pap.

Published biennially, this directory lists and describes grants and fellowships in the fields of language and linguistics sponsored by institutions, associations, foundations, and government agencies located in the United States. Nearly 200 programs are covered. They are arranged by sponsoring organization. In each entry, the folowing information is provided; program title, sponsoring organization name, address, and telephone number, purpose, eligibility, restrictions, duration, stipend, and application procedures. All the information presented is supplied by the sponsoring organizations. Prior to 1983, the directory was issued as a supplement to the *Linguistic Reporter* (Arlington, VA: Center for Applied Linguistics. 83–11337).

Literature

600 Children's Media Market Place. Ed. by Carol A. Emmens. 2d ed. New York: Neal-Schuman, 1982. 353p. 82–82058. ISBN 0–918212–33–2. ISSN 0734–8169. $29.95. Pap.

In focusing on print and nonprint children's materials, this directory identifies state and federal agency officals concerned with library and media services, grants for children's programming, and national awards for children's materials. For more information about the publication, see the annotation in the "Awards and Prizes—Humanities—Literature" section of this bibliography.

601 Coda: Poets & Writers Newsletter. New York: Poets & Writers, 1973– . 5 times/yr. 73–649056. ISSN 0091–5645. $18/yr.

Published five times each year, this is a good resource for current information on grants and awards deadlines of interest to poets and writers as well as on recipients of those awards. The "deadline" section tells when to apply for upcoming competitions and provides brief program descriptions.

602 Dramatists Sourcebook: Complete Opportunities for Playwrights, Translators, Composers, Lyricists, and Librettists. Ed. by M. Elizabeth Osborne. New York: Theatre Communications Group, 1982– . Annual. 82–644562. ISSN 0733–1606. $10.95 (1985–86 ed.). Pap.

There are a number of separate sections in this sourcebook that describe financial aid programs for dramatists, including grants, scholarships, fellowships, colonies and residencies, and emergency funds. For more information about the publication, see the annotation in the "Awards and Prizes—Humanities—Literature" section of this bibliography.

603 Grants and Awards Available to American Writers. New York: P.E.N. American Center, 1973– . Annual. 73–648098. ISSN 0092–5268. $6/ yr., individuals; $9/yr., libraries and institutions (13th ed.). Pap.

Grants and awards in excess of $500, available to American writers for use in the United States and abroad, are described in this directory. For a more complete annotation, see the description of *Grants and Awards Available to American Writers* in the "Awards and Prizes—Humanities—Literature" section.

604 How to Enter and Win Fiction Writing Contests. By Alan Gadney. New York: Facts On File, 1981. 200p. 81–2181. ISBN 0–87196–319–4, cloth; -552–6, pap. $14.95, cloth; $6.95, pap.

More than 400 national and international grants, scholarships, and contests for literature are covered in this guide. For more information about the publication, see the annotation in the "Awards and Prizes—Humanities— Literature" section of this bibliography.

605 How to Enter and Win Non-Fiction & Journalism Contests. By Alan Gadney. New York: Facts On File, 1981. 205p. 81–2179. ISBN 0–87196–518–6, cloth; -553–4, pap. $14.95, cloth; $6.95, pap.

Nearly 400 national and international grants, scholarships, contests, and festivals open to nonfiction writers are identified and described in this directory. For more information about the publication, see the annotation in the "Awards and Prizes—Humanities—Literature" section of this bibliography.

606 List of Grants and Awards Available to American Writers. New York: P.E.N. American Center, 1969–1972. 72–200103. ISSN 0075–983X. Pap.

In 1973, this publication was superseded by *Grants and Awards Available to American Writers* (described in the "Awards and Prizes—Humanities— Literature" section).

607 Literary Market Place: The Directory of American Book Publishing with Names & Numbers. New York: Bowker, 1972– . Annual. 81–640008. ISSN 0161–2905. $59.95 (1986 ed.). Pap.

Originaly designed as a register of personnel in publishing and allied fields, over the years this annual has been expanded to include 12,000 entries in a dozen major sections. One of these sections focuses on awards, scholarships, fellowships, and grants-in-aid of interest to the American writer. For more information about the publication, see the annotation in the "Awards and Prizes—Humanities—Literature" section of this bibliography.

608 PEN American Center Newsletter. New York: PEN International, 1978– . Quarterly. 80–657. ISSN 0197–5498. $5/yr.

In addition to articles of interest to writers and conference reports, the newsletter includes announcements of grants and awards open to writers. For more information about the publication, see the annotation in the "Awards and Prizes—Humanities—Literature" section of this bibliography.

609 Poet's Marketplace: The Definitive Sourcebook on Where to Get Your Poems Published. By Joseph J. Kelly. Philadelphia: Running Press, 1984. 174p. 84–2053. ISBN 0–89471–257–8, cloth; -264–0, pap. $19.50, cloth; $9.95, pap.

One chapter of this directory designed "to help serious poets find the right outlets for their work" identifies writers' grants and associations. For a more complete description, see the annotation in the "Awards and Prizes—Humanities—Literature" section of this bibliography.

Music

610 British Music Yearbook. London: Adam & Charles Black (dist by Schirmer Books), 1975– . Annual. 75–649724. ISSN 0306–5928. $29.95 (1984 ed.).

In addition to information about awards and prizes, this yearbook also describes music grants and scholarships tenable either in Britain or abroad. For more information about the publication, see the annotation in the "Awards and Prizes—Humanities—Music" section of this bibliography.

611 Career Guide for Young Singers from the United States and Canada. 5th ed. New York: Central Opera Service, 1985. 80p. $9.50. Pap.

One of the eight sections in the 1985 edition of this irregularly-issued directory describes grants for Canadian and American singers. For more information about the publication, see the annotation in the "Awards and Prizes—Humanities—Music" section of this bibliography.

Performing Arts

612 Dance Magazine Annual: Catalog of Performing Artists and Attractions, Programs, Resources and Services. New York: Dance Magazine, 1967– . Annual. 86–25454. ISSN 0070–2684. $30 (1986 ed.). Pap.

From 1958 through 1964, *Dance Magazine Annual* was published as the December issue of *Dance Magazine*. Since 1965, it has been issued annually as a separate publication. Currently, it provides extensive listings of dance companies, artists, programs, organizations, and sources in the field of dance. Over 10,000 entries are covered in the 1986 edition. One of the sections identifies funding agencies in the United States and Canada. Brief entries specify address, telephone number, and contact person only. The small print and the lack of subject headings or bold-face subheadings make the material hard to read.

613 Lively Arts Information Directory. Ed. by Steven R. Wasserman and Jacqueline Wasserman O'Brien. 2d ed. Detroit: Gale, 1985. 1,040p. 81–20060. ISBN 0–8103–0321–3. $165.

Over 6,700 grants, foundations, scholarships, awards, publications, special libraries, and schools offering study in theater, music, dance, filmmaking, radio, and television are described in the second edition of this directory. For more information about the publication, see the annotation in the "Awards and Prizes—Humanities—Performing Arts" section of this bibliography.

614 Musical America: International Directory of the Performing Arts. New York: ABC Leisure Magazines, 1969– . Annual. 83–713. ISSN 0560–308X. $40.

There are two chapters devoted to financial assistance in this annual directory of the performing arts, one which covers foundation awards and contests for the United States and the other which covers them for the rest of the world. For more information about the publication, see the annotation in the "Awards and Prizes—Humanities—Performing Arts" section of this bibliography.

615 Whole Film Sourcebook. Ed. by Leonard Maltin. New York: New American Library, 1983. 454p. (A Plume Book). 82–19085. ISBN 0–452–25361–6. $9.95. Pap.

Also included in this potpourri listing of academic institutions, organizations, distributors, producers, libraries, and bookstores are grants and awards dealing with filmmaking. Generally, each entry includes the following information: organization address and telephone number, description of offerings, application requirments, and deadlines.

Philosophy

616 Grants and Fellowships of Interest to Philosophers. Newark, DE: American Philosophical Association, 1972– . Annual. $2.50. Pap.

This annually-issued directory identifies fellowships and grant opportunities for graduate and postdoctoral study and research in the United States and abroad available from approximately 30 sources. Entries, arranged alphabetically by sponsoring organization, supply information on deadline, fields of study, purpose, qualifications, tenure, stipend, number, application procedures, and contact person. The list is contained in no. 5 of each volume of the Association's *Proceedings and Addresses of the American Philosophical Association.*

Religion

617 Agencies for Project Assistance: Sources of Support for Small Church and/or Lay Sponsored Projects in Africa, Asia, Latin America, and the Pacific. By Pierre Aubin and George Cotter. 2d ed. New York: Mission Project Service, 1984. 330p. 84–62380. $50. Pap.

This directory identifies international organizations (private foundations, public charities, government agencies, and church agencies) that provide socio-economic and pastoral development assistance to small church or lay-sponsored projects in Latin America, Asia, Africa, and the Pacific. Entries contain information on sponsoring organization address and telephone number, sources of income, financial activities, fields of interest, geographical areas of interest, and application deadlines. The types of assistance described range from funds and research to training, marketing, livestock, and personnel. The first edition of the directory was published in 1982 (346p. 82–199292); the most recent edition was released in 1984.

618 Foundation Guide for Religious Grant Seekers. Ed. by Francis J. Butler and Catherine E. Farrell. 2d ed. Chico, CA: Scholars Press, 1984. 139p. (Scholars Press Handbook Series). 84–10593. ISBN 0–89130–756–7. $11.95. Pap.

The majority of this book consists of a set of introductory essays for religious grantseekers. In addition, there is a list of 384 foundations with a history of religious grantmaking, with only minimal information provided for each of these foundaitons: address, telephone number, contact, geographic giving patterns, and areas of special interest. The entries are divided into four sections (Protestant, Catholic, Jewish, and Interfaith) and subdivided by state. There is no index. The bibliography printed at the end of the volume has not been updated from the first edition (1979. 99p. 79–19006), and most of the editions cited are very much out of date.

619 Foundations That Support Roman Catholic Activities. Comp. by Anthony L. Robinson. Washington, DC: Campaign for Human Development, U.S. Catholic Conference, 1984. 89p. First copy free; $4 for each additional copy. Pap.

This directory identifies 80 foundations whose "grant activity suggest some preference for supporting Roman Catholic activities." The listed foundations either annually awarded $100,000 or more in grants or had assets of at least $1 million. The focus is on nongovernmental, nonprofit organizations. The entries are arranged by sponsoring organization, within state divisions, and specify address and telephone number, contact person, type of assistance, funding interests, application procedures, and examples of funded projects. Organization names are indexed.

SCIENCES

General

620 ARIS Funding Messenger: Social and Natural Sciences Report. San Francisco: Academic Research Information System, 1976– . 8 times/yr., plus supplements. 84–8697. ISSN 0747–9921. $79, individuals; $165, institutions.

This current awareness service presents up-to-date information on hundreds of grant and fellowship opportunities in the sciences and social sciences. For more information about the publication, see the annotation in the "Grants—Social Sciences—General" section of this bibliography.

621 Financial Aid for Minorities in Science. Ed. by Ruth N. Swann and Sharon F. White. Garrett Park, MD: Garrett Park Press, 1980. 49p. $2. Pap.

This booklet, published in 1908, lists grants, fellowships, and scholarships open to minorities interested in the sciences. For more information about the publication, see the annotation in the "Scholarships—Sciences—General" section of this bibliography.

622 Free Money for Science Students. By Laurie Blum. New York: Barnes & Noble, 1985. 204p. (Blum's Guides to College Money). 85–42724. ISBN 0–06–464108–0. $5.95. Pap.

This guide identifies state-based organizations awarding grants and scholarships to their residents, miscellaneous awards available to special applicants (e.g., deaf children, veteran's dependents), and selected financial aid programs specifically of interest to science students. For more information about the publication, see the annotation in the "Scholarships—Sciences—General" section of this bibliography.

623 National Science Foundation Guide to Programs. Washington, DC: National Science Foundation. Annual. Free. Pap.

The National Science Foundation (NSF) was founded in 1950 to promote and advance scientific progress. Over the years, it has established a wide range of programs to support scientific and engineering research and education. These programs are described in this annual booklet, which is distributed without charge by the foundation (1800 G Street, N.W., Washington, DC 20550). Entries provide information on program title, contact address, eligibility requirements, application deadline, program purpose, application procedure, and type and amount of assistance available. Also covered in the booklet are programs administered in cooperation with foreign countries. The criteria for selection of NSF research projects is described in the introduction. To identify the recipients of the grants and contracts awarded each year, use the annually issued *National Science Foundation Grants and Awards.*

Engineering

624 Financial Aid for Minorities in Engineering. Ed. by Clayton G. Holloway and Ruth N. Swann. Garrett Park, MD: Garrett Park Press, 1981. 52p. 81–161268. $3. Pap.

This booklet, published in 1981, lists grants, fellowships, and scholarships open to minorities interested in engineering. For more information about the publication, see the annotation in the "Scholarships—Sciences—Engineering" section of this bibliography.

Health Sciences

625 ARIS Funding Messenger: Medical Sciences Report. San Francisco: Academic Research Information System, 1976– . 8 times/yr., plus supplements. 84–8696. ISSN 0747–9913. $79, individuals; $165, institutions.

Started in 1976, this current awareness service presents up-to-date information on grant and fellowship opportunities, agency activities, new programs, and funding policies in the medical sciences. The emphasis is on biomedical research, health care and services, and the general biological sciences. Both public and private programs are described. Each entry provides address, telephone numbers, concise guidelines, and deadline dates. Reports are issued every six weeks and supplements are issued as needed, to list program deadlines and RFPs announced after a report's publication date. While the price for this service may seem a little steep, its comprehensiveness and currency are worth it.

626 Directory of Biomedical and Health Care Grants. Phoenix: Oryx, 1985– . Annual. 85–15562. $74.50 (1986 ed.). Pap.

The 1986 edition of this directory, (432p. ISBN 0–89774–336–9) describes 2,000 health-related funding programs (500 more than the first edition), ranging from nutrition to health-care delivery needs for the aged. Each program profile describes purpose, remuneration, eligibility, renewability, application deadlines, and sources of additional information. The entries are arranged by topic and indexed by sponsoring organization, sponsoring organization by type (e.g., business and professional organizations, government agencies), and 344 specific subject terms. The programs listed in the directory are taken from Oryx's *GRANTS* database, which is also the source for the *Directory of Research Grants* (described in the "Grants— General—United States" section of this bibliography); consequently, many of the programs included in the two publication are duplicates.

627 Directory of Federal Aid for Health and Allied Fields: A Guide to Federal Assistance Programs for Health and Allied Fields. Santa Monica, CA: Ready Reference, 1982. 315p. 81–23515. ISBN 0–916270–35–1. $47.50. Pap.

The purpose of this directory is to provide information on federal funding, services, and activities related to the health and allied fields. As with the other Ready Reference directories of federal aid (described in various sections of this bibliography), the listings in this volume on the health fields are taken directly from the *Catalog of Federal Domestic Assistance* (described in the "Grants—General—United States" section). The information presented here, in fact, even follows the format of the catalog (which costs less, covers more areas, and is more current). For a more expensive but much more comprehensive single volume covering grants (both public and private) in the health area, see Oryx Press' *Directory of Biomedical and Health Care Grants* (described elsewhere in this section of the bibliography).

628 Directory of Psychiatry Residency Training Programs. Ed. by Carolyn B. Robinowitz and Zebulon Taintor. Washington, DC: American Psychiatric Association, 1982– . Biennial. 84–1012. ISSN 0740–8250. $15 (1986 ed.). Pap.

Aimed at medical students interested in applying for a general or child psychiatry residency program, this directory also identifies applicable postgraduate grants. For more information about the publication, see the annotation in the "Internships—Sciences—Health Sciences" section of this bibliography.

629 **Financial Aid for Minorities in Allied Health.** Ed. by Lois S. Cofield and Ruth N. Swann. Garrett Park, MD: Garrett Park Press, 1980. 58p. 81–129225. $2. Pap.

This booklet, published in 1980, lists grants, scholarships, and fellowships open to minorities interested in health care. For more information about the publication, see the annotation in the "Fellowships—Sciences—Health Sciences" section of this bibliography.

630 **Financial Aid for Minorities in Medicine.** By Sterling H. Hudson III and Ruth N. Swann. Garrett Park, MD: Garrett Park Press, 1981. 66p. 81–184828. $3. Pap.

This booklet focuses on grants, fellowships, and some scholarships that were open to minorities interested in the medical field prior to 1981. For more information about the publication, see the annotation in the "Fellowships—Sciences—Health Sciences" section of this bibliography.

631 **Foundation Profiles: A Guide to Foundation Giving in the Health Field.** By G. Ramey, Dan Feshbach, and Susan Hagadorn. San Francisco: Consortium for the Health Professions, 1982. n.p. (Health Care Fundraising series, 5). $20. Pap.

The purpose of this directory is "to provide grant seekers with quick access to information on major foundations which gave grants in the field of health." The listing covers the most prominent national foundations in the health care field as well as a select group of community and corporate foundations with a reputation for giving in the Western United States. The information provided was current as of March, 1982. The entries are arranged by sponsoring organization and contain the following information: address, telephone number, contact person, program priorities, types of programs funded, areas of interest, restrictions, amount awaded, number awarded, sample grants, and application procedures. There are no indexes, but a list of foundations covered is printed in the front of the book.

632 **Free Money for Professional Studies.** By Laurie Blum. New York: Barnes and Noble, 1985. 204p. (Blum's Guides to College Money). 85–42725. ISBN 0–06–464104–0. $5.95. Pap.

This guide identifies state-based organizations awarding grants and scholarships to their residents, miscellaneous awards available to special applicants (e.g., deaf children, veterans' dependents), and selected financial aid programs appropriate for "professional studies" (dentistry, medicine, nursing, optometry, pharmacology, psychiatry, veterinary medicine, business, and law). For more information about the publication, see the annotation in the "Fellowships—Sciences—Health Sciences" section of this bibliography.

633 Health Grants & Contracts Weekly. Arlington, VA: Capitol Publications. Weekly (51 issues). ISSN 0194–2352. $179/yr.

Similar in purpose and format to *Federal Grants and Contracts Weekly*, this 10–page weekly newsletter provides details on requests for proposals (RFPs), deadline dates for grant competitions, procurement-related news, and newly-issued regulations for health grants and contracts. RFP entries include the following information: title of project, brief description, length of project, date proposal due, RFP number, date appearing in *Commerce Business Daily*, and name and address of contact in agency. This information used to be available online through NewsNet as *Grants & Contracts Weekly*; however, the online version was recently suspended. Another useful source of current information on federal funding in the health fields is the monthly *Health Funds Government Letter: Sharing Information on Federal and Foundation Fund Sources*, issued by Health Resources Publishing (Main P.O. Box 206, Long Beach, NJ 07740. $72/yr).

634 Medical and Health Information Directory. Ed. by Anthony T. Kruzas. Detroit: Gale, 1978– . Irreg. 85–645724. ISSN 0749–9973. $320 (1984/85 ed.).

Published irregularly since 1977, the third edition of this directory was issued (in two volumes) in 1984/85. In volume one of the set, typical directory-type information is supplied for various organizations in the medical and health fields, including foundations and grant-awarding organizations. Provided in the entries are names, addresses, key personnel, and descriptions of services, facilities, and functions.

635 Medical Research Funding Bulletin. Bronxville, NY: Science Support Center, 1972– . 3 times/month. 85–14532. $48/yr.

Each issue (published on the 10th, 20th, and 30th of the month) identifies (1) up to 40 research grants and fellowships in medical sciences offered by federal and private organizations and (2) up to 30 federal research contracts in the science and health care fields. The programs are listed chronologically by deadline (two months lead time is usually given). Entries generally specify sponsoring organization address and telephone number, contact person, acronym, program requirements, and application deadline.

Physical Sciences

636 Guide to Federal Energy Development Assistance Programs, 1981. Washington, DC: Northeast-Midwest Institute, 1982. 120p. 81–643162. ISSN 0275–6064. Pap.

In 1982, this publication was issued under the title *User's Guide to Government Energy Programs* (described below).

637 Guide to Financing: Small-Scale Geothermal Energy Projects. Salem, OR: Department of Energy (dist. by National Technical Information Service), 1982. $8, pap.; $4.50, microfiche.

This directory identifies (1) agencies and organizations that provide technical assistance (arranged geographically) and (2) sources of public and private sector financial support for geothermal energy projects (arranged by type of agency or organization). The information supplied is limited to address and telephone number only. A new edition is planned for 1987.

638 User's Guide to Government Energy Programs, 1982. Washington, DC: Northeast-Midwest Institute, 1982. 142p. (Economic Growth series). 81–2666. ISSN 0730–627X. $7.50. Pap.

Covered in this guide are 60 grants, loans, loan guarantees, tax incentives, technical assistance programs, and other forms of aid for the energy field. The programs are open to businesses, local governments, community groups, homeowners, renters, and entrepreneurs. Both federal and state programs are covered. In addition, there are separate sections that identify energy strategies in urban, rural, and community settings, government and private information sources, directories, national and regional federal offices, state agencies, and related vocabulary. Indexing is by applicant, agency, and subject. An earlier edition of this work was issued under the title *Guide to Federal Energy Development and Assistance Programs.*

Technology

639 Computer Resource Guide for Nonprofits. 3d ed. San Francisco: Public Management Institute, 1985. 2v. 83–63275. ISBN 0–916664–42–2. $225. Pap.

This directory provides information on two types of computer resources. The first, of little interest to the seeker of financial aid, describes computer software packages that provide special services (e.g., accounts receivable, donor history) to nonprofit organizations. The second section identifies foundations, corporations, and federal agencies that have made computer-related grants, loans, and in-kind donations. The following information is provided for each: name, address, telephone number, contact person, trustees, board members or contribution committee members, geographic limitations, types of grants awarded, areas of interest, number of grants awarded, total amount of grants award, funder's giving patterns in the computer area, and typical grants. The entries are indexed by geographic focus, grant recipients, vendor locations, types of support, board and committee members, computer software, contact person, and sponsoring organization headquarters. The first edition of the directory was published in 1982 (Comp. by Kenneth L.

Gilman. 355p. 82–235690). To update the data presented here, use *Nonprofit Computer Connection* (described below).

640   Federal Biotechnology Funding Sources. Ed. by Oskar R. Zaborsky and Brenda K. Young. Washington, DC: OMEC Publishing, 1984. 262p. ISBN 0–931283–23–X. $45.

This is the most current separate listing available of federal programs funding biotechnological research and/or development. Over 300 programs and activities in 33 federal agencies and departments are described. The entries are arranged alphabetically. Generally, contact names and research interests are included in each entry. The directory is indexed by sponsoring organization and by contact personnel. Small business programs are covered in a separate section.

641   Nonprofit Computer Connection. San Francisco: Public Management Institute, 1985– . Monthly. $127/yr.

This monthly eight-page newsletter devotes one of its five regular sections to computer-related philanthropy. Use it to update the listings in the *Computer Resource Guide for Nonprofits* described above.

SPECIAL POPULATION GROUPS

The Disabled

642   Directory of Federal Aid for the Handicapped: A Guide to Federal Assistance Programs Serving the Handicapped. Santa Monica, CA: Ready Reference, 1982. 280p. 81–23547. ISBN 0–916270–30–0. $47.50. Pap.

The purpose of this directory is to provide information on federal funding, services, and activities relating to the needs of the disabled. As with other Ready Reference directories of federal aid (described in various sections of this bibliography), the listings in this volume are taken directly from the *Catalog of Federal Domestic Assistance* (see the annotation in the "Grants— General—United States" section). The information presented here, in fact, even follows the format of the catalog (which costs less, covers more areas, and is more current).

643   Federal   Assistance   for   Programs   Serving   the   Handicapped.
Washington, DC: U.S. Office for Handicapped Individuals, 1976– .
Annual. 79–647376. ISSN 0198–9367.

Although planned as an annual, the latest edition of this directory was
published in 1980. It covers more than 140 programs addressing the needs of
handicapped individuals. The program descriptions are excerpted from the
Catalog of Federal Domestic Assistance (described elsewhere). The entries are
grouped into four categories (project grants, formula grants, direct payments,
and nonfinancial assistance) and indexed by subject area and applicant
eligibility. Included as supplementary information are descriptions of a
number of private sector resource organizations concerned with fund raising,
approximately 50 publications of interest to grantseekers, and a directory of
state offices that deal with special education, crippled children's services,
developmental disabilities, and vocational rehabilitation. Two other
publications that are useful in identifying financial assistance programs for
the disabled are *Handicapped Funding Directory*, which lists both foundation
and federal sources of support, and *Programs for the Handicapped*, a
bimonthly newsletter issued by the U.S. Department of Education's
Clearinghouse on the Handicapped. To identify financial aid programs
available directly to the disabled themselves, see the *Directory of Financial
Aids for the Disabled and Their Dependents*, described in the "Scholarships—
Special Population Groups—The Disabled" section of this bibliography.

644   Financial Aid for the Disabled and Their Dependents. By Gail Ann
Schlachter. Los Angeles: Reference Service Press, 1987– . Biennial.
(Directories of Financial Aid for Special Needs Groups). $29.95 (1987/
88 ed.).

This is the first comprehensive and up-to date listing of grants-in-aid, loans,
awards, scholarships, and fellowships that have been established for disabled
individuals and their dependents. For more information about the
publication, see the annotation in the "Scholarships—Special Population
Groups—The Disabled" section of this bibliography.

645   Financial Resources for Disabled Individuals. Falls Church, VA:
Institute for Information Studies, 1980. 75p. 80–84166. ISBN
0–935294–06–6. $1. Pap.

Supported in part by a research grant from the National Institute of
Handicapped Research, this guide is "intended to provide a practical source
of information on financial resources for disabled individuals." A broad range
of national programs are described, including those related to basic living
needs, education, and employment. Many of the programs profiled are aimed
specifically at individuals with disabilities; a number of others, however, are
targeted at a broader audience. Among the 40 resources covered are Social

Security Disability Insurance, the Railroad Retirement Act, workmen's compensation, the Internal Revenue Code exemption for the blind, and College Work Study. The information provided for each program is limited to purpose, eligibility requirements, benefits available, and some additional comments. Much of the information presented is now out of date and should be used with care. A more current list of similar programs can be found in the *Pocket Guide to Federal Help for the Disabled Person*, described elsewhere in this section of the bibliography.

646 Handicapped Funding Directory: A Guide to Sources of Funding in the United States for Handicapped Programs and Services. Ed. by Richard M. Eckstein. Marina del Rey, CA: Research Grant Guides, 1978– . Biennial. 82–642077. ISSN 0733–4752. $23.50 (1986–87 ed.). Pap.

Published biennially since 1978, this guide identifies foundations, corporations, associations, and agencies (700 in the 1986–1987 edition) that have funded programs and services in the following areas: mentally retarded, speech impaired, emotionally disturbed, health impaired, hard of hearing, deaf, visually handicapped, orthopedically impaired, and learning disabled. However, only very brief information is provided for the agencies, many of which do not have ongoing funding programs for the disabled but only a record of having issued at least one grant at least one time during the past in at least one of the areas listed above. The organizations are grouped by type (associations, foundations, and federal agencies) and indexed by name and area of service. Also provided are a selected bibliography of financial aid directories and selected lists of directories of state/local grantmakers and organizations publishing information on handicaps. Programs for individuals with disabilities are not covered in this directory; for that information, see *Financial Aid for the Disabled and Their Dependents* (described in the "Scholarships—Special Population Groups—The Disabled" section of this bibliography).

647 Pocket Guide to Federal Help for the Disabled Person. Rev. ed. Prep. by the Office of Information Resources for the Handicapped. Washington, DC: U.S. Department of Education, 1985. 23p. Free. Pap.

Similar in purpose to but less extensive in coverage than *Financial Resources for Disabled Individuals* (described elsewhere in this section), this free booklet provides information on "federal programs designed to assist the disabled in making the most of their abilities." It describes benefits applicable to blind, deaf, and developmentally disabled persons. Also included are the names and addresses of various federal agencies that can identify state and/or local counterpart offices. The entries are arranged by area of assistance offered (education, employment, housing). There is no index. Previous editions of the pamphlet were published in 1979, 1980, and 1983.

Ethnic Groups

648 **Directory of Federal Aid for Women & Minorities: A Guide to Federal Assistance Programs Serving Women & Minorities.** Santa Monica, CA: Ready Reference, 1982. 250p. ISBN 0–916270–32–7. $47.50. Pap.

The descriptions of federal domestic assistance projects, programs, and services for minorities and women included here are taken directly from the *Catalog of Federal Domestic Assistance* (described in the "Grants—General—United States" section). For more information about the directory, see the annotation in the "Grants—Special Population Groups—Women" section of the bibliography.

649 **Directory of Financial Aids for Minorities.** By Gail Ann Schlachter. Los Angeles: Reference Service Press, 1984– . Biennial. (Directories of Financial Aid for Special Needs Groups). 83–25068. ISBN 0–918276–03–9. ISSN 0738–4122. $37.50 (1986–1987 ed.).

The latest edition of this biennial directory includes a descriptive list of more than 1,200 grants, scholarships, fellowships, loans, awards, prizes, and internships set aside for Asian Americans, Black Americans, Hispanic Americans, Native Americans, and minorities in general. For more information about the publication, see the annotation in the "Scholarships—Special Population Groups—Ethnic Groups" section of this bibliography.

650 **Federal Programs of Assistance to American Indians: A Report Prepared for the Senate Select Committee on Indian Affairs of the United States Senate.** By Richard S. Jones. Washington, DC: G.P.O., 1985. 295p. (Committee Print 99th Congress, 1st Session). Free. Pap.

Described in this committee report are (1) programs specifically designed to benefit Indian tribes and individuals; (2) programs that specifically include Indians or Indian tribes as eligible beneficiaries; and (3) programs that may not specifically name Indians or Indian tribes as eligible beneficiaries but which are of special interest to Indians. The programs are arranged by sponsoring organization. The entries contain the following information: name, nature and purpose of program; eligibility requirements; application procedures; contact person; printed information available; authorizing legislation; administering agency; available assistance; use restrictions; appropriations for recent years; obligations incurred; Washington contacts; local contacts throughout the United States; and related programs. This is the most comprehensive single source of information on programs of assistance for Native Americans from the federal government. Earlier editions were published in 1975 (Congressional Research Service, Library of Congress. 159p.), 1978 (Congressional Research Service, Library of Congress. 339p.),

1981 (97th Congress, 1st Session. 345p. 81–602544), and 1983 (97th Congress, 2d Session. 279p. 83–601818).

651 Financial Aid for Minorities in Allied Health. Ed. by Lois G. Cofield and Ruth N. Swann. Garrett Park, MD: Garrett Park Press, 1980. 58p. 81–129225. $2. pap.

Now considerably out of date, this directory provides a selective listing of fellowships, scholarships, and grants available in 1980 to minorities interested in allied health fields. For more information about the publication, see the annotation in the "Scholarships—Sciences—Health Sciences" section of this bibliography.

652 Financial Aid for Minorities in Business. Ed. by Howard F. Wehrle, III and Ruth N. Swann. Garrett Park, MD: Garrett Park Press, 1980. 48p. 80–14474. $3. Pap.

Selected grants, fellowships, and scholarships in the field of business that were available to minorities in 1980 are listed in this directory. For more information about the publication, see the annotation in the "Scholarships— Social Sciences—Business and Economics" section of this bibliography.

653 Financial Aid for Minorities in Education. Ed. by Mary T. Christian and Ruth N. Swann. Garrett Park, MD: Garrett Park Press, 1980. 58p. 80–153221. $3. Pap.

One in a series of booklets covering financial assistance programs for minorities, this compilation identifies selected grants, fellowships, and scholarships in the field of education that were available in 1980. For more information about the publication, see the annotation in the "Scholarships— Social Sciences—Education" section of this bibliography.

654 Financial Aid for Minorities in Engineering. Ed. by Clayton G. Holloway and Ruth N. Swann. Garrett Park, MD: Garrett Park Press, 1981. 52p. 81–161268. $3. Pap.

Focusing on the field of engineering, this mostly unannotated list selectively identifies grants, scholarships, and fellowships open to minority students prior to 1981. For more information about the publication, see the annotation in the "Scholarships—Sciences—Engineering" section of this bibliography.

655 Financial Aid for Minorities in Law. Ed. by Novelle J. Dickensen and Ruth N. Swann. Garrett Park, MD: Garrett Park Press, 1981. 63p. 80–153225. $3. Pap.

Aimed at minorities interested in legal studies, this (mostly unannotated) list identifies grants, fellowships, and scholarships that were available in 1981.

For more information about the publication, see the annotation in the "Fellowships—Social Sciences—Law" section of this bibliography.

656 Financial Aid for Minorities in Mass Communications. By Leslie L. Lawton and Ruth N. Swann. Garrett Park, MD: Garrett Park Press, 1981. 62p. 81–211245. $3. Pap.

Included in this listing are references to grants, scholarships, and fellowships open to minorities interested in the fields of mass media and communications. For more information about the publication, see the annotation in the "Scholarships—Humanities—Communications and Mass Media" section of this bibliography.

657 Financial Aid for Minorities in Science. Ed. by Ruth N. Swann and Sharon F. White. Garrett Park, MD: Garrett Park Press, 1980. 49p. $2. Pap.

Published in 1980, this mostly unannotated listing selectively identifies grants, fellowships, and scholarships open to minorities interested in the sciences. For more information about the publication, see the annotation in the "Scholarships—Sciences—General" section of this bibliography.

658 Foundations That Provide Support for Health and Human Services: A Selected List. 2d ed. Washington, DC: Public Health Service, 1981. 75p. Free. Pap.

A revision of the 1978 edition (*Foundations That Provide Support for Human Services.* 45p.), this guide identifies 150 private foundations that provide support for health and human services. Although not indicated in the title, the list is intended to be used by persons working with Native American groups and communities. It emphasizes financial assistance for health projects, social services, training, environmental activities, and construction. However, it should be noted that the programs described here do not necessarily exclude other groups from applying. The entries are arranged by state and supply the following information: name of foundation, address (no telephone number), and statement of general purpose (one to two sentences). At the end of the volume, there is a briefly annotated bibliography, primarily of Foundation Center publications and state directories of foundations, and a set of three appendices: Indian Health Service Area and program officers; Indian Health Service Area office contacts; and Department of Health and Human Services Regional Office contacts for Native American Funding.

659 Funding Guide for Native Americans. By Dean Chavers. 2d ed., rev. Broken Arrow, OK: DCA Publishers, 1985. 398p. $54.95. Looseleaf.

Like Fincher's *Funds for Hispanics* (described elsewhere in this section), this guide does not identify financial aid programs for individual Native

Americans. Rather, it lists 170 foundations, corporations, and religious groups that "have expressed an interest in Native Americans in the past five years." The entries are arranged by foundation and specify address, contact person, application procedures and deadlines, financial support, numbers awarded, policy statement, purpose of grant, limitations, officers/trustees, and typical grants funded. An asterisk is placed beside the names of foundations that specify Native Americans in their basic policy statements. There are only eight of these. A five-page "Fund Raiser's Bibliography" completes the volume. The first edition of the listing was issued in 1983 (399p.). For similar but retrospective coverage, see *Grants to Indians, 1972–1983* (described elsewhere in this section).

660 Funds for Hispanics. Comp. by Beatrice Fincher. Austin, TX: Spanish Publicity, 1981. 36p. 81–90470. ISBN 0–9607386–0–6. $9. Pap.

Despite what its title might suggest, this booklet does not identify financial aid programs for individual Hispanic Americans. Rather, it lists private foundations that made grants either for projects that benefited Hispanics or for projects sponsored by Hispanic groups between 1978 and 1980. About 90 foundations are covered, much fewer than the number covered in the Foundation Center's *COMSEARCH* on Hispanics (see the annotation in the "Grants—General—United States" section of this bibliography). The entries are arranged by foundation name and give brief information on purpose, limitations, financial support, and typical grants awarded. Also included is a table that indicates how to apply for funding from the foundations listed.

661 Grants to Indians, 1972–1983. By Robert J. Swann. Broken Arrow, OK: DCA Publishers, 1984. 138p. $49.95. Pap.

Similar to *Funding Guide for Native Americans* (which is issued by the same publisher), but retrospective in its coverage, this directory describes nearly 900 grants given to or in support of American Indians. Only grants over $5,000 are identified. The entries are grouped into 61 topical categories and are indexed by subject and chronology. The foundations awarding these grants are listed in a separate section, with address, telephone number, and contact person provided. This listing has limited value as a funding resource, since such aspects as agency guidelines, application procedures, and geographic limitations are not given.

662 Guide to Federal Minority Enterprise and Related Programs. Rev. ed. Washington, DC: Minority Business Development Agency, U.S. Department of Commerce, 1982. 44p. 83–644813. ISSN 0739–6066. Free. Pap.

This pamphlet is divided into eight sections, one of which deals specifically with federal grants available to minority businesses. For more information about the publication, see the annotation in the "Grants—Social Sciences—Business and Economics" section of this bibliography.

663 Hispanic Financial Resource Handbook. Comp. by the Hispanic Student Program. Columbus: Office of Student Life, Ohio State University, 1982– . Annual. $5 (1985 ed.). Pap.

This comb-bound handbook was first compiled in 1982 (and revised annually since then) to "assist Hispanic students and professionals in obtaining financial aid information which is especially geared toward Hispanic and other minorities." Brief descriptions are provided for applicable grants, fellowships, scholarships, and loans. For more information about the publication, see the annotation in the "Scholarships—Special Population Groups—Ethnic Groups" section of this bibliography.

664 A Study of Foundation Awards to Hispanic-Oriented Organizations in the U.S., 1981–1982; Preliminary Report. By Armando Valdez. Stanford, CA: Stanford University, 1984. 36p. $3. Pap.

Similar to but a little more up to date than Fincher's *Funds for Hispanics* (described elsewhere in this section), this preliminary report identifies 94 foundations that have made grants to Hispanic-oriented organizations and projects. In addition, the pamphlet includes numerous tables that chart the geographic distribution of awards, types of services supported, foundations making the largest number of awards, major recipients, and number of awards by subject category. The final report has not yet been issued.

Foreign Students

665 Private Sector Funding Available to Foreign Scholars and Students in the United States. Prep. by Ellen Wise Sivon. Rev. ed. Washington, DC: National Association for Foreign Student Affairs, 1985. 54p. 84–242345. ISBN 0–912207–09–4. $2.95. Pap.

Approximately 50 private sector-sponsored grants, scholarships, and fellowships for foreign scholars and students already in the United States are described in this directory. For more information about the publication, see the annotation in the "Scholarships—Special Population Groups—Foreign Students" section of this bibliography.

Military Personnel and Veterans

666 **Educational Assistance and Opportunities Information for Army Family Members.** Alexandria, VA: Adjutant General's Office, U.S. Department of the Army, 1984. v.p. Free. Looseleaf.

This directory identifies associations and other groups that provide grants-in-aid, scholarships, fellowships, and loans to army personnel and relatives of military personnel. For more information about the publication, see the annotation in the "Scholarships—Special Population Groups—Military Personnel and Veterans" section of this bibliography.

667 **Federal Benefits for Veterans and Dependents.** Prep. by the U.S. Veterans Administration. Washington, DC: G.P.O., 1969– . Annual. 85–641702. ISSN 0883–3370. $1.75 (1986 ed.). Pap.

This booklet provides a comprehensive summary of benefits available to veterans and their dependents. It is updated annually and contains information on alcoholism treatment programs, aid for the blind, burial assistance, clothing allowances, compensation for service-connected disabilities, death payments, dental treatment, dependents' education, education and training loans, medical benefits, pensions for nonservice-connected disabilities, etc. Three lists appear in the back of the publication for the benefit of the veteran: (1) VA facilities: where to go for help; (2) Veterans Administration centers; and (3) Veterans Administration national cemeteries. Each of these lists is arranged alphabetically by state and includes names of facilities, addresses, and telephone numbers. Over the years, the pamphlet has been issued under a number of titles, including *Handbook on Federal Benefits for Veterans* and *Federal Benefits for Veterans.*

668 **Once a Veteran: Benefits, Rights, Obligations. 1985 Edition.** Washington, DC: American Forces Information Service, U.S. Department of Defense (for sale by G.P.O.), 1985. 43p. $2. Pap.

This inexpensive pamphlet provides up-to-date information on the benefits, rights, and obligations of American veterans. It includes program descriptions (covering the loans, scholarships, fellowships, and grants-in-aid available), specifies application procedures, covers eligibility requirements, and indicates ways to collect benefits while remaining in the armed services. This pamphlet supersedes DoD PA-5D, DA Pam 360–526, NAVPERS-46682B (rev. 1978). It is more general in its coverage than *Federal Benefits for Veterans and Dependents* (described elsewhere in this section of the bibliography).

669 State Veterans' Laws: Digests of State Laws Regarding Rights, Benefits, and Privileges of Veterans and Their Dependents. Washington, DC: G.P.O., 1945– . Irreg. 60–62289. Free. Pap. Microfiche to depository libraries.

This congressional report presents digests of veterans' rights, benefits, and privileges provided at the state level. The publication serves as a complement to the listing of federal programs described in the annual *Federal Benefits for Veterans and Dependents* (described elsewhere in this section of the bibliography).

670 United States Code, Title 38: Veteran's Benefits. Washington, DC: G.P.O. Irreg. $25, U.S.; $31.25, elsewhere. Looseleaf.

This looseleaf subscription service consists of a basic manual and one supplement. It contains the exact text of the laws relating to veterans' benefits that come under the jurisdiction of the House Committee on Veterans' Affairs. Use this publication when you need the official wording of the authorizing legislation. For a more readable and considerably less expensive description of available veterans' benefits, see the annually revised *Federal Benefits for Veterans and Their Dependents* (described elsewhere in this section of the bibliography).

671 The Viet Vet Survival Guide: How to Get through the Bureaucracy and Get What You Need and Are Entitled To. Ed. by Craig Kubey, et al. New York: Facts On File, 1986. 256p. ISBN 0–8160–1379–9. $19.95.

This is the first self-help book to address the needs of the nine million men and women who served in Southeast Asia. Written with the support of the Vietnam Veterans of America, it provides practical information on problems that remain a legacy of the war: e.g., Post-Traumatic Stress Disorder, Agent Orange, and drug and alcohol dependence. However, most of the financial information—on disability compensation, housing assistance, and other benefits and services available to Vietnam veterans—is not new or unique to this book. It is available, at much less cost, in *Federal Benefits for Veterans and Dependents* (described elsewhere in this section of the bibliography).

672 What Every Veteran Should Know. East Moline, IL: Veterans Information Service, 1937– . Annual, with monthly supplements. ISSN 0083–9108. $6.00; $18, with supplements (1981 ed.). Pap.

Published since 1937, the latest edition of this guide (1981. ISBN 0–346–32464–5) describes the federal benefits that veterans and their dependents are eligible to receive. Instructions are provided on the best ways to obtain assistance. Entries are arranged by subject and thoroughly indexed.

Women

673   **Directory of Federal Aid for Women & Minorities: A Guide to Federal Assistance Programs Serving Women & Minorities.** Santa Monica, CA: Ready Reference, 1982. 250p. ISBN 0–916270–32–7. $47.50. Pap.

The program descriptions included in this directory are extracted directly from the *Catalog of Federal Domestic Assistance* (see entry in the "Grants— General—United States" section of this bibliography). Only federal domestic assistance projects, programs, and services for women and minorities are covered. Grouped into two sections—programs serving women and minorities and programs of interest to them—the entries provide information on sponsoring agency, authorization, objectives and goals, remuneration, eligibility, uses and restrictions, application process, regulations and guidelines, related programs, sample funded projects, selection criteria, and agency policies pertaining to the program. Also included are five appendices: programs requiring circular coordination, suggestions for proposal writing and application submission, commonly-used abbreviations and acronyms, agency regional and local office addresses, and sources of additional information contacts. A brief subject index completes the volume.

674   **Directory of Financial Aids for Women.** By Gail Ann Schlachter. Los Angeles: Reference Service Press, 1978– . Biennial. (Directories of Financial Aid for Special Needs Groups). 84–24582. ISSN 0732–5215. $37.50.

This is the only extensive and regularly updated listing of grants, loans, fellowships, scholarships, awards/prizes, and internships designed primarily or exclusively for women. For more information about the publication, see the annotation in the "Scholarships—Special Population Groups—Women" section of this bibliography.

675   **Financial Aid: A Partial List of Resources for Women.** Prep. by the Project on the Status and Education of Women. Washington, DC: Association of American Colleges, 1984. 15p. $2.50. Pap.

Selected grants and scholarships available to women students are briefly described in this pamphlet. For more information about the publication, see the annotation in the "Scholarships—Special Population Groups—Women" section of this bibliography.

676 **Public and Private Sources of Funding for Sexual Assult Treatment Programs.** Prep. by the National Center for the Prevention and Control of Rape. Rockville, MD: U.S. National Institute of Mental Health, 1981. 35p. (DHHS Publication No. (ADM) 81–1117). Free. Pap.

The purpose of this publication is "to assist rape crisis centers and other sexual assult treatment and service programs in obtaining financial support." Not intended to be a comprehensive listing, the guide attempts only to identify some possible resources in the federal government and the private sector. The booklet is divided into three sections. The first section provides brief descriptions of selected federal agencies or programs administered on the federal level, as well as those dispersed in block grants through the individual states. The second section highlights foundations that have an interest in projects for women and those programs that can assist individuals and organizations in researching foundations and preparing grant proposals. The final section, the appendices, consists of citations of additional sources of information, an annotated grant proposal outline, and suggested fundraising approaches. While this pamphlet provides a unique listing, much of the information (particuarly the addresses) is now out of date.

Awards and Prizes

Awards—including prizes, competitions, and honoraria—are granted on local, state, regional, national, and international levels to recognize, reward, or support notable achievement. Included in this chapter are 95 references to directories listing awards and prizes. Of these, 15 are general in nature (covering either international or American awards); 8 deal with the social sciences; the vast majority focus on the humanities (69 entries), particularly fine and applied arts, journalism, and literature; and 3 cover special population groups. If you are looking for a specific awards directory and you do not find it in this chapter, be sure to check the Title Index to see if it is covered elsewhere in the Guide.

GENERAL

International

677 Annual Register of Grant Support: A Guide to Support Programs of Government Agencies, Foundations, and Business and Professional Organizations. Wilmette, IL: National Register, 1969– . Annual. 69–18307. ISSN 0066–4049. $87 (1985–86 ed.).

Although it focuses on North American programs, the *Annual Register* also describes a number of awards sponsored abroad. A more comprehensive list of international awards can be found, however, in the latest edition of *Awards, Honors, and Prizes*, described elsewhere in this section. For more information on the *Annual Register*, see the annotation in the "Grants— General—United States" section of this bibliography.

678 Awards, Honors, and Prizes: An International Directory of Awards and Their Donors. Ed. by Gita Siegman. 6th ed. Detroit: Gale, 1985–1986. 2v. 78–16691. ISBN 0–8103–0445–7. $145, v. 1; $160, v. 2.

Volume two of the sixth edition of this widely-used reference work provides comprehensive international coverage of awards and prizes given in countries other than the United States. For more information about the publication, see the annotation in the "Awards and Prizes—General—United States" section of this bibliography.

679 The Grants Register: Postgraduate Awards in the English Speaking World. Ed. by Norman Frankel. New York: St. Martin's Press, 1969– . Biennial. 77–12055. $39.50 (1985–87 ed.).

This biennial directory describes prizes, fellowships, and grants open to nationals of the United States, Canada, the United Kingdom, Ireland, Australia, New Zealand, South Africa, and the developing countries. For more information about the publication, see the annotation in the "Grants— General—International" section of this bibliography.

680 Winners: The Blue Ribbon Encyclopedia of Awards. By Claire Walter. Indexed by Felice D. Levy and Cynthia Crippen. Rev. ed. New York: Facts On File, 1982. 916p. 80–22177. o.p.

While this directory focuses on major American honors in all fields of endeavor, it also covers important awards granted abroad, particularly those of international scope. For more information about this publication, see the annotation in the "Awards and Prizes—General—United States" section of this bibliography.

United States

681 Annual Register of Grant Support: A Guide to Support Programs of Government Agencies, Foundations, and Business and Professional Organizations. Wilmette, IL: National Register, 1969– . Annual. 69–18307. ISSN 0066–4049. $87 (1985–86 ed.).

Despite its title, this annual covers awards and prizes as well as grant opportunities. For more information about the publication, see the annotation in the "Grants—General—United States" section of this bibliography.

682 Awards, Honors, and Prizes: An International Directory of Awards and Their Donors. Ed. by Gita Siegman. 6th ed. Detroit: Gale, 1985–1986. 2v. 78–16691. ISBN 0–8103–0445–7. $145, volume 1; $160, volume 2.

The sixth edition of this widely-used reference work is intended to completely supersede the fifth edition, published in 1982. Volume 1, *United States and Canada*, contains up-to-date information on more than 8,600 awards, honors, and prizes given in the United States and Canada in the areas of advertising and public relations, art, business, government, finance, science, engineering, literature, technology, sports, religion, public affairs, law, publishing, international affairs, transportation, architecture, journalism, music, photography, theater, and the performing arts. Excluded from the listing are scholarships, fellowships, study awards to students, prizes received as a result of entering contests where something is achieved only for the purpose of the contest, and local and regional awards. The volume is divided into four sections: 1) the main listing for each award, where the following information is given: name, address, title of award, purpose, eligibility, form of award, frequency, date established, and who established the award; 2) a list of subjects and "see also" references (each award is indexed by subject and/or areas of interest); 3) an alphabetical index to the specific names of each award; and 4) an organization index. Volume 2 adds international coverage by describing organizations and awards given in countries other than the United States. The first and second editions of this title were published in 1969 and 1972 as one-volume works. Beginning in 1975, with the third edition, the publication has been issued as a two-volume work. In between editions, the publishers have been issuing a *Supplement* volume (the sixth edition supplement is $85).

683 Chronicle Student Aid Annual. Moravia, NY: Chronicle Guidance Publications, 1978– . Annual. 79–640–360. ISSN 0190–339X. $16.50 (1985 ed.). Pap.

In addition to scholarship programs, a number of awards, grants, loans, and fellowships are described in this annual directory. For more information about the publication, see the annotation in the "Scholarships—General—United States" section of this bibliography.

684 Financial Aids for Higher Education. Prep. by Oreon Keeslar. Dubuque, IA: William C. Brown, 1963– . Biennial. 76–645208. ISSN 0364–8877. $32.95 (1986 ed.). Pap.

Each biennial edition of this directory contains detailed information on over 5,000 programs (contests, scholarships, and loans) open to students interested in postsecondary education. For more information about the publication, see the annotation in the "Scholarships—General—United States" section of this bibliography.

685 For Us Women Newsletter. Washington, DC: For Us Publications, 1983– . Monthly. 83–7501. ISSN 0737–5395. $16.50/yr.

This eight-page monthly newsletter provides information on contests and grants of interest to individuals as well as nonprofit organizations. On the average, 20 to 30 competitions are described in each issue. Despite the newsletter title, most of the programs listed are open equally to men and women.

686 The Grants Register: Postgraduate Awards in the English Speaking World. Ed. by Norman Frankel. New York: St. Martin's Press, 1969– . Biennial. 77–12055. $39.59 (1985–87 ed.).

This biennial directory describes prizes, fellowships, and grants open to nationals of the United States, Canada, the United Kingdom, Ireland, Australia, New Zealand, South Africa, and the developing countries. For more information about the publication, see the annotation in the "Grants—General—International" section of this bibliography.

687 NASSP National Advisory List of Contests and Activities. Reston, VA: National Association of Secondary School Principals, 1940– . Annual. $1 (1986 ed.). Pap.

This annually-issued advisory list of regional and national contests and activities suitable for inclusion in a school program or curriculum is prepared by the National Association of Secondary School Principals' Committee on National Contests and Activities. The contests and activities listed here are "designed solely to benefit secondary school youth in educational, civic, social and ethical development." They are open to all secondary students,

215

regardless of race, creed, sex, or national origin. Excluded from the compilation are unsupervised essay and poster contests, scholarship programs, and national contests that require team or group competition at a common site. Some music festivals and music-travel programs are included. The contests and activities are divided into national and regional categories, listed alphabetically by sponsoring organization and indexed by program type (e.g., speech and debate programs, performing groups). The following information is provided for each entry: sponsors' address, program title, date registration closes, and program dates.

688   The Scholarship Book: The Complete Guide to Private-Sector Scholarships, Grants and Loans for Undergraduates. By Daniel J. Cassidy and Michael J. Alves. Englewood Cliffs, NJ: Prentice-Hall, 1984. 391p. 84–11683. ISBN 0–13–792342–2, cloth; -334–1, pap. $28.50, cloth; $14.95 pap.

Included in this extensive but rather unfocused directory are competitions, grants, internships, loans, scholarships, and fellowships for undergraduate and (despite its subtitle) graduate students. For more information about this publication, see the annotation in the "Scholarships—General—United States" section of this bibliography.

689   Student Aid Annual. Moravia, NY: Chronicle Guidance Publications, 1955–1975. Annual. ISSN 0580–4555.

From 1955 through 1974, this publication was known as *Student Aid Annual*, from 1975 through 1977 as *Student Aid Manual*, and since 1979 as *Chronicle Student Aid Annual* (described in the "Scholarships—General—United States" section of this bibliography).

690   Winners: The Blue Ribbon Encyclopedia of Awards. By Claire Walter. Indexed by Felice D. Levy and Cynthia Crippen. Rev. ed. New York: Facts On File, 1982. 916p. 80–22177. o.p.

Winners was first issued in 1978 (731p. 78–10247) by Facts On File to fill "a gap in reference material by compiling and indexing available information about awards, the organizations that give them, and the people or institutions that have received them." The work was also released by Harcourt Brace Jovanovich, in 1979, as *The Book of Winners* (731p. 79–14237). It was revised in 1982 by Facts On File and issued under its original title. In the latest edition (now out of print), 1,000 awards given on the basis of judgment rather than measurable or objectively defined achievements are included. The emphasis is on major American honors in all fields of endeavor, as well as important awards granted abroad, particularly those of international scope. Both serious and humorous honors are covered. The following information for each award is provided: name of awarding body, address, name of award, nature of the award, frequency, founding date, and names of winners by year. The entries are grouped by category (e.g., books and literature, theater, librarianship and information science, beauty and fashion, culinary arts and homemaking) and indexed by award.

691 Winning Money for College: The High School Student's Guide to Scholarship Contests. By Alan Deutschman. Princeton, NJ: Peterson's Guides, 1984. 209p. 83–22151. ISBN 0–87866–261–8. $7.95. Pap.

Written by a Princeton student who won several awards himself, this guide covers 50 national scholarship competitions that award cash prizes for use at any college chosen by the winner. For more information about the publication, see the annotation in the "Scholarships—General—United States" section of this bibliography.

SOCIAL SCIENCES

Education

692 The Teacher's Almanac, 1986—1987. By Sherwood Harris and Lorna B. Harris. New York: Facts On File, 1986. 300p. ISBN 0–8160–1369–1. $24.95.

The first annual reference of its kind published for American educators, *The Teacher's Almanac* provides a potpourri of information, ranging from facts and figures to personalities in the teaching profession today. One section covers awards and prizes available in the field of education.

History

693 Fellowships and Grants of Interest to Historians. Washington, DC: American Historical Association, 1976–1977. Annual. Pap.

Since 1978, this annual publication has been issued as *Grants and Fellowships of Interest to Historians* (described in the "Grants—Social Sciences—History" section).

694 Grants and Fellowships of Interest to Historians. Washington, DC: American Historical Association, 1978– . Annual. 83–644237. ISSN 0275–830X. $4, members; $5, nonmembers (1985/86 ed.). Pap.

This annual listing identifies and describes nearly 200 awards, prizes, internships, fellowships, and travel grants of interest to graduate students, postdoctoral researchers, and scholars in history. For a more complete annotation, see the description of *Grants and Fellowships of Interest to Historians* in the "Grants—Social Sciences—History" section.

Librarianship

695   The Bowker Annual of Library and Book Trade Information. New York: Bowker, 1955– . Annual. 55–12434. ISSN 0068–0540. $79.95 (1986 ed.).

This annual focuses on library and book trade developments. The specific aspects covered vary somewhat from year to year. Generally, each edition contains a section on book statistics, prices, and prizes as well as a list of library scholarship sources and up-to-date information on library legislation, funding, and grantmaking agencies. Over the years, the annual has been issued under various titles, including *American Library Annual* and *American Library and Book Trade Annual*.

696   Library Resources Market Place: LRMP 204 New York: Bowker, 1980– . Irreg. 81–640040. ISSN 0000–0442. $35 (1981 ed.). Pap..

One section of this directory is devoted to library awards. Listed there are approximately 150 awards given either by libraries and library associations or to librarians and libraries in the United States and Canada. Each entry specifies only award title, sponsoring organization, address and telephone number, founding date, and purpose. More detail on the programs listed in this section can be found in the latest edition of Bowker's *Literary and Library Prizes* (described in the "Awards and Prizes—Humanities—Literature" section of this bibliograpy).

697   Literary and Library Prizes. New York: Bowker, 1935– . Irreg. 59–11370. ISSN 0075–9880. $26.95 (1980 ed.).

The latest edition of this directory (1980. ISBN 0–8352–1249–1) lists 454 representative major literary and library awards offered on an international and national basis. For more information about *Literary and Library Prizes*, see the description in the "Awards and Prizes—Humanities—Literature" section of this bibliography.

698   Literary Prizes and Their Winners. New York: Bowker, 1935–1939. Annual. 59–11370. ISSN 0730–5850.

Since 1940, the directory has been published as *Literary and Library Prizes* (described in the "Awards and Prizes—Humanities—Literature" section of this bibliography).

699   Opportunities and Honors for You and Your Colleagues. Chicago: American Library Association, 1986. 4p. Free. Pap.

The American Library Association sponsors more than 80 awards, fellowships, and grants "to honor distinguished service and foster professional growth." In this booklet, the association's programs are grouped by purpose (e.g., achievement/distinguished service, intellectual freedom, public relations, research), and each entry contains a brief description covering purpose, donor, and amount awarded. Most of these awards are also described in the American Library Association's annual *Handbook of Organization.*

HUMANITIES

General

700   ARIS Funding Messenger: Creative Arts and Humanities Report. San Francisco: Academic Research Information Systems, 1976– . 8 times/ yr., plus supplements. 84–8702. ISSN 0747–993X. $46, individuals; $96, institutions.

This current awareness service provides up-to-date information about hundreds of regional, national, and international awards, grants, and fellowships in the humanities, performing arts, and visual arts. For more information about the publication, see the annotation in the "Grants— Humanities—General" section of this bibliography.

701   Gadney's Guide to 1800 International Contests, Festivals & Grants in Film & Video, Photography, TV-Radio Broadcasting, Writing, Poetry, Playwriting, Journalism. By Alan Gadney. 2d ed. Glendale, CA: Festival Publications, 1980. 610p. 80–66803. ISBN 0–930828–03–8, cloth; -02–X, pap. $22.95, cloth; $15.95, pap.

This guide, prepared by an independent filmmaker and updating a 1978 edition (578p. 77–89041), contains over 1,800 entries describing national and international festivals, competitions, prizes, awards, grants, loans, and fellowships, divided into six sections: film; video, audio, and TV broadcasting; photography; writing, print, and journalism; general; and all media. Within each of these sections, the entries are grouped into 166 "special interest" categories and contain varying amounts of information (covering such points as deadlines, purpose, eligibility criteria, and judging process). A cross index of the five media categories and special interest subcategories, along with an alphabetical index of entries, completes the work. While still in print, this listing is basically subsumed by Gadney's 1980 through 1983 *How to Enter and Win* series (check the index for names of specific titles).

702 The National Directory of Grants and Aid to Individuals in the Arts, International. By Daniel Millsaps. 5th ed. Washington, DC: Washington International Arts Letter, 1983. 246p. (The Arts Patronage series, no. 11). 70–11269. ISBN 0–912072–12–1. ISSN 0270–5966. $15.95. Pap.

According to its editors, this paperback directory lists "most grants, prizes, and awards for professional work in the United States and abroad, and information about universities and schools which offer special aid to students." For more information about the publication, see the annotation in the "Grants—Humanities—General" section of this bibliography.

703 Ocular: The Directory of Information and Opportunities for the Visual Arts. Denver: Ocular, 1976– . Quarterly. $14/yr.

Provided in each issue of this quarterly journal is a section identifying financial aid for visual artists, including awards, grants, and fellowships. For more information about this publication, see the annotation in the "Grants—Humanities—General" section of this bibliography.

704 Washington International Arts Letter. Washington, DC: Washington International Arts Letter (WIAL), 1962– . 10 issues/yr. 68–6506. ISSN 0043–0609. $54/yr.

This monthly newsletter provides information on fellowships, scholarships, awards, and grants open to institutions and individuals involved in the arts. For more information about the publication, see the annotation in the "Grants—Humanities—General" section of this bibliography.

Applied Arts

705 Artweek. Oakland, CA: Artweek, 1970– . Weekly, September-May (44 issues/yr.). ISSN 0004–4121. $19.50/yr., individuals; $23/yr., institutions.

The competitions section of *Artweek* identifies approximately 50 art contests and festivals each week (from September through May). International, national, and regional competitions are covered. Entries for each competition specify event name, address, telephone number, contact persons, deadline, location, dates, eligibility, media accepted, entry fees, awards offered, and whether or not juried. The weekly lists are arranged by geographic restrictions, subdivided by deadline dates.

706 **Craftsworker's Market.** Ed. by Lynne Lapin. Assist. by Connie Archabal. Cincinnati, OH: Writer's Digest, 1978–1981. Annual. 79–640463. ISSN 0161–0554.

This publication supersedes Writer's Digest's *Art and Crafts Market* (ISSN 0147–2441) which, in turn, had superseded *Artist's and Photographer's Market* (ISSN 0140–8294). In each of the annual editions of *Craftsworker's Market*, entries are divided into three main sections: The Profession (information on functioning as a craftsworker), The Markets (e.g., architectural and interior design firms, colleges and universities, manufacturers, shows and fairs), and Opportunities and Services. The directory ceased publication in 1981 and has been replaced by the *National Directory of Shops/Galleries, Shows/Fairs* (described elsewhere in this section of the bibliography).

707 **How to Enter and Win Black & White Photography Contests.** By Alan Gadney. New York: Facts On File, 1982. 204p. 81–12594. ISBN 0–87196–571–2, cloth; -577–1, pap. $14.95, cloth; $6.95, pap.

708 **How to Enter and Win Color Photography Contests.** By Alan Gadney. New York: Facts On File, 1982. 204p. 81–12591. ISBN 0–87196–572–0, cloth; -578–X, pap. $14.95, cloth; $6.95, pap.

These publications—similar in format to others in the *How to Enter and Win* series—each cover over 500 national and international photography contests, photofairs, festivals, apprenticeships, grants, and awards. Program profiles specify names, addresses, judging rules, eligibility requirements, deadlines, and remuneration. Access to the numbered entries is through alphabetically arranged event/sponsor/award and subject/category indexes.

709 **How to Enter and Win Clay and Glass Crafts Contests.** By Alan Gadney. New York: Facts On File, 1983. 204p. 81–19561. ISBN 0–87196–661–1, cloth; -662–X, pap. $14.95, cloth; $6.95, pap.

Described here are national and international contests involving china, raku, earthenware, enameling, plaster, ceramics, pottery, porcelain, stoneware, glass art, stained and leaded glass, mosaic, plastic sculpture, and glassblowing. Among the competitions included are festivals, shows, exhibitions, markets, and trade fairs. Program entries specify eligibility, selection criteria, application deadlines, entry fees, technical requirements, and contact persons. Indexing is by event/sponsor/award and subject/category. A helpful introduction discusses how to analyze, enter, and—possibly—win clay and glass contests.

710 **How to Enter and Win Fabric and Fiber Crafts Contests.** By Alan
     Gadney. New York: Facts On File, 1983. 202p. 81–19563. ISBN
     0–87196–657–1, cloth; -658–1, pap. $14.95, cloth; $6.95.

The fabric and fiber crafts described here involve soft sculpture, embroidery,
quilting, stichery, weaving, spinning, papercrafts, crochet, doll making,
knitting, needlepoint, tapestry, macrame, basketry, tie-dye, textile craft, and
batik. For each national and international contest, the following information
is supplied: eligibility, judging criteria, "catch-clauses," deadlines, names and
addresses, entry fees and forms, subject categories, and technical
requirements. Both alphabetical and subject indexes provide access to the
entries.

711 **How to Enter and Win Jewelry and Metal Crafts Contests.** By Alan
     Gadney. New York: Facts On File, 1983. 204p. 81–19562. ISBN
     0–87196–659–X, cloth; -660–3, pap. $14.95, cloth; $6.95, pap.

This directory, like the other Gadney *How to Enter and Win* guides, focuses
on national and international festivals, competitions, salons, shows,
exhibitions, markets, trade fairs, and other award events and sales outlets. All
contests identified here involve jewelry and metal crafts, including
goldsmithing, gemology, enameling, jewelry making, metal sculpture,
metalsmithing, blacksmithing, ornamentation, and lapidary. Entries cover
eligibility, judging criteria, "catch-clauses," deadlines, names and addresses,
entry fees and forms, subject categories, and technical requirements.
Completing the work are indexes by event/sponsor/award and subject/
category.

712 **How to Enter and Win Wood and Leather Crafts Contests.** By Alan
     Gadney. New York: Facts On File, 1983. 204p. 81–19558. ISBN
     0–87196–655–7, cloth; -656–5, pap. $14.95, cloth; $6.95, pap.

Covered in this directory are national and international festivals,
competitions, salons, shows, exhibitions, markets, trade fairs, and other
award events and sales outlets for wood and leather crafts. Included are
contests for decoy carving, whittling, wood sculpture, upholstery, furniture
making, leather design, leather picture art, belt making, hide tanning, egg art,
scrimshaw, and toy and doll making. Entries for each program describe
eligibility, selection criteria, "catch-clauses," deadlines, entry fees, subject
categories, technical requirements, and contact names and addresses.
Completing the volume are indexes by event/sponsor/award and subject/
category.

713 National Directory of Shops/Galleries, Shows/Fairs: Where to Exhibit and Sell Your Work. Coral Springs, FL: B. Klein Publications, 1982– . Annual. 82–643819. ISSN 0730–9309. $25. Pap.

Replacing Writer's Digest's *Craftsworker's Market*, this annual groups 2,200 shops, galleries, shows, and fairs by region. The detailed information provided in each entry covers contacts, terms, establishment hours, owner's philosophy, and typical customers.

714 Photographer's Market: Where to Sell Your Photographs. Ed. by Robin Weinstein. Cincinnati, OH: Writer's Digest, 1978– . Annual. 78–643526. ISSN 0147–247X. $16.95 (1986 ed.).

Included in each annual guide to the photography market are chapters that (1) identify a total of 2,500 organizations making awards or grants to photographers (state arts council funding programs receive special emphasis) and (2) list foundations and grants of interest to photographers. For more information about the publication, see the annotation in the "Grants—Humanities—Fine Arts" section of this bibliography.

715 Sunshine Artists U.S.A. Longwood, FL: Sun Country Enterprises, 1972– . Monthly. 80–9204. ISSN 0199–9370. $20/yr.

While there are a number of state and regional guides to arts and crafts competitions, this is the most comprehensive of the national listings found in a serial. In the course of a year, the monthly identifies over 1,000 photography and arts and crafts shows in the United States and seven foreign countries. Entries are arranged chronologically and cover dates, location, contact persons, application procedures, awards, and fees. Using the information supplied by 800 "secret" auditors (generally artists, crafts persons, and photographers themselves), the magazine also rates the attendance, management, and value of the shows.

Communications and Mass Media

716 Audio Video Market Place: A Multimedia Guide. New York: Bowker, 1969– . Annual. 85–651452. ISSN 0067–0553. $49.95 (1985–86 ed.). Pap.

From 1969 through 1983, this annual was published under the title *Audiovisual Market Place*. Beginning with the 14th edition, in 1984, the title was changed to *Audio Video Market Place*, to better reflect the content of the listings. The latest edition of this standard reference source (1985–86. 822p. ISBN 0–8352–2069–9) identifies 4,500 audio/video producers, distributors, and other services, plus associations, film commissions, unions, and other organizations active in or serving the audio/video fields. The volume is divided into six sections. One of the sections, "Awards & Festivals," lists four pages of events open to professional, student, educational, and industrial media products in the United States. The entries are arranged by program name and specify address, telephone number, media, award, date presented, deadline, and entry fee (if any). For more complete lists of media contests, see *How to Enter and Win Film Contests* and *How to Enter and Win Video/Audio Contests*, described elsewhere in this section of the bibliography.

717 **Children's Media Market Place.** Ed. by Carol A. Emmens. 2d ed. New York: Neal-Schuman, 1982. 353p. 82–82058. ISBN 0–918212–33–2. ISSN 0734–8169. $29.95 Pap.

In focusing on print and nonprint children's materials, this directory identifies state and federal agency officals concerned with library and media services, grants for children's programming, and national awards for children's materials. For more information about the publication, see the annotation in the "Awards and Prizes—Humanities—Literature" section of this bibliography.

718 **Editor & Publisher Journalism Awards Directory.** Ed. by Jerome H. Walker. New York: Editor & Publisher Company. Annual. $3. Pap.

Each year, this directory describes over 200 awards, scholarships, and fellowships available in the United States and abroad for reporters, columnists, editors, cartoonists, and photographers. For more information about the publication, see the annotation in the "Scholarships—Humanities—Communications and Mass Media" section of the bibliography.

719 **Honor Awards Handbook.** Ed. by Milton L. Levy. Berkeley, CA: Honor Awards Handbook, 1957–1964. 3v. 84–7113.

Published in 1957, 1960, and 1964 under the title *Honor Awards Handbook*, this directory changed its name in 1968 to *Media Awards Handbook* (described elsewhere in this section of the bibliography).

720 **How to Enter and Win Film Contests.** By Alan Gadney. New York: Facts On File, 1981. 195p. 81–2183. ISBN 0–87196–517–8, cloth; -524–0, pap. $14.95, cloth; $6.95, pap.

Designed to appeal to both the amateur and professional filmmaker, this reference source covers over 350 film contests, festivals, screenings, and grants. Coverage is international. The programs are grouped by subject and described in terms of eligibility rules, entry fees, categories, and deadlines. Helpful tips on how to increase the chances of winning and a thorough index are also provided.

721 How to Enter and Win Video/Audio Contests. By Alan Gadney. Ed. by Carolyn Porter. New York: Facts On File, 1981. 193p. 81–2221. ISBN 0–87196–520–8, cloth; -551–8, pap. $14.95, cloth; $6.95, pap.

This volume covers the fast-growing field of video and television, with entries on over 400 national and international contests, festivals, fellowships, and grants open to television and video tape producers. The following information is provided for each of the programs covered: eligibility, names and addresses, financial reward, award category, technical requirements, "catch-clauses," deadlines, entry fees, and judging criteria. An extensive introduction provides suggestions for competing in and winning video/audio contests. Entries are indexed by subject/category and event/sponsor/award.

722 Media Awards Handbook: Radio, Television, Newspaper, Magazine, Allied Fields & Industries. Ed. by Milton L. Levy. Danville, CA: Media Awards Handbook, 1980. n.p. 68–24272. ISBN 0–910744–03–3. $20. Pap.

Published in 1957, 1960, and 1964 as *Honor Awards Handbook*, this directory was released under the current title in 1968, 1974, and 1980. It is intended as a "workbook for those professionals who want to know as much detail as possible about the various Contests and Awards with the thought of entering them for their work." No attempt is made to indicate which of the prizes are more prestigious or notable. The awards (national, regional, and sectional) are listed by official program title and indexed by variant name and deadline. Some fellowships, scholarships, and grants are also included. The entries are arranged alphabetically and identify sponsor address, application procedures, deadlines, purpose, remuneration, and rules. A four-page addendum provides addresses for the sponsoring organizations whose awards are not covered. A deadline index completes the volume. Last published in 1980, the listing is now quite out of date and incomplete.

Fine Arts

723 Artist's Market: Where to Sell Your Commercial Art. Ed. by Diana L. Martin-Hoffman. Cincinnati, OH: Writer's Digest, 1974– . Annual. ISSN 0161–0546. $16.95 (1986 ed.).

This directory has had a complex publication history. It was issued from 1974 to 1976 as the *Artist's Market*, from 1976 to 1978 as *Artist's and Photographer's Market* (74–28735. ISSN 0146–8294), in 1978 as *Art & Crafts Market* (78–645385. ISSN 0147–2461), from 1979 through 1981 again as *Artist's Market* (79–640253. ISSN 0161–0546), and since 1982 as *Artist's Market: Where to Sell Your Artwork*. The annual identifies 10,000 market opportunities (in 4,000 listings) for the freelance artist. The volume is divided into 13 major sections (e.g., advertising and public relations, architecture, record companies, manufacturers, paper products). In some editions, a separate section deals with competitions and exhibitions of interest to artists in the United States and abroad.

724 Artweek. Oakland, CA: Artweek, 1970– . Weekly, September-May (44 issues/yr.). ISSN 0004–4121. $19.50/yr., individuals; $23/yr., institutions.

The competitions section of *Artweek* identifies approximately 50 art contests and festivals each week (from September through May). International, national, and regional competitions are covered. Entries for each competition specify event name, address, telephone number, contact persons, deadline, location, dates, eligibility, media accepted, entry fees, awards offered, and whether or not juried. The weekly lists are arranged by geographic restrictions, subdivided by deadline dates.

725 Fine Arts Market Place. New York: Bowker, 1974–1983. Biennial. 73–2497. ISSN 0000–0361.

Published from 1974 through 1983, each biennial edition of *Fine Arts Market Place* listed thousands of firms, organizations, and individuals involved in the fine arts field, specifying their names, locations, telephone numbers, specialties, and products or activities. Each edition was divided into approximately 30 sections (e.g., restorers and conservators, insurers, custom brokers, arts councils, art associations, art presses, auction houses, art dealers). Two of these sections dealt with competitions, one in the United States and the other abroad.

726 How to Enter and Win Design & Commercial Art Contests. By Alan Gadney. New York: Facts On File, 1982. 204p. 81–12582. ISBN 0–87196–570–4, cloth; -576–1, pap. $14.95, cloth; $6.95, pap.

Another in Gadney's series of contest guides focusing on a specific artistic medium, this volume provides information of interest to the contest competitor in graphic design, fashion design, architecture, advertising, cartooning, commerical illustration, postermaking, and printmaking. Nearly 400 national and international events (over 2,000 prizes) are covered here. The entries are arranged by subject and medium and indexed by event/ sponsor and subject/category. Event profiles specify address and telephone number, entry month, entry regulations and categories, eligibility requirements, awards, judging aspects, sales terms, entry fees, and deadline.

727 How to Enter and Win Fine Arts & Sculpture Contests. By Alan Gadney. New York: Facts On File, 1982. 205p. 81–12580. ISBN 0–87196–573–9, cloth; -579–8, pap. $14.95, cloth; $6.95, pap.

Updating Gadney's 1980 general guide to artistic contests, festivals, and grants (described in the "Awards and Prizes—Humanities—General" section of this bibliography), this volume identifies 343 national and international competitions in fine arts and sculpture. Program profiles cover size requirements, types of awards, number of judges, eligibility, sponsors' addresses and telephone numbers, and number of entries submitted to earlier competitions. The volume is organized by "special-interest subject categories." Indexing is by event/sponsor/award and subject/category.

Literature

728 Book Publishing Annual: Highlights, Analysis, Trends. New York: Bowker, 1984– . Annual. 85–645245. ISSN 0000–0787. $60 (1985 ed.).

Each *Book Publishing Annual* provides a detailed view of that year in publishing through a series of original articles covering such topics as religious publishing, trends in paperback publishing, rights and permissions, people on the move, and the book industry abroad. One of the sections usually identifies awards and prizes (both children's and adult awards) in the United States and abroad. In the 1985 edition, this section was 20 pages long and briefly described several hundred awards (giving sponsoring organization, program title, purpose, and winner). The first edition of this serial, issued in 1983, was published under the title *Publisher's Weekly Yearbook*. For more extensive coverage of current literary prizes for American and Canadian writers, see *Grants and Awards Available to American Writers* (described elsewhere in this section of the bibliography).

729 Children's Books: Awards & Prizes. New York: Children's Book Council, 1969– . Irreg. 68–4275. ISSN 0069–3472. $35 (1981 ed.).

Described in the latest edition (1981. 215p.) are approximately 75 different prizes and awards granted to illustrators and/or authors of children's books. The entries, arranged alphabetically within three geographic divisions (United States, British Commonwealth, and International) provide the following information: history of the award, criteria for selection, and recipients of the award in chronological order. Indexing is by title and name. Access by type of award is provided through an appendix.

730 Children's Literature Awards and Winners: A Directory of Prizes, Authors, and Illustrators. Ed. by Dolores Blythe Jones. 1st ed. New York: Neal-Schuman (in assoc. with Gale), 1983. 495p. 84–643512. ISBN 0–8103–0171–7. ISSN 0749–3096. $90.

731 **Children's Literature Awards and Winners: A Directory of Prizes, Authors, and Illustrators. Supplement.** By Dolores Blythe Jones. New York: Neal-Schuman (in assoc. with Gale), 1984. 136p. ISBN 0–8103–0173–3. ISSN 0749–3096. $55. Pap.

This work covers awards granted to authors and illustrators of children's books in English-speaking countries. International awards that are open to English-language books are also included. In all, 144 awards and 3,500 winners are listed. Entries give name of award, award-granting group, address, criteria and rules, purpose, history, categories, presentation, winners (year of award, title, author, illustrator, publisher, year of publication), and runners-up. In addition, there is a listing of authors and illustrators who won the awards listed (with title, publisher, date of publication, and name and date of award given) and a selected bibliography of books, articles, chapters, dissertations, and reports of children's book awards. The *Supplement* updates information on the awards covered in the main volume. Of the 144 awards described in the first edition, only 109 are still active and listed in the *Supplement*. In addition, the *Supplement* includes 32 new awards.

732 **Children's Media Market Place.** Ed. by Carol A. Emmens. 2d ed. New York: Neal-Schuman, 1982. 353p. 82–82058. ISBN 0–918212–33–2. ISSN 0734–8169. $29.95. Pap.

This directory focuses on print and nonprint children's materials. It lists hundreds of book clubs, bookstores, publishers, audiovisual producers and distributors, periodicals, wholesalers, agents, television stations, radio stations, and organizations interested in media for children. In addition, the directory identifies state and federal agency officials concerned with library and media services, grants for children's programming, and national awards for children's materials. The first edition was published under the same title in 1978 by Gaylord Professional Publications.

733 **Children's Prize Books: An International Listing of 193 Children's Literature Prizes.** Ed. by Jess R. Moransee. With an into. by Walter Scherf. 2d ed. New York: K.G. Saur, 1983. 620p. (Catalogues of the International Youth Library, no. 2). 83–153848. ISBN 3–598–03250–1. $32.

Listed in this second edition are 187 children's literature prizes awarded in 38 countries (plus six international awards). The arrangement is by country, with prizes listed alphabetically. Each entry provides a history of the award (in both English and German) and a chronological listing of award winners. The author, illustrator, publisher, and place and date of publication are also given. Supplementing the text are 50 illustrations taken from various prizewinning books. Completing the volume are three indexes: authors, illustrators, and translators.

734   Coda: Poets & Writers Newsletter. New York: Poets & Writers, 1973– . 5 times/yr. 73–649056. ISSN 0091–5645. $18/yr.

Published five times each year, this is a good resource for current information on grants and awards deadlines of interest to poets and writers as well as on recipients of those awards. The "deadline" section tells when to apply for upcoming competitions and provides brief program descriptions.

735   Dramatists Sourcebook: Complete Opportunities for Playwrights, Translators, Composers, Lyricists, and Librettists. Ed. by M. Elizabeth Osborne. New York: Theatre Communications Group, 1982– Annual. 82–644562. ISSN 0733–1606. $10.95 (1985–86 ed.). Pap.

While one half of this directory focuses on "script opportunities" (theaters willing to review unpublished plays), there are separate sections that relate directly to financial aid programs: prizes, fellowships and grants, colonies and residencies, and emergency funds. The entries in these sections are arranged by sponsoring organization and subdivided by specific programs. The information presented includes eligibility, financial arrangements, purpose, application process, and deadlines. The sourcebook also contains a short bibliography of useful publications, a submission calendar for the programs described, a special interests index, a sponsoring organization index, and several helpful essays in the prologue. Use the Theatre Communications Group's monthly magazine, *American Theater*, to update the listings in the sourcebook. Prior to 1982, this publication was issued as *Information for Playwrights*.

736   Fiction Writer's Market. Cincinnati: Writer's Digest, 1981– . Annual. 82–643314. ISSN 0275–2123. $17.95 (1985 ed.).

Compiled in response to requests from users of *Writer's Market* (described elsewhere in this section), the bulk of this annual consists of advice and tips to fiction writers. One chapter lists and describes relevant contests and awards. Program entries provide the following information: sponsoring organization address, contact person, year established, frequency, purpose, requirements, remuneration, and submission fees.

737   Foreign Literary Prizes: Romance and Germanic Languages. Ed. by E. C. Bufkin. New York: Bowker, 1980. 300p. 79–25113. ISBN 0–8352–1243–2. $24.95.

This book identifies and describes representative literary prizes for writings in Romance and Germanic languages. The selection presented includes awards famous and obscure, old and recent, discontinued and continuing. Excluded are awards for journalism and literature for children; works in English awarded in the United States, Great Britain, or Canada; and prizes for works in French awarded in Canada (for these, see *Literary and Library Prizes*). The entries are grouped by countries in which the awards are given and include a complete list of laureates. The information is complete only through 1978. Supplementing the main body of the work are a bibliography and an index of recipients.

738 **Grants and Awards Available to American Writers.** New York: P.E.N. American Center, 1973– . Annual. 73–648098. ISSN 0092–5268. $6/ yr., individuals; $9.50/yr., libraries and institutions (13th ed.). Pap.

Grants and awards in excess of $500, available to American writers for use in the United States and abroad, are described in this much used directory. According to the editors, this is the only reference work "which combines both domestic and foreign grants for American writers." Additional sections identify grants and awards available to Canadian writers and state arts councils. The listing is wide-ranging but not comprehensive. The 600 to 700 entries each year are arranged alphabetically by organization and indexed by award title, type of literature, and sponsoring organization. There is no subject index. Each listing specifies purpose of the award, amount available, eligibility, and application procedures. The programs covered are open to playwrights, poets, journalists, fiction writers, researchers, and scholars. Since many of the awards described here require prior publication or are open only to nominees, this listing will prove most useful to writers with experience and reputation. To update the annual listing, use the *P.E.N. American Center Newsletter* (described elsewhere in this section of the bibliography). The directory was first published in 1973. It supersedes the *List of Grants and Awards Available to American Writers* that was issued from 1969 through 1972.

739 **How to Enter and Win Fiction Writing Contests.** By Alan Gadney. New York: Facts On File, 1981. 200p. 81–2182. ISBN 0–87196–319–4, cloth; -552–6, pap. $14.95, cloth; $6.95, pap.

More than 400 national and international contests, scholarships, and grants for short stories, poetry, scripts, plays, and novels are covered in this source. Each entry provides information on prize money, names, addresses, and deadlines. Cross-references and indexes complete the work. This book and the other *How to Enter and Win* compilations by Gadney revise and expand the original *Gadney's Guide* (described in the "Awards and Prizes— Humanities—General" section of this bibliography).

740 **How to Enter and Win Non-Fiction & Journalism Contests.** By Alan Gadney. New York: Facts On File, 1981. 205p. 81–2179. ISBN 0–87196–518–6, cloth; -553–4, pap. $14.95, cloth; $6.95, pap.

Nearly 400 national and international contests, festivals, grants, and scholarships open to nonfiction writers are identified and described in this directory. Entries include information on addresses, judging rules, eligibility requirements, deadlines, and prize money. Indexing is by subject category and event/sponsor/award.

741 **International Directory of Children's Literature.** Comp. by Mary Beth Dunhouse. New York: Facts On File, 1986. 128p. 85–29372. ISBN 0–8160–1411–6. $29.95.

The successor to the 1973 *Children's Literary Almanac*, this international directory is intended "to serve as a resource for people working in various capacities in the children's literature field," to provide "access to information that has previously been difficult, if not impossible to find in other reference tools," and to provide "a survey of global children's literature." Over 80 countries are covered. Entries are grouped into eight chapters (e.g., children's magazines, children's literature organizations), one of which covers children's literature prizes (pp. 107 to 119). The prize descriptions are arranged by sponsoring country and provide very brief information on sponsor's address, frequency, purpose, and eligibility. Over 200 awards are listed (more than 25 percent of these are from the United States). There is no index.

742 **International Directory of Writers Groups & Associations, 1984–1985.** Comp. by John Hall. Alexandria, MN: Inkling, 1984. 186p. ISBN 0–915521–04–6. $19.50. Pap.

Over 2,000 writers clubs and organizations (including their chapters) are covered in this international directory, which was published in 1984 and has not been updated since then. In addition to providing typical directory-type information for many of the listed organizations, some of the entries also indicate sponsored fellowships and awards; however, the information provided is so brief that neither purpose nor eligibility is generally specified. The entries are arranged geographically. There is an index of officers and contact persons.

743 **International Literary Market Place.** New York: Bowker, 1971/72– . Annual. 77–70295. ISSN 0074–6827. $95 (1886/87 ed.). Pap.

The 1985/86 edition of this guide (576p. ISBN 0–8352–2081–8) identifies more than 13,000 publishers, booksellers, and book-related organizations in 160 countries outside of the United States and Canada. It serves as a companion volume to *Literary Market Place* (described elsewhere in this section of the bibliography). Entries in each annual volume are arranged by country and subdivided by 15 subject headings (e.g., book trade organizations, remainder dealers, book clubs, major libraries, literary periodicals). One of these subsections covers literary awards. In addition, a separate section is provided at the end of the volume for international literary prizes. Between 1965 and 1970, this publication was issued under the title

International Literary Market Place. European Edition (Annual. 65–28326. ISSN 0538–8562).

744 International Writers' and Artists' Yearbook. London: Adam & Charles Black (dist. by Writer's Digest), 1906– . Annual. 84–7972. ISSN 0084–2664. $12.95 (1986 ed.). Pap.

Emphasizing the United Kingdom (but covering several other English-speaking countries, including India, New Zealand, South Africa, and the United States), the latest annual (1986. 530p. ISBN 0–7136–2742–5) describes and lists publishing outlets and sources of interest to writers and artists. Its principal components are brief descriptions of newspapers and magazines for the professional writer; materials in book publishing; writing for the theater, films, and television; sources for artists, designers, and photographers; and miscellaneous other topics, including a subsection devoted to literary prizes offered (primarily in the United Kingdom). From 1906 through 1982, this publication was issued by Adam & Charles Black under the title *Writers' and Artists' Year-book* (Annual. 8–22320. ISSN 0084–2664). In 1983, the annual changed its name to *International Writers' and Artists' Yearbook.*

745 List of Grants and Awards Available to American Writers. New York: P.E.N. American Center, 1969–1973. Annual. 72–200103. ISSN 0075–983X. Pap.

In 1973, this annual publication was superseded by *Grants and Awards Available to American Writers* (described elsewhere in this section).

746 Literary and Library Prizes. New York: Bowker, 1935– . Irreg. 59–11370. ISSN 0075–9880. $26.95 (1980 ed.).

Not intended to be inclusive, the latest edition of the directory (1980. ISBN 0–8352–1249–1) lists only 454 representative major literary and library awards offered on an international and national basis. Each prize listed includes a description of its origins, an indication of its criteria, and an identification of all winning authors and works. The book is divided into four major sections: International Prizes; American Prizes; British Prizes; and Canadian Prizes. The American Prizes section has been subdivided into: Drama, Short Story, and Library Prizes. Within these categories, entries are listed alphabetically by name of award. There is a name index (recipient and prize). Over the years, this directory has been published under various titles. From 1935 through 1939, it was issued as *Famous Literary Prizes and Their Winners.* The 1946 edition was entitled *Literary Prizes and Their Winners* (81–2056. ISSN 0730–5850). Taken as a whose, the editions have identified over 675 prizes and 10,000 winners. To update the listings in the latest

Literary and Library Prizes, check the "Annual Summary and Highlights" section of *Publishers Weekly*, which appears in early March each year.

747 Literary Market Place: The Directory of American Book Publishing with Names & Numbers. New York: Bowker, 1972– . Annual. 81–640008. ISSN 0161–2905. $75.00 (1987 ed.). Pap.

Originally designed as a register of personnel in American publishing and allied fields, over the years this annual has been expanded to include 13,000 entries in a dozen major sections (e.g., book trade events, book manufacturing, agents and agencies). In the 1987 edition (900p. ISBN 0–8352–2072–9), one of the major sections focuses on "Literary Awards, Contests & Grants." Covered here are selected major awards given to books, authors, publishers, libraries, or librarians by various organizations; prizes that may be applied for by writing to the sponsor; and scholarships, fellowships, and grants-in-aid of interest to the American writer. The present title was formed in 1972 by the union of two publications: *Literary Market Place* (1940–1971/72. 41–51575. ISSN 0161–1891) and *Names & Numbers: The Book Industry Telephone Directory* (1952/53–1971/72. 61–1000. ISSN 0075–9899). For international coverage, see *International Literary Market Place*, described elsewhere in this section of the bibliography.

748 Literary Markets. Ed. by Bill Marles. Point Roberts, WA: Literary Markets, 1983– . Bimonthly. ISSN 0712–4384. $10/yr.

This six-page newsletter devotes more than one third of each issue to announcements of American and Canadian literary contests. Emphasis is on the smaller, lesser-known awards. For example, in the November-December 1985 issue, 20 contests were announced, most of which were not covered in the basic award directories. Thus, the newsletter provides an inexpensive way to update and supplement the listings included in such sources as *How to Enter and Win Fiction Writing Contests, Grants and Awards Available to American Writers*, and *Literary and Library Prizes* (each described elsewhere in this section of the bibliography).

749 Magazine Industry Market Place: The Directory of American Periodical Publishing. New York: Bowker, 1980– . Annual. 80–648262. ISSN 0000–0434. $59.95 (1987 ed.). Pap.

Patterned after Bowker's successful *Literary Market Place* (described elsewhere in this section), the annual *Magazine Industry Market Place* was first issued in 1980 and is intended to serve as a standard reference source for information on the magazine and allied industries. The directory is arranged in more than 30 sections (e.g., micropublishers, national associations, messenger services, translators, editorial services). One of these sections in the 1987 edition (712p. ISBN 0–8352–2073–7) identifies approximately 50 "major awards made by publications to publishers; to authors of best articles, short stories, etc., published in periodicals; and for excellence in graphics." No indexing to these entries is provided anywhere in the volume.

750 PEN American Center Newsletter. New York: PEN International, 1978– . Quarterly. 80–657. ISSN 0197–5498. $5/yr.

This quarterly publication, issued by the American Center of PEN International (a world association of writers), was formerly titled *American PENewsletter*. In addition to articles of interest to writers and conference reports, the newsletter includes announcements of grants and awards open to writers. Use this listing to update the annual *Grants and Awards Available to American Writers* (described elsewhere in this section of the bibliography).

751 Poet's Market. Ed. by Judson Jerome. Cincinnati, OH: Writer's Market, 1985– . Annual. 85–7245. ISSN 0883–5470. $16.95 (1986 ed.).

This is the newest member of the Writer's Digest annual directory collection. It is compiled by poetry authority Judson Jerome. Included are detailed market analyses of more than 1,300 poetry publishers. In addition, the annual also contains listings of contests and awards for poetry.

752 Poet's Marketplace: The Definitive Sourcebook on Where to Get Your Poems Published. By Joseph J. Kelly. Philadelphia: Running Press, 1984. 174p. 84–2053. ISBN 0–89471–257–8, cloth; -264–0, pap. $19.50, cloth; $9.95, pap.

Similar in scope and format to other "marketplace" directories, this publication attempts "to help serious poets find the right outlets for their work and gain appropriate rewards for it." Nearly 400 magazines, journals, and publishers are identified. One chapter describes contests and awards for poets and another identifies writers' grants and associations.

753 Publishers Weekly Yearbook. By the staff of Publishers Weekly in collab. with the Book Division, R.R. Bowker. New York: Bowker, 1983. 1v. 83–647876. ISSN 0000–0469.

Only one volume of the serial was issued under this title. Since 1984, the yearbook has been published as *Book Publishing Annual: Highlights, Analysis, Trends* (described elsewhere in this section of the bibliography).

754 The Writer. Boston: The Writer, 1897– . Monthly. ISSN 0043–9517. $19/yr.

Included each month in this journal is a "Prize Offers" column, which announces literary contests. A special "Opportunities for Playwrights" section is presented annually in the September issue. In both sections, entries include name of prize, sponsoring organization, address, a brief description of contest terms, and deadline date.

755 The Writer's Handbook. Boston: The Writer, 1936– . Annual. 36–28596. ISSN 0084–2710. $21.95 (1986 ed.).

In addition to identifying 2,000 markets for the sale of literary manuscripts, this annual presents a number of special lists, including a brief list of awards and prizes open to American writers.

756 Writer's Market: Where to Sell What You Write. Ed. by Paula Deimling. Cincinnati, OH: Writer's Digest, 1922– . Annual. 31–20772. ISSN 0084–2729. $19.95 (1986 ed.).

Described in the 1986 edition (1,056p. ISBN 0–89879–198–7) are 4,000 places for authors to sell their books, articles, poetry, and features. Listings include the names and addresses of editors, how much they pay, their needs, and how to contact them. There are more than 700 new listings provided each year. In addition, annual volumes present interviews with magazine and book editors, tips on how to analyze the markets and subject manuscripts, a postal chart, and answers to frequently asked questions about copyright. A separate section lists and describes the most important literary contests and awards.

Music

757 British Music Yearbook. London: Adam & Charles Black (dist. by Schirmer Books), 1975– . Annual. 75–649724. ISSN 0306–5928. $29.95 (1984 ed.).

Issued annually, this reference source provides information and statistics on musical developments in Britain, plus numerous directory listings (e.g., offices and societies, professional services, libraries and museums). Each year, an entire chapter is devoted to festivals and competitions in the United Kingdom and several other countries. The entries are arranged in alphabetical order of location. For each, the address of the director or secretary of the sponsoring organization is given along with the month(s) when the event is normally held. In addition, brief information on scholarships and grants tenable either in Britain or abroad is included elsewhere in each volume. Over the years, the publisher of the yearbook has varied. From 1973 to 1974, when the publication was issued as *The Music Yearbook*, it was published by Macmillan in London and St. Martin's in New York. From 1975 until 1980, the yearbook was issued by Classical Music. Since 1980, the annual has been published by Adam & Charles Black in London and, beginning in 1984, by Schirmer Books in New York.

758   Career Guide for Young Singers from the United States and Canada.
5th ed. New York: Central Opera Service, 1985. 80p. $9.50. Pap.

Since its founding in 1954, the Central Opera Service (COS) has been
concerned with helping young American and Canadian singers build
professional careers. In 1958, COS published its first compilation of *Awards
for Singers* (then a four-page pamphlet). Since there were only a few programs
geared to the needs of young singers, most of the listings were devoted to
scholarships available at academic institutions. The scene changed slowly and
it was not until 1969 that the brochure contained a small section on "Special
Opportunities for the Young Professional." By 1978, however, the *Career
Guide for the Young American Singer* contained many programs bridging the
gap between education and professional engagements. The latest edition
(1985. 80p.) consists of eight sections: grants for singers; regional, national,
and international competitions in the United States and Canada; foreign
competitions open to American and Canadian singers; additional audition
opportunities; opera/musical theater companies in the United States and
Canada (with details on apprentice, training, and educational/tour programs,
and on audition and hiring policies); institutes for advanced training (new to
this edition); apprentice programs in fields other than singing; and
educational institutions with major opera workshops. For the first time,
information in this edition has been expanded to reflect the interests of
Canadian singers as well as American singers. Each section is arranged by
state. Entries provide information on the address and telephone number of
the sponsoring organizations, program title, contact person, qualifications,
remuneration, entrance fees, and residency requirements. The *Career Guide* is
a special directory of the *COS Bulletin* (New York: Central Opera Service,
1960– . Quarterly). In 1986, COS began issuing an annual addenda to keep
the irregularly-released guide current.

759   Music Directory Canada. Toronto: Norris-Whitney Communications,
1982– . Annual. 84–646941. ISSN 0820–0416. $19.95 Canadian (1985
ed.).

Over 4,000 organizations in Canada's music industry are covered in this
annual directory. In addition to competitions, the entries describe publishers,
libraries, lawyers, radio stations, opera companies, recording studios, etc. The
following information is provided: organization name, address, telephone
number, and services provided. The entries are grouped by service area and
indexed by organization name.

760   Music Industry Directory. Chicago: Marquis Professional Publications,
1983– . Irreg. 83–645913. ISSN 0740–476X. $67.50 (1983 ed.).

The first six volumes of the directory were published by Music Information
Service, from 1954 through 1980, as *The Musician's Guide*. In 1983, Marquis

began issuing the publication. To date, only the 1983 (7th ed.) has been published; it is currently out of print. The 1983 edition provides comprehensive coverage of the music industry. It contains descriptive listings for service and professional organizations, schools and colleges, competitions, periodicals, festivals, libraries, and foundations. Three chapters describe various financial aid programs and awards available to musicians. One chapter consists of a reproduction of the National Federation of Music Clubs' scholarships and awards chart. The second details country music awards, and the third (and largest) lists music competitions by country, providing information on type of award, eligibility, remuneration, and contact person.

761 The Musician's Guide. New York: Music Information Service, 1954–1980. Irreg. 54–14954. ISSN 0580–3160.

From 1954 through 1980, Music Information Service published six volumes of this directory. In 1983, Marquis began issuing the publication as an annual, under the title *Music Industry Directory*. For more information, see the annotation for *Music Industry Directory* in this section of the bibliography.

762 Songwriter's Market: Where to Sell Your Songs. Ed. by Rand Ruggeberg. Cincinnati, OH: Writer's Digest, 1979– . Annual. 78–648269. ISSN 0161–5971. $15.95 (1986 ed.).

Songwriter's Market was first introduced in 1978 as a guide for songwriters seeking markets for their songs. The bulk of the 1986 annual (432p. ISBN 0–89879–201–0) consists of 2,000 markets seeking songs or songwriters' services. Listings feature the name and address of the person to contact, special requirements, and payment arrangements. In addition, there is a separate section on opportunities and services available to songwriters. One of the subsections included here covers relevant contests and awards.

Performing Arts

763 Film/Video Festivals and Awards. Comp. by Christina Spilsbury and Deborah Davidson Boutchard. 2d ed. Los Angeles: American Film Institute, 1984. 88p. (FACTFILE, v. 3). $6. Pap.

Formerly issued under the title *Student Film Festivals and Awards*, this directory covers U.S. and foreign festivals and awards for all types of films— from super-8mm through videotape. Both competitive and noncompetitive programs are described, including some by invitation only. No attempt has been made to separate cash awards from noncash competitions. Entries for American film competitions are brief but contain all relevant details, including name, address, telephone number, contact persons, dates, location, eligibility requirements, deadline for entry, fees, length of film, and categories of competition. Less complete information is provided for festivals which are by invitation only or are held outside the United States. The indexing is extensive and provides a number of access points: e.g., program title, festivals awarding cash prizes, student festivals, videotape festivals. The first edition of this publication was issued in 1980 (30p.).

764   Information for Playwrights. New York: Theater Communications Group, 1979–1981. Irreg. 2v. 83–10658.

Two editions of this small pamphlet (approximately 20 pages each) were published in 1979 and 1981. In 1982, the publication changed its title to *Dramatists Sourcebook* (described elsewhere in this section of the bibliography).

765   Lively Arts Information Directory. Ed. by Steven R. Wasserman and Jacqueline Wasserman O'Brien. 2d ed. Detroit: Gale, 1985. 1,040p. 85–6949. ISBN 0–8103–0321–3. $165.

This directory serves as the single most comprehensive source book for the fields of music, dance, theater, film, radio, and television in the United States and Canada. Over 6,700 foundations, grants, scholarships, awards, publications, special libraries, and schools offering study in the performing arts are described. The entries are grouped into 12 chapters, 11 of which have their own indexes. The largest sections are those covering festivals, colleges and universities, and non-degree granting schools. This expensive but useful source of information on the performing arts was revised in 1985. Its 9,000 entries represent a 35 percent increase over the first edition, which was issued in 1982 (846p. 81–20060).

766   Musical America: International Directory of the Performing Arts. Great Barrington, MA: ABC Leisure Magazines, 1969– . Annual. 83–713. ISSN 0735–7788. $40.

There are two chapters devoted to musical awards in this annual directory of the performing arts, one which covers contests and foundation awards for the United States and the other which covers them for the rest of the wrold. In each of these chapters, the competitions are arranged alphabetically and grouped by country. Program profiles include the following information: name, sponsoring organization, telephone number, address, frequency, eligibility, remuneration, entrance fee, competition dates, and application deadline dates. From 1969 through 1973, the directory was published annually as an issue of the journal *Musical America*. Since 1974, it has been released as a separate publication.

767   Student Film Festivals. Washington, DC: American Film Institute, 1980. 30p. Pap.

The latest edition of this publication was issued in 1984 under the file *Film/ Video Festivals and Awards* (described elsewhere in this section of the bibliography).

768   Whole Film Sourcebook. Ed. by Leonard Maltin. New York: New American Library, 1983. 454p. (A PLUME BOOK). 82–19085. ISBN 0–452–24361–6. $9.95. PAP.

Also included in this potpourri listing of academic institutions, organizations, distributors, producers, libraries, and bookstores are descriptions of awards and grants dealing with filmmaking. For more information about the publication, see the annotation in the "Grants—Humanities—Performing Arts" section of this bibliography.

SPECIAL POPULATION GROUPS
The Disabled

769   Financial Aid for the Disabled and Their Dependents. By Gail Ann Schlachter. Los Angeles: Reference Service Press, 1987– . Biennial. (Directories of Financial Aid for Special Needs Groups). $29.95 (1987/ 88 ed.).

This is the first comprehensive and up-to-date listing of awards, grants-in-aid, loans, scholarships, and fellowships that have been established for disabled individuals and their dependents. For more information about the publication, see the annotation in the "Scholarships—Special Population Groups—The Disabled" section of this bibliography.

Ethnic Groups

770   Directory of Financial Aids for Minorities. By Gail Ann Schlachter. Los Angeles: Reference Service Press, 1984– . Biennial (Directories of Financial Aid for Special Needs Groups). 83–25068. ISBN 0–918276–03–9. $37.50 (1986–1987 ed.).

The latest edition of this biennial directory includes a descriptive list of more than 1,200 awards/prizes, scholarships, fellowships, loans, grants, and internships set aside for Asian Americans, Black Americans, Hispanic Americans, Native Americans, and minorities in general. For more information about the publication, see the annotation in the "Scholarships— Special Population Groups—Ethnic Groups" section of this bibliography.

Women

771   **Directory of Financial Aids for Women.** By Gail Ann Schlachter. Los
       Angeles: Reference Service Press, 1978– . Biennial. (Directories of
       Financial Aid for Special Needs Groups). 84–24582. ISSN 0732–5215.
       $37.50. (1985—86 ed.).

This is the only extensive and regularly updated listing of awards/prizes,
fellowships, scholarships, grants, loans, and internships designed primarily or
exclusively for women. For more information about the publication, see the
annotation in the "Scholarships—Special Population Groups—Women"
section of this bibliography.

Loans

Loan programs represent the only type of financial assistance that eventually must be repaid—with or without interest. Loans constitute one of the most important sources of financial assistance, but because most of the money tends to come only for education and from a few large-scale public programs on the state or federal levels, there are relatively few directories that list only loan programs and only a few more that include any sizeable number of individual loans in their listings. Included in this chapter are 66 references to directories that focus exclusively or substantially on loan programs. Of these listings, over half (35 entries) are general in nature, describing loans on either the international, national, or state level; the rest are divided in focus among the social sciences (6 entries), humanities (1 entry), sciences (6 entries), and special population groups (18 entries). If you are looking for a specific loan directory and you do not find it in this chapter, be sure to check the Title Index to see if it is covered elsewhere in the Guide.

GENERAL

International

772 Annual Register of Grant Support: A Guide to Support Programs of Government Agencies, Foundations, and Business and Professional Organizations. Wilmette, IL: National Register, 1969– . Annual. 69–18307. ISSN 0066–4049. $87 (1985–86 ed.).

Although it focuses on North American programs, the *Annual Register* also describes a number of loans sponsored abroad. For more information about the publication, see the annotation in the "Grants—General—United States" section of this bibliography.

773 College Blue Book. New York: Macmillan, 1923– . Biennial. 79–66292. $185 (20th ed.).

A number of the loans described in Volume 5 of the *Blue Book*'s 20th edition may be used for research or study abroad. For more information about this publication, see the annotation in the "Scholarships—General—United States" section of this bibliography.

774 Directory of Research Grants. Phoenix: Oryx, 1975– . Annual. 76–47074. ISSN 0146–7336. $74.50 (1986 ed.). Pap.

Although the emphasis is on U.S. programs, some loans, scholarships, fellowships, and research grants sponsored by other countries are also included. For more information about the publication, see the annotation in the "Grants—General—United States" section of this bibliography.

United States

775 Alphabetic List of Lenders. Washington, DC: Bureau of Student Financial Assistance, U.S. Department of Education, 1979– . Irreg. 79–644935. ISSN 0192–3455. Free. Pap.

For a list of the universities, associations, companies, financial institutions, and others that make the federal loans described in *Five Federal Financial Aid Programs: A Student Guide* (described in the "Scholarships—General—United States" section of this bibliography), use this alphabetical list of lenders issued by the Department of Education's Bureau of Student Financial Assistance. Entries are listed alphabetically by sponsoring organization and include the following brief information: organization name, address, type of lender, agency identification number, parent type, available loans, and reasons for ineligibility. First published in 1979, the most recent edition of the list was issued in 1985 (584p.).

776 **Annual Register of Grant Support: A Guide to Support Programs of Government Agencies, Foundations, and Business and Professional Organizations.** Wilmette, IL: National Register, 1969– . Annual. 69–18307. ISSN 0066–4049. $87 (1985–86 ed.).

Despite its title, this annual covers loans, fellowships, and scholarships as well as grant opportunities. For more information, see the annotation in the "Grants—General—United States" section of this bibliography.

777 **Catalog of Federal Domestic Assistance.** Prep. by the General Services Administration. Washington, DC: G.P.O., 1965– . Annual. 73–60018. ISSN 0097–7799. $36. Looseleaf.

Over 1,000 domestic assitance programs and activities, administered by 60 different federal agencies and departments, are described in this annual publication, including loans, loan guarantees and shared revenue programs, and grants. For more information about the publication, see the annotation in the "Grants—General—United States" section of this bibliography.

778 **Catalog of Federal Loan Guarantee Programs.** By the Subcommittee on Economic Stabilization, Committee on Banking, Finance and Urban Affairs, U.S. House of Representatives, 97th Congress, First Session. Rev. ed. Washington, DC: G.P.O., 1982. 228p. 82–601279.

This listing of presently authorized federal loan guarantee programs updates a 1977 Committee Print of the same title (32p. 78–600564). The entries are arranged by agency and type of loan regulated. The following information is provided: purpose, authorization, type of credit aid, interest rates, size of loan guarantee authorized, extent of U.S. liability, instrument form, and marketing arrangement.

779 **Chronicle Student Aid Annual.** Moravia, NY: Chronicle Guidance Publications, 1978– . Annual. 79–640360. ISSN 0190–339X. $16.50 (1985 ed.). Pap.

In addition to scholarship programs, a number of loans, grants, awards, and fellowships are described in this annual directory. For more information about the publication, see the annotation in the "Scholarships—General—United States" section of this bibliography.

780 **The College Aid Checkbook: A Guide to College Financial Aid.** Clifton, NJ: Army ROTC, 1985. n.p. Free. Pap.

This checkbook-sized pamphlet was written as a starting point to identify major private and public loans, grants, scholarships, and work programs. For more information about the free publication, see the annotation in the "Scholarships—General—United States" section of this bibliography.

781 College Blue Book. New York: Macmillan, 1923– . Biennial. 79–66191. ISSN 0069–5572. $185 (20th ed.).

Volume 5 of the 20th edition (718p. $44. ISBN 0–02–695790–6) identifies over $100 million in loans, scholarships, fellowships, and grants available to graduate and undergraduate students. For more information about this publication, see the annotation in the "Scholarships—General—United States" section.

782 College Loans from Uncle Sam: The Borrower's Guide That Explains All. Alexandria, VA: Octameron Associates, 1981– . Annual. $2 (1986 ed.). Pap.

Described in this brief booklet (1986 edition was approximately 25 pages) are the following federal loan programs: Guaranteed Student Loans, National Direct Student Loans, PLUS Loans, Nursing Loans, Health Professions Student Loans, Health Education Assistance Loans, and Loan Consolidation Programs. The text summarizes interest rates, repayment provisions, grace periods, deferment conditions, and forbearance. There is a directory of guaranteeing agencies appended. The Pell Grant is not covered here; it is included in another small Octameron booklet, *College Grants from Uncle Sam* (1986 edition: 28p. ISBN 0–917760–62–X. $2. Pap.). Both of these booklets are also reprinted in their entirety in Peterson's Guide's *Your Own Financial Aid Factory: The Guide to Locating College Money* (described in the "Scholarships—General—United States" section of this bibliography).

783 The College Money Handbook: The Complete Guide to Expenses, Scholarships, Loans, Jobs, and Special Aid Programs at Four-Year Colleges. Princeton, NJ: Peterson's Guides, 1983– . Annual. 83–62921. ISSN 0883–5578. $15.95 (1987 ed.). Pap.

Both loans and scholarships are indicated in the tabular "College Cost and Aid Profiles" that make up the bulk of this annual. For more information about the publication, see the annotation in the "Scholarships—General—United States" section of this bibliography.

784 Directory of Research Grants. Phoenix: Oryx, 1975– . Annual. 76–47074. ISSN 0146–7336. $74.50 (1986 ed.). Pap.

Loans, fellowships, and some scholarships are described in this annual directory, in addition to research grants. For more information about the publication, see the annotation in the "Grants—General—United States" section of this bibliography.

785   **Directory of Scholarships and Loan Funds.** Irving, TX: Boy Scouts of
      America, 1985. 9p. Free. Pap.

Approximately 40 loans and scholarships aimed at current and former
members of the Boy Scouts are identified in this free booklet. For more
information about the publication, see the annotation in the "Scholarships—
General—United States" section of the bibliography.

786   **Don't Miss Out: The Ambitious Student's Guide to Scholarships and
      Loans.** By Robert Leider and Anna Leider. Alexandria, VA:
      Octameron, 1976– . Annual. 84–643340. ISSN 0277–6987. $4 (1986
      ed.). Pap.

One of the sections of this annually-issued pamphlet briefly identifies sample/
representative loans and scholarships. For more information about the
publication, see the annotation in the "Scholarships—General—United
States" section of this bibliography.

787   **Encyclopedia of U.S. Government Benefits: A Complete, Practical, and
      Convenient Guide to United States Government Benefits Available to
      the People of America.** Ed. by Beryl Frank. 11th ed. New York: Dodd
      Mead, 1985. 518p. 84–8018. ISBN 0–396–08438–9. $22.95.

Among the benefits described in this publication are small business, veterans,
and individual loans available from the federal government. For more
information about the publication, see the annotation in the "Grants—
General—United States" section of this bibliography.

788   **Financial Aid for College through Scholarships and Loans: A Guide to
      Meeting College Expenses.** By Elizabeth Hoffman. 4th ed. Wellesley
      Hills, MA: Richards House, 1985. 169p. 85–185928. ISBN
      0–930702–03–4. $7.95. Pap.

This directory focuses on loans and scholarships funded by federal and state
governments and by privately-sponsored groups (businesses, churches, clubs,
the health professions, trade unions, private trusts and foundations, and
veterans organizations). The emphasis is on programs open to Massachusetts
residents. For more information about the publication, see the annotation in
the "Scholarships—General—United States" section of this bibliography.

789   **Financial Aids for Higher Education.** Prep. by Oreon Keeslar.
      Dubuque, IA: William C. Brown, 1963– . Biennial. 76–645208. ISSN
      0364–8877. $32.95 (1986 ed.). Pap.

Each biennial edition of this directory contains detailed information on over
5,000 programs (loans, scholarships, and contests) open to students interested
in postsecondary education. For more information about the publication, see

the annotation in the "Scholarships—General—United States" section of this bibliography.

790 Financing College Education. By Kenneth A. Kohl. 3d ed. New York: Harper, 1983. 288p. 82–48232. ISBN 0–06–090994–3. $5.95. Pap.

In this concise guide, Kohl reviews and evaluates various sources of financial assistance, including loans and scholarship funds available to middle- and low-income students. For more information about the publication, see the annotation in the "Scholarships—General—United States" section of this bibliography.

791 Five Federal Financial Aid Programs: A Student Guide. Washington, DC: U.S. Department of Education, 1985. 43p. Free. Pap.

This booklet describes the five major programs of student assistance available from the federal government: National Direct Student Loans, Guaranteed Student Loans/PLUS Loans, Supplemental Educational Opportunity Grants, Pell Grants, and College Work-Study. For more information about the publication, see the annotation in the "Scholarships—General—United States" section of this bibliography.

792 Foundation Grants to Individuals. Ed. by Claude Barilleaux. 4th Ed. New York: Foundation Center, 1984. 242p. 84–185951. ISBN 0–87954–097–4. $18. Pap.

Many of the grant opportunities for individual applicants identified in the fourth edition of this directory are, in fact, loan programs and scholarships. For more information about the publication, see the annotation in the "Grants—General—United States" section of this bibliography.

793 Getting Yours: The Complete Guide to Government Money. By Matthew Lesko. Rev. Ed. New York: Penguin, 1984. 292p. 84–60953. ISBN 0–14046–652–5. $7.95. Pap.

There are hundreds of government programs annually providing $190 billion in loans and guarantees to individuals, nonprofit organizations, and state and local governments. Many of these are described here. For more information about the publication, see the annotation in the section on "Grants—General—United States."

794 Need a Lift? To Educational Opportunities, Careers, Loans, Scholarships, Employment. Prep. by the American Legion Educational and Scholarship Program. Indianapolis: American Legion, 1969– . Annual. $1 (1986 ed.). Pap.

This annually revised booklet presents descriptions of loans, scholarships, fellowships, and state educational benefits valued at over $4 billion. For more information about the publication, see the annotation in the "Scholarships—General—United States" section of this bibliography.

795 Peterson's State and Federal Aid Programs for College Students. Princeton, NJ: Peterson's Guides, 1986. 56p. ISBN 0–87866–525–0. $3. Pap.

This concise booklet contains a description of the five major federal aid programs available to undergraduate students: Pell Grants, College Work-Study, National Direct Student Loans, Guaranteed Student Loans, PLUS Loans, and Supplemental Educational Opportunity Grants. For more information about the publication, see the annotation in the "Scholarships—General—United States" section of this bibliography.

796 The Scholarship Book: The Complete Guide to Private-Sector Scholarships, Grants and Loans for Undergraduates. By Daniel J. Cassidy and Michael J. Alves. Englewood Cliffs, NJ: Prentice-Hall, 1984. 391p. 84–11683. ISBN 0–13–792342–2, cloth; -334–1, pap. $28.50, cloth; $14.95, pap.

Included in this extensive but rather unfocused directory are loans, scholarships, fellowships, grants, competitions, and internships for undergraduate and (despite its title) graduate students. For more information about the publication, see the annotation in the "Scholarships—General—United States" section of this bibliography.

797 Scholarships, Fellowships and Loans. Prep. by S. Norman Feingold and Marie Feingold. Bethesda, MD: Bellman Publishing, 1949– . Irreg. 49–49180. $80 (v. 8, 1986).

This comprehensive guide to student aid provides detailed information on fellowships, scholarships, grants, and loans available to undergraduate and graduate students in the United States. For more information about the publication, see the annotation in the "Scholarships—General—United States" section of this bibliography.

798 Scholarships, Fellowships and Loans News Service and Counselors Information Services. Bethesda, MD: Bellman Publishing, 1980– . Quarterly. 81–642576. ISSN 0277–6502. $32/yr.

Use this newsletter to update Feingold's *Scholarships, Fellowships and Loans* (described above). For more information on the newsletter, see the annotation in the "Scholarships—General—United States" section of this bibliography.

799 Selected List of Fellowship Opportunities and Aids to Advanced Education for United States Citizens and Foreign Nationals. Washington, DC: National Science Foundation, 1984. 76p. Free. Pap.

Despite its title, this free pamphlet presents concise descriptions of loans, scholarships, and work-study assignments for undergraduate and graduate students as well as fellowship opportunities. For more information about this publication, see the annotation in the "Fellowships—General—United States" section of this bibliography.

800 Student Aid Annual. Moravia, NY: Chronicle Guidance Publications, 1955–1975. Annual. ISSN 0580–4555.

From 1955 through 1974, this publication was known as *Student Aid Annual*, from 1975 through 1978 as *Student Aid Manual*, and since 1979 as *Chronicle Student Aid Annual* (described in the "Scholarships—General—United States" section of this bibliography).

801 Your Own Financial Aid Factory, 1985–1986: The Guide to Locating College Money. By Robert Leider. 5th ed. Princeton, NJ: Peterson's Guides, 1985. 212p. 80–11185. ISBN 0–87866–295–2. $7.95. Pap.

This is an anthology of Octameron Associates' separately issued pamphlets on financial aid. One section reprints *College Loans from Uncle Sam*, a description of the $10 billion loan program available from the federal government. For more information about the scope and coverage of *Your Own Financial Aid Factory*, see the annotation in the "Scholarships—General—United States" section; for more information about the Octameron Associates' pamphlet describing federal loan programs, see the entry for *College Loans from Uncle Sam* provided elsewhere in this section of the bibliography.

Maryland

802 Catalog of State Assistance Programs. Baltimore: Maryland Department of State Planning, 1985. 600p. 75–642476. ISSN 0097–9309. $5. Pap.

More than 200 loans, grants, and services available from the state and federal government to public sector agencies and the general public in Maryland are described in this directory. For more information about the publication, see the annotation in the "Grants—General—Maryland" section of this bibliography.

Massachusetts

803 **Financial Aid for College through Scholarships and Loans: A Guide to Meeting College Expenses.** By Elizabeth Hoffman. 4th ed. Wellesley Hills, MA: Richards House, 1985. 169p. 85–185928. ISBN 0–930702–03–4. $7.95. Pap.

Despite the general nature of the title of this publication, the emphasis is on loans and scholarships open to Massachusetts residents. For more information on the publication, see the annotation in the "Scholarships—General—United States" section of this bibliography.

Michigan

804 **Michigan Local Assistance Manual.** Lansing: Michigan State Department of Commerce, 1981. 750p. $11. Looseleaf.

This directory identifies Michigan agencies, federal offices, and state universities that offer loans, grants, information, and services to local government units. For more information about the publication, see the annotation in the "Grants—General—Michigan" section of this bibliography.

Minnesota

805 **Dollars for Scholars Student Aid Catalog: Minnesota Edition.** By Marlys C. Johnson and Linda J. Thompson. Princeton, NJ: Peterson's Guides, 1982. v.p. 81–23503. ISBN 0–87866–194–8. $7.95. Pap.

Both loans and scholarships open to Minnesota residents (sponsored by either state or national sources) are briefly described in this directory. For more information about the publication, see the annotation in the "Scholarships—General—Minnesota" section of this bibliography.

New Hampshire

806 **Dollars for Scholars Student Aid Catalog: New Hampshire Edition.** By Linda J. Thompson and Marlys C. Johnson. Princeton, NJ: Peterson's Guides, 1982. v.p. 81–23502. ISBN 0–87866–193–X. $5.95. Pap.

Both loans and scholarships open to New Hampshire residents (sponsored by either state or national sources) are briefly described in this directory. For more information about the publication, see the annotation in the "Scholarships—General—New Hampshire" section of this bibliography.

SOCIAL SCIENCES

Anthropology

807 Funding for Anthropological Research. Ed. by Karen Cantrell and Denise Wallen. Phoenix: Oryx, 1986. 308p. 85–43472. ISBN 0–89774–154–4. $74.50. Pap.

Published in 1986, this directory identifies 700 loans, scholarships, fellowships, and grants from 200 government agencies, private and corporate foundations, associations, institutes, museums, libraries, and professional societies that would be of interest to "professional anthropologists and graduate anthropology students." For more information about the publication, see the annotation in the "Grants—Social Sciences—Anthropology" section of this bibliography.

Business and Economics

808 Guide to Government Resources for Economic Development: A Handbook for Nonprofit Agencies and Municipalities. Washington, DC: Northeast-Midwest Institute, 1979– . Irreg. 83–9394. ISSN 0735–6226. $19.95 (1983 ed.). Pap.

This guide focuses on those federal loans and grants "most important to developing overall economic development strategies." For more information about the publication, see the annotation in the "Grants—Social Sciences—Business and Economics" section of this bibliography.

809 How to Finance Your Small Business with Government Money. By Rick Stephan Hayes and John Cotton Howell. 2d ed. New York: Wiley, 1983. 258p. 82–16060. ISBN 0–471–86563–X. $19.95. Pap.

The first edition of this guide was published in 1980 (165p. 80–12016). The 1983 edition (up to date as of 1982) provides general information on loans available from the U.S. Small Business Administration and other sources. Because of the coverage date, this publication should be used with care.

810 The User's Guide to Government Resources for Economic Development. Washington, DC: Northeast—Midwest Institute, 1982. 168p. 82–644121. ISSN 0730–6288. Pap.

The first two editions (1979, 1981) of this directory were issued under the title *Guide to Federal Resources for Economic Development*. It was released in 1982 as *The User's Guide to Government Resources for Economic Development*. Since 1983, the listing has been published as *Guide to Government Resources for Economic Development: A Handbook for Nonprofit*

Agencies and Municipalities (described in the "Grants—Social Sciences—Business and Economics" section of this bibliography).

Librarianship

811 **Financial Assistance for Library Education.** Chicago: American Library Association, 1970– . Annual. 73–649921. ISSN 0569–6275. $1 (1986 ed.). Pap.

This annual directory identifies loans, scholarships, fellowships, grants-in-aid, and other financial aids for library education in the United States and Canada. For more information about this publication, see the annotation in the "Fellowships—Social Sciences—Librarianship" section in this bibliography.

Law

812 **Barron's Guide to Law Schools.** Woodbury, NY: Barron's Educational Series, 1967– . Irreg. 84–9316. $8.95 (1984 ed.). Pap.

In addition to indicating the financial aid available at each of the law schools covered here, this directory also includes a separate chapter devoted to loans and fellowships available from private and public sources to low-income students interested in legal studies.

HUMANITIES

General

813 **Gadney's Guide to 1800 International Contests, Festivals & Grants in Film & Video, Photography, TV-Radio Broadcasting, Writing, Poetry, Playwriting, Journalism.** By Alan Gadney. 2d ed. Glendale, CA: Festival Publications, 1980. 610p. 80–66803. ISBN 0–930828–03–8, cloth; -02–X, pap. $22.95, cloth; $15.95, pap.

This guide describes over 1,800 national and international loans, fellowships, festivals, competitions, prizes, awards, and grants open to those interested in film, video, photography, TV-radio broadcasting, writing, poetry, playwriting, and journalism. For more information about the publication, see the annotation in the "Awards and Prizes—Humanities—General" section of this bibliography.

SCIENCES

Health Sciences

814 Scholarships and Loans for Nursing Education. New York: National League for Nursing, 1984– . Annual. 80–102098. ISBN 0–88737–128–0. $7.25 (1985 ed.). Pap.

This booklet describes six federal financial aid programs and 50 sources of private aid available to students interested in nursing (grouped into the following categories: resources for registered nurses only; for RNs and beginning students of nursing; for beginning students only; for minority students only; and scholarships and loans for constitutent leagues). For more information about this publication, see the annotation in the "Scholarships— Medical Sciences—Health Sciences" section of this bibliography.

815 Student Financial Aid: Speech-Language Pathology and Audiology. Rockville, MD: American Speech—Language—Hearing Association, 1981. 21p. Free. Pap.

Aimed at students planning careers in speech-langauge pathology and audiology, this listing identifies loans, scholarships, and aids for graduate education. For more information about the publication, see the annotation in the "Scholarships—Sciences—Health Sciences" section of this bibliography.

Physical Sciences

816 Guide to Federal Energy Development Assistance Programs, 1981. Washington, DC: Northeast-Midwest Institute, 1982. 120p. 81–643162. ISSN 2075–6064. Pap.

In 1982, this publication was issued under the title *User's Guide to Government Energy Programs* (for information about the publication, see the annotation in the "Grants—Sciences—Energy Resources" section of the bibliography).

817 User's Guide to Government Energy Programs, 1982. Washington, DC: Northeast-Midwest Institute, 1982. 142p. 81–2666. ISSN 0730–627X. $7.50. Pap.

Covered in this guide are loans, loan guarantees, grants, tax incentives, technical assistance programs, and other forms of aid for the energy field. For more information about this publication, see the annotation in the "Grants— Sciences—Energy Resources" section of this bibliography.

Technology

818   **Computer Resource Guide for Nonprofits.** 3d ed. San Francisco: Public Management Institute, 1985. 2v. 83–63275. ISBN 0–916664–42–2. $225. Pap.

The third edition of this directory identifies foundations, corporations, and federal agencies that have made computer-related loans, grants, and in-kind donations. For more information about the publication, see the annotation in the "Grants—Sciences—Technology" section of this bibliography.

819   **Nonprofit Computer Connection.** San Francisco: Public Management Institute, 1985– . Monthly. $127/yr.

This monthly eight-page newsletter devotes one of its five regular sections to computer-related philanthropy (including loans). Use it to update the listings in the *Computer Resource Guide for Nonprofits* (described above).

SPECIAL POPULATION GROUPS

The Disabled

820   **Financial Aid for the Disabled and Their Dependents.** By Gail Ann Schlachter. Los Angeles: Reference Service Press, 1987– . Biennial. (Directories of Financial Aid for Special Needs Groups). $29.95 (1987/88 ed.).

This is the first comprehensive and up-to-date listing of loans, awards, grants-in-aid, scholarships, and fellowships that have been established for disabled individuals and their dependents. For more information about the publication, see the annotation in the "Scholarships—Special Population Groups—The Disabled" section of this bibliography.

Ethnic Groups

821   **Black Resource Guide.** Photos. by Robert Sengstacke. Washington, DC: Black Resource Guide, 1981– . Annual. 85–645223. ISSN 0882–0643. $25 (1985 ed.).

First published in 1981, the latest edition of this annual black directory (1985. 217p. ISBN 0–9608374–2–6) is designed "to inform the public of available sources of assistance and information in black America." The guide is divided into sections, e.g., accounting firms, adoption agencies, book publishers and book stores, executive recruiters, fraternal organizations, media. One of these sections, "Financial Institutions," (banks and savings and loan associations) provides information to readers interested in financial assistance in the form of loans. This listing, as well as the other sections in the directory, is available on mailing labels from the publisher.

822 Directory of Financial Aids for Minorities. By Gail Ann Schlachter. Los Angeles: Reference Service Press, 1984– . Biennial. (Directories of Financial Aid for Special Needs Groups). 83–25068. ISBN 0–918276–03–9. ISSN 0738–4122. $37.50 (1986–1987 ed.).

The latest edition of this biennial directory includes a descriptive list of more than 1,200 loans, scholarships, fellowships, grants, awards, prizes, and internships set aside for Asian Americans, Black Americans, Hispanic Americans, Native Americans, and minorities in general. For more information about the publication, see the annotation in the "Scholarships— Special Population Groups—Ethnic Groups" section of the bibliography.

823 Directory of Special Programs for Minority Group Members: Career Information Services, Employment Skills Banks, Financial Aid Sources. Prep. by Willis L. Johnson. 3d ed. Garrett Park, MD: Garrett Park Press, 1980. 612p. 73–93533. ISSN 0093–9501. $20. Pap.

In addition to listing career information services and employment skills banks, this directory identifies a number of sources of loans, scholarships, and fellowships for minority groups members that were available in 1980. For more information about the publication, see the annotation in the "Scholarships—Special Population Groups—Ethnic Groups" section of this bibliography.

824 Higher Education Opportunities for Minorities and Women...Annotated Selections. Washington, DC: G.P.O., 1982– . Annual. 84–11125. Free. Pap.

Issued annually, this pamphlet describes loans, scholarships, and fellowships open to minorities and women at the postsecondary level. For more information about the publication, see the annotation in the "Scholarships— Special Population Groups—Ethnic Groups" section of this bibliography.

825 Hispanic Financial Resource Handbook. Comp. by the Hispanic Student Program. Columbus: Office of Student Life, Ohio State University, 1982– . Annual. $5 (1985 ed.). Pap.

This comb-bound handbook was first compiled in 1982 (and revised annually since then) to "assist Hispanic students and professionals in obtaining financial aid information which is especially geared toward Hispanic and other minorities." Brief descriptions are provided for applicable loans, grants, fellowships, and scholarships. For more information about the publication, see the annotation in the "Scholarships—Special Population Groups—Ethnic Groups" section of this bibliography.

Foreign Students

826 Selected List of Fellowship Opportunities and Aids to Advanced
    Education for United States Citizens and Foreign Nationals.
    Washington, DC: National Science Foundation, 1984. 76p. Free. Pap.

This free pamphlet presents concise descriptions of loans, scholarships,
fellowships, and work-study experiences available to foreign students in the
United States as well as to American citizens. For more information about
the publication, see the annotation in the "Fellowships—General—United
States" section of this bibliography.

Military Personnel and Veterans

827 Educational Assistance and Opportunities Information for Army
    Family Members. Alexandria, VA: Adjutant General's Office, U.S.
    Department of the Army, 1984. v.p. Free. Looseleaf.

This directory identifies associations and other groups that provide
scholarships, fellowships, loans, and grants to army personnel and relatives of
military personnel. For more information about the publication, see the
annotation in the "Scholarships—Special Population Groups—Military
Personnel and Veterans" section of this bibliography.

828 Federal Benefits for Veterans and Dependents. Prep. by U.S. Veterans
    Administration. Washington, DC: G.P.O., 1969– . Annual.
    85–641702. ISSN 0883-3370. $1.75 (1986 ed.). Pap.

This booklet provides a comprehensive summary of benefits (including loans)
available to veterans and their dependents. For more information about the
publication, see the annotation in the "Grants—Special Population Groups—
Military Personnel and Veterans" section of this bibliography.

829 Once a Veteran: Benefits, Rights, Obligations. 1985 Edition.
    Washington, DC: American Forces Information Service, U.S.
    Department of Defense (for sale by G.P.O.), 1985. 43p. $2. Pap.

This inexpensive pamphlet provides up-to-date information on the benefits
(including loans available), rights, and obligations of American veterans. For
more information about the publication, see the annotation in the "Grants—
Special Population Groups—Military Personnel and Veterans" section of this
bibliography.

830   **State Veterans' Laws: Digests of State Laws Regarding Rights, Benefits, and Privileges of Veterans and Their Dependents.** Washington, DC: G.P.O., 1945– . Irreg. 60–62289. Free. Pap. Microfiche to depository libraries.

This congressional report covers the loans, fellowships, scholarships, and grants available to veterans on the state level. For more information about the publication, see the annotation in the "Grants—General—United States" section of this bibliography.

831   **United States Code, Title 38: Veteran's Benefits.** Washington, DC: G.P.O. Irreg. $25, U.S.; $31.25, elsewhere. Looseleaf.

This looseleaf subscription service contains the exact text of laws relating to veterans' benefits (including the financial aid programs established by the federal government). For more information about the publication, see the annotation in the "Grants—Special Population Groups—Military Personnel and Veterans" section of this bibliography.

832   **The Viet Vet Survival Guide: How to Get through the Bureaucracy and Get What You Need and Are Entitled To.** Ed. by Craig Kubey, et al. New York: Facts On File, 1986. 256p. ISBN 0–8160–1379–9. $19.95.

Included in this first self-help book for Vietnam veterans is information on loans, scholarships, fellowships, and grants-in-aid that are available for this group from the federal government. For more information about the publication, see the annotation in the "Grants—Special Population Groups—Military Personnel and Veterans" section of this bibliography.

833   **What Every Veteran Should Know.** East Moline, IL: Veterans Information Service, 1937– . Annual, with monthly supplements. ISSN 0083–9108. $6.00; $18, with supplements (1981 ed.). Pap.

Published since 1937, the latest edition of this guide (1981. ISBN 0–346–32464–5) describes the federal benefits that veterans and their dependents are eligible to receive. Instructions are provided on the best ways to obtain assistance. Entries are arranged by subject and thoroughly indexed.

Reentry Students

834   **Finding Financial Resources for Adult Learners: Profiles for Practice.** New York: College Entrance Examination Board, 1985. 56p. 85–172422. ISBN 0–87447–206–7. $8.95. Pap.

In this selective guide, 70 community- and campus-based sources of financial aid are identified and described, including loans, work programs, credit for prior learning, tuition plans, and scholarships. For more information about the publication, see the annotation in the "Scholarships—Special Population Groups—Reentry Students" section of this bibliography.

Women

835   Directory of Financial Aids for Women. By Gail Ann Schlachter. Los Angeles: Reference Service Press, 1978– . Biennial. (Directories of Financial Aid for Special Needs Groups). 84–24582. ISSN 0732–5215. $37.50.

This is the only extensive and regularly updated listing of loans, awards/ prizes, fellowships, scholarships, grants, and internships designed primarily or exclusively for women. For more information about the publication, see the annotation in the "Scholarships—Special Population Groups—Women" section of this bibliography.

836   Educational Financial Aids: A Guide to Selecting Fellowships, Scholarships, and Internships in Higher Education. Washington, DC: American Association of University Women, 1984. 35p. $5. Pap.

In the 1984 edition (earlier versions were published in 1976 and 1981), loans are covered along with scholarships, fellowships, and internships. For more information about the publication, see the annotation in the "Fellowships— Special Population Groups—Women" section of this bibliography.

837   Higher   Education   Opportunities   for   Minorities   and Women...Annotated Selections. Washington, DC: G.P.O., 1982– . Annual. 84–11125. $5.50 (1986 ed.). Pap.

Issued annually, this pamphlet describes loans, scholarships, and fellowships open to women and minorities at the postsecondary level. For more information about the publication, see the annotation in the "Scholarships— Special Population Groups—Ethnic Groups" section of this bibliography.

Internships

Internships provide work experience opportunities and often monetary support for students (high school through postdoctoral), professionals, and other workers who are interested in short-term placements. Some internships can be held while pursuing other activities (e.g., school, job), but most of the programs listed in commercially available directories require a concentrated commitment for a limited time period (one month, a summer, intersession, a semester, or a year). Many students find internships to be an excellent source of financial assistance. Included in this chapter are 47 references to directories listing work experience programs. Of these, 19 are general in coverage, 8 focus on the social sciences, 7 cover the humanities, 4 deal with the sciences, and 9 are aimed at special population groups. If you are looking for a specific internship directory and you do not find it in this chapter, be sure to check the Title Index to see if it is covered elsewhere in the Guide.

GENERAL

International

838 Directory of Summer Jobs Abroad. Oxford, Eng.: Vacation-Work (dist. by Writer's Digest), 1980– . Annual. 85–20062. ISSN 0308–7123. $8.95 (1986 ed.). Pap.

Revised annually, this directory lists and provides career information on more than 50,000 summer jobs located outside of the United States, from Australia to Yugoslavia. The employment opportunities covered are particularly suitable for high school graduates, college students, and teachers. Each listing specifies who to contact, length of employment, number of openings available, how and when to apply, rates of pay, duties, and qualifications sought. Supplemental information on visa and work permit regulations and procedures is also provided. The entries are arranged by country. From 1969 through 1979, this publication was issued under the title *Directory of Overseas Summer Jobs* (Annual. 72–204826. ISSN 0070–6051). For similar but more comprehensive coverage of employment opportunities in Scotland, Wales, and England, see *Summer Jobs in Britain* (described below).

839 Summer Jobs in Britain. Ed. by Susan Griffith. Oxford, Eng.: Vacation-Work (dist. by Writer's Digest), 1970– . Annual. 79–645164. ISSN 0143–3490. $8.95 (1986 ed.). Pap.

More than 30,000 summer jobs in Scotland, Wales, England, the Channel Islands, and Northern Ireland are listed in this annual directory. In the 1986 edition (174p. ISBN 0–907638–48–1), these jobs range from farm hand to office worker to lorry driver. Entries specify all information needed to apply for each job. Also included in the volume are procedures to follow in applying for visas and work permits. Over the years, the title has varied slightly; at one point, it was issued as the *Directory of Summer Jobs in Britain*.

United States

840 The College Aid Checkbook: A Guide to College Financial Aid. Clifton, NJ: Army ROTC, 1985. n.p. Free. Pap.

This checkbook-sized pamphlet was written as a starting point to identify major private and public work programs, loans, grants, and scholarships. For more information about the free publication, see the annotation in the "Scholarships—General—United States" section of this bibliography.

41   Directory of Undergraduate Internships. Raleigh, NC: National
Society for Internships and Experiential Education, 1975– . Irreg.
83–11516. Pap.

The latest (1980) edition of this directory lists 150 internship opportunities
throughout the country. The entries, arranged alphabetically by sponsoring
organization, provide information on program design, admissions
requirements, application procedures, remuneration, and academic credit.
The directory also includes a clearinghouse section at the beginning that lists
central organizations that refer or place students into a variety of agencies
based on career interests and academic background. A bibliography,
geographical index, and alphabetical index complete the work. The directory
is now completely out of date and is not available for distribution. A new
edition is being considered but has not yet been issued. For a more current
and inclusive listing of undergraduate internships, see *1981— Internships*
(described elsewhere in this section of the bibliography).

**842   Earn & Learn: Cooperative Education Opportunities Offered by the
Federal Government.** Ed. by Joseph Re. Alexandria, VA: Octameron
Associates, 1979– . Annual. $2.50 (1986 ed.). Pap.

"Cooperative education" is a blend of classroom instruction and on-the-job
work experiences related to formal instruction. The main part of this
annually-issued pamphlet (1986 edition: 28 pages) consists of a name/address
list of over 700 colleges participating in cooperative education programs. Also
included is a name/address list of federal agencies—from Agriculture to
Treasury—that act as program sponsors. In addition to being issued as a
separate publication, this work is also reprinted in its entirety in Peterson's
Guide's *Your Own Financial Aid Factory: The Guide to Locating College
Money* (described in the "Scholarships—General—United States" section of
this bibliography). Although the 1986 edition of the *Earn & Learn* pamphlet
costs only $2.50, an even less expensive way to obtain similar information is
to write to the National Commission for Cooperative Education (360
Huntington Avenue, Boston, MA 02115) for their free list of all colleges and
universities in the United States that offer cooperative education.

**843   Getting Work Experience: The Student's Directory of Professional
Internship Programs.** By Betsy Bauer. New York: Dell, 1985. 336p.
85–16142. ISBN 0–440–52815–1. $7.95. Pap.

This handbook lists more than 10,000 paid internships (while *1987
Internships* identifies more opportunities, many of those are unpaid
placements). The entries in Bauer's book provide address, telephone number,
and company profiles. Opportunities in business, technology, and government
are stressed.

844   Guide to Apprenticeship Programs. By William F. Shanahan. New York: Arco, 1983. 217p. (An Arco Occupational Guide). 82–24277. ISBN 0–668–05454–9, cloth; -05461–1, pap. $12.95, cloth; $7.95, pap.

Using the *Occupational Outlook Handbook*, local programs, unions, and the U.S. Bureau of Apprenticeship and Training (BAT) as sources, this guide identifies 700 "apprenticeable" programs and describes 125 of them. Entries (each a page or less in length) provide information on the nature of the work, qualifications, length of program, employment outlook, wages, working conditions, and contact for additional information. In addition, one section of the volume defines apprenticeship and describes programs in general (eligibility, standards and myths, openings, application procedures, and opportunities for women, minorities, and the disabled) and seven appendices list occupations meeting the criteria for apprenticeships, BAT offices and state offices, and state apprenticeship agencies; provide statistics on apprenticeships between 1941 and 1979; and supply answers to common questions about apprenticeships. There is an index to occupations, ranging from air conditioning to water treatment plants. Use the *Occupational Outlook Handbook* to update the information in the guide.

845   An Independent Sector Resource Directory of Education and Training Opportunities and Other Services. By Sandra Trice Gray. Washington, DC: Independent Sector, 1986– . Annual. $18 (1986 ed.). Pap.

Independent Sector represents more than 600 foundations, corporations, and voluntary organizations. One goal of the coalition is to improve the management and overall effectiveness of voluntary and philanthropic organizations. To that end, Independent Sector conducted a survey of organizations and institutions that offer training for nonprofit organization work. The data collected in the survey is reported in this directory, planned as an annual. It is divided into four sections, one of which identifies internships, fellowships, and grants for individuals interested in this "independent sector." The less than 40 programs included here are grouped by type (internships, fellowships) and arranged by sponsoring organization. Brief descriptions are provided for each program.

846   National Directory of Internships. Ed. by Barbara A. Coluni. Raleigh, NC: National Society for Internships and Experiential Education, 1984. 315p. ISBN 0–536–04852–5. $15. Pap.

This directory identifies "internships and fellowship opportunities throughout the United States for high school students, undergraduate students, graduate students, and persons with career experience." The volume is divided into organizational categories, such as museums, fine arts, business and finance, communications, education, medicine and health care, and human services. Each program is listed only once, under the category that best describes the organization. However, the internships are cross-referenced by functional area in the back of the book. Program profiles specify name, address, telephone number, activities of the sponsoring organization, eligibility requirements, number of interns accepted, duration, and application procedures. The entries are indexed alphabetically and by geographic location. The listing is less comprehensive than but somewhat complementary to *1987 Internships* (described elsewhere in this section of the bibliography).

847 **National Directory of Summer Internships for Undergraduates.** Prep. by the Career Planning Offices of Bryn Mawr and Haverford Colleges. Ed. by John Blackwood, et al. Haverford, PA: Career Planning Office, Haverford College, 1981. 181p. 83–11450. ISSN 0098–1451. o.p.

This directory lists specific summer internships available to undergraduates across the United States. The opportunities described are available in public service, health, communications, education, the arts, and a number of other fields. The entries, arranged in 10 subject areas with a cross-reference index, provide information on location, duration, eligibility, remuneration, duties, and application procedures. A bibliography of additional sources of information completes the work. The listing is now quite a bit out of date, and it is out of print. A more current list of summer opportunities can be found in *Summer Employment Directory of the United States* and by browsing through the latest edition of *Internships: 34,000 On-the-Job Training Opportunities for All Types of Careers* (both described elsewhere in this section of the bibliography).

848 **The Scholarship Book: The Complete Guide to Private-Sector Scholarships, Grants and Loans for Undergraduates.** By Daniel J. Cassidy and Michael J. Alves. Englewood Cliffs, NJ: Prentice-Hall, 1984. 391p. 84–11683. ISBN 0–13–792342–2, cloth; -334–1, pap. $28.50, cloth; $14.95, pap.

Included in this extensive but rather unfocused directory are internships, grants, loans, scholarships, fellowships, and competitions for undergraduate and (despite its subtitle) graduate students. For more information about the publication, see the annotation in the "Scholarships—General—United States" section of this bibliography.

849 **Selected List of Fellowship Opportunities and Aids to Advanced Education for United States Citizens and Foreign Nationals.** Washington, DC: National Science Foundation, 1984. 76p. Free. Pap.

Despite its title, this free pamphlet presents concise descriptions of work-study assignments, loans, and scholarships for undergraduate and graduate students as well as fellowship opportunities. For more information about this publication, see the annotation in the "Fellowships—General—United States" section of this bibliography.

850 The Student Guide to Fellowships and Internships. By students of Amherst College. New York: Dutton, 1980. 402p. 80–67575. ISBN 0–5256–3155–4, cloth; -3147–3, pap. $15.95, cloth; $7.95, pap.

A group of Amherst students prepared this guide to internships in architecture, business, government, and law. The guide contains two different kinds of information: general advice on internship and fellowship hunting, and descriptions of specific programs (grouped by particular field or discipline). The entries are meant to be "suggestive, not exhaustive." Despite its title, only one chapter in the book addresses fellowships, and only national fellowships are described there. The volume concludes with a short bibliography of additional sources of information. There is no index.

851 Summer Employment Directory of the United States. Ed. by Rand Ruggeberg. Cincinnati, OH: Writer's Digest, 1952– . Annual. 82–403. ISSN 0081–9352. $9.95 (1986 ed.). Pap.

For over 30 years, *Summer Employment Directory* (title varies slightly) has been providing college students, high school students, and teachers with detailed information on 50,000 summer jobs at resorts, camps, parks, businesses, and government offices in the United States. Since the 1983 edition, a short international section has also been included. Job information is supplied by the employers. Arrangement is geographical and then by type of employer (camp, restaurant, etc.). Each listing specifies who to contact, application address, payment rates, qualifications needed, and number of openings available. Suggestions on how to write a resume and a cover letter are also presented.

852 Summer Opportunities for Kids and Teenagers. Ed. by Christopher Billy. Princeton, NJ: Peterson's Guides, 1983– . Annual. ISSN 0739–9006. $12.95 (1986 ed.). Pap.

The first edition of this annual was issued in 1983. Its stated purpose was to provide "information on the growing number of summer educational opportunities for children and teenagers." The fourth edition, covering 1986 (650p. ISBN 0–87866–444–0), provides information (obtained through questionnaires) on 1,100 camps, summer schools, college- and university-sponsored programs, travel groups, and special programs for the gifted, mentally retarded, and the physically disabled. Nearly 600 of the camps and programs described offer employment opportunities for high school and college students in a variety of internship-like capacities.

853   Undergraduate Programs of Cooperative Education in the United States and Canada. Boston: National Commission for Cooperative Education, 1972– . Irreg. Free. Pap.

This free publication, available from the National Commission for Cooperative Education (360 Huntington Ave., Boston, MA 02115), identifies over 1,000 colleges and universities that offer cooperative education. These programs provide students with the opportunity of alternating periods of off-campus career-related work with on-campus, academic study. Full information on each program is provided. The latest edition of the directory was issued in 1982 (83p.).

854   Your Own Financial Aid Factory, 1985–1986: The Guide to Locating College Money. By Robert Leider. 5th ed. Princeton, NJ: Peterson's Guides, 1985. 212p. 80–11185. ISBN 0–87866–295–2. $7.95. Pap.

This is an anthology of Octameron Associates' separately issued pamphlets on financial aid. One section reprints *Earn & Learn: Cooperative Education Opportunities*, a description of the cooperative education programs supported by the federal government. For more information about the scope and coverage of *Your Own Financial Aid Factory*, see the annotation in the "Scholarships—General—United States" section; for more information about the Octameron Associates' pamphlet describing cooperative education programs supported by the federal government, see the entry for *Earn & Learn* provided elsewhere in this section of the bibliography.

855   1981—Internships: 34,000 On-the-Job Training Opportunities for All Types of Careers. Ed. by Lisa S. Hulse. Cincinnati, OH: Writer's Digest, 1981– . Annual. 81–649753. ISSN 0272–5460. $14.95 (1987 ed.). Pap.

Internships provide a valuable way of acquiring on-the-job experience, testing a career, or getting practical training. One of the best ways to find an internship is with a copy of the latest edition of this directory. Published annually since 1981, this publication identifies over 34,000 short-term career-oriented positions in major American firms. The jobs cover a wide range of fields, including architecture, business, communications, and sciences. Program entries describe length and season of the position, rates of pay, desired qualifications, duties, training involved, availability of college credit, and application contacts, procedures, and deadlines. International internships are also listed, as well as specific information for interns working abroad and non-U.S. citizens applying for U.S. internships. The book is arranged by categories of job sponsors as they relate to college disciplines; to narrow down your search, use the General or the Geographic-Cross Index. Completing the volume are helpful articles on selecting, applying for, and interviewing for an internship position.

Washington, DC

856 **Directory of Washington Internships.** Raleign, NC: National Society for Internships and Experiential Education, 1974– . Irreg. 84–1454. $9.50 (1983 ed.). Pap.

Revised and updated irregularly, this directory focuses on approximately 200 internship opportunities available to undergraduate and graduate students in the Washington, D.C. area. The entries are divided into general fields of interest and then arranged alphabetically by sponsoring organization. They contain the following information: program design, requirements, remuneration, and academic credit. In addition, separate sections identify internship clearinghouses and describe housing accomodations in Washington, D.C. The latest edition was published in 1983 (112p.).

SOCIAL SCIENCES
Business and Economics

857 **Advertising Career Directory.** New York: Career Publishing, 1985– . Annual. (A Career Directory Series Book). 86–643000. ISSN 0882–8253. $24.95. Pap.

While most of this book is devoted to a discussion of the education for and practice of advertising as a career, one chapter (Chapter 28, pp. 275–301) lists "1986 Internships and Training Programs." Both salaried and nonsalaried postiions are covered.

History

858 **Fellowships and Grants of Interest to Historians.** Washington, DC: American Historical Association, 1976–1977. Annual. Pap.

Since 1978, this publication has been issued as *Grants and Fellowships of Interest to Historians* (described in the "Grants—Social Sciences—History" section).

859 **Grants and Fellowships of Interest to Historians.** Washington, DC: American Historical Association, 1978– . Annual. 83–644237. ISSN 0275–830X. $4, members; $5, nonmembers (1985/86 ed.). Pap.

This annual listing identifies and describes nearly 200 internships, fellowships, awards, prizes, and travel grants of interest to graduate students, postdoctoral researchers, and scholars in history. For a more complete annotation, see the description of *Grants and Fellowships of Interest to Historians* in the "Grants—Social Sciences—History" section.

Law

860 Summer Legal Employment Guide. Chicago: American Bar
   Association, 1982– . Annual. 83–643535. ISSN 0738–1921. $12. Pap.

More focused than *Summer Jobs: Opportunities in the Federal Government*
(described in the "Internships—General—United States" section), this
annual directory from the American Bar Association identifies federal
agencies, international organizations, nonprofit organizations, and public
interest groups offering summer internship opportunities for law students.
The entries are arranged by sponsoring organization and contain the
following information: sponsoring organization, address, contact person,
number of interns accepted, eligibility requirements, scope of assignments,
and comments from previous interns. In 1982, this directory was issued under
the title *Summer Federal Legal Employment Guide* (82–644745. ISSN
0278–6737). In 1983, the annual changed its name to *Summer Legal
Employment Guide.*

Political Sciences

861 International Directory of Youth Internships. Ed. by Cynthia T.
   Morehouse. 4th ed. New York: Learning Resources in International
   Studies, 1984. 48p. ISBN 0–8936876–44–1. $4.75. Pap.

This fourth revised editon provides fairly current coverage of approximately
400 intern and volunteer opportunities within the United Nations Secretariat
and its specialized and related agencies, as well as within selected
nongovernmental organizations. Sections are also included on the World
Federation of United Nations Associations and some university programs
related to the United Nations. A concluding bibliography identifies additional
sources of information on work, study, and travel within the United States
and abroad.

Psychology

**862 Internship Programs in Professional Psychology, Including Post-
   Doctoral Training Programs.** Knoxville, IA: Association of Psychology
   Internship Centers, 1967– . Annual. $10 (1985 ed.). Pap.

Issued annually, this directory identifies institutions offering internship and
postdoctoral training programs in psychology. The listing is arranged
geographically. Program entries specify institution address, contact person,
internship characteristics, number of internships available, stipend, and
admission requirements.

Public Administration

863 Directory of Public Service Internships: Opportunities for the Graduate, Post-graduate, and Mid-Career Professional. Raleigh, NC: National Society for Internships and Experiential Education, 1973– . Irreg. $12 (1981 ed.). Pap.

The 1981 edition lists and describes 127 internship and fellowship opportunities for graduates, postgraduates, and mid-career professionals in 24 states and Washington, D.C. (where nearly half of the programs are located). The entries, which are arranged into 14 fields, contain information on program design, supervision, recruitment strategies, selection requirements, and remuneration. The entries are indexed by geographic location and organization name. Also included in each volume are a bibliography of related publications and a list of clearinghouses of internship information.

864 Summer Jobs: Opportunities in the Federal Government. Washington, DC: U.S. Office of Personnel Management, 1971– . Annual. Free. Pap.

This pamphlet is distributed free each fall by the Office of Personnel Management (1900 E Street, N.W., Washington, DC 20415). It describes jobs available throughout the country the following summer in various federal agencies. These range from office jobs to Park Ranger assignments. Most listed jobs, however, are in large metropolitan areas, particularly Washington, D.C. The entries are arranged by job level (GS-1 through GS-5 and above) and then alphabetically by agency name. In the past, this pamphlet was issued under the title *Summer Jobs in the Federal Agencies.*

HUMANITIES

General

865 Directory of Undergraduate Internships in the Humanities. Comp. by the Washington Center. New York: Modern Language Association of America, 1984. 139p. 84–25486. $11. Pap.

The title of this publication is misleading. This is not a listing of internship opportunities open to undergraduate students interested in the humanities. Rather, this directory "lists departments and campus offices that provide humanities undergraduates with access to academic internships." The directory is based on 915 responses received from a college-level survey of "internship attitudes and practices in the humanities" (a full report of the survey, *Preparing Humanists for Work: A National Study of Undergraduate Internships in the Humanities,* is available from the National Society for Internships and Experiential Education for $8). The entries prepared from the participants' responses supply the following information for each office: school address, contact persons, telephone number, "access" (who is responsible for conducting the office's work with internships), prerequisites for the students interested in participating in internships, and services offered by the offices. The entries are alphabetized by institution and indexed by state and by department or campus office. While the information included here will not help undergraduate students find humanities internships, it will assist staff in humanities deaprtments who are interested in creating internship options or who wish to compare their current internship activity with the range available to humanities undergraduates nationally.

866 Survey of Arts Administration Training in the U.S. New York: American Council for the Arts, 1976– . Irreg. 84–21593. $7.50 (1985–86 ed.). Pap.

In the 1985–86 edition (86p. ISBN 0–915400–49–9), there are approximately 25 institutions offering internships, seminars, graduate programs, or other special programs available to train administrators for performing arts companies, museums, and other organizations in the arts. The entries are arranged by type of program and include the following information: sponsoring organization address and telephone number, program description (including eligibility requirements), degrees offered, degree requirements, and internships, seminars, or workshops offered.

Applied Arts

867 How to Enter and Win Black & White Photography Contests. By Alan Gadney. New York: Facts On File, 1982. 204p. 81–12594. ISBN 0–87196–571–2, cloth; -577–1, pap. $14.95, cloth; $6.95.

868 How to Enter and Win Color Photography Contests. By Alan Gadney. New York: Facts On File, 1982. 204p. 81–12591. ISBN 0–87196–572–0, cloth; -578–X, pap. $14.95, cloth; $6.95, pap.

These twin directories each cover over 500 national and international photography apprenticeships, contests, photofairs, festivals, grants, and awards. For more information about the publications, see the annotation in the "Awards and Prizes—Humanities—Applied Arts" section of this bibliography.

Communications and Mass Media

869   Journalism Career Guide for Minorities. Prep. by the American
Society of Newspaper Editors. Princeton, NJ: Dow Jones Newspaper
Fund, 1984. 48p. Free. Pap.

One section of this free booklet deals with internships, scholarships,
fellowships, and special training programs for minorities interested in
journalism as well as with general scholarship/fellowship opportunities. For
more information about the publication, see the annotation in the
"Scholarships—Humanities—Communications and Mass Media" section of
this bibliography.

870   The Student Guide to Mass Media Internships. Comp. by Ronald
Claxton. Boulder: Intern Research Group, University of Colorado,
1977– . Annual. ISSN 0730–5117. $40 (1986 ed.). Pap.

Since 1985, this annual internship directory has been issued in two volumes:
Print and *Broadcast*. The first volume, *Print*, covers internship opportunities
in daily and weekly newspapers, newspaper groups, specialty newspapers,
news services and syndicates, newspaper organizations, magazines, inhouse
publications, and book publishers. The second volume, *Broadcast*, covers
broadcast groups, television stations, cable television, and radio stations. In
all, about 10,000 internships offered by 2,700 mass media agencies are
identified. The program listings provided in both volumes contain general
descriptions of the internships and basic information about their operation
(e.g., remuneration, duration, eligibility). Not all of the internships covered
are salaried. There is no index.

Music

871   Career Guide for Young Singers from the United States and Canada.
5th ed. New York: Central Opera Service, 1985. 80p. $9.50. Pap.

Two of the eight sections in the 1985 edition of this irregularly-issued
directory describes apprenticeship opportunities for Canadian and American
singers. For more information about the publication, see the annotation in the
"Awards and Prizes—Humanities—Music" section of this bibliography.

SCIENCES

Biological Sciences

872 Student Employment and Internships at Botanical Gardens and Arboreta for 1986. Comp. by Woody Frey. Swathmore, PA: American Association of Botanical Gardens and Arboreta, 1985. 17p. $1.50. Pap.

Included in this booklet are descriptions of 235 internships and 100 summer employment positions at 78 botanical gardens, arboreta, and other horticultural institutions. Each entry contains the following information: sponsoring organization address and telephone number, contact person, number, duration, stipend, eligibility, and deadline date.

Health Sciences

873 Directory of Pathology Training Programs: Anatomic, Clinical, Specialized. Bethesda, MD: Intersociety Committee on Pathology Information, 1970– . Annual. 75–5589. ISSN 0070–6086. $45 (1986/ 87 ed.). Pap.

More than 200 postgradaute pathology training programs in the United States and Canada are described in this annual directory. The listing overlaps to a great extent with the American Medical Association's *Directory of Residency Training Programs* (described elsewhere in this section of the bibliography). More detail, however, is provided in this directory. Entries specify facilities, methods, staff, application procedures, and stipends.

874 Directory of Psychiatry Residency Training Programs. Ed. by Carolyn B. Robinowitz and Zebulon Taintor. Washington, DC: American Psychiatric Association, 1982– . Biennial. 84–1012. ISSN 0740–8250. $15 (1986 ed.). Pap.

Aimed at medical students interested in applying for a general or child psychiatry residency program, this directory lists programs by geographic location (by states, for the United States; by provinces, for Canada) and provides detailed program descriptions that are followed by narrative information and the name of a contact person. In addition, the directory includes a list of postgraduate fellowships, board requirements, names of program directors, brief descriptions of the subspecialties of psychiatry and the settings in which they are practiced, a description of the methods to use to select a residency, and a section on "Careers in Psychiatry." Use this source to supplement ths listings in the American Medical Association's *Directory of Residency Training Programs* (described elsewhere in this section of the bibliography).

875 Directory of Residency Training Programs Accredited by the Accreditation Council for Graduate Medical Education. Chicago: American Medical Association, 1981– . Annual. 82–222065. ISSN 0164–1670. $23.50 (1986/87 ed.).

Over the years, this directory has been issued under a variety of titles. From 1952 through 1974, it was published as the *Directory of Approved Internships and Residencies* (76–539. ISSN 0419–2141); in 1975 as the *Directory of Approved Residencies* (76–916. ISSN 0097–899X); from 1976 through 1978 as the *Directory of Accredited Residencies* (77–647051. ISSN 0147–2291); in 1979 and 1980 as the *Directory of Residency Training Programs Accredited by the Liaison Committee on Graduate Medical Education* (79–640143. ISSN 0164–1670); and since 1981 as the *Directory of Residency Training Programs Accredited by the Accreditation Council for Graduate Medical Education.* This annual provides the most comprehensive listing available of residencies open to medical school graduates. It contains less detail, however, than either the *Directory of Pathology Training Programs* or the *Directory of Psychiatry Residency Training Programs* (both described elsewhere in this section of the bibliography).

SPECIAL POPULATION GROUPS

Ethnic Groups

876 Directory of Financial Aids for Minorities. By Gail Ann Schlachter. Los Angeles: Reference Service Press, 1984– . Biennial. (Directories of Financial Aid for Special Needs Groups). 83–25068. ISBN 0–918276–03–9. ISSN 0738–4122. $37.50 (1986–1987 ed.).

The latest edition of this biennial directory includes a descriptive list of over 1,200 internships, scholarships, fellowships, loans, grants, and awards and prizes set aside for Asian Americans, Black Americans, Hispanic Americans, Native Americans, and minorities in general. For more information about the publication, see the annotation in the "Scholarships—Special Population Groups—Ethnic Groups" section of this bibliography.

877 Directory of Special Programs for Minority Group Members: Career Information Services, Employment Skills Banks, Financial Aid Sources. Prep. by Willis L. Johnson. 3d ed. Garrett Park, MD: Garrett Park Press, 1980. 612p. 73–92422. ISSN 0093–9501. $20. Pap.

In addition to listing career information services, employment skills banks, and selected financial aid sources, this directory identifies 160 summer employment and internship opportunities and 280 job training programs that were available in 1980. For more information about the publication, see the annotation in the "Scholarships—Special Population Groups—Ethnic Groups" section of this bibliography.

878 **Journalism Career Guide for Minorities.** Prep. by the American Society of Newspaper Editors. Princeton, NJ: Dow Jones Newspaper Fund, 1984. 48p. Free. Pap.

One section of this free booklet deals with scholarships, fellowships, internships, and special training programs for minorities interested in journalism as well as with general scholarship/fellowship opportunities. For more information about the publication, see the annotation in the "Scholarships—Humanities—Communications and Mass Media" section of this bibliography.

Foreign Students

879 **Selected List of Fellowship Opportunities and Aids to Advanced Education for United States Citizens and Foreign Nationals.** Washington, DC: National Science Foundation, 1984. 76p. Free. Pap.

This free pamphlet presents concise descriptions of loans, scholarships, fellowships, and work-study experiences available to foreign students in the United States as well as to American citizens. For more information about the publication, see the annotation in the "Fellowships—General—United States" section of this bibliography.

Reentry Students

880 **Finding Financial Resources for Adult Learners: Profiles for Practice.** New York: College Entrance Examination Board, 1985. 56p. 85–172422. ISBN 0–87447–206–7. $8.95. Pap.

In this selective guide, 70 community- and campus-based sources of financial aid are identified and described, including work programs, credit for prior learning, loans, tuition plans, and scholarships. For more information about the publication, see the annotation in the "Scholarships—Special Population Groups—Reentry Students" section of this bibliography.

Women

881 **Directory of Financial Aids for Women.** By Gail Ann Schlachter. Los Angeles: Reference Service Press, 1978– . Biennial. (Directories of Financial Aid for Special Needs Groups). 84–24582. ISSN 0732–5215. $37.50.

This is the only extensive and regularly updated listing of internships, loans, awards/prizes, fellowships, scholarships, and grants designed primarily or exclusively for women. For more information about the publication, see the annotation in the "Scholarships—Special Population Groups—Women" section of this bibliography.

882 Educational Financial Aids: A Guide to Selecting Fellowships, Scholarships, and Internships in Higher Education. Washington, DC: American Association of University Women, 1984. 35p. $5. Pap.

This updated pamphlet (earlier versions were issued in 1976 and 1981) "divides financial aid offerings according to educational level: undergraduate, graduate, postdoctdoral, and internships/traineeships." For more information about the publication, see the annotation in the "Fellowships— Special Population Groups—Women" section of this bibliography.

883 Internship Programs for Women. By Kathryn L. Mulligan. Raleign, NC: National Society for Internships and Experiential Education, 1980. 80p. $7. Pap.

Approximately 40 internship programs open primarily or exclusively to women are described in this directory. Most of the opportunities covered are nonsalaried. The entries are grouped by eligibility (e.g., re-entry women, low-income women) and contain the following information: name, address, telephone number, purpose, requirements, stipend, academic credit, fees, source of funding, and contact person. A list of program names completes the work. There has been no new edition since 1980 and the publication is now suspended indefinitely. The Women's Equity Action League published a similar list in 1982, *Internships in Washington D.C. with a Focus on Women*, which is described elsewhere in this section.

884 Internships in Washington D.C. with a Focus on Women. Washington, DC: Women's Equity Action League, 1982. 30p. $2.50. Pap.

This small publication describes about 30 internship programs in the Washington, D.C. area. The emphasis is on programs open to nontraditional women students. Entries include information on program title, sponsoring organization, address and telephone number, contact person, time and length of internship, eligibility requirements, salary, and number of openings. Although the 1982 listing is no longer being distributed by WEAL, a new edition is in process.

Databases and Search Services

Automated lists of financial aid take two forms: as databases that may be accessed by computer (some of these are also available as print products) and as scholarship search services that are accessed upon customer request. Included in this chapter are 21 entries identifying "automated" financial aid directories. Of these listings, 14 describe databases and 7 cover search services. Whenever appropriate, references are made from the automated products to the print versions of the directories. If you are looking for a particular automated service and you do not find it in this chapter, be sure to check the Title Index to see if it is covered elsewhere in the Guide.

DATABASES

885 CASHE/3000. Gaithersburg, MD: College Student Financial Aid Services. Updated quarterly.

CASHE/3000 is a computerized scholarship search program that can help students identify financial aid programs sponsored by public agencies and private organizations. It is available both in microform and as a database. The programs included here are taken from the database used by College Student Financial Aid Services in its scholarship search service business (see a description of this business in the "Scholarship Search Services" section of this chapter).

886 CBD Plus. Washington, DC: Data Resources. Files covers 1981 to present. Updated daily; replaced weekly. Available through Data Resources.

Like *Commerce Business Daily (CBD Online)*, which is described elsewhere in this section, this database contains the full text of *Commerce Business Daily* print version (see annotation in "Grants—General—United States" section)—including contract awards, special notices, requests for proposals, and quotations. Also in the database are the full texts of the U.S. Department of Defense's daily contract award press releases.

887 Commerce Business Daily (CBD Online). Chicago: Commerce Business Daily. File covers 1982 to present. Updated daily and monthly. Available through Dialog Information Services (Files 194 and 195) and United Communications Group.

There are over 700,000 records in this database, which is the online equivalent of *Commerce Business Daily* (described in the "Grants—General—United States" section of this bibliography). Among the items included in the file are all federal contract awards of at least $25,000 from civilian agenices or at least $100,000 from military agencies as well as notifications of the U.S. government's interest in specific research and development fields and programs. File 195 on Dialog is updated daily, so that announcements are searchable on the same day they appear in the printed publication. Daily updates remain in file 195 for a period of 60 to 90 days, at which time the oldest material is transfered to file 194. The database is also available through United Communications Group under the title *CBD Online*. A special service offered through the database, called "RFP Request," allows users to order RFPs online via United Communciations Group.

888   **Federal Assistance Programs Retrieval System (FAPRS).** Washington, DC: U.S. Office of Management and Budget. File covers current year. Updated monthly. Available through Control Data Corporation/ Business Information Services and General Electric Information Services Company.

This is the online version of the *Catalog of Federal Domestic Assistance* (described in the "Grants—General—United States" section of this bibliography). It contains more than 1,000 summaries of federal assistance grant and loan programs available to communities in the areas of housing, education, employment, planning and technical assistance, business and industrial development, social services, health, and community facilities. Records provide detailed information on each assistance program, including types of assistance, eligibility requirements, financial support available, matching requirements, application process, and sponsoring agency. Users can access the information by eligibility characteristics, categories of interest, and program applicant. Most states have FAPRS services available through state, county, and local agencies as well as through federal extension services. For a list of these locations, contact the Federal Program Information Branch at this address: Office of Management and Budget, 6001 New Executive Office Building, Washington, DC 20503.

889   **Federal Register Abstracts (Database).** Washington, DC: Capitol Services. File covers 1977 to present. Updated weekly. Available through Dialog Information Services, Public Affairs Information, and SDC Information Services.

There are nearly 250,000 records in this database, which is updated weekly. The listings provide online access to federal regulatory agency actions as published in the *Federal Register* (described in the "Grants—General— United States" section of this bibliography), the official record of U.S. regulations, proposed rules, and legal notices issued by federal agencies. The text of Presidential proclamations and executive orders are available here. Also included are references to meetings and hearing notices, public laws, and rules taking effect each day. This is the online equivalent of Capitol Services' print product, *Federal Register Abstracts*. The title of the database at Dialog and Public Affairs Information is *Federal Register Abstracts*; at SDC, it is *FEDREG*.

890   **Federal Research in Progress (FEDRIP).** Springfield, VA: National Technical Information Serivce (NTIS). Covers 1975 to the present. Updated semi-annually. Available through Dialog.

This database provides coverage of current federally-funded research projects in engineering, the physical sciences, and the life sciences. It focuses on awardees, not on the provisions of specific funding programs. The information included in the database is submitted to NTIS by sponsoring federal government agencies. Recently, a subfile was added of summaries of 400 research projects funded by the National Science Foundation's Engineering Directorate from 1975 to the present. Data elements in the file records vary, depending on the submitting agency, but generally they provide project title, project scope, principle investigator, sponsoring and performing organization, and a summary of the funded project.

891 Federal Research Report (Database). Silver Spring, MD: Businesss Publishers. Covers 1982 to present. Updated weekly. Available through NewsNet.

This database, the online equivalent of the printed newsletter by the same name (described in the "Grants—General—United States" section of this bibliography), covers federal research and development funding. The records provide the addresses, contact names, and deadlines for grants and other funding opportunities. The data are updated weekly.

892 Foundation Directory (Database). New York: Foundation Center. File covers current year. Semi-annual updates. Available through Dialog Information Services.

This is the online version of the Foundation Center's *Foundation Directory* (described in the "Grants—General—United States" section of this bibliography). The 3.500 records in this database identify foundations with assets of $1 million or more or which annually award grants of $100,000 or more. Only a "nongovernmental, nonprofit organization, with funds and programs managed by its own trustees or directors, and established to maintain or aid social, educational, charitable, religious, or other activities serving the common welfare, primarily through the making of grants" qualify for inclusion. Foundations meeting these criteria account for nearly 90 percent of the assets of all American foundations and 80 percent of all foundation giving. In descending order, the grants given by these foundations are in the following fields: education, health, welfare, sciences, international activities, and religion. The information included in the database is taken from voluntary reports by the foundations to the Foundation Center and from annual public information returns filed with the Internal Revenue Service.

893 Foundation Grants Index. New York: Foundation Center. File covers 1973 to present. Bimonthly updates. Available through Dialog Information Services.

Information on the grant giving activity of more than 400 major American philanthropic foundations is available in this database. There are over 240,000 records in the database and approximately 20,000 new grants are added to the file each year. The listing is restricted to nongovernmental, nonprofit organizations, with funds and programs managed by their own trustees or directors, that have been established "to maintain or aid social, educational, charitable, religious, or other activities serving the common welfare, primarily through the making of grants." Specifically excluded are grants to individuals and grants of less than $5,000. The grants awarded have been primarily in the fields of education, health, welfare, sciences, international activity, and religion. The printed equivalent of this database is the Foundation Center's *Foundation Grants Index Annual*, described in the "Grants—General—United States" section of this bibliography.

894 GRANTS. Phoenix: Oryx. File covers current year. Updated monthly. Available through Dialog Information Services and SDC Information Services.

The online equivalent of Oryx Press' annual *Directory of Research Grants* (described in the "Grants—General—United States" section) and various other subject-based directories (described throughout this bibliography), this database provides information on more than 4,000 available grants offered by federal, state, and local governments; commercial organizations; associations; and private foundations. The information is updated monthly. These programs cover all academic disciplines as well as performance and program grants in the sciences, social sciences, humanities, and arts. Entries specify sponsoring organization address and telephone number, purpose, eligibility qualifications, money available, and renewability. Subject access to the records in the database is provided through 1,660 terms. To aid online searchers of the *GRANTS* database, Oryx Press recently published the *Grants Thesaurus* (1986. 48p. ISBN 0–89774–335–0. $15. Pap.), which provides a guide to the keywords indexed in the database.

895 Guidance Information System. New York: Houghton Mifflin Company. File covers current year. Updated semi-annually. Available from Houghton Mifflin Company, TSC Division.

This system was originally produced for use on the Apple III personal computer. Of the five files that make up the database system (occupational information, armed services information, two-year and four-year college information, graduate school information, and financial aids information), the latter three provide information on financial assistance. The Two-Year and Four-Year College Information File consists of data on 1,800 two-year colleges and technical institutions and over 1,700 four-year colleges and universities. Financial aid at each school is indicated, along with majors offered, size of surrounding community enrollment, religious affiliation, admission requirements, application procedures, deadlines, and fees. Similar information is provided for more than 1,500 and professional schools in the

Graduate School Information File. The Financial Aids Information File covers federal, state, and private sources (foundations, businesses, labor organizations, religious groups) of financial assistance; records indicate type of aid avaialble, eligibility requirements, application deadlines, and sources of additional information. The database is updated twice a year.

896 Illinois Researchers Information System (IRIS). Urbana: Campus-Wide Research Services Office, University of Illinois.

This online computerized information retrieval system was designed for grantseeking individuals and institutions in higher education. Included in the file are over 3,500 funding opportunities sponsored by federal agencies, private and corporate foundations, and other organizations that support research and scholarship activities. Only subscribers can access the system. For more information, contact the Illinois Researchers Information System at the Campus-Wide Research Services Office, University of Illinois, Urbana, IL 61801.

897 National Foundations. New York: Foundation Center. File covers current year. Updated annually. Available through Dialog Information Services.

Over 22,000 American foundations that annually award grants (of any amount) are described in this database. Only a "nongovernmental, nonprofit organization, with funds and programs managed by its own trustees or directors, and established to maintain or aid social, educational, charitable, religious, or other activities serving the common welfare, primarily through the making of grants" is eligible for inclusion. More than 75 percent of the foundations coverd here are excluded from the Foundation Center's *Foundation Directory* database (described elsewhere in this section of the bibliography), since their assets total less than $1 million. Because many of these smaller foundations limit their giving to local or regional applicants, grantseekers interested in funding local projects will find *National Foundations* particularly useful. This database is the online eqivalent of the Foundation Center's *National Data Book* (described in the "Grants— General—United States" section of this bibliography).

898 Peterson's College Database. Princeton, NJ: Peterson's Guides. File covers current year. Updated annually. Available from BRS, CompuService Consumer Information Service, Dialog Information Services, and Dow Jones.

Online access to current information on approximately 3,000 two- and four-year colleges and universities in the United States and Canada is provided through this database, which is available from BRS (as *National College Databank*); CompuServe (as *Peterson's College Database*), Dialog (as

Peterson's College Database); and Dow Jones (as *Peterson's College Selection Service*). It is also available for purchase directly from Peterson's Guides. In addition to information on financial aid (including availability of athletic scholarships), each record covers college size and location, enrollment, admissions requirements, graduation requirements, athletics, majors offered, special services, and availability of housing. The data included here correspond, in part, to *Peterson's Annual Guide to Undergraduate Study* (described in the "Scholarships—General—United States" section of this bibliography).

SEARCH SERVICES

899 Academic Guidance Services. 300 State Highway 73, Marlton, NJ 08053.

There are more than 70 franchises using the Academic Guidance Services scholarship database (claimed by the company to be the largest in the United States). Each operates under a different name (e.g., Scholarships Finders, Scholarship Clearing House, Scholarships Unlimited). They all send the questionnaires received from clients to New Jersey to be processed. There is no consistency in the prices charged by the franchises; they range from under $30 to over $200, depending on the services offered (some provide counseling, application assistance, products associated with SAT preparation). If you write to Academic Guidance Services in New Jersey, they will provide the address of the franchise closest to you.

900 College Scholarship Information Bank. College Entrance Examination Board, 888 Seventh Avenue, New York, NY 10106.

Like the College Selection Service (described below), this service helps students identify postsecondary schools with scholarship programs for which they may be eligible. In addition, the service also assists in determining a family's eligibility for selected need-based scholarships.

901 College Selection Service. Peterson's Guides, P.O. Box 2123, Princeton, NJ 08540.

This program is offered as part of a broader college selection service, which costs $45. The computer-assisted process helps students identify schools that offer scholarship programs for which they may be eligible.

902 College Student Financial Aid Services. 16220 South Frederick Road, Suite 208, Gaithersburg, MD 20877.

A search and report at this service costs $40 for the first family member and substantially less for searches for additional family members. Questionnaires completed by clients are run through the service's CASHE program (Computer Assisted Scholarships for Higher Education). Appropriate programs are identified on the basis of the academic plans, hobbies, clubs, career objectives, and personal background indicated on the questionnaire. The entire list of the service's scholarships is also available on a subscription basis, which costs approximately $400 a year.

903 Financial Aid Finders. 77 Gristmill Road, Randolph, NJ 07869.

Drawing on the National Scholarship Research Service database (200,000 college money sources valued at over $8 billion), this scholarship search service guarantees to find "at least 20 private sector college money sources" for each applicant (at a cost of $55 per search). The service also provides a sample form letter to use in contacting the award sources, tips and suggestions on how to apply for awards, and lists of publications and organizations that can help with the applicant's college and career interests.

904 National Scholarship Research Service. 122 Alto, San Rafael, CA 94912.

This search service claims to have a databank of over 200,000 listings for scholarships, fellowships, grants, and loans, representing over $10 billion in private sector funding. After receiving a completed questionnaire from a client, NSRS supplies a computer printout containing a list averaging 40 sources of programs matched to the application, tips and suggestions on applying for awards, a list of general publications containing further postsecondary and financial aid information, a list of specific publications that could prove useful in finding financial assistance, a list of national organizations and special interest groups that can provide further assistance, a sample form letter requesting scholarship information, and a semi-annual newsletter to keep clients informed of financial aid developments during the year. This service costs $45 for either undergraduate or graduate listings. Updates cost an additional $10 each. The NSRS database was used by its president, Daniel Cassidy, to develop *The Scholarship Book* (described in the "Scholarships—General—United States" section), which covers over 1,000 programs at half the cost. According to a press release recently issued by the search service, NSRS's datahbase will also be available online, through Lockheed's Dialog Information Service.

905   Scholarship Search Service. 407 State Street, Santa Barbara, CA 93101. According to their literature, Scholarship Search Service originated the first nationwide computer research and marketing system for college funds (in 1970). Like the National Scholarship Research Service, they specialize in private sector sources of funding. Like Academic Guidance Services, they claim to have the largest database of programs in the nation. For a $57 fee, the service matches applicant characteristics (e.g., geographic residence, religious affiliation, ethnic background, college major) against 250,000 scholarships, grants, and financial aid donor award source items. The service guarantees to identify up to 25 money sources for which each applicant is eligible (although no promise is made that the applicant will receive financial aid from any of the leads provided). Because the service updates its database on a continuous basis, its information is potentially more current than can be found in printed sources.

Publishers Directory

Over 300 publishers are responsible for the more than 700 directories of financial aid that have been published since 1980 and described in this Guide. These companies constitute a virtual "who's who" in the area of financial aid directory publishing. They are listed here alphabetically, word by word, with "see" references provided for variant names. The most recently available address and telephone number is included in each publisher entry. As a special feature, toll free numbers (when available) are also cited.

A.A.U.W. *See* American Association of University Women.

ABC Leisure Magazines. 825 Seventh Avenue, New York, NY 10019. *(212) 765-8360.*

Academic Guidance Services. 3001 State Highway 73, Marlton, NJ 08053. *(609) 983-3737.*

Academic Research Information System. Redstone Building, 2940 16th Street, Suite 314, San Francisco, CA 94103. *(415) 558-8133.*

Action Agenda Project. University for Man, Kansas State University, 1221 Thurston, Manhattan, KS 66502. *(913) 532-5866.*

Adam & Charles Black. 35 Bedford Row, London WC1R 4JH England.

Adams Company. *See* John L. Adams Company.

Adelphi University Press. South Avenue, Garden City, NY 11530. *(516) 663-1120.*

Advanced Acceptance Program, Inc. 2010 Oak Street, Quincy, IL 62301. *(217) 224-1172.*

AFL—CIO. 815 16th Street, N.W., Washington, DC 20006. *(202) 637-5000.*

Alu Like. 401 Kamakee Street, Third Floor, Honolulu, HI 96814. *(808) 521-9571.*

American Association of Botanical Gardens and Arboreta. P.O. Box 206, Swathmore, PA 19081. *(215) 328-9145.*

American Association of Fund-Raising Counsel. 25 West 43rd Street, New York, NY 10036. *(212) 354-5799.*

American Association of State Colleges and Universities. One Dupont Circle, Suite 700, Washington, DC 20036. *(202) 293-7070.*

American Association of University Women. 2401 Virginia Avenue, N.W., Washington, DC 20037. *(202) 785-7700.*

American Bar Association. 750 North Lake Shore, Chicago, IL 60611. *(312) 988-5000.* There is also a toll free number: *(800) 621-6159.*

American Council for the Arts. 570 Seventh Avenue, New York, NY 10018. *(212) 354-6655.*

American Federation of Labor—Congress of Industrial Organizations. *See* AFL-CIO.

American Field Service. 313 East 43rd Street, New York, NY 10017. *(212) 949-4242.* There is also a toll free number: *(800) AFS-INFO.*

American Film Institute. 2021 N. Western Avenue, Los Angeles, CA 90027. *(213) 856-7600.*

American Forces Information Service. *See* U.S. American Forces Information Service.

American Historical Association. 400 A Street, S.E., Washington, DC 20003. *(202) 544-2422.*

American Jewish Committee. c/o Institute of Human Relations, 165 East 56th Street, New York, NY 10022. *(212) 751-4000.*

American Legion. 700 N. Pennsylvania Street, P.O. Box 1055, Indianapolis, IN 46206. *(317) 635-8411.*

American Library Association. 50 East Huron Street, Chicago, IL 60611. *(312) 944-6780.* There are also toll free numbers: *(800) 545-2433 (outside of Illinois); (800) 545-2444 (in Illinois); (800) 545-2455 (in Canada).*

American Library Association. Washington Office. 100 Maryland Avenue, N.E., Washington, DC 20002. *(202) 547-4440.*

American Medical Association. 535 N. Dearborn Street, Chicago, IL 60611. *(312) 645-5000.*

American Philosophical Association. c/o University of Delaware, Newark, DE 19716. *(302) 451-1112.*

American Political Science Association. 1527 New Hampshire Avenue, N.W., Washington, DC 10026. *(202) 483-2512.*

American Psychiatric Association. 1400 K Street, N.W., Washington, DC 20005. *(202) 682-6000.*

American Psychological Association. P.O. Box 2710, Hyattsville, MD 20784. *(703) 247-7702.* There is also a toll free number: *(800) 336-4980.*

American Sociological Association. 1722 N Street, N.W., Washington, DC 20036. *(202) 833-3410.*

American Speech—Language—Hearing Association. 10801 Rockville Pike, Rockville, MD 20852. *(301) 897-5700.*

Arco Publishing Inc. 215 Park Avenue South, New York, NY 10003. *(212) 777-6300.*

Artists Foundation, Inc. 110 Broad Street, Boston, MA 02110. *(617) 482-8100.*

Artweek, Inc. 1628 Telegraph Avenue, Oakland, CA 94612. *(415) 763-0422.*

Associated Grantmakers of Massachusetts. 294 Washington Street, Suite 840, Boston, MA 02108. *(617) 426-2606.*

Association for Computing Machinery. 11 West 42nd Street, Third Floor, New York, NY 10036. *(212) 869-7440.*

Association for Education in Journalism and Mass Communications. c/o College of Journalism, University of South Carolina, 1621 College Street, Columbia, SC 29208. *(803) 777-2005.*

Association for Intercollegiate Athletics. 1201 16th Street, N.W., Washington, DSC 20036. *(202) 833-5485.*

Association of American Colleges. 1818 R Street, N.W., Washington, DC 20009. *(202) 387-3760.*

Association of American Geographers. 1710 16th Street, N.W., Washington, DC 20009. *(202) 234-1450.*

Association of American Medical Colleges. One Dupont Circle, N.W., Washington, DC 20036. *(202) 828-0400.*

Association of Commonwealth Universities. John Foster House, 36 Gordon Square, London WClJ OPF England. There is a toll free U.S. number: *(800) 521-0707.*

Association of Psychology Internship Centers. Box 574, Knoxville, IA 50138. *(515) 842-3101.*

Association of Universities and Colleges of Canada. 151 Slater Street, Ottawa K1P 5N1 Canada. *(613) 563-1236.*

Atlanta—Fulton Public Library. One Margaret Mitchell Square, Atlanta, GA 30303-1089. *(404) 688-4636.*

Audio Independents. 1232 Market Street, San Francisco, CA 94102.

B. Klein Publications. P.O. Box 8503, Coral Springs, FL 33065. *(305) 752-1708.*

Barnes & Noble Books. 10 East 53rd Street, New York, NY 10022. *(212) 207-7655.* There is also a toll free number: *(800) 242-7737.*

Barron's Educational Series, Inc. 113 Crossways Park Drive, Woodbury, NY 11797. *(516) 921-8750.* There is also a toll free number: *(800) 645-3476.*

Bellman Publishing Company. P.O. Box 34937, Bethesda, MD 20817. *(301) 897-0033.*

Bernan/Unipub. 10033—F Martin Luther King Highway, Lanham, MD 20706. *(301) 459-7666.* There is also a toll free number: *(800) 233-0506.*

Bibliographic Retrieval Services. *See* BRS.

Birmingham and Jefferson County Free Library. 2100 Park Place, Birmingham, AL 35203. *(205) 226-3600.* There is also a toll free number: *(800) 292-3895.*

Black (Adam & Charles). *See* Adam & Charles Black.

Black Resource Guide, Inc. 501 Oneida Place, N.W., Washington, DC 20011. *(202) 291-4373.*

Bowker Company. *See* R. R. Bowker Company.

Boy Scouts of America. 1325 Walnut Hill Lane, Irving, TX 75038. *(214) 659-2000.*

British Council. 10 Spring Gardens, London SW1A 2BN England.

BRS. 1200 Route 7, Latham, NY 12220. *(518) 783-1161.* There are also toll free numbers: *(800) 833-4707 (outside New York); (800) 553-5566 (in New York).*

Bureau of Indian Affairs. *See* U.S. Bureau of Indian Affairs.

Bureau of Inter-governmental Management. 125 North Mid-America Mall, Room 508, Memphis, TN 38103.

Business Committee for the Arts. 1775 Broadway, New York, NY 10019. *(212) 921-0700.*

Business Publishers, Inc. 951 Pershing Drive, Silver Spring, MD 20910. *(301) 587-6300.*

Caldwell Public Library. 1010 Dearborn Street, Caldwell, ID 83605-4195. *(208) 459-3242.*

California Community Foundation. 3580 Wilshire Boulevard, Suite 1660, Los Angeles, CA 90010. *(213) 738-7377.*

California State Library. 914 Capitol Mall, Library and Courts Building, P.O. Box 2037, Sacramento, CA 95809-2037. *(916) 445-2585.*

Canada Council. 255 Albert Street, P.O. Box 1047, Ottawa K1P 5V8 Canada. *(613) 237-3400.*

Canadian Centre for Philanthropy. 185 Bay Street, Suite 504, Toronto M5J 1K6 Canada. *(416) 364-4609.*

Capitol Publications, Inc. 1300 N. 17th Street, Suite 1600, Arlington, VA 22209. *(703) 528-1100.* There is also a toll free number: *(800) 847-7772.*

Career Publishing Corp. 505 Fifth Avenue, Suite 1003, New York, NY 10017. *(212) 840-7011.*

Center for Arts Information. 625 Broadway, New York, NY 10012. *(212) 677-7548.*

Center for Research and Advanced Study. University of Southern Maine, 246 Deering Avenue, Portland, ME 04102. *(207) 780-4411.*

Central Opera Service. Metropolitan Opera, Lincoln Center, New York, NY 10023. *(212) 957-9871.*

Central Resarch Systems. 320 North Meridian, Suite 515, Indianapolis, IN 46204. *(317) 635-1400.*

Charities Aid Foundation. 48 Pemburg Road, Tonbridge, Kent TN9 2JD England.

Charles Black. *See* Adam & Charles Black.

Charles Scribner's Sons. 597 Fifth Avenue, New York, NY 10017. *(212) 486-2700.* There is also a toll free number: *(800) 257-5755.*

Children's Book Council. 67 Irving Place, New York, NY 10003. *(212) 254-2666.*

Chronicle Guidance Publications, Inc. Aurora Street Extension, P.O. Box 1190, Moravia, NY 13118-1190. *(315) 497-0330.*

Chronicle of Higher Education. 1255 23 Street, N.W., Suite 700, Washington, DC 20037. *(202) 466-1000.*

Clairol Loving Care Scholarship Program. 345 Park Avenue, Fifth Floor, New York, NY 10022. *(212) 546-5000.*

Clark County Library District. 1401 East Flamingo Road, Las Vegas, NV 89109-6160. *(702) 733-7810.*

College Entrance Examination Board. 888 Seventh Avenue, New York, NY 10106. *(212) 713-8000.*

College Student Financial Aid Services. 16220 South Frederick Road, Suite 208, Gaithersburg, MD 20877. *(301) 258-0717.*

Columbia Books, Inc. 1350 New York Avenue, N.W., Suite 207, Washington, DC 20005. *(202) 737-3777.*

Community Foundation of Greater Washington. 3221 M Street, N.W., Washington, DC 20007. *(202) 338-8993.*

CompuServe Consumer Information Service. 5000 Arlington Centre Boulevard, Columbus, OH 43220. *(614) 457-8600.* There is also a toll free number: *(800) 848-8990.*

Conference Board, Inc. 845 Third Avenue, New York, NY 10022. *(212) 759-0900.* There is also a toll free number: *(800) US-BOARD.*

Consortium for the Health Professions. 703 Market Street, San Francisco, CA 94103.

Contemporary Books, Inc. 180 N. Michigan Avenue, Chicago, IL 60601. *(312) 782-9181.*

Control Data Corporation/Business Information Services. Box D, Minneapolis, MN 55437-1194. *(612) 861-0165.*

Council for Advancement and Support of Education. 11 Dupont Circle, N.W., Suite 400, Washington, DC 20036. *(202) 328-5900.*

Council for Community Service. 229 Waterman Street, Providence, RI 02906.

Council for European Studies. 1509 International Affairs Building, Columbia University, 420 West 118th Street, New York, NY 10027. *(212) 280-4727.*

Council for Financial Aid to Education. 680 Fifth Avenue, New York, NY 10019. *(212) 541-4050.*

Council for International Exchange of Scholars. 11 Dupont Circle, Suite 300, Washington, DC 20036. *(202) 833-4950.*

Dallas Public Library. 1515 Young Street, Dallas, TX 75201-9987. *(214) 749-4100.*

Dance Magazine, Inc. 33 West 60th Street, New York, NY 10023. *(212) 245-9050.*

Data Resources, Inc. Data Products Division Headquarters, 1750 K Street, N.W., Suite 1060, Washington, DC 20006. *(202) 862-3760.*

DCA, Inc. 7001 S. 234th E Avenue, Broken Arrow, OK 74012. *(918) 251-0727.*

de Gruyter, Inc. *See* Walter de Gruyter, Inc.

Dell Publishing Company, Inc. 245 East 47th Street, New York, NY 10017. *(212) 605-3000.*

Department of Commerce. *See* U.S. Department of Commerce. Commerce Business Daily.

Department of Education. *See* U.S. Department of Education.

Department of Justice. *See* U.S. Department of Justice.

Department of the Army. *See* U.S. Department of the Army. Adjutant General's Office.

Department of the Navy. *See* U.S. Department of the Navy. Naval Military Personnel Command.

Dialog Information Services. 3460 Hillview Avenue, Palo Alto, CA 94304. *(415) 858-2700.* There is also a toll free number: *(800) 3-DIALOG.*

Dodd, Mead & Co. 79 Madison Avenue, New York, NY 10016. *(212) 685-6464.* There is also a toll free number: *(800) 251-4000.*

Donors Form. 208 S. LaSalle Street, Chicago, IL 60604. *(312) 726-4877.*

Douglas M. Lawson Associates, Inc. 39 East 51st Street, New York, NY 10022. *(212) 759-5660.*

Dow Jones & Company. Box 300, Princeton, NJ 08540. *(609) 452-2000.* There is also a toll free number: *(800) 257-5114.*

Dow Jones Newspaper Fund. Box 300, Princeton, NJ 08540. *(609) 452-2820.*

Dutton, Inc. *See* E. P. Dutton, Inc.

E. P. Dutton, Inc. 2 Park Avenue, New York, NY 10016. *(212) 725-1818.* There is also a toll free number: *(800) 526-0175.*

Eastern Montana College Foundation. Eastern Montana College Library, 1500 North 30th Street, Billings, MT 59101-0298. *(406) 657-2244.*

Economics Institute. 1030 13th Street, Boulder, CO 80302. *(303) 492-8419.*

Editor & Publisher Company. 11 West 19th Street, New York, NY 10011. *(212) 675-4380.*

Education Funding Research Council. 1611 N. Kent Street, Suite 508, Arlington, VA 22209. *(703) 528-1082.*

Education Unlimited. P.O. Box 146, Orland, IN 46776.

Ellen Roberts Press. 7 Noth Drive, Livingston, NJ 07039.

Europa Publications. 18 Bedford Square, London WC1B 3JN England. There is a toll free number: *(800) 521-0707.*

Facts On File, Inc. 460 Park Avenue South, New York, NY 10016. *(212) 683-2244.* There is also a toll free number: *(800) 322-8755.*

Feminist Press. 311 East 94th Street, New York, NY 10128. *(212) 360-5790.*

Festival Publications. 24425 Woolsey Canyon Road, Canoga Park, CA 91304. *(818) 887-0034.*

Financial Aid Finders. 77 Gristmill Road, Randolph, NJ 07869. *(201) 361-2567.*

Florida Department of Community Affairs. Bureau of Local Government Assistance, Tallahassee, FL 32301. *(904) 488-8466.*

Florida Department of Education. Office of Student Financial. Assistance Tallahasse, FL 32301. *(904) 488-4095.*

Foggy Bottom Publications. Box 57150 West End Station, Washington, DC 20037. *(202) 337-435.*

For Us Publications. P.O. Box 33147, Farragut Station, Washington, DC 20036. *(202) 462-1463.*

Forum Institute. 1225 15th Street, N.W., Washington, DC 20005. *(202) 347-2931.*

Foundation Center. 79 Fifth Avenue, New York, NY 10003. *(212) 620-4230.* There is also a toll free number: *(800) 424-9836.*

Free Library of Philadelphia. Logan Square at 19th Street, Philadelphia, PA 19103. *(215) 686-5322.*

Funding Information Center of Texas. 507 Brooklyn, San Antonio, TX 78215. *(512) 227-4333.*

G.P.O. *See* U.S. Government Printing Office.

Gale Research Company. Book Tower, Detroit, MI 48226. *(313) 961-2242.* There is also a toll free number: *(800) 521-0707.*

Garrett Park Press. Garrett Park, MD 20896. *(301) 946-2553.*

General Electric Information Services Company. 401 North Washington Street, Rockville, MD 20850. *(301) 294-5405.*

Georgia Department of Natural Resources. 270 Washington Street S.W., Atlanta, GA 30334. *(404) 656-2840.*

Gorsuch Scarisbrick Publications. 8233 Via Paseo del Norte, Suite E, Scottsdale, AZ 85258. *(602) 991-7881.*

Government Information Services. 1611 North Kent, Suite 508, Arlington, VA 22209. *(703) 528-1082.*

Government Printing Office. *See* U.S. Government Printing Office.

Graduate Careers Council of Australia. P.O. Box 28, Parkerville, Victoria 3052, Australia.

Grants Advisory Service, Inc. Box 122, Newton Center, MA 02159.

Grants Resource Library. Hampton, VA. *(804) 727-6496.*

Grantsmanship Center. 1031 South Grand Avenue, Los Angeles, CA 90015. *(213) 749-4721.*

Greater Minneapolis Council of Churches. 122 West Franklin Avenue, Room 218, Minneapolis, MN 55405. *(612) 870-3660.*

Greenwood Press. 88 Post Road West, Box 5007, Westport, CT 06881. *(203) 226-3571.*

Harper & Row. Keystone Industrial Park, Scranton, PA 18512. There is a toll free number: *(800) 242-7737.*

Hartman Planning and Development Group. 14645 N. E. 34th Street, Suite C-24, Bellevue, WA 98007. *(206) 328-1893.*

Haverford College. Career Planning Office. Haverford, PA 19041-1392. *(215) 896-1000.*

Hope Press. P.O. Box 40611. Washington, DC 20016-0611. *(202) 337-4507.*

Houghton Mifflin Company, TSC Division. Box 683, Hanover, NJ 03755. *(603) 448-3838.* There is also a toll free number: *(800) 225-3362.*

Hunt Publishing Company. *See* Kendall/Hunt Publishing Company.

Illinois Office of Education. 100 North First Street, Springfield, IL 62701. *(217) 782-7913.*

Independent Community Consultants, Inc. Box 141, Hampton, AR 71744. *(501) 798-4510.*

Independent Sector. 1828 L Street, N.W., Washington, DC 20036. *(202) 223-8100.*

Indian Resource Development. Box 3 IRD, Las Cruces, NM 88003. *(505) 646-1347.*

Inkling Publications. P.O. Box 128, Alexandria, MN 56308. *(612) 762-2020.*

Institute for Information Studies. 200 Little Falls Street, Suite 104, Falls Church, VA 22046. *(703) 533-0383.*

Institute of International Education. 809 United Nations Plaza, New York, NY 10017. *(212) 984-5410.*

Intern Research Group. Box 52, Regent Hall, University of Colorado, Boulder, CO 80309. *(303) 492-5007.*

Internal Revenue Service Center. *See* U.S. Internal Revenue Service Center.

International Communications Industries Association. 3150 Spring Street, Fairfax, VA 22031-2399. *(703) 273-7200.*

International Publications Service. 242 Cherry Street, Philadelphia, PA 19106-1906. *(215) 238-0939.*

International Reading Association. 800 Barksdale Road, P.O. Box 8139, Newark, DE 19714. *(302) 731-1600.*

International Research and Exchanges Board. 655 Third Avenue, New York, NY 10017. *(212) 490-2002.*

Intersociety Committee on Pathology Information. 4733 Bethesda Avenue, Suite 735, Bethesda, MD 20814. *(301) 656-2944.*

James H. Taylor Associates. 804 Main Street, Williamsburg, KY 40769. *(606) 549-1639.*

John L. Adams Company. P.O. Box 561565, Miami, FL 33156.

John Wiley and Sons. 605 Third Avenue, New York, NY 10158. *(212) 850-6465.*

Junior League of Denver. 6300 East Yale Avenue, Denver, CO 80222. *(303) 692-0270.*

Junior League of Omaha. 808 South 74th Plaza, Omaha, NE 68114. *(402) 391-8986.*

K. G. Saur Inc. 175 Fifth Avenue, New York, NY 10010. *(212) 982-1302.*

Kendall/Hunt Publishing Company. 2460 Kerper Boulevard, P.O. Box 539, Dubuque, IA 52001. *(319) 589-2833.*

Klein Publications. *See* B. Klein Publications.

Laramie County Community College Library. 1400 East College Drive, Cheyenne, WY 82007. *(307) 634-5853.*

Lawson Associates, Inc. *See* Douglas M. Lawson Associates, Inc.

Learning Resources in International Studies. 777 United Nations Plaza, New York, NY 10017. *(212) 972-9877.*

Libraries Unlimited. Box 263, Littleton, CO 80160. *(303) 770-1220.*

Linguistic Society of America. 3520 Prospect Street, N.W., Washington, DC 20007. *(202) 298-7120.*

Literary Markets. 725 South Beach Road, Suite 105, Point Roberts, WA 98281.

Lockheed/Dialog Information Services. *See* Dialaog Information Services.

Log Cabin Publishers. 620 Washington Street, P.O. Box 1536, Allentown, PA 18105. *(215) 434-2448.*

Logos Associates. 7 Park Street, Room 212, Attleboro, MA 02703. *(617) 226-3085.*

Louisville Foundation. 623 West Main Street, Louisville, KY 40202.

Macmillan Publishing Company. 866 Third Avenue, New York, NY 10022. *(212) 702-2000.* There is also a toll free number: *(800) 257-5755.*

Marquette University Memorial Library. Foundation Collection. 1415 W. Wisconsin Avenue, Milwaukee, WI 53233. *(414) 224-1515.*

Marquis Who's Who, Inc. 200 E. Ohio Street, Chicago, IL 60611. *(312) 787-2008.* There is also a toll free number: *(800) 621-9669.*

Maryland Attorney General. 7 N. Calvert Street, Baltimore, MD 21202. *(301) 576-6491.*

Maryland Department of State Planning. 301 W. Preston Street, Baltimore, MD 21201-2365. *(301) 838-7875.*

Media Awards Handbook. 621 Sheri Lane, Danville, CA 94526. *(415) 837-7562.*

Mercer—Meringer. Meidinger Tower, Louisville, KY 40202. *(502) 561-4500.*

Michigan League for Human Services. 300 N. Washington Square, Suite 311, Lansing, MI 48933. *(517) 487-5436.*

Michigan State Department of Commerce. Box 30004. Lansing, MI 48909. *(517) 373-8363.*

Minority Business Development Agency. *See* U.S. Minority Business Development Agency.

Mission Project Service. 204 West 97th Street, New York, NY 10025. *(212) 678-0836.*

Mitchell Guides. 195 Nassau Street, P.O. Box 413, Princeton, NJ 08542. *(609) 921-9468.*

Modern Language Association of America. 62 Fifth Avenue, New York, NY 10011. *(212) 741-7861.*

Monarch Press. 215 Park Avenue South, New York, NY 10003. *(212) 777-6300.*

Moyer Bell Ltd. Colonial Hill, RFD 1, Mt. Kisco, NY 10549. *(914) 666-0084.*

NACME. *See* National Action Council for Minorities in Engineering, Inc.

National Action Council for Minorities in Engineering, Inc. 3 West 35th Street, New York, NY 10001. *(212) 279-2626.*

National Association for Sport and Physical Education. 1900 Association Drive, Reston, VA 22091. *(703) 476-3410.*

National Association of Foreign Student Affairs. 1860 19th Street, N.W., Washington, DC 20009. *(202) 462-4811.*

National Association of Secondary School Principals. 1904 Association Drive, Reston, VA 22091. *(703) 860-0200.*

National Association of Towns and Townships. 1522 K Street, N.W., Suite 730, Washington, DC 20008. *(202) 737-5200.*

National Commission for Cooperative Education. P.O. Box 775, Boston, MA 02117. *(617) 437-3778.*

National Endowment for the Arts. *See* U.S. National Endowment for the Arts.

National Endowment for the Humanities. *See* U.S. National Endowment for the Humanities.

National Fire Protection Association. Batterymarch Park, Quincy, MA 02269. *(617) 770-3000.*

National Institute of Corrections. Information Center. 1790 30th Street, Suite 130, Boulder, CO 80301. *(303) 444-1101.*

National Institute of Mental Health. *See* U.S. National Institute of Mental Health.

National Institute on Drug Abuse. *See* U.S. National Institute on Drug Abuse.

National League of Nursing. 10 Columbus Circle, New York, NY 10019. *(212) 582-1022.*

National Network of Grantmakers. 2000 P Street, N.W., Suite 410, Washington, DC 20036. *(202) 822-9236.*

National Register Publishing Company, Inc. 3004 Glenview Road, Wilmette IL 60091. *(312) 256-6067.* There is also a toll free number: *(800) 323-6772.*

National Scholarship Research Service. 122 Alto, San Rafael, CA 94912. *(415) 456-1577.*

National Science Foundation. 1800 G Street, N.W., Washington, DC 20550. *(202) 357-9859.*

National Society for Internships and Experiential Education. 124 St. Mary's Street, Raleigh, NC 27605. *(919) 834-7536.*

National Technical Information Service. *See* U.S. National Technical Information Service.

Naval Military Personnel Command. *See* U.S. Department of the Navy. Naval Military Personnel Command.

Neal—Schuman Publishers, Inc. 23 Leonard Street, New York, NY 10013. *(212) 620-5990.*

New American Library. 120 Woodbine Street, Bergenfield, NJ 07621. *(201) 387-0600.* There is also a toll free number: *(800) 526-0275.*

New Hamphsire Attorney General's Office. State House Annex, Concord, NH 03301. *(603) 271-3591.*

New Jersey Department of Community Affairs. 363 West State Street, CN 800, Trenton, NJ 08625. *(609) 292-6055.*

New Moon Consultants. P.O. Box 532, Tijeras, NM 87059.

New York State Department of Audit and Control. A. E. Smith Building, 10th Floor, Albany, NY 12236. *(518) 474-4377.*

NewsNet, Inc. 945 Haverford Road, Bryn Mawr, PA 19010. *(215) 517-8030.*

Norris—Whitney Communications. 832 Mount Pleasant Road, Toronto M4P 2L3 Canada.

Northeast—Midwest Institute. 218 D Street, S.E., Washington, DC 20003. *(202) 544-5200.*

Northern California Grantmakers. 334 Kearny Street, San Francisco, CA 94108. *(415) 788-2982.*

NTIS. *See* U.S. National Technical Information Service.

Octameron Associates. Box 3437, Alexandria, VA 22302. *(703) 823-1882.*

Ocular Publishing. 640 Broadway, Denver, CO 80202. *(303) 426-4426.*

Office for Handicapped Individuals. *See* U.S. Department of Education. Office of Special Education and Rehabilitative Services.

Office of Management and Budget. *See* U.S. Office of Management and Budget.

Office of Personnel Management. *See* U.S. Office of Personnel Management.

Office of Special Education and Rehabilitative Services. *See* U.S. Department of Education. Office of Special Education and Rehabilitative Services.

Ohio Office of the Attorney General. 30 East Broad Street, First Floor, Columbus, OH 43215. *(614) 466-3180.*

Ohio State University. Office of Student Life. 347 Ohio Union, 1739 North High Street, Columbus, OH 43210. *(614) 422-6446.*

OMEC International, Inc. 1126 16th Street, N.W., Washington, DC 20036. *(202) 833-4161.*

Oregon Arts Commission. 835 Summer Street, NE, Salem, OR 07301. *(503) 378-3625.*

Oregon Department of Energy. Labor and Industries Building, No. 102, Salem, OR 97310. *(503) 378-2773.*

Oryx Press. 2214 N. Central Avenue, Phoenix, AZ 85004-1483. *(602) 254-6156.* There is also a toll free number: *(800) 457-6799.*

OUA/DATA. 81 Saltonstall Avenue, New Haven, CT 06513. *(203) 776-0797.*

PEN American Center Publications. 568 Broadway, New York, NY 10012. *(212) 334-1660.*

Penguin Books. 299 Murray Hill Parkway, East Rutherford, NJ 07073. *(201) 933-1460.* There is also a toll free number *(800) 631-3577.*

Perigee Books. 200 Madison Avenue, New York, NY 10016. *(212) 576-8900.*

Peterson's Guides, Inc. 166 Bunn Drive, P.O. Box 2123, Princeton, NJ 08543-2123. *(609) 924-5338.* There is also a toll free number: *(800) 225-0261.*

Pilot Books. 103 Cooper Street, Babylon, NY 11702. *(516) 422-2225.*

Poets & Writers, Inc. 201 East 54th Street, New York, NY 10019. *(212) 757-1766.*

Prentice Hall, Inc. P.O. Box 500, Englewood Cliffs, NJ 07632. *(201) 592-2000.* There is also a toll free number: *(800) 262-6868.*

Preservation League of New York State. 307 Hamilton Street, Albany, NY 12210. *(518) 462-5658.*

Preservation Reports, Inc. 1620 I Street, N.W., Washington, DC 20036. *(202) 466-4234.*

Project on the Status and Education of Women. Association of American Colleges, 1818 R Street, N.W., Washington, DC 20009. *(202) 387-1300.*

Public Affairs Inc. 1024 Tenth Street, Suite 300, Sacramento, CA 95814. *(916) 444-0840.*

Public Health Service. *See* U.S. Public Health Service.

Public Management Institute. 358 Brannan Street, San Francisco, CA 94107. *(415) 896-1900.*

Public Media Center. 466 Green Street, San Francisco, CA 94133. *(415) 434-1403.*

Public Service Materials Center. 111 N. Central Avenue, Hartsdale, NY 10530. *(914) 949-2242.*

Putnam Publishing Group, Inc. 200 Madison Avenue, New York, NY 10016. *(212) 576-8900.* There is also a toll free number: *(800) 631-8571.*

R. R. Bowker Company. P.O. Box 1807, Ann Arbor, MI 48106. There is a toll free number: *(800) 521-8110.*

Rawson Associates. 115 Fifth Avenue, New York, NY 10003. *(212) 614-1300.* There is also a toll free number: *(800) 257-5755.*

Ready Reference Press. P.O. Box 5879, Santa Monica, CA 90405.

Reference Service Press. 3540 Wilshire Boulevard, Suite 310, Los Angeles, CA 90010. *(213) 251-3743.*

Regional Young Adult Project. 330 Ellis Street, No. 506, San Francisco, CA 94012. *(415) 771-8375.*

Research Grant Guides. Box 10726, Marina del Rey, CA 90295.

Revenue Sharing Advisory Service. 1725 K Street, N.W., Suite 200, Washington, DC 20006. *(202) 872-1766.*

Richards House. P.O. Box 208, Wellesley Hills, MA 02181. *(617) 235-1142.*

Roberts Press. *See* Ellen Roberts Press.

Running Press Book Publishers. 125 S. 22 Street, Philadelphia, PA 19103. *(215) 567-5080.* There is also a toll free number: *(800) 428-1111.*

Saur Inc. *See* K. G. Saur.

Schirmer Books. 7101 Westfield Avenue, Pennsauken, NJ 08110. *(609) 665-2500.* There is also a toll free number: *(800) 524-1137.*

Scholars Press. 101 Salem Street, P.O. Box 2268, Chico, CA 95927. *(916) 891-4541.*

Scholarship Search Service. 407 State Street, Santa Barbara, CA 93101. *(805) 963-1311.*

Science Support Center. Box 587, Bronxville, NY 10708.

Scribner's Sons. *See* Charles Scribner's Sons.

SDC Information Services. 2525 Colorado Avenue, Santa Monica, CA 90406. *(213) 453-7229.* There are also toll free numbers: *(800) 421-7229 (outside California); (800) 352-6689 (inside California).*

Smithsonian Institution Press. 955 L'Enfant Plaza, Room 2100, Washington, DC 20560. *(202) 287-3765.*

Social Science Research Council. 605 Third Avenue, New York, NY 10158. *(212) 661-0280.*

South Carolina State Library. 1500 Senate Street, P.O. Box 11469, Columbia, SC 29211. *(803) 758-3181.*

Spanish Publicity. 200 Prairie Dell, Austin, TX 78752.

St. Martin's Press, Inc. 175 Fifth Avenue, New York, NY 10010. *(212) 674-5151.* There is also a toll free number: *(800) 221-7945.*

State Agency Grantspeople Exchange. P.O. Box 2037, Sacramento, CA 95809.

Sun Country Enterprises, Inc. 1700 Sunset Drive, Longwood, FL 32750-9697. *(303) 323-5927.*

Sun Features, Inc. Box 368-P, Cardiff, CA 92007. *(619) 753-3489.*

Swift Associates. P.O. Box 28033, St. Louis, MO 63119. *(314) 962-2940.*

System Development Services Information Services. *See* SDC Information Services.

Taft Group. 5130 MacArthur Boulevard, N.W., Washington, DC 20016. *(202) 966 7086.* There is also a toll free number: *(800) 424-3761.*

Ten Speed Press. P.O. Box 7123, Berkeley, CA 94707. *(415) 845-8414.*

Thompson Publishing Group. 1725 K Street, N.W., Suite 200, Washington, DC 20006. *(202) 872-1766.*

Toft Consulting. P.O. Box 3553, Arlington, VA 22203. *(703) 241-2783.*

Transnational Investments, Ltd. Box 56049, Washington, DC 20011. *(202) 829-0002.*

Trumpet Associates. P.O. Box 172, Dubuque, IA 52001.

U.S. American Forces Information Service. Department of Defense, Room 210, 1735 N. Lynn Street, Arlington, VA 22209. *(202) 696-5284.*

U.S. Bureau of Indian Affairs. Department of the Interior, Washington, DC 20240. *(202) 343-7445.*

U.S. Catholic Conference. Campaign for Human Development. 1312 Massachusetts Avenue, N.W., Washington, DC 20005. *(202) 659-6600.*

U.S. Department of Commerce. Commerce Business Daily. 433 W. Van Buren Street, Room 1304, Chicago, IL 60607. *(312) 353-2950.*

U.S. Department of Education. 400 Maryland Avenue, S.W., Washington, DC 20202. *(202) 245-3192.*

U.S. Department of Education. Office of Special Education and. Rehabilitative Services Switzer Building, Room 3018, 330 C Street, S.W., Washington, DC 20202. *(202) 245-3192.*

U.S. Department of Justice. Constitution Avenue and Tenth Street, N.W., Washington, DC 20530. *(202) 633-2000.*

U.S. Department of the Army. Adjutant General's Office. The Pentagon, Washington, DC 20310. *(202) 545-6700.*

U.S. Department of the Army. ROTC. c/o 75 Harmon Gym, U.C. Berkeley, Berkeley, CA 94720.

U.S. Department of the Navy. Naval Military Personnel Command. NMPC-121D, Washington, DC 20370. *(202) 545-6700.*

U.S. Government Printing Office. USGPO Stop SSMP, Washington, DC 20401. *(202) 783-3238.*

U.S. Internal Revenue Service Center. Box 245, DP 536, Philadelphia, PA 19255. *(215) 574-9900.*

U.S. Minority Business Development Agency. U.S. Department of Commerce, 14th and Constitution, N.W., Washington, DC 20230. *(202) 377-2414.*

U.S. National Endowment for the Arts. 1100 Pennsylvania Avenue, N.W., Washington, DC 20506. *(202) 682-5400.*

U.S. National Endowment for the Humanities. 1100 Pennsylvania Avenue, N.W., Washington, DC 20506. *(202) 786-0438.*

U.S. National Institute of Mental Health. Department of Health and Human Services, 200 Independence Avenue, S.W., Washington, DC 20201. *(301) 443-1910.*

U.S. National Institute on Drug Abuse. Public Health Service, Department of Health and Human Services, 5600 Fishers Lane, Rockville, MD 20857. *(301) 443-4373.*

U.S. National Technical Information Service. 5285 Port Royal Road, Springfield, VA 22161. *(703) 487-4929.*

U.S. Office for Handicapped Individuals. *See* U.S. Department of Education. Office of Special Education and Rehabilitative Services.

U.S. Office of Management and Budget. 6001 New Executive Office Building, Washington, DC 20503. *(202) 395-3112.*

U.S. Office of Personnel Management. 1900 E Street, N.W., Washington, DC 20415. *(202) 254-7540.*

U.S. Public Health Service. Department of Health and Human Services, 5600 Fishers Lane, Rockville, MD 20857. *(301) 443-2404.*

Unipub. *See* Bernan/Unipub.

United Communications Group. 4550 Montgomery Avenue, Suite 700N, Bethesda, MD 20814. *(301) 656-6666.*

United States Tennis Association. 729 Alexander Road, Princeton, NJ 08540. *(609) 452-2580.*

United Way of Delaware. 701 Shipley Street, Wilmington, DE 19801. *(302) 573-2400.*

United Way of the Columbia—Willamette. 718 West Burnside, Portland, OR 97209. *(503) 228-9131.*

University of Illinois. Campus-Wide Research Service Office. Urbana, IL 61801. *(217) 333-0284.*

University of Minnesota Press. 2037 University Avenue, S.E., Minneapolis, MN 55414. *(612) 373-3266.*

University of Minnesota. Office of International Programs. 201 Nolte West, 315 Pillsbury Drive, S.E., Minneapolis, MN 55455. *(612) 373-3793.*

University of Oklahoma Press. 1005 Asp Avenue, Norman, OK 73019. *(405) 325-5111.* There is also a toll free number: *(800) 242-7737.*

University of Tennessee. Center for International Education. 201 Alumni Hall, Knoxville, TN 37996-0620. *(615) 974-3475.*

University of Utah Press. 101 University Services Building, Salt Lake City, UT 84112. *(801) 581-6771.*

University of Wyoming. Division of Financial Aid. P.O. Box 3335, University Station, Laramie, WY 82071.

Urban Institute Press. 2100 M Street, N.W., Washington, DC 20037. *(202) 833-7200.*

Vacation—Work. 9 Park End Street, Oxford OX1 1AJ England.

Veterans Information Service. Box 111, East Moline, IL 61244.

VU/TEXT Information Services, Inc. 1211 Chestnut Street, Phiadelphia, PA 19107. *(215) 665-3300.* There is also a toll free number: *(800) 258-8080.*

Walter de Gruyter, Inc. 200 Saw Mill River Drive, Hawthorne, NY 10532. *(914) 747-0110.*

Warren, Gorham, & Lamont, Inc. 1633 Broadway, New York, NY 10019. *(212) 977-7400.* There is also a toll free number: *(800) 225-2363.*

Washington International Arts Letter. P.O. Box 15240, Washington, DC 20003. *(202) 488-0800.*

Washington Office of the Attorney General. Temple of Justice, Olympia, WA 98504. *(206) 753-6299.*

Wiley, Inc. *See* John Wiley and Sons, Inc.

Name Index

Indexed here are authors, editors, compilers, translators, and illustrators listed on the title pages of the specific directories cited in this guide. Since not all directories credit individual authors, a number of the publications described in the Guide (particularly those that are serial in nature or those prepared by organizations) are not represented here. Indexed names are arranged alphabetically, word by word. The numbers following each name refer to the entries that contain the fullest annotation of the individual's work.

Name Index

Name Index

Title Index

The current, previous, and variant names of all publications covered in the Guide (either as separate entries or as references in annotations describing other titles) are indexed here. Over 700 individual titles are listed alphabetically, word by word (except in the cases of certain prefixes, such as "A," "An," and "The"). The numbers following each title identify the entries where the publication is cited and/or described.

Title Index

320

Title Index

Geographic Index

This index provides access to the geographic coverage provided by the directories listed in the Guide. Country, state, province, region, county, and city terms are used. They are arranged in alphabetical order (word by word) and subdivided by type of programs covered in that area: scholarships, fellowships, grants, awards, loans, and/or internships. The numbers included in the index identify the entries where the publications are cited and/or described. Liberal cross-references provide access to broader or more specific geographic index terms.

Geographic Index

Subject Index

This index identifies the subject emphasis of the more than 700 directories covered in the Guide. Over 125 subject terms are used. They are arranged in alphabetical order, ranging from "Advertising" to "Writers and writing" and are subdivided by type of program described: scholarships, fellowships, grants, awards, loans, and/or internships. The numbers included in the index identify the entries where the publications are cited and/or described. Liberal cross-references provide access to broader, more specific, or variant subject terms.

Language and linguistics: **Scholarships**, 81, **Fellowships**, 221, 268, **Grants**, 505, 599, **Loans**, 807 *See also* General programs; Literature

Law. *See* Legal studies and services

Law enforcement. *See* Criminal justice

Leadership. *See* Management

Learning disabilities. *See* Disabilities, learning

Legal studies and services: **Scholarships**, 98-99, **Fellowships**, 218-219, 239-241, 276, **Grants**, 499, 552-553, 620, **Loans**, 812, **Internships**, 850, 860 *See also* Criminal justice; General programs

Libraries and librarianship: **Scholarships**, 97, **Fellowships**, 235-238, **Grants**, 545-550, 569, 592, **Awards and Prizes**, 695-699, **Loans**, 811 *See also* Computer sciences; General programs

Linguistics. *See* Language and linguistics

Literature: **Scholarships**, 116, **Fellowships**, 253, 271-272, **Grants**, 399, 570, 605, **Awards and Prizes**, 701, 728, 740, 742-744, 746, 753, **Loans**, 813 *See also* Fiction; General programs; Humanities; Language and linguistics; Literature, children's; Literature, American; Literature, Canadian; Literature, French; Literature, German; Plays; Poetry; Short stories; Writers and writing

Literature, American: **Scholarships**, 104, 115-117, **Fellowships**, 260, 269-271, 273, **Grants**, 575, 601-609, **Awards and Prizes**, 718, 728, 734-736, 738-740, 745-756, 764 *See also* General programs; Literature

Literature, Canadian: **Fellowships**, 249, **Grants**, 563, **Awards and Prizes**, 746, 748 *See also* General programs; Literature

Literature, children's: **Grants**, 589, 600, **Awards and Prizes**, 717, 728-729, 731-733, 741, 753 *See also* General programs; Literature

Literature, English: **Awards and Prizes**, 746 *See also* General programs; Literature

Literature, French: **Awards and Prizes**, 737 *See also* General programs; Literature

Literature, German: **Awards and Prizes**, 737 *See also* General programs; Literature

Macrame: **Awards and Prizes**, 710 *See also* Arts and crafts; General programs

Magazines. *See* Journalism; Literature

Management: **Fellowships**, 226 *See also* Business administration; General programs; Public administration

Mass communications. *See* Communications

Mathematics: **Fellowships**, 219, 276, 292, **Grants**, 499, 620 *See also* Computer sciences; General programs

Media. *See* Communications; Radio; Television

Medical sciences: **Scholarships**, 126-128, **Fellowships**, 281-283, 285-290, **Grants**, 625-627, 630, 632, 635, **Internships**, 873, 875 *See also* General programs; Health and health care; Nurses and nursing; Sciences

Mental health. *See* Health and health care; Psychiatry

Mental retardation: **Grants**, 646 *See also* Disabilities; General programs

Mexican American affairs. *See* Hispanic American affairs

Microcomputers. *See* Computer sciences

Military affairs: **Scholarships**, 69, 154-161, **Fellowships**, 312-316, **Grants**, 556, 666-672, **Loans**, 791, 827-833 *See also* General programs

Minority affairs: **Scholarships**, 133-134, 136-144, 146-147, **Fellowships**, 289, 295-305, 307-308, **Grants**, 359, 582, 648-649, 651-657, 662, **Awards and Prizes**, 770, **Loans**, 822-824, **Internships**, 876-878 *See also* General programs; names of specific ethnic minority groups

Missionary work. *See* Religion and religious activities

Museums: **Scholarships**, 102, **Fellowships**, 256, **Grants**, 359, 384, 569, 576-577, 580-581, 592, **Awards and Prizes**, 702, **Internships**, 866 *See also* General programs; Libraries and librarianship

Music: **Scholarships**, 102, 118-121, **Fellowships**, 256, 269, 274, **Grants**, 575-577, 580-581, 602, 610-611, 613-614, **Awards and Prizes**, 702, 735, 757-762, 765-766, **Internships**, 871 *See also* Fine arts; General programs; Humanities; Performing arts

Narcotics. *See* Drug use and abuse

Native American affairs: **Scholarships**, 132-133, 135, 148-149, **Fellowships**, 295, **Grants**, 649-650, 658-659, 661, **Awards and Prizes**, 770, **Loans**, 822, **Internships**, 876 *See also* General programs; Minority affairs

Natural sciences: **Fellowships**, 219, 276, **Grants**, 499, 620 *See also* General programs; Sciences; names of specific sciences

Newspapers. *See* Journalism

Nurses and nursing: **Scholarships**, 128-129, **Fellowships**, 287, **Grants**, 632, **Loans**, 814 *See also* General programs; Health and health care; Medical sciences

Opera. *See* Music

Optometry: **Scholarships**, 128, **Fellowships**, 287, **Grants**, 632 *See also* General programs; Medical sciences

334